THE GREAT POST OFFICE SCANDAL

THE FIGHT TO EXPOSE A MULTIMILLION POUND SCANDAL WHICH PUT INNOCENT PEOPLE IN JAIL

Nick Wallis

Published October 2021

ISBN 978-1-9163023-8-9

Bath Publishing Limited
27 Charmouth Road
Bath
BA1 3LJ
Tel: 01225 577810
email: info@bathpublishing.co.uk
www.bathpublishing.co.uk

Bath Publishing is a company registered in England: 5209173
Registered Office: As above

To Mum, Dad, Nic, Amy, Abi and James.

Thanks for everything.

SUBPOSTMASTERS' FUND

Many of the Subpostmasters featured in the book – and many more not mentioned – are still fighting for proper compensation or having to seek damages through malicious prosecution claims. Some will not have the resources to raise a claim, find the documents they need or travel to meet their lawyers or parliamentary representatives. Others may be suffering in silence, without peace of mind.

To help those directly affected by the Horizon scandal, 10% of the revenue generated by this book will be directed to a new fund. The fund will distribute money to assist people who have suffered as a result of the Post Office's punitive methods. This could include helping with expert and legal advice, travel (to meetings, court or evidence sessions of the statutory inquiry), medical help, counselling, media and creative projects and basic hardships. Thank you for buying this book. It will make a difference.

CONTENTS

PART 1

PART 2

PART 3

READER NOTE

For most of the last century the Post Office was known corporately as the General Post Office. The initials GPO were ubiquitous and well-understood. The GPO governed the activities of Royal Mail and Britain's telephony network (which later became British Telecom).

When the GPO was scrapped the Post Office went through various reorganisations. At one stage it was known as Post Office Counters Limited – or POCL (pronounced 'pockell'). Soon afterwards it became Post Office Limited, often written up in documents as POL (pronounced 'poll'). Many Subpostmasters therefore call the Post Office 'POL,' though Post Office employees tend to just call it 'the business.'

If it's not being called POL or 'the business,' there is a habit (mainly among its representatives) of dropping the definite article, so 'the' Post Office becomes 'Post Office.'

The various official and unofficial names the Post Office has gone by are reflected in the hundreds of documents and interviews which have informed this book.

To save confusion and to be as consistent as possible, I have added, where appropriate, the definite article and changed many (but not all) of the POLs and POCLs to 'the Post Office.' I hope this aids the reader.

FOREWORD BY SEEMA MISRA

I have always been a spiritual person. When I was convicted of theft in 2010, my faith and my belief in justice was shattered. I was pregnant at the time. My despair caused me to think of suicide. I wondered if God wanted me to have something in prison to worry about. Thoughts of my unborn child kept a bit of hope, and me, alive.

The Hindu religion has a concept of *Ramarajya*. That is the realm of what Ghandi called the moral authority of the people. It is a realm in which peace, honesty, prosperity and security prevail. I had come to England like many, believing Britain was a place of *Ramarajya* which offered the opportunity to work, to thrive and to prosper.

In 2005, Davinder and I invested our own money in a Post Office branch and retail business. We were proud to have become part of such a famous British institution. When I was sentenced to prison on my eldest son's tenth birthday, all our dreams and hopes were destroyed.

The Post Office did not quite get away with it. They almost did. It was reassuring and comforting to know that others believed something had gone wrong. They have kept the story alive when the Post Office very much wanted the story to die.

Throughout our journey, we have made many wonderful friends who have been like lights in the darkness. Some have helped to restore a bit of faith in English justice. They never believed, even for one moment, that I was a thief.

Reading this book made me cry. Nick brings to life what the Post Office did to me and to my family in a way that makes reading it feel like re-living it. It is a story which broke my heart.

You may think it could never happen to you – or to someone you love. This book shows that you would be wrong. It happened to me.

Seema Misra, former West Byfleet Subpostmaster, July 2021

INTRODUCTION

Seema Misra was sacked as Subpostmaster at the West Byfleet Post Office in Surrey and then charged with theft. A jury at Guildford Crown Court found her guilty of stealing £74,000 from her own Post Office. As Seema says in her foreword to this book, she was sentenced to jail for a crime she didn't commit, on her eldest son's tenth birthday.

When I met Davinder Misra, Seema's husband, his wife was still in prison. Davinder was adamant the case against her was wholly false. Seema, he told me, had been convicted on the basis of evidence from a faulty computer system called Horizon. It took more than ten years for Davinder to be proved right.

The Misras were not alone. In the first decade of this century, accounting evidence generated by the IT system at the heart of the Post Office branch network was being used to bring private prosecutions against counter staff and branch Subpostmasters on an industrial scale. Between 2000 and 2015, more than 700 people were given criminal convictions.

Yet the 'largest non-military IT system in Europe,' as Horizon was proudly described, was riddled with bugs and coding errors. The Post Office – a government-owned company – was using the shaky electronic data produced by Horizon to wrongfully charge its own Subpostmasters with crimes which simply did not exist.

Even if Horizon worked as it should, the sheer number of Post Office-led prosecutions during this fifteen year period (more than one a week) should have raised eyebrows. But no one in the justice system or government seemed to be aware of what was going on. Worse still, when the Post Office realised it might have been responsible for unsafe prosecutions, it orchestrated a cover-up, hiding crucial information from MPs and campaigners.

By 2020, enough details had come to light for the MP Julian Lewis to describe the affair in parliament as 'one of the worst disasters in public life since the infected blood scandal.'

Despite this, no one has been held responsible. Not a single person has been officially censured or blamed for the misery heaped on so many lives.

Over the last decade or so I've spoken to countless Subpostmasters, Post Office workers, politicians, union officials, lawyers, IT experts, accountants and fraud investigators. I've spent hundreds of hours digging through transcripts, parliamentary inquiry evidence, audit reports and court documents. I've also met dozens of innocent people who were criminally prosecuted by the Post Office, some of whom – like Seema – were sent to prison. They were put at the mercy of an organisation stuffed with managerial incompetents, who exercised their responsibilities with a toxic mixture of prejudice and indifference.

The Great Post Office Scandal is an attempt to unravel exactly what went wrong, and determine who is to blame. It also documents the heroics of those who fought long and hard against a powerful and well-resourced opponent to get the truth into the public domain.

It's quite a story.

'When we came to office, there was probably no greater shambles than the Horizon project.'

Tony Blair, Prime Minister's Questions, 12 April 2000.

PART 1

BUILDING AN EMPIRE

Clint parked up outside the lo-rise glass and concrete office block situated on the edge of Hanworth Park in Hounslow. He announced himself at reception and collected an ID pass. As he waited to be accompanied into the building, he reflected on what he'd been told about the project he would soon be getting a direct handle on.

He knew it was in trouble – that's why he was there. How much trouble, he could not begin to imagine.

The late nineties were a good time to be in IT. The globally-connected future, foretold by wide-eyed seers and digital visionaries, was no longer the stuff of fantasy. The dot com boom was, well, booming, and the information super-highway, or World Wide Web, was becoming part of everyday life. Smartphones, Google and Facebook were still a while off, but dial-up modems, Netscape and email had worked their way into Britain's businesses and homes.

Empires need construction workers, and jobs were easy to come by. The IT world was full of brilliant minds, but there were plenty of chancers talking themselves into jobs they weren't qualified to do. Coders, testers, and systems and network engineers were all in demand, alongside the usual project managers, sales and marketing people. There were also plenty of middle-ranking execs with little understanding of what the young turks in their charge were up to, but had learned just about enough to bluff their way through.

Clint was no chancer. Clint was the real deal. He'd been working in IT development his entire career. He knew how to code a system and he knew how to manage a team.

After spending most of the nineties in Brussels developing complex financial systems for the European Parliament and European Commission, Clint had been called by a former colleague who was working on a project to automate the Post Office network. The project's name was Horizon.

TRACY FELSTEAD

In November 1999, 17-year-old Tracy Felstead nervously stepped through the door of her local Crown Post Office[1] in Camberwell Green, South London. She was young, keen, just out of school and had been invited to an interview for the post of counter assistant. Luckily, Tracy had been recommended to the branch manager by a family friend, and the interview went well. She was offered and accepted the job.

Tracy was sent on a two day training course to learn her way round Horizon, the new computerised till system which hadn't long been installed in the branch. Soon, Tracy was using it to serve customers.

There were 12 counter positions at Camberwell Green. Tracy was the youngest assistant, so she was taken under the wing of the experienced staff.

'To be fair, everybody seemed lovely,' she remembers. 'Everybody seemed pretty much on the ball. If you needed any help, you could just ask.'

Each member of staff had their own login, allowing them to switch between counters, but the regime was lax. No one minded if you used somebody else's login. If someone needed a break during a busy period, another member of staff would 'jump on' their Horizon terminal without going through the process of logging off and logging back in again. This ensured minimum disruption for customers, but it had obvious security implications.

Every day, after each shift, Tracy would cash up, checking the money in her till tray against the figures on the Horizon screen. She would then print off and sign a receipt displaying the till tray balance. One day, she found herself with a small deficit. Tracy said her manager was not in the least bit concerned.

'I think because I was the baby, all of them mothered me. She said, "Oh, it's fine, it will rectify itself." I suppose I was a bit naïve, being 17, but I trusted her.'

Tracy was a happy girl and a popular employee. She flew through the hectic pre-Christmas period without any serious mishaps. Her understanding of her responsibilities – handling cash, handling Horizon and handling customers – was coming on in leaps and bounds. Outside work, Tracy was getting serious with her partner Jon, who worked as a

[1] Crown Post Offices – usually shortened to Crown Offices – are directly owned and managed by the Post Office.

reprographics manager in the City. They bought a house in Penge and were planning to get married. Life was all set.

Half way through 2000 Tracy suffered another spate of discrepancies. 'I did a cash up at the end of the week and I had a £1,300 loss,' she says. Again, her boss seemed relaxed. Tracy said the manager took over at the terminal, 'did something' and the loss went up to £1,800. 'And then she said, "Oh, leave it, I'll sort it out."'

Tracy did leave it, but she was concerned.

In February 2001 Tracy locked her till tray in the office safe and went on a family holiday. It was her parents' 15th wedding anniversary, so they chose somewhere special – the Dominican Republic. While Tracy was away her cash tray could be used by someone else, so long as all the stock and cash was checked before and after each session, and the counter assistant entered the figures under their own login into Horizon.

The day before Tracy got back from holiday, a loss of £11,503.28 was found on her stock unit.[2] On her return to work, Tracy was questioned about the loss. Her manager's demeanour was not motherly any more.

'I'm looking at this woman like, "What on earth is going on?," and she said, "Oh, another member of staff used the till while you were away and found a discrepancy."'

Tracy was asked if she knew how the discrepancy had come about. She remembers shaking her head and firmly telling her manager she had 'no idea.'

The next day, Tracy cashed up and signed off her stock unit with the £11,503.28 discrepancy still outstanding.

There appeared to be a serious amount of money missing from Tracy's till position, but as nothing more was said, she put it to the back of her mind. Tracy continued serving customers, but the atmosphere had

---

2 Stock units are usually related to, and the responsibility of, individual Horizon users. A counter assistant or Subpostmaster will log in to a Horizon terminal and assign themselves, or be assigned to, a stock unit (usually lettered AA, AB etc). The stock unit will relate to a physical till tray containing cash and stamps. Horizon registers electronic transactions and transfers in, out and through stock units over the course of the day. So, if I take a book of stamps out of my till tray and you pay for it by card, my till tray and my stock unit is down one book of stamps, and the amount of electronic money in my stock unit is up by the cost of a book of stamps (even though there is nothing physical in my till tray). If you give me a £50 note and I change it for 5 x £10 notes from my till tray I would also have to manually register that physical transfer electronically on Horizon, so that the physical cash denominations in my stock unit match those in my till tray.

changed. Two weeks later she walked into work and was given a shock.

'I've got two strapping, great big guys sitting there waiting for me, and they want to interview me. And I said, "Okay, that's absolutely fine." They asked whether I wanted legal representation and I told them, "No, I haven't done anything wrong, so I don't need anybody. Happy to be interviewed. Not a problem." '

The two strapping guys were from the Post Office's internal security unit. Tracy's interview turned into an interrogation. 'They were constantly asking, "What did you spend the money on?" And I remember looking at them and saying, "Seriously, I haven't taken any money. You can have access to anything you want. Bank accounts … whatever. I haven't taken any money." '

Tracy was suspended. 'They said they needed to do some more investigation. I was distraught, absolutely distraught. But part of me actually thought – well, they'll get me sorted because I haven't stolen any money. So they'll fix this.'

Three weeks later, at 8am, the same Post Office investigators knocked on the door of Jon's parents' home in Peckham, where Tracy was staying. The investigators were accompanied by two police officers.

'The police told me they were there to keep the peace. What they thought I was going to do, I'm not quite sure. I'm only 5'3" and small, you know, a size 10. And I'm not gonna … these men are massive, intimidating, huge men. And they said, "Could you escort us down to the police station for interviewing?" And I said, "Yeah, fine." '

On this occasion Tracy did ask for a solicitor.

THE MAGIC BULLET

The full automation of Post Office systems was set in motion in 1992, initially as part of a solution to rampant fraud.

In those days benefits were paid at the Post Office by exchanging vouchers from social security order books for cash. Between 1991 and 1992, £230m worth of order books were lost, of which £85m had been found to be fraudulently cashed. A further £16m was lost through fraudulent encashment of girocheques. The paper system was vulnerable, and needed upgrading.

After a few experiments with barcoded order books, the Department of Social Security decided it wanted to use a magnetic-strip swipe-card as a vehicle for dispensing benefits payments. The cards would be given to claimants, who would have their use of the card electronically registered at a central database each time they were swiped at a Post Office. This ensured each card could only be used once a week, and deactivated if lost. Swipe-cards were an established technology. The problem was, the Post Office had nowhere to swipe them.

For decades the Post Office had been the place where British citizens did their admin with the state. Each day millions of people would visit their local branch to buy stamps, tax discs, traveller's cheques, premium bonds or TV licences. They would cash benefits and pensions, or make utility bill payments, National Savings Bank account withdrawals or deposits, or apply for passports or driving, fishing or game licences or any number of other permits and services.[1]

Important documents were stamped, signed, shown or submitted, and cash would be paid or received accordingly. These transactions, made in their millions every day, gave the Post Office a multi-billion pound annual turnover. It was an established system and it worked, but it was costly.

---

1 A recent request to a Postmasters' online forum about the extent of permits and services available through a Post Office in the early nineties returned a wealth of information, for which I am grateful. The following were available: TV savings stamps, general savings stamps, milk tokens, Red Star parcels, Canadian money order encashment, Littlewoods pools, flowers and chocolates by post, WH Smith, Kingfisher and Boots gift vouchers, electoral register applications, viewing of public telephone directories, viewing of the London Gazette (to see premium bond winners), National Railcards, National Savings Certificates, film developing by post, Transcash payments abroad, prescription charge exemption forms and no doubt much, much more…!

Although attempts had been made to automate various parts of the network, by the mid-nineties most village and suburban branches were still handing over paper forms, stamping dockets, transferring physical cash and generally operating more or less along the same lines they had in Queen Victoria's day. Especially when it came to filing branch accounts.

At the end of each trading week, every Subpostmaster would fill out a giant paper spreadsheet, recording their transactions in the relevant, designated column. The sheet would be signed, folded and posted back to the Post Office's financial HQ in Chesterfield.

By the 1990s this antiquated system was in need of an overhaul. With the race for digitisation happening everywhere, the Post Office, government and many Subpostmasters felt that automating the Post Office network was a nettle which needed to be grasped. The DSS swipe-card idea provided the impetus for starting to wrestle with the eye-watering cost and logistics of doing so. The eventual solution was a £1bn PFI contract. This was tendered in 1994 by both the DSS-owned Benefits Agency and the Post Office. It would deliver the swipe-card scheme and automate the front and back end of Britain's twenty thousand Post Offices – a transformative project.

The candidates were whittled down to a shortlist of three. In May 1996, the winner was announced. Pathway, a consortium owned almost entirely by a company called International Computers Ltd – better known as ICL – got the gig. ICL once saw itself as Britain's answer to the American computing giant IBM, but its glory days were long gone. In 1990, the Japanese tech corp Fujitsu had taken an 80% stake in ICL with a view to outright ownership. Whilst Pathway was being tendered, Fujitsu was in the process of swallowing ICL whole.

Pathway managed to come bottom in eight of the 11 scoring criteria drawn up to quantify the strengths of each bid, but it was the cheapest in terms of its cost to the government. Fujitsu's business model for Pathway saw it shouldering almost all the project's commercial risk by paying for its development and rollout. In return Pathway would get a transaction fee every time a shiny new Benefits Agency card was swiped through a shiny new Post Office card-swiper, for a guaranteed period of eight years. If all went according to plan, Project Pathway would deliver automation of the Post Office and vast sums of cash to Fujitsu, without any risk to the public purse. As an incentive to get things operational as soon as possible, the eight year guaranteed transaction fee period would start the moment the PFI deal was signed.

Almost as soon as the ink on the contract was dry, Pathway ran into difficulties. Serious, big-picture difficulties. It seemed everyone had badly underestimated the complexity of automating 20,000 geographically isolated and disparate Post Offices carrying out multiple (and sometimes region-specific[2]) transactions which were many times more complicated than the average bank.

The logistics of building, testing and installing a bespoke IT system of this size was uncharted territory for the government, and Fujitsu. 20,000 Post Offices would need 40,000 terminals. 67,000 people with variable technical skills would have to be trained to successfully keep handing out £56 *billion* in benefits *alone* to their 28 million annual customers.

The hardware would have to be robust. The software would have to process millions of transactions a year. Training and support would have to be first rate. Fujitsu had bid for IT's Operation Moonshot by undercutting the competition. Having won the contract, they were realising how complex and expensive moonshots can be.

Conceptually, Horizon was relatively straightforward. The front-end terminals would be custom-specced PCs running Microsoft's Windows NT operating system. These would sit in a box under each Post Office counter window. Each PC would be connected to a custom keyboard, a barcode scanner, a 3.5 inch receipts printer and a touchscreen, which would sit on top of the counter. Running bespoke Horizon software, each counter PC would write both manually- and barcode-inputted transactions into the branch accounts. Every night all the information collected from the branch would be uploaded via ISDN or (in some cases) satellite to a centrally-located Post Office mainframe.

That was the theory. Writing the code to make this system work reliably appeared to be completely beyond Fujitsu. Despite burning through £10m a month, by the middle of 1997, Fujitsu was not able to deliver an (already renegotiated) contractual obligation to demonstrate Horizon's 'satisfactory, sustained' operation. Even in a controlled environment, they simply could not get it to work.

Fujitsu was not helped by its clients, two state-owned entities with different and sometimes competing priorities. Goalposts for the project were constantly being moved. Fujitsu would later tell parliament that over three years, Pathway's 366 original contractual requirements had been subject to 323 formal change requests by the Post Office and the Benefits

---

2 For example: local authority rent and council tax services, local authority home care services, parking permits, market trader permits.

Agency. This was exacerbated, it said, by numerous informal changes and 'clarifications' which necessitated 'significant system re-design.'

Frustrated with the delays, in December 1997, the Benefits Agency and the Post Office served Fujitsu with a formal notice of breach of contract. Fujitsu, fed up with the way it was being treated, refused to accept the notice. It then upped the ante by threatening to stop work on the Horizon project altogether unless it received a guaranteed hike in the fee it was going to get from each swipe of the DSS benefits card.

The stand-off turned critical when the Benefits Agency responded by announcing it no longer wished to use swipe-cards to dispense benefits payments. Instead, it was going to encourage claimants to have their benefits delivered direct to their bank accounts. In one swoop, Fujitsu's potential income from the project had been reduced to zero. On top of that, the Post Office was looking at losing a third of its customer base overnight.

In January 1998, serious consideration was given to abandoning Horizon altogether, but the project limped on. Despite a shifting brief and its lack of operability, there was a feeling in Whitehall that Horizon had become too expensive to kill. Someone was going to have to find a way through, because the fallout caused by cancelling the project would be politically disastrous.

When Clint joined Fujitsu in April 1998, he was vaguely aware of the political wrangling going on around the Horizon project, but it was of no real concern to him. His job was to find out what was stopping Horizon from working and fix it. More than twenty years later, after a couple of lengthy telephone conversations, I travelled to meet Clint for lunch at The Grand Hotel in York. Clint had got in touch with me using a messaging app, but was something of a terse communicator when it came to email. I was keen to ensure that before I made the trip he understood the terms on which we were meeting – to record an interview about his experiences at Fujitsu. I also needed some documentation from him. He seemed cagey, but genuine. I was prepared to take a punt. I got on a commuter train to London, crossed the city to Kings Cross and then travelled to York in a near-empty train carriage, a tiny bit unsure as to whether Clint was going to turn up. I needn't have worried. Clint arrived bang on time and produced enough paperwork to prove he was indeed who he said he was.[1] I found him to be a blunt-speaking individual who is keen to keep his identity private. Over lunch he opened up about his experience of working on Horizon.

Clint, as you may have already guessed, is not his real name.

'Everybody in the building by the time I got there knew it was a bag of shit,' he told me. 'Everybody. Because it had gone through the test labs God knows how many times, and the testers were raising bugs by the thousand, including category As.'

Software code is written by human beings who make mistakes. Computer bugs are errors mistakenly written by developers into the lines of software code which tell electronic devices what to do. One misplaced character can make a computer do the wrong thing, or set off a chain of routines and sub-routines which could lead to something very serious happening. This is why software code needs to be tested in a variety of different environments, almost to destruction, before it can be let loose in the wild. If it is not properly written or properly tested your computer will crash, and sometimes, in extreme circumstances, so will the planes reliant on it.

During testing and operation, the problems bugs create are traditionally classified according to severity. Category C is okay, Category B is

---

[1] Which I then had independently corroborated, checking out his job roles and the technical accuracy of his allegations with other computer experts.

serious and Category A means the system might be unusable. Clint told me Horizon, when he first encountered it, was infested.

'There were thousands, *thousands* of bugs in the system. You could not see for leaping antelopes, and a lot of them were As and Bs.'

Clint's initial role was undefined.

'My manager knew enough about computers to realise he was in the shit, so when he saw I came from a technical background and how much experience I had, he just said, "Go in there and find out what the developers are doing." '

Clint said what he saw was not pretty. 'They had a team of eight developers who were some of the worst people I've ever seen. There were a couple of good lads in there who knew how to code properly and were interested in learning and having a properly structured development project, but the rest … it was just … it was like kindergarten. They didn't know, they weren't interested in knowing and it was just about filling their pockets with money and going home at the end of the day.'

It seemed to Clint that some managers didn't know the difference between a good developer and a bad developer, because they weren't developers themselves. This included the former Post Office man who'd been put in charge of developing Horizon's Electronic Point of Sale (EPoS) system – the front-end terminal which would sit inside each Post Office branch, recording the transactions. Clint was aghast.

'He didn't have any experience, to my knowledge, in running a development team, writing code, how to make sure the guys knew what they were doing, recruiting the right people, putting them in the right place, system testing, volume testing, any of this stuff that you really need to be doing in a development team.'

He was, according to Clint, in the wrong job.

'He was a Post Office guy. He should have been there as a business advisor, and they should have had a proper development manager in charge of running that development team. There were no specs getting written, there were no development controls going on, there was no design written down, there was nothing.'

Clint told me that after spending a few weeks trying to properly understand the project, he had a decent handle on most of the problems. He reckoned Horizon's third-party touchscreen interface software worked well, but the code behind the touchscreen buttons (written in a mixture of three programming languages: Visual Basic, C and C++), was not good. The biggest problem, however, was the information being written to something called a message store.

The Riposte message store was a powerful piece of third-party software within the Horizon system, containing some of its fundamental operating instructions. Riposte also functioned to ensure the important financial data being inputted was safely transferred and duplicated to off-site mainframe storage computers.

'The first thing that you should always do with a system like that,' said Clint, 'is design and agree a data dictionary and a message library repository, basically to say, "These are the messages that are allowed to be written to the message store and they all provide the following function… " '

Clint continued, 'It's almost like an API – a programming interface[2] – so that you have a list of allowed messages, agreed messages, which can all be written to the correct format with the correct content. You should also have a layer of software that lies on top of the message store which checks any application above it that's trying to write a message conforms to the agreed data dictionary. Otherwise, you can just write freestyle to the message store, which is what they were doing. There was no application interface in there, no agreed data catalogue or anything.'

According to Clint, Horizon's developers had spent the last couple of years 'firing any old shit' into the message store as they changed and developed the product. Clint explained that this was a recipe for disaster. If a message was given a new data field, but this wasn't retrospectively applied, the counter software could retrieve an old message with what it would now perceive to be a missing data field. The reaction of the application would be unpredictable. It could crash. It could send the wrong information to the wrong place, unnoticed. It could cause the wrong values to be applied to a transaction. It could cause values to halve, or double, or multiply.

Knowing exactly what code is in your system is essential. 'If the application's not checking that the contents are correct, which they weren't because they weren't writing them properly, then the message store is completely corrupted with garbage,' Clint told me. This meant the software had no integrity. It was unreliable.

---

[2] Literally, an Application Programming Interface, a set of definitions and protocols for building and integrating application software. APIs allow two applications to talk to each other.

I wondered how this could have happened. It was a question Clint was asking himself at the time. He said that from talking to people around the project he gathered the Horizon software at the EPoS end was originally written by a small nucleus of people as a prototype, to show what a Riposte-based counter system might look like. It was this which won them the contract.

'And what you should do when you get the contract,' Clint said, 'is throw the prototype away and start from the beginning, because all that prototype is, is proof of concept – the architect's cardboard model. You don't start putting roof tiles on the cardboard building – which is what they were doing.'

Having reviewed the whole EPoS side of the Horizon project, and tested his theories with some developers he trusted, Clint says he went back to his bosses with a few home truths.

'I broke it down and said, "You can keep these bits at a push if you have to. But that bit in the middle, these bits of the engine, the gearbox, you need to throw them away and rebuild them. Starting with the cash account. You've got to throw the cash account away and you've got to rewrite it." '

The cash account wasn't an account in the traditional sense of the word. It was a program which crawled through every transaction on each Horizon terminal in each branch at the end of the day's trading. It then came up with a figure which should correspond exactly with the amount of physical cash on the premises. That figure was then automatically uploaded to the Post Office's central servers overnight. It is a relatively simple task to describe, but not necessarily to execute. Given its central importance to the financial integrity of the Horizon system, it had to be bullet-proof. It wasn't. The code was not good enough.

Clint told his bosses at Fujitsu the cash account had to be completely scrapped and rebuilt from scratch. They refused his request, saying it would take too long and cost too much. He was told to repair it. Clint told me he convened and ran a team of hand-picked developers who did what they could, before internal politics saw him shifted to working on the back-end of the Horizon project.

I listened to Clint with rising levels of alarm. When he had finished, I asked him to sum Horizon up. Without hesitation, he replied:

'It was a prototype that had been bloated and hacked together afterwards for several years, and then pushed screaming and kicking out of the door. It should never have seen the light of day. *Never*.'

Over the first six months of 1999, whilst Clint was still there, Horizon's PFI contract was reorganised once more. The Benefits Agency, having almost fatally holed the project with its decision to take swipe-cards off the table, walked away completely. The government decided Horizon would become the Post Office's baby. Fujitsu (which had written off £180m on the project and hadn't yet worked out how it was going to get it back) would continue to develop Horizon on a fixed payment basis. A subsequent National Audit Office report estimated the botched procurement had wasted ***half a billion pounds*** of government money. So much for Fujitsu shouldering nearly all of the risk.

Once the decision had been made by government, the Post Office's IT and business impact teams were understandably concerned about taking responsibility for Horizon. They wanted the opportunity to test it properly before it went anywhere near the Post Office estate.[3]

On 4 March 1999, the Post Office's Horizon Programme Board examined the risks associated with the project. It scored them up to 25, multiplying their 'impact value' by their 'probability value', and graded them green, amber and red. Anything over 15 was a red. The first five risks listed were red. All of them were scored at the maximum 25. The authors wrote:

> 'Due to lack of adequate visibility of the ICL Pathway [read: Horizon] design, and the lack of support from the contract to leverage this visibility, we have been unable to gain a high level of assurance in the adequacy or suitability of the service.'

Under 'Action' it rather desperately states:

> 'All other approaches having failed – final entreaty has been made for cooperation from Pathway [read: Fujitsu] to make available appropriate level of documentation.'

Fujitsu saw this concern from their clients as yet more interference, which could lead to yet more changes and yet more cost. Also, they still couldn't

[3] A word regularly used to describe either the Post Office systems networks and/or its physical estate (including Crown and sub-Post Offices and its administrative buildings).

get Horizon to work. Fujitsu put up a shield of commercial confidentiality, citing the terms of the PFI project, and shut everyone out.

Behind that shield, Fujitsu's developers, testers and engineers feverishly bashed their new IT system into something that looked like it might work.

Although Horizon was clearly not ready to go live, in July 1999 the government announced the Post Office would start its switch to full automation in October the same year. A joint Working Group was convened. Base units, touchscreens and keyboards were bought and specced up. Teams were hired. A live trial began.

Margaret Davison's Post Office in West Boldon was one of the branches selected for the trial. In a short, but vivid memoir, written long after her retirement in 2006, Margaret describes what it was like:

> 'The installation took place over some days when a constant stream of electricians, Post Office staff and computer geeks climbed or sat all around my office whilst I tried to keep my counter and business running. Looking back I wonder how I retained my sanity or my strength... There were so many faults in the system which you were expected to cope with, learning on your feet with a queue of customers in front of you ... not to mention helpline staff so inexperienced and under pressure it often took over an hour to get a call to them answered. How I avoided a nervous breakdown at the age of 60 in a one-position very busy little village Post Office, I do not know. From day one the system was flawed.'[4]

In August 1999, *two months* before the project would go live, a Post Office 'business impact analysis' of Horizon listed six high severity problems, including, 'TIP [Transaction Information Processing] derived cash account not equal to electronic cash account received by TIP.'

In other words, the cash account Clint was so exercised about still didn't work.

Under 'Business Impact', the report's authors wrote that the Post Office 'has not seen a detailed description of the faults creating the missing data, neither has it seen any description of how and when these faults

---

[4] As published on former Subpostmaster Tim McCormack's blog, ***Problems with POL***.

will be fixed.'

The effect was clear: 'These gaps in data will ultimately be reflected in balance sheet accounts.'

The seriousness of the situation was underscored by the startling revelation that Fujitsu had admitted to the report's authors that they 'do not yet understand the root cause of the problem.'

Other high severity problems included back-end data losses causing accounting discrepancies, transactions being lost before they could even be written to the cash account, system freezes and 'lock ups,' printer failures, and general losses of accounting integrity.

It is perhaps no surprise that in September 1999 the Post Office board refused to sign off the project, noting 'serious doubts' over the reliability of the software.

Yet, a month later, in October 1999, the minutes note, 'Following remedial work around two issues which had previously prevented acceptance … the system had now been accepted with implementation proceeding at a rate of 200 offices per week.'

How Horizon's serious system problems could be fixed to the satisfaction of the Post Office board so quickly (and conveniently) is a mystery. The document, presentation or written assurance which gave them this comfort has not yet been made public. Nevertheless, the board had signed it off, rollout was underway, and Horizon would soon be wreaking its havoc across the Post Office network.

THE FIRST GOVERNMENT AGENCY

To understand how the Horizon scandal could happen, it's worth trying to understand what the Post Office actually is.

If you have spent any time in the UK, you are likely to have some sort of concept of the Post Office. Depending on where you live, and possibly how old you are, that concept will vary. The image of a middle-aged husband and wife team running a village branch as their last job before retirement still just about holds true; but the network has changed significantly over the last 20 years. There are now hundreds of busy suburban outlets in the hands of limited companies, or entrepreneurial Subpostmasters with multiple branches seeking profit in economies of scale. In recent years the Post Office has also retreated from many of its imposing city-centre Crown Office buildings, and chosen instead to inhabit the basements and back ends of newsagents and stationery chains.

Unfortunately, a down-at-heel shabbiness characterises many Post Offices. In 2018, the journalist Patrick Collinson wrote an article for The Guardian entitled: 'How did we allow our Post Offices to become so grotty?' You only have to drive by a few urban branches in large cities to see what he means.

Yet the Post Office still holds (and undoubtedly trades off) a unique position in the British psyche. In the alleyway behind my house there is a wooden telegraph pole. Carved into the pole at just about head height are the initials 'GPO.' This stands for General Post Office – a brand which pre-dates the industrial revolution, the British Empire, and, indeed, Britain itself.[1]

There has been a Master of the Post since Henry VIII's time, and in 1660, Charles II approved an 'Act for Erecting and Establishing a Post Office,' which created the role of Postmaster General, and 'one Generall Post Office … soe that speedy and safe dispatches may be had.'

The General Post Office formally survived as a directly-controlled government department until 1969. But the Post Office isn't just old, it is everywhere.

During the eighteen hundreds, the Post Office's activities grew

---

[1] Established in 1707 with the Acts of Union between Scotland and England.

exponentially on the back of huge railway expansion, democratising long-distance communication and accelerating Britain's capacity to conduct business between its great cities. Nineteenth and twentieth century developments in telecommunications – telegrams, and then telephones – were monopolised by the GPO, which required thousands of operators and engineers to keep these new technologies going. By 1936, the Post Office (along with its glamorous, liveried sub-brand, the Royal Mail) was the largest employer in the country, with a quarter of a million staff.

The Post Office as a concept is therefore more than just a retail presence on the High Street. It can legitimately be said to be the oldest government agency, and at least until recently, the main physical interface between the British state and its citizens. Even now, Post Office paraphernalia retains certain *romantic* associations which are bound up with concepts of national identity. Think about images of Penny Blacks, post boxes, mail trains, switchboard operators, postcards and telegrams. The apparatus of the networked state has been lionised in poetry, literature, film and television. More often than not, they were presented as symbols of British greatness, representing notions of trust, efficiency, stability and security.

But the Post Office's eternal presence has been preserved by something with an altogether more sinister edge. As well as being part of the fabric of the nation, the efficient and secure operation of the Post Office is protected by its proximity to power. Interrupting or defrauding Post Office business comes with severe penalties.

For most of the last three centuries, the Post Office has maintained a specialised investigative unit. This unit has direct access to the criminal justice system through the Post Office's in-house prosecutors. In fact, the Post Office Investigation Branch (known by the start of the twentieth century as 'IB') is the oldest recognised criminal investigation force in the world. It pre-dates the police. In the eighteenth and nineteenth centuries, postal workers caught stealing from the mail could expect to be hanged. The Post Office Museum website proudly states that the Investigation Branch 'has worked to detect offences against the post and prosecute the perpetrators.' These could be highwaymen, robbers, clerks or delivery boys. Or even spies.

During the twentieth century IB personnel worked with the security services to identify mail sent by internal subversives. When suspicious letters reached Royal Mail sorting offices, they would be picked up by IB security staff and taken to the first floor of the Post Office's Headquarters in St Martin's-le-Grand, near St Paul's Cathedral. Here, technicians would carefully open the letters to photograph the contents. The photographs were passed to government spooks. The letters were carefully re-sealed and dropped back into the system with their intended recipients none the wiser. In addition, whilst the GPO had responsibility for the nation's phone lines, the Post Office Investigation Branch supplied the security services with phone-taps.

This creepy element to the Post Office's activities wound down as perceived post-war and cold-war threats to the internal stability of the nation dissipated. In 1969, the office of Postmaster General was abolished and the GPO ceased to exist as a brand, though the Post Office and Royal Mail remained state-owned, with a monopoly on the business of shifting letters from one part of the country to another.

In the latter half of the twentieth century IB went through various reorganisations (first becoming an Investigations Division, then a Department). By the eighties it had largely ceded its external investigative activities to the police and was focusing its attention and resources on the internal activities of Royal Mail, Post Office and Parcelforce staff. There were thousands of people within the Post Office network who came into daily contact with large volumes of mail and tempting wads of notes at sorting offices, cash centres and Post Office branches around the country. They needed to be watched.

By all accounts the Post Office Investigations Department (with more than its fair share of burly ex-coppers), was something of a law unto itself. POID[2] had the authority to interview staff under caution. As with its historical predecessors, if POID believed a criminal offence had taken place, instead of handing everything over to the police, or the newly-formed Crown Prosecution Service, Post Office investigators passed their evidence to the Post Office's own in-house prosecutors, who would bring charges directly. In the 1990s the department was renamed POSIS – Post Office Security and Investigation Services – and then, finally, Security Group.

By 2010, when the Post Office's prosecution frenzy was still in full swing, Royal Mail Group (which had turned the tables on its older sibling

2 Pronounced 'pee-oh-eye-dee,' not 'poyed.'

and now counted the Post Office as one of *its* sub-brands) employed 287 investigators and security managers. A five page document informing the public about the activities of RMG Security stated bluntly, 'Those who steal must expect to be detected and prosecuted.'

The process of calling in the heavies when suspicions were raised about nefarious activities at a Post Office branch varied. In a Crown Office it was relatively straightforward. A branch manager would spot or be informed about suspected criminal activity and refer that information directly to the Security team. Things were a little different when it came to the Post Office's network of Subpostmasters.

This is because Subpostmasters are not, and never have been, Post Office staff. They are small business owners, acting as agents for the Post Office.

Every Subpostmaster is security-checked before being appointed. They are, as a rule, unlikely to be dishonest. But there are thousands of Subpostmasters, employing tens of thousands of counter assistants. Billions of pounds in cash wash through the Post Office network on a monthly basis. Criminal activity at some level, by someone, is a given. Detecting and stopping it is another matter altogether. Pre-Horizon, once a tranche of cash had been received by a branch from a Post Office cash centre, the Post Office essentially lost sight of it, becoming wholly reliant on the weekly filed accounts to know where it had gone. Close monitoring of what was happening in any one of the Post Office's 20,000+ branches was impossible. There was no CCTV or electronic data collection. Almost everything was done on trust.

The only way of knowing if a Subpostmaster's filed accounts had any bearing on reality was by paying them a visit. This was done by the Post Office's UK-wide squad of 'auditors' who would descend on a branch without warning, lock the door and conduct a full stock-take and cash count, with the Subpostmaster present. Auditors chose which branch to visit either at random, on the basis of a tip off, or if someone in Chesterfield had flagged something alarming. If everything was in order, the auditors would leave and the branch could reopen. If a small amount of money was missing, the Subpostmaster would be required to make it good before being allowed to reopen. Some kind of warning might be issued. If a large amount of money was missing, the Subpostmaster would be suspended by their local contract manager and the Security team's feared investigators would be summoned. It was a rather agricultural approach, but right up until the end of the twentieth century, it was all the

Post Office had.

Horizon was going to be the Post Office's Big Bang. Instead of being in the dark about what was going on in their thousands of branches, every transaction put through every Post Office till in the country would now be recorded and downloaded onto the Post Office's central servers every night. A window onto the activities of Subpostmasters and their assistants had been opened. The lights had come on.

ROLLING OUT HORIZON

Sio Lohrasb is a former technical lead at Fujitsu, responsible for the live rollout of Horizon. I found his details on social media and thought it was worth chancing my arm to see if he was willing to be interviewed for this book. Being an amiable chap, he saw no reason why not. It was fascinating to have a lengthy chat with someone who had the job of introducing Horizon to hundreds of Subpostmasters across the country. Unfortunately, due to the coronavirus pandemic, we couldn't meet in person.

'I thought Horizon was state of the art,' Sio told me, when we finally got our Zoom link working. 'I actually really liked the solution, and the hardware we were delivering was quite high spec. I mean, it didn't run so well, but that's because it was being asked to do so much. But it was very forward-thinking.'

It was Sio's job to help Subpostmasters make sense of Horizon, both as a piece of kit and as a concept. 'It was really daunting to the older generation,' Sio told me. 'Some of them just weren't ready for it. One guy was selling postcards in his shop, and I said to him, "You see all these individual postcards? Each one of these could be a holiday, that you could sell through Horizon." But he couldn't grasp it. He called it a sledgehammer to crack a nut.'

Sio had a team of installers who would help Subpostmasters switch from paper accounts to touchscreen data entry, working with them to patiently input their existing figures into Horizon, and holding their hands as they came to terms with this brave new world. There were plenty of Subpostmasters who welcomed the arrival of the new IT system, but a few found it genuinely terrifying.

Sio recalled 'one old dear' who went to press her new Horizon touchscreen 'with her finger shaking, bless her. I really felt sorry for her. But we never rushed anybody. We gave her as much time as she needed to make her comfortable and make sure she was all right.'

Even so, Sio admits there was a problem from the start. 'Yeah, there was incompatibility there with the older generation.'

WHAT IS A SUBPOSTMASTER?

Today, the terms Postmaster and Subpostmaster are used interchangeably. They describe exactly the same job. This is a recent conflation. The role of Head Postmaster, distinct from a *Sub*postmaster, survived well into the 1980s. In the nineteenth century, there was a clear hierarchical divide between the two. Head Postmasters were regional appointees of the Postmaster General, responsible for the receipt and distribution of the entire mail operation in a given area. Subpostmasters were an altogether less fortunate breed.

Unlike Head Postmasters, Subpostmasters were not employed by the Post Office. Their role attracted no pension, holiday or sick pay. They were self-employed, and on their appointment were expected to install their Post Office counter and telegraph communications fixtures at their own expense. In Queen Victoria's time, they received no extra allowance for working Sundays – or up to twelve hours on Christmas Day – and often found the cost of running a branch outweighed its income. In short, Postmasters – full time members of Post Office staff – were the haves; Subpostmasters were the have nots.

There was also a not-so-subtle class distinction at work. Within the Post Office, Postmasters were seen and treated as, maybe not quite *gentlemen* (after all, they worked for a living), but an altogether better sort of person, going about the Queen's business in service of their country and Empire. Subpostmasters were traders, shopkeepers – lower-middle class sorts opportunistically seeking to improve their social standing by association with a national institution. Subpostmasters were accepted by the Post Office hierarchy on sufferance, mainly because their contribution to a functioning network was essential, but they were never quite trusted or embraced.

In 1896, Joseph Ramms, a stationer living in Wakefield, wrote, 'I was desirous of the appointment as Subpostmaster, in the belief that to have employment from the Government was a direct road to success in commercial life.'

Ramms' application succeeded, but he soon discovered it wasn't everything it was cracked up to be. 'I was doing the work of a Subpostmaster,' he wrote, 'and paying for the privilege, as the working expenses of the office were decidedly more than the income from all sources.'[1]

This was not sustainable. In 1897, aggrieved Subpostmasters, led by Ramms, formed a trade association – the National Federation of Subpostmasters. Campaigns, threatened strikes and wider social advances led to some improvements in working conditions, but the lot of a Subpostmaster in the first half of the twentieth century was not a happy one.[2]

In the 1950s, after substantial lobbying, the government awarded Subpostmasters a series of salary increases. For the first time it was just about possible to make a living. The hours were long, and you had to be a savvy retailer, but there were perks. You had a government stipend, your retail business got plenty of footfall, and as a holder of public office you became a visible and respected pillar of your local community.

Throughout the technological and retail revolutions of the seventies and eighties, branch sub-Post Offices barely changed. So long as their biggest client (the government), kept putting business their way (for example, pensions, tax discs, housing benefit, social security stamps) and as long as that gave the general public an incentive to regularly visit their local Post Office (which it did), a Subpostmaster could make a living. During the latter part of the twentieth century, the National Federation of Subpostmasters seemed to spend a lot of their lobbying efforts resisting initiatives which could take government business away from their members. To run a profitable business, Subpostmasters needed to be the middle man between state and citizen. On many occasions, trading on their central importance to the High Street, they won the argument with both politicians and the public.

Despite this, and despite the official abolition of Head Postmasters at the end of the twentieth century, the Post Office's cultural snobbery towards, and lack of trust in, their Subpostmasters never quite disappeared.

---

1 '100 years of proud history 1897–1997' – The National Federation of Subpostmasters.

2 It has also come full circle – in 2019, the Post Office's interim CEO Alisdair Cameron admitted to MPs that cuts to income and the removal of salaries meant it was no longer possible to make a living from running a Post Office. 'We are very clear and we have been clear for years that standalone Post Offices are not usually financially viable. It needs that retail support.' With staff costs (borne by a Subpostmaster) factored in, a Post Office counter is nowadays loss-making, but it gives the gift of footfall to a retail premises.

Whilst Subpostmasters were treated like employees and given some of the benefits employees might enjoy (including a guaranteed salary), the Post Office took the view that, contractually, Subpostmasters were business agents, operating sub-Post Offices as franchises.

This is legally set down in the document which underpins the relationship between a Subpostmaster and the Post Office – the Subpostmasters Contract. It spells out exactly what is expected of a Subpostmaster in return for the privilege of having a sub-Post Office. It is completely non-negotiable.

The contract makes clear the extent to which the office of Subpostmaster is in the gift of the Post Office. Once bestowed, it can be removed for any perceived infraction, or transferred to a more deserving candidate on receipt of three months' notice. A Subpostmaster is in a position of responsibility, and therefore has to abide by strict rules. The Subpostmasters Contract makes it clear the Post Office has the right to query, audit or investigate a Subpostmaster's branch at any time.

The most notorious clause in the Subpostmasters Contract is Section 12 (Responsibility for Post Office Stock and Cash), Clause 12 (Losses). It states:

> 'The Subpostmaster is responsible for all losses caused through his own negligence, carelessness or error, and also for losses of all kinds caused by his Assistants. Deficiencies due to such losses must be made good without delay.'

The Post Office took this to mean that if a Subpostmaster had a negative discrepancy in their accounts, and could not prove it was *not* caused by their 'negligence, carelessness or error', it was on them. The clause also meant that if a Subpostmaster's assistant messed up, or looted the safe, it was on the Subpostmaster too. Section 12:12 was designed as a clear contractual incentive to make sure each Subpostmaster ran a tight ship, employed the right assistants and trained them well.

On the day Subpostmasters took control of their branches, it was expected they would sign their contract in situ, along with the Official Secrets Act and several other legally binding documents. The contents of these documents were often a mystery to both the incoming Subpostmaster and the Post Office Contract Manager who proffered them. Subpostmasters often had no idea what they were signing up to and even if they asked, were unlikely to get a sensible answer.

The Subpostmasters who went into business with the Post Office tended to be bright and diligent, proud to work for a national institution with an illustrious history. Before applying to run a branch, many Subpostmasters had successful careers and led innocuous and blameless lives. Some had been police officers, or served in the military. Others were done with being middle-managers in large businesses. Most had built up a modest nest egg and were looking to invest in a solid proposition as their last job before retirement. Another typical group already ran small retail businesses and were looking to invest their savings into a brand which would bring them more visibility and footfall.

You might think anyone who doesn't read a contract before they sign it is an idiot, but it comes down to how well you understand the risks involved, and the consequences of something going wrong. Downloading an app to your phone might require giving it permission to access your address book, location, camera, microphone, operating system and personal details. This carries a significant risk. But most of us don't even read the legally binding agreement which comes with the app. We just tick the box without any idea what the app developer intends to do with the access we've just granted it.

This is because we think whatever could happen, won't happen to us. Or even if it does, the outcome won't be catastrophic, because we can probably rely on some kind of unspecified legislation to protect us.

A few years ago, a BBC colleague of mine asked Geoffrey Sturgess, a laconic and worldly-wise franchise lawyer, to review the Subpostmasters Contract for a TV piece we were making. Geoffrey had a good read of it before stating on camera it was 'unfair.' He caveated this by saying that being unfair is par for the course with this type of contract. 'What's unusual,' he noted, 'is the really unfair way in which the Post Office enforces it.'

Pre-Horizon, the Subpostmaster/Post Office relationship worked on a combination of trust, the threat of penalties and the expectation of mutual benefit. Subpostmasters had to keep tabs on the cash that came into and went out of their branches. They filled in their own accounts, signed them and sent them to the Post Office for examination. There are strong disincentives to filing false accounts. It is a criminal offence.

Horizon, when it came, subtly adjusted the dynamic between the Post Office and Subpostmaster by inserting a third party into it. Horizon didn't just combine a branch's till transactions and accounts, it took *control* of them. This was not acknowledged by the Post Office. Certainly, the Subpostmasters Contract was not redrawn to reflect it. The 152-page version I have from 2002 (which is the 1994 version with a lot of extra rules front-loaded onto it) acknowledges Horizon only in passing.[1]

[1] Twice in the context of linking it to an ISDN line, and twice in terms of giving assistants their own Horizon login.

TRACY IS SENT TO PRISON

The Post Office's investigators seemed fascinated by Tracy Felstead's family holiday. 'They said, "Did you pay for everybody to go?"' she remembers.

Tracy's mum and dad got involved. 'We said, "Right, you can have access to everybody's bank accounts so you can see exactly how people have paid for the holiday and where the money's come from."'

The investigators were not satisfied.

Three weeks later, at the end of April 2001, Tracy was sacked. She was charged by the Post Office's criminal prosecutors with theft and false accounting 'because my signature was on the paperwork.'

Tracy's solicitor was unamused. The Post Office investigators had no evidence of theft. The prosecution didn't make sense.

Although Tracy was devastated, she remembers thinking things would work out. The Post Office would realise its mistake and drop the charges, or if the worst happened, the justice system would allow her to prove her innocence.

Word of the prosecution leaked into the local community. Tracy found herself the victim of a whispering campaign.

'Family friends, like the guy who got me the job – his family refused to talk to me. They just totally ignored me. And I had people looking at me as if I was a thief. You know – "*She's done this.*"'

Tracy's self-belief began to crumble alarmingly quickly.

'The only way to explain it is that you're in a black hole. You feel trapped … suffocated. I couldn't understand how anyone could think I would steal anything. My mental health, my whole life took a hit. I was a bubbly girl. I would go out. I had a decent life, I enjoyed life. And then all of a sudden … I didn't want to go out.'

Things escalated. 'Because I had time on my hands, because I wasn't working, because I'd been dismissed, I got stuck in a rut. The more I was indoors and the more my mind wasn't occupied, the more frantic I became.'

Tracy went to see her GP, who prescribed Prozac anti-depressants. They didn't work. Over the summer of 2001, Tracy tried to kill herself.

'I didn't want to have to answer questions I couldn't answer. I didn't want people to see me. I didn't want to go to court. The stigma was very strong. I didn't want to feel like that. I wanted me back. I wanted to be me again and I didn't feel I was me. I just wanted to die.'

Tracy took an overdose in her room. She was found by a friend while she was still conscious and rushed to hospital, where she had her stomach pumped.

A few weeks later Tracy took another overdose. 'I thought *I can't deal with this anymore. I can't cope*. I just didn't want to be alive. I didn't want to feel the pain.'

Alone in the house, Tracy slipped out of consciousness. By luck, her fiancé Jon came home early from work and found her. She was rescued by the emergency services again. This time she was not sent home but committed to a secure psychiatric unit at the Princess Royal Hospital in Bromley.

Tracy was given intensive psychotherapy treatment and responded well, but once she was out, she had to deal with the reality of being prosecuted. Tracy was not a well woman, but the Post Office clearly felt it was important to nail her.

First there was a hearing at Guildford magistrates' court, where Tracy pleaded not guilty to both theft and false accounting. Then came the three-day trial in front of a jury at Kingston Crown Court.

Tracy was a wreck. She remembers shivering in the dock as she watched the trial happen around her. She can't recall much about what was said, but she remembers a point that came up during her cross-examination.

'Basically, they were saying, "You did take the money. Your signature is there. It's your till. You've taken the money." I said, "I went to the manager and explained, and I was told it would be okay." But it didn't seem like they wanted to listen. I couldn't answer the prosecution's questions because I didn't know what had happened.'

Tracy was convicted by a majority verdict. 'I was just in disbelief. I just couldn't believe what I was hearing.'

Tracy wasn't sentenced immediately. Because of her fragile mental state and previous suicide attempts the judge wanted psychiatric reports completed. Without Tracy's knowledge her family were also told if they paid the Post Office the 'missing' £11,503.28, a prison sentence was less likely. Between Tracy's family and Jon's parents they raised the total, and handed it over.

When Jon's mum told Tracy she hit the roof. 'I was like, "Why are you paying them something I haven't taken?" They were trying to save me, but I was so strong-willed… I thought people would see it as a sign of guilt.'

On her sentencing date, Tracy was told by the judge that she was a liar, that she had stolen money from pensioners and she had disgraced her family. Tracy was invited to apologise. She refused.

'I said in court, "I'm not saying sorry for something I have not done. I'm not saying sorry because I haven't done anything wrong." '

The judge decided this lack of remorse required a custodial sentence and sent her to prison for six months. Tracy's father had to watch his daughter being led from the dock to the cells in handcuffs.

'I was absolutely petrified,' remembers Tracy. 'Petrified. My barrister came and saw me. He said, "Something's not right, but I don't know how to prove it." We didn't know how to prove it. We almost didn't know how to defend ourselves, in a way. Because we've got these big guys, they're saying, "Well, you've signed that piece of paper and used that till and it's a discrepancy and you're the only one that uses that till and blah, blah, blah." As much as you can say, "Well, actually, no, I wasn't, other people used that till as well," and they just didn't want to listen.'

On 20 June 2002, Tracy was taken away in an armoured van to HMP Holloway. She was put on suicide watch.

'I was in a high-security prison at the age of 19. I walked in and … you go through all the protocol. You've got to strip. You've got to be searched.'

As with all new inmates, Tracy was brought before the prison governor. 'I sat down, and I was obviously very, very distraught because they had to give me medication to calm me down. And he said to me, "What are you doing here? A girl like you shouldn't be here." '

Tracy was assigned to a cell but she was not allowed to be left on her own. She became even more desperate listening to the tales of prisoners who had 'murdered people. I'm with people that … it's their home if that makes sense. You listen to their stories and you think, "Oh my goodness, it's all they've got." They actually go out and re-offend because that's all they've got.'

One afternoon, Tracy walked into a cell to find the body of a girl who had hanged herself. She began to have nightmares. 'There were fights – people screaming they're going to kill someone.'

Tracy spent three months in Holloway. On the day of her release, Jon and her parents were waiting outside.

'I got in the car and I remember I was shaking. Jon gave me my engagement ring back and I put it on my finger. I'd lost a tremendous amount of weight, and all I wanted to do ... I just needed to get home. When I got in, I was conscious about the door going. I said, "Don't close the door." And still to this day I can't have doors closed in my house ... because it takes me back to that sound of the prison door slamming.'

Tracy spent the next 20 years battling the mental health repercussions of her experience. In 2020, the Post Office admitted her prosecution was an abuse of process. The following year, the Court of Appeal ruled it was more than that. It was an affront to the entire justice system and should never have happened.

In the four years leading up to the rollout of the Horizon system, the Post Office prosecuted 52 Subpostmasters or Post Office staff for shortfall-related offences. In the four years after the rollout, the number more than quadrupled to 220. No one outside the Post Office queried this leap in prosecution activity because no one was aware of it. The Post Office was not required to publish its numbers.

Tracy Felstead was not the only Crown Office worker to be prosecuted using Horizon evidence. Horizon was of course capable of going wrong in Crown Offices the same as it was everywhere else[1] but Crown Office employees had more protection. Managers could use their discretion to park small discrepancies in a suspense account and the business would swallow the loss.

If large discrepancies in a Crown Office arose, as in Tracy's case, things would get serious,[2] but as the years went on the Communication Workers Union, which represented directly-employed Crown Office staff, learned to take a sceptical view of any allegation which relied solely on Horizon data.

Horizon's real killing fields were out in the branch sub-Post Offices, where a different union operated – the National Federation of Subpostmasters.

---

1 Post Office internal document, September 2008 - *Losses and Gains: A Quick Guide.*

2 And they did. 121 people working in Crown Offices were convicted of Horizon-related shortfall offences between 2000 and 2015.

THE NFSP

Years ago, when I first started digging into this story, I needed to find some independent evidence there was a problem with Horizon. I was speaking to a small number of Subpostmasters with harrowing stories, but most of them had criminal convictions. It was all very well me believing they might be telling the truth, but without compelling documentary evidence, the case for a BBC investigation was weak. Especially as most viewers could walk into their local Post Office and see this supposedly dysfunctional Horizon IT system working without any problems.

I had no paperwork or independent witnesses. I also had flat denials from the Post Office. A journalist who has met someone with a story to tell will often seek information from a variety of sources before approaching their commissioning editor. If the story is a complaint about industrial malpractice, a quick phone call to one of the trade unions operating in that sector can throw up useful contextual information. The complainant might be raising something a union is already alive to, or believes is symptomatic of a wider problem. Unions act like canaries down a coal mine, bringing issues or potential issues to the attention of management. If management isn't interested, a union might go to the media, either as part of a campaign or through individual officials briefing their contacts.

So what of the Postmasters' union, the National Federation of Subpostmasters? As befits a membership comprised of people who are not traditional employees, the NFSP – otherwise known as 'the Fed' – is not a traditional union.

'It's more like a Rotary Club than anything else,' a rival union rep once explained to me. 'They seem to be far more interested in holding annual dinners and congratulating each other than doing much else.'

That could be unfair both to the Fed and Rotary Clubs, but I could see what he was getting at. Unlike stereotypical union activists, Postmasters do not see themselves as oppressed shop-floor workers who want to fight management. They want to *be* management. They are employers themselves, entrepreneurial, self-reliant, small-'c' conservatives who instinctively trust officialdom and state institutions. Although they expect their membership body to look after their interests, Subpostmasters want their relationship with the Post Office to be understood as a partnership of equals. It is a self-image the NFSP likes to reflect and project, and one the Post Office is only too happy to take advantage of. The key, and fatal, word in all of this, is pride.

In 1996, the NFSP's then General Secretary, Colin Baker, posed for photographs in front of a Post Office branch in Stroud. He was standing alongside the Secretary of State for Business, Peter Lilley, and the Post Office Managing Director, Stuart Sweetman. There were smiles all round. The three men had set up this PR opportunity to announce a vastly ambitious scheme to put a networked computer system into every Post Office branch in the country. It was presented as a silver bullet which would future-proof every Postmaster's business (and income) for decades.

Automation would not only accommodate proposed changes to the way government benefits were delivered, but it would open up a lucrative world of digital versatility – banking, bill payments, product sales and cost efficiencies were all within reach. It was the deal of the century, and the NFSP were at the very heart of it, selling the network to members at national and regional conferences, promising a golden future.

'I cannot help but be optimistic,' murmured a dewy-eyed Baker. 'Members,' he said, 'were gazing at a new dawn, a new horizon [clever] unfurling before our eyes. The scope for new business is probably as wide as our imagination.'

The Post Office, with the full support of the NFSP, had bet the farm on Horizon. It could not fail. Protecting the credibility, integrity and operability of the Horizon system was therefore paramount.

From day one of Horizon's rollout, the NFSP refused to countenance any public criticism of the system. To do so could undermine confidence in the Post Office network, and its ability to attract new business.

As the Post Office went on its prosecution spree, any journalist approaching the NFSP would be told (in language strikingly similar to the Post Office's) that Horizon was 'robust.' Requests for off-the-record steers about potentially unsafe convictions were met with dark hints that the individuals concerned might well be spinning a yarn. Conversations of that nature can have a chilling effect on the publication of any story, especially if the people bringing it to the journalists' attention had pleaded guilty to the crimes they were now saying they hadn't committed.

When I was investigating this story for the first time in late 2010, I had already been warned by campaigners that the NFSP was worse than useless. My colleagues at the BBC approached them directly. They were sent the following statement:

> 'We have complete confidence in the Horizon system, which carries out hundreds of millions of transactions every week at 12,000 Post Office outlets across the country. The NFSP has seen no evidence to suggest that Horizon has been at fault – we believe it to be robust, as does Post Office Ltd, with whom we have regular discussions on the system.'

The Post Office has never been slow to weaponise the NFSP's position, telling us in their statement to the same programme:

> 'The National Federation of Subpostmasters, which vigorously represents the views and interests of Subpostmasters around the entire country, has gone on record on a number of occasions to express its full confidence in the accuracy and robustness of the Horizon system.'

The message could not be clearer: if you don't believe what we're saying about Horizon, talk to the organisation which exists solely to represent its members' interests.

That's not to say the NFSP was entirely supine. On the ground, the picture could be different. Individual area reps would travel to meet suspended Subpostmasters, and act as a sounding board or advocate during formal interviews. Some would be as bad as the executive (many Postmasters believe their reps actively connived with Post Office managers). Others would try to push the issue up the chain to a local branch secretary who may or may not have tried to assist. In the main, though, from the experiences related to me by almost every single former Postmaster *I've* spoken to, any Postmaster raising the issue of Horizon as a potential source of their discrepancies was told by their NFSP rep to forget it, and think of some other reason they might be losing cash.

The decision taken by the NFSP to avoid voicing any public concerns or criticism of Horizon is beyond reprehensible. It made the Fed complicit in the misery and chaos that became the Post Office Horizon IT scandal. Over the next two decades, desperate Subpostmasters, under threat of prosecution or losing their livelihoods, would look to the NFSP for help. Having put its faith in the Horizon system to protect the wider interests of the network, the NFSP publicly cut those Subpostmasters loose, and let them drown.

NOEL THOMAS

Anglesey is a famously wild and beautiful island, which sits just off the north western coast of Wales, linked in two places across the Menai Strait by road and rail bridge to the mainland.[1] Its northern peninsular points like a finger across the Irish Sea towards Belfast, but the island's main ferry links are with Dublin. The Irish capital city lies directly west, 60 miles across the water. Anglesey's main industries are tourism and agriculture. It remains a Welsh-language stronghold.

Noel Thomas was an Anglesey lad, born and bred. He left school at 15, and in 1963 went to work at the marine yard in Holyhead. After a few adventures, he returned home to the tiny village of Bodorgan on the south western side of the island, joining the Royal Mail as a postman on 6 June 1965. Noel became a fixture in Bodorgan and nearby Malltraeth, riding 17 miles a day on his Post Office bike, delivering letters and parcels to his neighbours. He married his sweetheart Eira, and over the next few years the couple had three children.

In 1976, when the Postmaster in Malltraeth retired, Noel spotted an opportunity. Noel's parents ran Malltraeth village stores, where they were helped by Eira. He suggested Eira apply to be the new Subpostmaster, and install a Post Office counter in his parents' shop. Noel's round was usually done by midday so he could help out in the afternoons. The plan was a success. Eira and Noel became the centre of another tight-knit, happy community. The couple's young sons were known in Bodorgan and Malltraeth as 'Postie' and 'Stamp.' Noel and Eira's daughter Sian became 'Sian-post.'

I got to know Noel much later in life. He's a good old boy who likes company, and, being Welsh, singing. He's also a very open and emotional man who cares a great deal about his family and the community around him.

In 1981 a bigger Post Office in Gaerwen – seven miles up the road from Malltraeth – became available, and the Thomases made their move.

---

1 Thomas Telford's Menai Suspension Bridge in 1826 – the world's first major suspension bridge – and Robert Stephenson's Britannia Rail Bridge in 1850.

For the first 13 years in Gaerwen, Eira was the Subpostmaster, while Noel continued as a postie. In 1994, Noel took on the Postmaster's job and Eira switched to managing the shop. By this time Noel had been a county councillor for eight years. He was becoming known and respected, not just by his local community, but across the island.

Horizon arrived at Gaerwen in 2000. Six months before it was installed Noel was sent to the Victoria Hotel in Llanberis, near Mount Snowdon. He was the youngest of six Postmasters who had gathered for three days training on the new machines. Noel had no IT experience of any kind.

'The other Subpostmasters were well into their sixties,' he remembers. 'And they all packed up except me. They decided to retire before Horizon came to their Post Offices. Couldn't be dealing with it, you see?'

Noel describes himself as a 'pen-and-paper man', but at the age of 53 he was too young to retire, and Horizon was not optional for his or anyone else's Post Office. Noel's trainers promised they'd visit him on site to help bed the system in, and they did, on three separate occasions.

Nonetheless, the switch from analogue to digital at Gaerwen Post Office was a culture shock. From the moment it was installed, Noel appears to have been engaged in a mutually antipathetic war of attrition with his new computer terminal.

I asked what he didn't like about it.

'As soon you pressed that button,' he replied, 'your work had gone. Before, you could go back into your paperwork and look over it. But once that button had been pressed you couldn't get anything back. You had no hard copy.'

Noel told me he couldn't get the system to generate automatic paper receipts for every transaction, which made it easy to lose track of things. And that's when the kit worked.

When serving customers, Noel's screen would regularly freeze mid-transaction. Sometimes the freeze became a crash, necessitating a complete reboot. The power supply to the terminal was prone to cutting out. Even when Horizon was functioning as it should, it was laggy and slow. Noel regularly called the Post Office Horizon helpline. The helpline notes for the Gaerwen branch acknowledge data transfer interrupts and several remote rebootings. In December 2001, the entire base unit was taken out and replaced.

Even when the hardware was working, Noel had a tough time

balancing his books.

Before 2005, Horizon trading periods were weekly. After closing up on a Wednesday, Subpostmasters would count the cash in the safe and till trays and then tot up the stamps, tax discs, traveller's cheques and other cash-value products. They would then manually enter all denominations, cheques and other values into the relevant boxes on the Horizon screen. Horizon would reconcile the Subpostmasters' data entries with their weekly transactions and deliver a figure which, in an ideal world, would match the total amount of cash and stock 'on hand' in the branch.

It was Post Office policy that every branch had to balance to zero before it started the next trading period. If you did manage to balance to zero – that is, Horizon's figures matched your cash and stock exactly – congratulations, you could go to bed. If they didn't, you had a problem.

Although very few Subpostmasters were ever told this, Horizon would actually let you roll a discrepancy over into the next trading period, but it didn't like it. Subpostmasters attempting to do so would get a screen warning that this was against procedure and they should not be doing it. If a Subpostmaster went ahead and did it anyway, an electronic red flag would be raised on the Post Office's systems. Before long, HQ (likely via a regional manager) would be on to you, requiring you to make good the discrepancy before the end of the next trading period.

If you had a surplus, you were contractually allowed to keep it.[1] Most Subpostmasters kept their surpluses in the safe, or in an 'unders and overs' tin. Like sensible business people, they knew surpluses didn't appear out of thin air, and were likely to be cancelled out somewhere along the line.

If the balance was negative by a few quid, a Subpostmaster might take that few quid out of the retail till, or the unders and overs tin, and 'make good' the difference. If a Subpostmaster was, say, more than ten pounds out of line, it might be time to start thinking about recounting the cash and stock, or going back through the paperwork looking for duplicate transactions, or mis-keyed entries. The latter was always a potential issue on a touchscreen – for instance, on Horizon, the 00 button is located right next to the 0 button. Screen misalignments, fat fingers and hurried

1 One Subpostmaster told me soon after Horizon had been installed in her branch her weekly balance gave her a £100,000 surplus. Whilst contractually entitled to keep it, she knew it was a ridiculous sum of money and an obvious Horizon error. She called the helpline and they removed the surplus, balancing her account to zero. When her branch later started getting negative discrepancies, the Post Office was not so quick to cancel them out.

counter assistants entering a £50 payment as £500 could cause a £450 discrepancy with one key stroke.

Depending on ability, the number of counter assistants (usually each with their own login/stock unit) and the number of transactions over the course of a week at any given branch, basic mistakes were *relatively* easy to find. To assist with locating possible sources of error, Horizon's rudimentary report-writing (printed on the same 3.5 inch till roll used to deliver customer receipts) was available to Subpostmasters who knew how to use it.

If a Subpostmaster checked their transactions, re-counted their cash and still had a discrepancy, or they had forgotten what to do, or didn't know how to use a piece of Horizon functionality – they could call the helpline. More on that later.

Despite finding things an uphill struggle, Noel slowly got to grips with Horizon. Over time, the more obvious hardware problems seemed to stabilise. But some accounting discrepancies could not be traced. They built up. By 2003, Noel had £6,000 sitting in his branch suspense account.

A Horizon branch suspense account was, on the face of it, a sensible solution for dealing with inexplicable discrepancies. If, like Noel, a Subpostmaster had a sum 'missing' from their branch accounts, and they could not find the source of that discrepancy, they had options. They could shrug their shoulders and make good the discrepancy themselves – from their own savings or retail takings – but no Subpostmaster liked doing that, especially if they knew the discrepancy was nothing to do with them or their assistants. The other option was to put the discrepancy into a local suspense account; that is, lift it out of the weekly figures and park it somewhere to be investigated. This had to be done with the authority of an area manager or the Post Office Suspense Account team.

But what happened then? Who was responsible for that discrepancy? The Subpostmaster or the Post Office? The Post Office was not obliged to investigate the cause of the discrepancy, and Subpostmasters were only responsible if the discrepancy was down to their carelessness, negligence or error.

After a few years of Horizon's operation, branch suspense accounts up and down the country were filled with disputed discrepancies. The sums involved were growing by the thousand. The Post Office was leaning on Subpostmasters to make the discrepancies good with some success (the threat of being sacked for refusing was an effective motivator), but many Subpostmasters were refusing to accept responsibility for gaps in branch accounts which they were certain had nothing to do with them. It was becoming a real headache for both Subpostmasters and the Post Office.

In 2005, the Post Office came up with an elegant solution. It removed the branch suspense account option from Horizon. Subpostmasters could no longer park discrepancies in suspense. They *had* to accept discrepancies as debts. Great for the Post Office. Not so good for Subpostmasters.

Under the post-2005 regime, the Horizon terminal screen presented a Postmaster with two choices to settle a discrepancy. They could either press the button marked 'Settle to Cash or Cheque', which meant the Postmaster had made good the discrepancy immediately, or they could press 'Settle Centrally' which acknowledged the debt was the Subpostmaster's, but to be paid at a later date. The Subpostmaster could then call the helpline to contest their debt. Once the Post Office had done as much or as little investigation it felt was necessary, it would either issue an error notice (later called a Transaction Correction[2]) to rebalance the books (effectively acknowledging the error was at the Post Office end) or require the Subpostmaster to make good the discrepancy, via a debt notice.

[2] Essentially a credit (or debit) note, manually generated by the Post Office, which electronically altered a branch's accounts.

NOT TO WORRY

Not knowing what to do with the £6,000 discrepancy he had been allowed to put in suspense, Noel called in the Post Office.

'The regional head manager came up to see me with my line manager, and we sorted it out in our back room,' Noel told me. 'It was settled between us. Half and half.'

For a man earning little more than £24,000 a year, swallowing a £3,000 loss was hard. Noel hoped that would be the end of it. But it wasn't. Inexplicable discrepancies began to build once more.

Each week the gap between the figures on Noel's Horizon screen and reality grew wider. Noel knew that if he raised the issue with his area manager again he could be held liable for at least half his discrepancy, if not all of it.

Noel continued to call the helpline, but neither rolled his losses over into the next weekly accounting period (because that was not allowed) nor sought permission to put them into suspense (because he'd seen how that ended). Instead, he signed off Horizon's figures, effectively agreeing that the number on the screen matched the value of cash and stock in the Gaerwen branch. Noel was later to discover the Post Office considered this to be falsifying accounts, making him liable for a criminal charge of false accounting.

I asked Noel why he decided to sign off Horizon figures which didn't match his cash and stock rather than go back to management to explain his concerns.

'At the time there was this big splurge of closing Post Offices,' he said, 'and I didn't want to lose my Post Office. I didn't want the village to lose its Post Office. And when I did tell the helpline about the problems, they told me to carry on. It would be sorted out by them.'

Ah, the helpline. In a scandal notable for lamentable failings at almost every level, the helpline's role as a facilitator of chaos within the Post Office network has probably not, even now, been fully appreciated.

The helpline, or as it became known, the 'hell-line', was the first point of contact for a frazzled Subpostmaster who had gone from serving customers behind their counter all day to working their way through a ten foot long strip of receipt paper trying to understand why they might be £60… £600… or £6,000 out of pocket. The advice Subpostmasters got from the helpline had a huge bearing on the decisions they took. Given it was coming directly from a representative of the Post Office, they could be forgiven for acting on it. Unfortunately, the helpline was under-staffed (which made it difficult to get through) and the staff were under-trained. When Horizon came in, the first line support operators knew little more about the system than the Subpostmasters themselves.

Subpostmasters who were having obvious technical problems – screen-freezes, printer failures and the like – would be referred by the helpline to technical support, run by Fujitsu. Fujitsu might arrange for a hardware 'swap-out' or a visit from an engineer. If the concern was thought to be more process or accounting driven, Subpostmasters would be diverted to a Post Office support team representative who would attempt to either talk them through the necessary screens and buttons, or offer advice.

If the telephone support provided by the Post Office couldn't help with a problem, a visit by a trainer or area manager might be arranged. If it became apparent what had looked like an accounting or process issue might actually be a software issue – that is, Horizon wasn't working properly – the Post Office or Fujitsu technical support could put a Subpostmaster through to specialist technical support. Software Support Centre, run out of Fujitsu HQ in Bracknell, dealt with complicated hardware issues, software errors and bugs. They could do anything from writing individual fixes to rolling out estate-wide software patches. When necessary, they could access a branch terminal remotely by taking it over and diving into it.

Sometimes a Subpostmaster would be put through to a Post Office helpline operator who didn't know enough about the system to diagnose a problem properly. The operator might suggest trying a few things. This occasionally ended up making a situation worse. Not just more confusing, but materially worse, by increasing a negative discrepancy. If the Subpostmaster was then unable to reverse the action taken, many have said they were told that they were liable for the (now larger) discrepancy.

Another common helpline nugget was telling Subpostmasters 'not to worry' because the problem a caller was facing would 'sort itself out,' which is what Noel says he was told. Sometimes this advice came with a suggestion to balance to zero (in other words to accept the Horizon discrepancy as an accurate record of cash and stock on hand, despite this not being the case) and wait for an error notice or transaction correction to be sent to them, rectifying the discrepancy. In 2014, the issue was raised in parliament, with one MP wondering if giving advice to balance to zero was a possible example of the Post Office breaking the law by encouraging its Subpostmasters to false account. This allegation was huffily rejected by the Post Office. No documentary evidence exists to back Subpostmasters' claims that they were occasionally encouraged to balance to zero in this way because the Post Office, until recently, didn't record calls to its helpline.

Noel told me he wasn't worried about the implications of what he was doing. Partly because he didn't understand them, and partly because he felt he'd done the right thing and informed his employers of what was going on, using the helpline. Despite what he'd been told, his balancing problems hadn't sorted themselves out. What was he supposed to do? Stop trading? That would reduce the number of customers coming into his shop and put him in breach of the same contract which held him responsible for any losses he couldn't prove weren't his fault. And besides, the village depended on him. In those days the local Post Office was an important community resource.

Noel now acknowledges he was sleepwalking into something very serious. With the benefit of hindsight he realises just how big a mistake it was to agree figures which weren't correct. 'If I'd closed the shop, it would have been better,' he said.

At the time, Noel blithely carried on accepting whatever weekly figure Horizon threw at him, and so long as no one from the Post Office noticed, he could carry on trading.

On 13 October 2005 the Post Office sprang a surprise audit on the Gaerwen branch. A discrepancy of £48,454.87 was recorded. Noel was immediately suspended.

During subsequent interviews with Post Office investigators, Noel was quite upfront about what he had been doing. He squarely blamed the IT system for what was going wrong. The Post Office investigators weren't sure. They told him he was the only person who had been having problems with Horizon. Noel couldn't believe it.

Being a big fish in a small pond, Noel's suspension was hot news in Anglesey.

'I got snide remarks. People would turn their backs. It was hard,' he remembers.

The gossip intensified in early 2006, when Noel was charged with false accounting and the theft.

It is not clear on what grounds the Post Office charged Noel with theft. No evidence has ever been produced to suggest he stole any money at all. The logic appears to have been that £48,000 was 'missing' from the branch and in the absence of any other explanation, Noel *must* have stolen it.

Noel was aware his situation was serious, but was equally adamant he wasn't guilty of any crime. Mistakes, perhaps, but not a criminal offence. Noel's lawyers took a different view. His interviews with Post Office investigators had been under caution. Whilst under caution, Noel had admitted to signing off false accounts. If he continued to plead not guilty to an offence he had admitted under caution, it was a slam dunk for the prosecution, and he would almost certainly go to jail.

In the background to this discussion there was some plea-bargaining going on. The Post Office told Noel's advisors that if he pleaded guilty to false accounting 'on a basis which made it clear that no blame was attributed to Horizon,' they would drop the theft charge. This could further reduce the likelihood of a prison sentence.

Faced with a very real prospect of going to jail, Noel wobbled.

He resigned the Plaid Cymru whip on the county council and ceased to be politically active. At his next court hearing, Noel pleaded guilty to false accounting. The Post Office dropped the theft charge.

Noel's sentencing took place at Caernarfon Crown Court on 6 November 2006. A local TV news crew was outside court to capture the occasion. Noel packed a bag of belongings, as he had been advised. In front of his family, who had come to support him in court, the judge told Noel the matter was so grave 'neither a fine nor a community service order is sufficient, and an immediate custodial sentence is appropriate.'

Noel was given nine months. He was led away from court in handcuffs to a waiting police van. As he left the building, Noel briefly looked towards the people gathered on the other side of the courtyard gates. The TV crew got their shot. The slow-motion image of a bewildered 59-year-old man staring forlornly at the camera was broadcast that evening across Wales.

Noel was taken to Walton prison in Liverpool. He is reluctant to talk in specifics about his time there, saying only, 'It was bloody horrible. There were very few people my age in prison. The majority were young people. And they could be pretty rough.'

Noel's full name is Hughie Noel Thomas. He's known as Noel

because he was born on Christmas Eve. Noel spent his 60th birthday, the Christmas of 2006, alone in prison as a convicted criminal, prosecuted by the organisation he had given 42 years of his life to.

On his release in 2007, Noel's nightmare continued. The Post Office succeeded in securing a Proceeds of Crime Act order against him which allowed them to go after his assets for the supposedly missing £48,000. After handing over his life savings, Noel declared himself bankrupt and went into retirement. He tells me the Post Office tried to retrieve the outstanding amount from his Post Office pension.

Noel's experience has left him permanently scarred. Long after he served his prison sentence he would go to bed at night and wake up screaming. Like Tracy Felstead, he still sleeps with his door open and a light on outside.

The mystery of what happened at Gaerwen remains to this day. Was there anything wrong with the Horizon terminals in Noel's branch, or was he just making basic mistakes? We don't know. After Noel's suspension, the Post Office removed both the Horizon terminals from Gaerwen Post Office. They were handed over to Fujitsu for 'testing' and never seen again. No record of any test results exist.

In fact, there's a lot of mystery about what happened to Noel. In 2013, when the Post Office were asked about the 50/50 deal they cut over Noel's initial £6,000 discrepancy, they were unable to find any record of this. Nor were the Post Office able to confirm whether or not Noel had received any training, nor could they produce any evidence of a signed Subpostmasters Contract. Nor were they able to refer to any of the documents they seized from Noel's Post Office when he was suspended in 2005, including Noel's personal diary detailing his problems with Horizon. Noel says when he asked for them back, he was told they had been lost in a fire.

THE SUBPOSTMASTERS' BIND

When attempting to explain this story to broadcast news editors, producers and taxi drivers, there are lots of 'but what' questions. No one really believes innocent people plead guilty, for a start. And no one really thinks an accounting system which consistently concludes two plus two equals four, would every now and then decide two plus two equals five, or eight. Furthermore, no one believes innocent people would deliberately declare incorrect accounting figures without raising their hands to ask for help. They do, it can, and they did, but understanding how requires some counter-intuitive thinking.

I realise lengthy explanations can derail a decent narrative, but unless you are fully satisfied a large IT network can appear to work perfectly well 99.9% of the time whilst malfunctioning quite seriously elsewhere (let alone accepting the idea that pleading guilty is a better option for an innocent person than pleading not guilty) then you, like my long-suffering newsroom colleagues, will have outstanding questions.

First of all, try to put aside the notion that computers are glorified calculators, and instead think of them as complex live ecosystems reliant on perfect humans, perfect hardware, perfect communication pathways, perfect environments and perfect software to ensure perfect outcomes.

As nothing is perfect, some level of failure, or malfunction, must therefore be an expected and normal outcome in any IT set-up. The larger and more complex the system, the more complex and likely the failure.

Where a malfunction manifests, and how long it takes to trace the manifestation *to* the malfunction can affect the operability of a system. If a malfunction is small in proportion to a system's general functionality, its manifestation may be equally small in its overall effect on the system, but disproportionally large in its consequence for an end user.

Every thousand lines of computer code is known as a KLOC.[1] A piece of commercial software is considered good if it contains 0.5 to 1 errors per KLOC. The more KLOCs, the more errors. Modern software

---

1 K = 1,000.
LOC = Lines of Code.
Pronounced 'kay-lock.'

applications run to several thousand KLOCs.

If a plane's computer software has one tiny bug in it – a dodgy line of source code amongst the thousands of KLOCs – and if certain inputs (for example sensor information combined with a pilot instruction inputted via specific interfaces within a specific time frame, at, say, a specific altitude) activate a routine containing that dodgy line of code, the plane's safety systems (also, obviously, running on code) might flag up a problem. Or the routine might cause the plane to do something unexpected. Or both. To respond, a pilot can input further instructions, but if the code implementing those further instructions has one dodgy line in it, and it is now trying to override an instruction in some code which itself isn't doing what it should, the new instruction could fail, or have the opposite intended effect, or not be told it is succeeding.

Planes rarely fall out of the sky just because of dodgy lines of code. In 2019, two Boeing 737 Max crashes led to the worldwide grounding of the 737 Max fleet. The crashes were not caused by bugs in source code but by fundamental errors in the software design, which, when combined with sensor failures, in specific circumstances, caused disaster. These were bad back-end inputs at a different level to coding inputs, but they were bad inputs which had terrible outputs – in this case, pilots not being in control of what they were flying.

Horizon's source code was never written or tested to anywhere near the same standard as the safety critical systems which keep planes in the air. It was also not a closed system. Multiple back-end inputs meant Horizon continually evolved. Security or product upgrades and software patches were written and released to fix, enhance or protect elements of the network. These were being introduced by imperfect humans on a weekly basis. These upgrades could change the data on the system, where it was being sent and what happened when it interacted with something else. Not all the upgrades and fixes were fully tested before being released. To do so would be too expensive. As a result, not all of them worked, and some of them caused odd problems in unexpected places.

Between 1999 and 2019, Fujitsu changed the software code which operated Horizon on 19,842 separate occasions, roughly equivalent to a thousand different changes per year. Subpostmasters were essentially using a slightly different computer system almost every time they logged in, and a different system might react to the same button pushes in slightly different ways.

Much of the new data swirling around the network each upgrade will have been small script changes and bug fixes, but every now and then, a new Horizon version was uploaded. These had exciting names like S06, S10 and B11.

In April 2003, Horizon version S30 was released by Fujitsu. It had not been properly tested, and it introduced a bug known as the Reversal bug. If a Subpostmaster inputted a series of transactions, and then for some reason wanted to cancel them, the transactions would have to be reversed out of Horizon. The Reversal bug *appeared* to reverse a transaction, but in fact doubled it. This was due to a plus sign in the code which should have been a minus sign. The Reversal bug was discovered by Fujitsu after Subpostmasters began to complain about the growing amount of non-existent money Horizon calculated as being in their accounts at the end of the week. When one Subpostmaster reversed an internal £13,910 cash transfer out of one stock unit and into another, he managed to create a £27,820 negative discrepancy in his accounts. Initially, Fujitsu engineers blamed the Subpostmasters for not going through the transaction reversal process properly. The number of calls they got on the matter began to disabuse them.

The Reversal bug was easy enough to fix (although it took two goes – one workaround caused the problem to manifest itself in a slightly different way) because it was relatively harmless to replicate and reverse engineer.

Another bug, the Callendar Square or Riposte Lock/Unlock bug[1] was, as the name suggests, a bug in the underlying Riposte message store software, which persisted in Horizon for years. It only appeared when certain circumstances (an unspecified 'event storm') conspired to 'lock' Riposte, and stop it replicating certain instructions and messages. Because the precise cause of the event storm wasn't clear, and the point at which Riposte became locked would differ, and the nature of the messages it failed to replicate didn't have much in common, it took years to track down and fix. Subpostmasters with holes in their accounts would have their calls logged by Fujitsu who, initially, could not diagnose the problem, so the Subpostmasters would be referred back to the Post Office, who would then decide whether or not to honour the mysterious discrepancies, put them in suspense or put them on the Subpostmaster. Until the source

---

1 A Horizon bug tended to be named after the branch first reporting it, its manifestation or its consequence. This one was known by two of the three.

of the problem was properly identified and communicated to the Post Office, the decisions as to who should be responsible for making good these Horizon-generated discrepancies appeared to be applied arbitrarily.

There were plenty of people (around 30 to 40) at Fujitsu working full time on catching, spotting and correcting many other errors within the Horizon system, but they too were imperfect humans, with limited resources, dealing with complex problems. Sometimes they would miss or misdiagnose the errors, or apply badly-written solutions. And whilst software was being tinkered with at the back end, hardware degradation and communication interrupts could also cause problems, leading to incomplete, erroneous transactions and recovery failures.

In the first ten years of Horizon's existence, no formal acknowledgment of specific bugs, even when fixed, was ever made to Subpostmasters in writing. The bugs specified above (the Reversal bug and the Riposte Lock/Unlock bug) were two of many which were finally established and confirmed in a multimillion pound court case. Until then, very little got outside a small circle of engineers and middle managers at the Post Office and Fujitsu.

It therefore became an article of faith within the Post Office that Horizon errors were (depending on your technical aptitude) either a thing of fantasy, or spotted and fixed before they caused any problems in Subpostmasters' branch accounts. All discrepancies were considered the Subpostmasters' fault, and their responsibility. It was the equivalent of Boeing blaming the 737 Max pilots for crashing their own planes.[2] The alternative was too reputationally toxic to contemplate.

As well as the IT, another key part of the Subpostmasters' bind is the contractual situation they were forced into on taking over a Post Office branch. We've covered some of these already, but to summarise:

- Subpostmasters were contractually liable for all cash and stock losses caused by 'negligence, carelessness or error.' This, in the Post Office's mind, meant all cash and stock losses which Subpostmasters couldn't prove as a Post Office or Horizon fault.
- Subpostmasters were required by the Post Office to balance to zero at the end of every accounting period. They were operating in breach of the rules if they didn't.

---

2 Which Boeing sort of did, on at least one occasion.

- Subpostmasters were not entitled to any investigative support from the Post Office. It was their responsibility to determine the cause of a discrepancy, even if they didn't have the relevant tools, knowledge or resources to do so. They were also not entitled to any documentation which might allow them to conduct their own investigation.
- The Post Office decided when a disputed discrepancy became a debt (whether put into suspense pre-2005 or not). Unless a Subpostmaster could *prove* a loss was not caused by 'negligence, carelessness or error', a demand to settle ('make good') the debt would usually follow.
- Shutting a branch and ceasing to use Horizon put a Subpostmaster in breach of contract.

Imagine you had invested your life savings, your career and your public reputation in a job which contractually bound you to the above. Then make your ability to stick to those rules reliant on a computer system you have no control over, which is believed by your employers to be incapable of material malfunction. You're done, aren't you?

GOING IN HARD

Whilst Subpostmasters were adapting to living with Horizon, the Post Office's punitive arm was watching closely. Horizon had given Post Office area managers, investigators and cash management teams a window into every single branch in the country.

Discrepancies were obviously a problem. Subpostmasters didn't like being told to cover losses they didn't want to take responsibility for, and would understandably kick up a fuss to the helpline or their area managers when it happened. The Post Office could take as much or as little notice of these complaints as it wanted to, but ultimately all it had to do was order the Subpostmaster to make the discrepancy good, holding that it was the Subpostmaster's contractual responsibility to do so. Anyone who didn't comply could be suspended, threatened with the loss of their business and/or pursued for 'missing' money with legal threats.

Suspected or unreported accounting discrepancies were an altogether different kettle of fish. Pre-Horizon these were almost impossible to spot, unless an unannounced visit from Post Office auditors brought them to light. Now, unusual patterns of activity on Horizon could trigger investigative action.

If, for example, a branch was declaring it held tens of thousands of pounds on the premises, and for some reason was not sending that surplus back to a Post Office cash centre, it was a red flag. It suggested the cash might not be there.

Any branch repeatedly calling the Horizon helpline with an IT or balancing problem which was then followed by a period of silence, during which the branch accounts balanced to the penny (as per Noel's situation), was also potentially suspicious. Perhaps a problem was now being covered up by false accounting.

Once unusual activity had been identified, auditors could arrive at a Post Office, demand access to a counter and assess what was happening for themselves.

Unfortunately, a lot of Post Office auditors weren't very good at their jobs.

Howe and Co, a firm of solicitors and forensic accountants, spelled it out in evidence submitted to a Parliamentary Select Committee inquiry in 2015. They told MPs:

> 'Instead of performing a real audit, Post Office "auditors" simply assume that the balances on Horizon are correct, compare them with those in the branch and prosecute the Subpostmasters if the balances in the branch are less than those on Horizon. Hence, in reality, no vouching of transactions whatsoever is undertaken by Post Office auditors.'

Howe and Co concluded: 'Using the term "audit" to describe the Post Office's intervention in the branches gives its actions a veneer of professionalism and depth of analysis which is in fact entirely absent.'

Contractually, this was not a situation Postmasters could do anything about. If Post Office auditors found a 'loss' they felt was not being reflected in the Horizon-generated branch trading statements, it would be reported to a Subpostmaster's area or contract manager. The contract managers had the power to suspend a Subpostmaster on the spot, and call in the security team. In some cases, Post Office investigators and contract managers (triggered by either of the red flags described above), would co-ordinate in advance. This could lead to a Subpostmaster being audited, suspended and subjected to a recorded interview (without a solicitor present) over the course of a few bewildering hours.

Although security team members are reluctant to speak to the media (at least, I have not yet managed to track down any chatty ones), I did speak to someone who knew one or two investigators well. He thinks they serve an important purpose. 'They go in hard, but it gets results. If someone working at a cash centre has got a bit sticky-fingered, they are pretty good at getting them to admit it.'

These intimidating tactics might be appropriate for someone caught on CCTV slipping a wad of notes into their trousers, but it isn't necessarily the right approach when it comes to dealing with Subpostmasters.

Unfortunately, the Post Office auditors' blind belief in Horizon's faultless operation was shared by Post Office investigators. One independent IT expert attached to a criminal trial interviewed an investigator who told him they did not 'as a matter of policy, consider system problems as a possible explanation for discrepancies.'

Another review, written in 2013, noted the Post Office's instructions to (and its training of) its investigators 'seems to have disregarded the possibility' that the Horizon system could ever be in any way relevant to their investigations.

ENTER ALAN

In the early 2000s, all over the country, pen-and-paper Postmasters like Noel were having varying degrees of luck with the Horizon system. Those who racked up huge discrepancies seem to have been terminated and prosecuted almost without a second's thought. Their honesty and good record counted for nothing. If Horizon's weekly totaliser declared more money should be behind the counter than there actually was, Subpostmasters were held liable until they made the discrepancy good. If they couldn't, they were hounded, suspended or sacked. If they tried to cover it up for fear of losing their livelihoods, they were prosecuted.

The one thing every Subpostmaster had in common was their isolation. Although Subpostmasters were visible within their communities, in the early days of Horizon they were unlikely to have much contact with any other Subpostmasters unless they were NFSP officials. Social media did not exist. Neither the Post Office nor the Fed's official publications would dream of publishing an article about problems with Horizon, and only the savviest Subpostmaster had an understanding of internet message boards and email groups. Despite the experience of individual Subpostmasters on the ground, there was no effective way of documenting Horizon problems to create a body of evidence. The NFSP simply did not encourage or keep any centralised record of Subpostmasters having problems with Horizon, a policy which allowed it to continue claiming none existed.

If ever a story was crying out for a hero, it is this one, so let's introduce him.

Before Alan Bates even thought about becoming a Subpostmaster, he was developing all the right skills to be a very good one. Alan was a specialist project manager working in the heritage sector, a job which involved revitalising ancient buildings. Alan worked on Winchester's *Domesday 900* project in the eighties before taking on a contract at *Cadw*, the organisation which looks after Welsh Historic Monuments.

Part of Alan's remit was adopting new technologies to give dusty old spaces a bit of razzle-dazzle. Boosting revenues and capturing visitor data was part of the process. A sensible way of doing this was to install

Electronic Point of Sale[1] systems at entrance gates and in gift shops. Mechanical tills registered cash sales in isolation. EPoS systems could collect all sorts of data about every transaction and collate the information into something useful. When *Cadw* wanted a new EPoS system for all its castles in Wales, Alan was part of a team which evaluated the possibilities, road-tested the candidates and implemented a suitable platform. Alan's last major project was in Halifax, in the mid-nineties. He worked on setting up a brand new children's museum called Eureka. The museum needed a site-specific solution and Alan worked with an IT company to design an EPoS system from the ground up. He learned a lot – not just about the development of the software and what it could do, but the staff training required to use it.

After project Eureka, both Alan and his partner Suzanne – a special needs teacher – were ready for new challenges. They wanted a bit more stability in their lives and thought it would be nice to see a bit of each other for a change. They knocked a few ideas about and landed on the idea of running a Post Office. To make it work financially, they would have to find a branch for sale in an attractive location, with a decent amount of footfall.

In May 1998, after a lot of to-ing and fro-ing, Alan and Suzanne finally took control of The Wool Post, a traditional Post Office counter and retail set-up in Craig-y-Don, close to Llandudno, where Alan grew up.

Alan went through the process of applying to the Post Office to become a Subpostmaster. He had to supply a business plan and be security checked. Once his application was successful, Alan was required to make a payment to the outgoing Subpostmaster of £65,000. This figure corresponded to 1.5 times the Craig-y-Don Subpostmaster's salary and reflected a notional level of value in the business. Alan and Suzanne also ploughed £40,000 of their own savings into refurbishing The Wool Post shop.

When three Horizon terminals arrived at Craig-y-Don in October 2000, Alan was looking forward to seeing what they could do. Alan is a capable, methodical thinker, and he had the benefit of knowing how EPoS systems worked. He got to grips with Horizon's user interface pretty quickly, but its accounting function was another matter. From very early on, when cashing up or rolling over one weekly accounting period

---

1 Shortened to EPoS, pronounced 'ee-poss.'

to the next, the system would misbalance. This is not necessarily unusual. Misbalancing means there has been at least one error, and Alan was keen to root any errors out.

Alan began by interrogating the system as an end-user – seeking to drill down into his transaction data and learn the processes required to fish out the information he needed.

He couldn't.

Most IT systems have a supervisor-level access function which, whilst it will allow more extensive access than the basic user level, doesn't allow anyone to do too much damage. You can have a look under the bonnet, or perhaps even change a tyre, but you're not an administrator or super-user, able to roam at will. Alan was completely locked out. He called the Horizon helpline, but the operator told him his current level of access was all he was going to get.

This presented Alan with a problem. He had a discrepancy. A small one, granted, but he needed to find out how it got there. After all, he was potentially responsible for it. Yet he was being told he did not have the authority to properly investigate his own accounts. Alan let the discrepancy roll over into the next balancing period.

The next episode was altogether more alarming, so much so that Alan felt the need to call his area manager and then write to him about it. It happened in December 2000, less than three months after Horizon had been introduced at Craig-y-Don. Alan told his boss, 'The balance at this office on Wednesday 13 December was not only very stressful but also very worrying.'

Horizon had produced a discrepancy of more than £6,000. Whilst his assistant attempted to serve customers, Alan spent more than an hour on the phone to the helpline, keeping one Horizon terminal active and dedicating the other two to producing reports. In the run up to Christmas, Post Offices tend to get busy. There were customers queueing out of the door.

Eventually, Alan was able to track down some transactions which had gone awry, bringing the discrepancy down to £1,182.81. Still a large amount of money. Eventually, Alan abandoned his search, though he was pretty certain £368.50 of the missing money was down to double-entered giro items, which 'I am unable to track,' he told his manager, 'because of the way Horizon is set up.' The remainder of the cash Alan had no idea about, because he couldn't get the information he wanted out of the system.

Alan's letter to his manager also mentioned Horizon's 'very poor layout of the screen and menus, the slowness of the printers, the lack of report writing facilities, the chaotic end of day and end of week procedures, and the problems of having to do "office work" at a terminal on the counter.'

He was clearly not a happy bunny, especially as the prospect of being held contractually liable for the undiscovered £1,182.81 was hanging over him. Alan wrote that he felt it was unreasonable for the Post Office to hold him liable for these losses 'until such time as 100% guarantee can be given about the accuracy of Horizon.'

Alan's area manager dealt with his pleas by ignoring them. Soon after writing his letter, Alan found the £368.50 worth of double-entered giro items. Seven months later, Alan received a demand for the outstanding £814.31.

Alan was not having this. He fired off another letter. 'It is nigh on impossible,' he wrote, 'to access the data I as a Subpostmaster need in order to track problems or accept responsibility for the processing through this office.'

Alan was quite sure that the information he needed was in Horizon. Knowing what he knew about EPoS systems, he was certain the Post Office's administrators would be able to access the information at Horizon's back end. He felt the right tools 'such as a report writer package ... to enable me to look for problems, duplications or errors, easily and effectively,' should be made available to him.

'The alternative,' Alan complained, 'is that I should subsidise the shortcomings of this system.'

That, it transpired, was *precisely* what the Post Office expected him to do.

And not just Alan. All over the country Postmasters whose Horizon systems were throwing up negative discrepancies were either having to subsidise them from their retail or personal income, or face demands from the Post Office to 'make good' the sums they had parked in their suspense accounts.

The reason helpline operators might have told exasperated Subpostmasters 'not to worry' is because even if a Subpostmaster had corrected every single transaction and stock-taking mistake at their branch and inputted perfect figures into their system, their branch could still have a discrepancy. This was because Horizon was a networked system. Data was being inputted into the back-end of Horizon by second and third parties all the time, and data inputs are vulnerable to error.

By the Post Office's own figures, around 80% of transaction corrections are required because of problems (e.g. mistakes, equipment failure) in branch. Camelot was a major issue for years as lottery and scratchcard transactions (and information about the activation of scratchcard packs) had to be taken from the Camelot system and manually inputted into Horizon. The remaining 20% of errors are caused outside branches, and can be the result of human error by Post Office back office/cash centre staff, IT error or third party client (human or technical) error, all of which impact on an individual Subpostmaster's branch accounts.

Data could also be lost due to communication or hardware failures, or end up in the wrong place due to digital reconciliation errors and software bugs. More often than not they would be spotted and fixed. Subpostmasters were given little or no information about all this. They would more likely just get an error notice or transaction correction which they were encouraged to accept into their Horizon account without demur.

A transaction correction is manually generated by the Post Office. 'TCs' can add money to an individual branch account or they can remove it. To take a random year – in 2010, the Post Office issued 46,460 credit transaction corrections to its 11,905 Post Offices, with a total value of £8,118,634. These credit TCs would be welcome to Subpostmasters as they would correct a loss to their accounts. The same year, the Post Office issued 103,984 debit transaction corrections to its 11,905 Post Offices with a total value of £19,454,770. These debit TCs would either remove a surplus or create a hole in a Subpostmaster's accounts.

Sometimes a Subpostmaster would apply for a transaction correction themselves. If a pin-pad machine crashed or took a transaction twice, or a printer produced a spoiled postage label, Subpostmasters could apply (via the helpline) to have a transaction correction sent to them. Given the size of the Post Office network, the number of things that could go wrong and the number of human interventions that had to take place before a transaction correction could be issued, an error notice or 'TC' could take a long time to arrive. This meant Subpostmasters could spend hours looking for discrepancies which were created off-site, which they had no knowledge of, and which they might not find out about for weeks or even months. Branch Horizon terminals only kept their data for 42 days (later extended to 60), which meant that if a transaction correction arrived six weeks after an error event, a Subpostmaster would be likely to have no idea what it was for. Fine if it's a credit, not so good if it isn't.

Transaction corrections can themselves be wrong and can be challenged. Although the Post Office does not have comprehensive records for the number of transaction corrections which have been successfully challenged, some numbers have come up in the courts which reveal the TC system of error correction was itself error-prone. An expert witness analysis found that 23% of transaction corrections issued to branches in relation to Santander bank in the 2016/7 financial year were successfully challenged as being erroneous. If nearly a quarter of corrective notices are themselves incorrect, your system probably sucks.

After introducing TCs to replace error notices, the Post Office later came up with Transaction Acknowledgements (TAs), which were exactly the same as TCs but they could not be contested by the Subpostmaster.

TCs and TAs added an Alice in Wonderland quality to branch accounting. No balance was quite what it seemed, and once things were in misalignment, getting them back on track required enormous effort, especially if multiple things were going wrong at once. A mysterious surplus could cover part of a mysterious loss, making the numbers difficult to spot. For a helpline operator to tell a Subpostmaster everything would likely 'sort itself out' was not just negligent but positively dangerous.

Former Subpostmaster Margaret Davison's memoir brings it alive so well:

> 'Advice to balance up obvious errors just created more errors, and sometimes greater misbalances which the helpline could not sort out. Often in exhausted desperation you balanced the books by making good the amount yourself. How many times and how many Subpostmasters have forked out some of their hard earned salary to achieve this so that the system could be rolled-over ready to trade

> the following morning after an office misbalance? In those days you naively and stupidly blamed yourself as being incompetent or that your staff may have made a mistake, which meant, as a Subpostmaster, you must make good.'

A few years ago, a Postmaster who ran a Post Office around the same time as Alan, Margaret and Noel got in touch with me. In an email she described the problems she had with Horizon in her village branch. She wants to stay anonymous.

'I had asked for help so so many times from the non-helpline,' she wrote. 'One time I tried to get the machine to balance from 12.30pm until 10pm. I had my area manager come and shadow me on cash account day only for the discrepancy to double before his eyes. He had no solution either.'

On a busy Thursday morning – pension day – my correspondent told me she was 'swooped upon' by Post Office auditors. They found a four-figure discrepancy. Her contract manager was called in.

'I took a breakdown of my phone bills to show at interview how much I had rung the helpline. I was suspended for three months. I went to a solicitor. He told me he could not get any information from the Post Office to help me.'

The Subpostmaster paid the four-figure discrepancy out of her own savings. She was reinstated, but she never got over the dread of cash account day.

'It was such a relief when I sold up,' she told me, 'but I'm sorry to say the new lady had the same problems after I had gone, with the debt doubling at rollover. To my shame, I never told her of my suspension, or my Horizon problems.'

I asked her why she got in touch. 'I hate them,' she said. 'I hate how they made me feel. I want the Post Office held to account.'

AS LONG AS IT TAKES

Over the course of 2001 Alan Bates continued trying to explain his problems with Horizon to the Post Office. He did not want to park his discrepancies in the local suspense account because he knew they would languish there without the Post Office investigating them. But the Post Office didn't want him to keep rolling them over from week to week because it was against policy.

Alan tried the helpline, of course, but decided they just 'read from a script and didn't actually understand the system, nor were they able to access data any further than I could.' Alan couldn't quite believe the situation he was in.

'It seemed mad,' he said. 'The data was meant to be within the system, but you had to wait weeks or months for a request for a specific piece of information to be answered after the request had been "escalated" up from the helpline. I was also starting to have serious concerns over the integrity of the system.'

In February 2002, the Post Office issued Alan a clear instruction. He was to keep his counter in agreement with Horizon's figures by balancing to zero, or he should apply to put his discrepancies into suspense.

Alan refused, setting out his position in yet another letter, in which he told his boss, 'I have always maintained the position that I am unable to accept any liabilities shown by the system until such time as I am able to access the data to check it.'

Alan felt that making good a discrepancy immediately and applying to put it into suspense were two different ways of acknowledging responsibility for figures he was refusing to accept. He refused to accept them because he could not get the information out of Horizon to tell him how his discrepancy had come about. As he told his area manager, 'The system does not actually log what the week's shortage or over was, or how it was arrived at anywhere on the documentation we print out and keep.'

Alan pointed out that the information he needed was lost from the screen the moment the weekly accounts were rolled over. He told the Post Office he was not going to balance to zero, and he was not going to put anything in suspense, because he wanted to track his position from week to week.

Again, the Post Office did not reply to Alan's letter.

In 2003, Alan's fifth area manager in three years, Mike Wakely, called to introduce himself. Alan raised his continuing concerns about Horizon and explained the reluctance to zero his balances without understanding why they were happening. Wakely heard Alan out, then went back to the regional office, from where he sent an ultimatum:

'I am now instructing you,' wrote Wakely, 'that with immediate effect, you are required to make good the outstanding loss and to cease with this current practice of rolling over any losses and gains.'

The area manager added a reference to Section 12:12 of the Subpostmasters Contract, a sure sign things were about to turn ugly.

'Please be advised that Subpostmasters are responsible for all losses caused through their own negligence, carelessness or error, and also for losses of all kinds caused by his Assistants. Deficiencies due to such losses must be made good without delay.'

Alan was bewildered. He was happy to make good mistakes he or his staff were responsible for – all he wanted was the tools to sort his Horizon problems out. He remembers slowly coming to the realisation 'that the people I was dealing with at the Post Office did not actually understand the Horizon system, how it really worked and what these types of systems could do.'

Alan is a man who knows when he's right, and he stuck to his guns, refusing to cave to the Post Office's ultimatum. In August 2003, the Post Office gave Alan three months notice of termination. He was no longer Craig-y-Don's Postmaster. Without the Post Office counter, the value of Alan and Suzanne's investment in their retail business evaporated. Alan felt the Post Office had 'just walked off' with their £100,000. Contractually, the Post Office didn't even need to give him a reason. 'In effect they had given away our investment to a third party without compensating us for our loss,' he said.

Alan consulted a lawyer. The advice was: don't bother. The Post Office's pockets are deeper than yours. You signed a contract which allows them to do more or less anything they want. Walk away.

Alan wisely realised the futility of someone in his position attempting to take on the Post Office through the courts *right then*, but that didn't mean he was going to shrug his shoulders and give up. Motivated by the loss of his savings and a stinging sense of injustice, Alan decided he was not going to allow the Post Office to get away with ruining his and Suzanne's future and, as he saw it, stealing their nest egg.

Alan's first move was to write a long letter to the North Wales News, which was published in October 2003. It stated, 'It is not just I who is the victim of their actions by losing my investment and livelihood, it is also the many loyal customers of all ages that Post Office Ltd have decided must also suffer.'

A letter like this is a gift to a local newspaper editor. Shortly after it was published, Alan received a visit from a North Wales News reporter. The resultant article (and photo of Alan outside his shop) painted the former Postmaster as a proud man wronged.

'I am going to fight this for as long as it takes,' he is quoted as saying, 'because of the grave injustice I feel has been done to myself and the people of Craig-y-Don in the way my contract was terminated.'

Alan took his campaign to a regional conference of the National Federation of Subpostmasters. He handed out leaflets to those who would take them, and a few people stopped for a chat. He told me he vividly remembers one NFSP rep walk past, saying, 'Don't talk to him, he's a thief.'

Undeterred, Alan set up an anonymous website called Post Office Victims. He publicised it by having the web address – www.postoffice-victims.org.uk – printed on a canvas canopy which extended over the pavement outside his shop.

The Post Office Victims website no longer exists, but in 2004 it was the only source of any public criticism of the Post Office Horizon system, and boy it was miffed.

Over a few basic text-based pages, Alan railed anonymously and furiously, stating his intention to 'expose the truth behind the extent Post Office Limited go to hide the flaws and weaknesses behind their Horizon system.'

Alan was also determined no one should fall into the same trap he did, hoping that publicising his plight would 'act as a warning for those considering purchasing a sub-Post Office.'

The defensive righteousness of Alan's prose ('I am not the only victim, if you look hard enough you will find the country is littered with bodies,' and, 'this has been a case of state sponsored corporate theft … not dissimilar to the robber barons of old who took their cut from the Crown'), gave the Post Office Victims website a slightly deranged tone, but the contact page came with a simple rallying call.

'Suffered at their hands?' it asked. 'Send me an email.'

A campaign to expose a scandal which would take 15 years, several parliamentary inquiries, an epic High Court litigation, two BBC Panoramas and end up costing the government and the Post Office more than a quarter of a billion pounds, was just about to get underway.

KAMRAN AND SIEMA

Not anyone can become a Subpostmaster. You have to be approved by the Post Office. This has the effect of limiting the number of people you can sell your business to when you no longer wish to carry on. It doesn't matter how much your premises are worth or how strong your retail trading is, the pool of potential buyers is limited to those who the Post Office deem suitable to take over the role.

Nine times out of ten, this works just fine. You might be one half of a husband and wife team who have built Little Itching Post Office into a successful and popular business. You are both in your mid-sixties and wish to retire. You advertise the retail space and adjoining residential premises for sale as a package, indicating you intend to move out of the domestic property, leave the business and hand over the role of Subpostmaster to the next incumbent. After assessing the offers, you accept the most favourable bid, telling the applicant they will have to be interviewed for the role of Subpostmaster by the Post Office before they can take control of the business. The Post Office requests business plans, conducts interviews, approves the favoured applicant and the sale goes through.

But ... what happens if the Post Office interviews your favoured applicant and discovers they have a conviction? The Post Office might not want someone with a criminal record on the books and so rejects their application to become Subpostmaster.

At that point your favoured applicant no longer wishes to pay the price they offered for your business because they are barred from getting their hands on the associated Post Office counter. The deal falls through and you approach the second highest bidder, accept the lower offer they made for your business and hope that, this time, the Post Office gives them the nod.

How long can this go on for? Well, the Post Office doesn't have to tell you why it rejected the candidate who was offering you the most money for your business, nor do you have any right of appeal. You just have to hope the Post Office likes your favoured applicant or, if not, an applicant who has offered you enough money to make the sale of your business worthwhile.

There are good reasons for the Post Office wishing to protect its position. After all, if the top bidder for Little Itching Post Office is a drug dealer, numerically inept or has been convicted of robbing a bank, it's probably a good thing they are not appointed as Little Itching's new Subpostmaster.

The point is, no matter how much of the value of your business is tied up in the fact you have a Post Office counter on your premises, you have next to no control over it. This somewhat bizarre situation was tolerated by existing and potential Subpostmasters because Post Office counters generated footfall and came with (in those days) a guaranteed monthly salary. It was also a 300-year-old government-owned brand. The contractual inequality was offset by a simple notion – trust.

Siema Mahmood was the 25-year-old daughter of Abid Mahmood, a successful businessman who had grown his London-based chicken shop empire through canny marketing and hard graft. One of his managers was a 23-year-old, called Kamran. Siema and Kamran became sweethearts and then engaged. Mr Mahmood gifted Siema a flat in London as a wedding present.

In 1999 Siema's first child was born, a boy. Siema asked her dad if he would mind if she sold the flat and used the money to get a mortgage on a house. Ever the strategic thinker, with an eye on the bottom line, Mr Mahmood suggested the couple use the money to buy a house and a business. Siema told him she was not about to go into the chicken shop trade, but she need not have worried. Her dad heard a family friend was selling their Post Office and shop on Hampstead Heath. The job of Subpostmaster came with a salary. Mr Mahmood encouraged Siema to put in a bid.

'I liked the fact it offered a secure income,' said Siema, 'and Hampstead is a lovely part of London. The positioning of the shop was really good, too. There was a park and hospital nearby, and not many banks. So it all seemed to be positive.'

Siema ended up using the proceeds from the sale of the flat to buy the Post Office business and get a mortgage on a separate, off-plan house which would become their family home. Siema didn't know much about Post Offices, but she had graduated with a degree in business management and marketing and felt she had the right aptitude to succeed. Kamran was no stranger to hard work – he had experience of retail management and of running a chicken shop which he felt would stand him in good stead. The young lovebirds decided to make a go of it.

In November 2001, Siema was approved as Subpostmaster and Kamran assumed the role of manager. Their son was nearly two.

The couple were each given three days off-site training on Horizon, during which they found Siema was pregnant with their second child. The pregnancy was difficult from the start and Siema became seriously ill, which meant she was unable to work within a few days of taking over the business. The couple decided to bring in their predecessor to help out behind the Post Office counter whilst Siema was absent.

I asked how that working relationship went. 'Let's put it this way,' said Kamran, 'we were paying her a very decent salary. She wasn't doing this for free. She demanded a substantial amount of money and we were not in a position to negotiate much.'

Kamran also brought in his younger brother to work on the retail side of the business so he could spend as much time as possible behind the Post Office counter, learning how Horizon worked. As branch manager, Kamran took responsibility for balancing the weekly accounts on a Wednesday under the previous Subpostmaster's guidance, but he could never get it to balance to zero.

'There were a couple of times when we were a few pounds up. But then there were times we were down. Sometimes it would be ten or twenty pounds, but sometimes it would be hundreds or thousands.'

Kamran's more experienced colleague was reassuring, but disengaged. 'She'd tell me not to panic or worry – that maybe there'd been a mistake somewhere along the line and hopefully I'd get an error notice. But these could take up to six weeks and that was a real problem. Because for six weeks you didn't know where you stood.'

Kamran had to make up the difference by borrowing money from the retail side of the business whilst he was waiting for the error notices to arrive. They didn't come.

'I was having to put more and more money in. Sometimes hundreds of pounds. I was basically taking money from the retail side of the business. It was all adding up very, very quickly.'

The experienced former Subpostmaster decided to leave in early 2002, leaving Kamran managing his assistants. Siema was still off work and her health was deteriorating badly. She became mentally unwell, so unwell she was having very dark thoughts at one point. Knowing how fragile Siema was, Kamran carefully told her about the discrepancies, and how he was having to plug the holes in the branch accounts with money from the retail business. The deficits were getting alarming. Siema began to borrow money from family members.

'I used to dread Wednesday,' said Kamran. 'I knew I would be there a long time, and I just used to hope that everything was going to be okay. We'd close, and I'd start counting. I'd get on the phone to the helpline … I'd be like "I've got a shortfall, are you able to help…?" but there was no help, no support, no guidance.'

Kamran alerted his area manager to the situation and was told his was the only Post Office experiencing shortfalls.

Siema's second child was born premature, weighing just over 4lb. Siema was still very ill with what turned out to be an under-active thyroid. Kamran tried his best to protect her from the worst of what was going on at the Post Office, but Horizon appeared to be completely out of control. The stress of trying to keep the business going led Kamran to develop depression and anxiety.

Eventually, at some point in the spring of 2002, Kamran put his hand up and told the Post Office he'd been making good discrepancies week after week and could no longer afford to do so. The Post Office sent in the auditors.

'When the auditors came,' Siema told me, 'we were happy. We thought they were going to find the problem and the money!'

The auditors found a deficit of around £4,000, and told Siema they were going to take it from her Subpostmaster salary.

'The shop shelves were getting emptier and emptier,' says Kamran. 'It was … embarrassing. My brother had to go to other shops to buy stock because we couldn't afford to go to the cash and carry. We had bailiffs turning up because we hadn't paid our business rates.'

Kamran did not once think the Horizon system itself might be to blame.

'When my father-in-law suggested [taking on] a Post Office, he said we couldn't go wrong. It was a government-owned body with a good reputation. I just kept wondering what I was doing wrong. What could I be doing that was causing so many problems?'

Over the 14-year period the Post Office was prosecuting people, dozens of Subpostmasters have reported they were told by Post Office contract managers, investigators and helpline operators that they were the only ones having problems with Horizon.

It was unforgivable corporate mendacity, and it had very serious, far-reaching effects. Firstly, it caused Subpostmasters to question their own competence, as well as the evidence of their own eyes. It was a short step from there to questioning their own sanity, with anxiety and depression a natural consequence. Today, there are plenty of web forums and WhatsApp or Facebook groups where Horizon problems are discussed by Subpostmasters. It was a very different world 20 years ago. The most serious effect of being told that no one else was having problems with Horizon came when Subpostmasters were prosecuted. They trusted the Post Office were telling the truth, and believing the lie, blamed themselves, their partners or their staff for the 'missing' cash.

'I felt there was a huge responsibility on my shoulders,' said Kamran. 'There was so much at stake. Siema had sold the flat that her father had gifted her to invest in the business. We had loans, a mortgage, two very young children.'

Kamran's mental health went into decline. He felt extremely helpless and hugely frustrated. Week after week went by with the Horizon deficits growing unabated. One morning, in September 2003, the Post Office auditors came back.

Siema took Kamran's call. 'I was at home in bed and my husband called to inform me that the auditors were at the Post Office. I said, "Okay, I'm coming – I'm the Subpostmistress so I should be there." '

By the time Siema arrived, the auditors had been through the Horizon accounts, checked the totals against the contents of the tills and safe and found a £25,000 discrepancy. Siema couldn't believe it. 'I said, "Well maybe they haven't counted properly – maybe they're missing something." '

The couple had exhausted the cash from their retail business, then they'd borrowed money from Siema's family and shovelled it into a black hole. Now they were being told they were contractually liable for £25,000 they didn't have.

Siema called the National Federation of Subpostmasters. Her local rep told her the only thing he could do was recommend a solicitor 'because you're going to need one.'

Siema was shocked and confused. 'The rep said, "She is a bitch, but she'll fight your corner." '

The auditors had called the Post Office investigators who arrived and asked Siema and Kamran if they could have a look round the family home. Siema let them. The couple had nothing to hide.

'They went through absolutely everything. They checked all the bedrooms, drawers, cupboards and even looked under the beds. I had a table full of paperwork which included all our bills and bank statements. After looking everywhere they said to me, "We cannot find a thing." '

Kamran was told he was no longer allowed to work behind the counter and that he was being investigated. Siema was suspended. She was ordered to attend a formal meeting.

'I explained the whole situation to them,' Siema said, 'but they wouldn't have it. They told me they were going to terminate my contract.'

Siema's dad said he would find the £25,000 the Post Office were demanding if necessary, but as Siema and Kamran were adamant they hadn't taken it, he wasn't inclined to gift it to the Post Office without 'a fight.'

The Post Office charged Kamran with theft.

According to Siema and Kamran, their solicitor seemed to think it was her job to organise a guilty plea as quickly and efficiently as possible. She told Kamran and Siema that a loss of £25,000 was going to get them a 'slap on the wrist' but 'you're just going to have to decide between you who gets the blame.'

The couple were mystified as to why they were being told one of them should admit to a criminal offence when neither of them had done anything wrong. The solicitor told them that maintaining their innocence could lead to one of them ending up in prison.

Siema and Kamran were astounded. They hadn't considered that either or even both of them might be sent to prison, yet here was a solicitor promising them that unless one of them took the rap, it was a real prospect.

'It felt unbelievable,' said Siema, remembering it as an almost out-of-body experience. 'How can people be talking about what they're going to do to you for things you haven't even done? We hadn't taken the money, so how could we be punished?'

Kamran was, by this stage, suffering from clinical depression.

'I don't think I was really taking in a lot of this information, because mentally I'd had enough. I was on medication. I was having panic attacks, I was having severe anxiety…'

To protect Siema against a possible prosecution, Kamran entered a guilty plea to the charge of theft. The night before sentencing, the couple went for a drive to get their eldest son off to sleep. They discussed what might happen. Kamran said he wasn't particularly worried, he just had to do what he'd been advised by the solicitor and everything would be okay. But the next morning he was in a bit of a state.

'He was running late,' Siema remembers, 'and my Dad said to me, "It's okay – I'll go with him – you stay at home with the kids and we'll be back soon." ' Kamran hugged and kissed Siema, told her he'd see her in a few hours and went with Abid to court.

On 26 February 2004, less than three months after Alan Bates had been booted out of Craig-y-Don Post Office, Kamran was sentenced to nine months in prison.

'When you've done something wrong,' said Kamran, 'it's easy for you to accept the consequence. When you know you haven't committed any crime, then it becomes really very difficult.'

Kamran regrets his guilty plea to this day. 'It was the worst decision I made in my life. In hindsight, I should never have taken the advice of my solicitor and pleaded guilty for something I hadn't done.'

Kamran was put in a prison van, and he remembers looking up through the one-way glass, completely confused.

'It was like I had died. I was expecting to go back and be with my family. But everything had just stopped. I could see outside the van, but people couldn't see in. I'm in a confined space … that's when I felt I was pretty much dead to the world.'

Between 2000 and 2004 more than two hundred Subpostmasters, Post Office managers and assistants were carted off to court, with many of them advised to plead guilty on the basis that the Horizon figures in their branch were evidentially sound. After all, computers do not lie.

ONCHING AND REMMING

An important, but often under-appreciated service provided by the UK's network of Post Offices is access to cash. Towards the end of the last century, as banks began to retreat from our high streets, the Post Office actively promoted its cash services, particularly its capacity to receive and bank it for local cash-oriented businesses.

Unfortunately, cash has inherent value and is difficult to trace, especially if it's passing through multiple hands in rapidly changing amounts on a minute-by-minute basis across the course of a working day. Storing it is another problem. Too little in the safe and you could run out the next day, too much and you might well find yourself a target.

To help Subpostmasters keep sensible amounts of money on their premises, the Post Office makes regular weekly (or even twice-weekly) cash collections from, or deliveries to, every branch. Some branches pay out far more than they take in (particularly when it comes to benefits in more deprived areas) and so need cash deliveries. Some take in more than they pay out because they might be receiving regular daily or weekly banking deposits. Moving notes and coins back and forth between Post Office branches and cash centres requires strong counting and handling protocols.

If Subpostmasters are instructed to or want to get rid of some of the physical cash on their premises, they count it up and put it into a rem (short for 'remittance') pouch. This is closed with a tamper-proof seal. The sum the pouch contains is entered into Horizon, which registers that the cash is ready to leave the branch, and produces a barcode sticker. This is attached to the rem pouch. When the security van arrives, the driver will scan the sticker to acknowledge the rem pouch is now under his or her control and no longer the responsibility of the Subpostmaster. It has been 'remmed out.' Once the rem pouch has arrived at a cash centre, the barcode is scanned to signal its collection. The pouch is opened and its contents are counted under CCTV. If there is a discrepancy between the contents of the pouch and the amount registered by the barcode, the Subpostmaster is notified and everyone is required to account for themselves. If all is well, the cash centre confirms it has received the declared amount, sending an acknowledgment to Horizon that the sum of money in the pouch is no longer being held by the sub-Post Office which remmed it out. When the process is reversed, and a Post Office takes delivery of pouches of cash, scanning barcodes and opening the tamper-proof seal, this process is known as 'remming in.'

The amount of money stored out of business hours on a Post Office premises is known as its Overnight Cash Holding, or 'onch.'[1] There is no standard maximum 'onch' value as each Post Office branch needs to keep varying volumes of cash in its safe according to the amount of business it does, but Post Office HQ will be concerned if it thinks a branch is holding more cash than it needs. This represents a security risk, not just to a Subpostmaster, but to the Post Office, whose cash it is. A reasonable onch value could be anything between £10,000 and £25,000. If it creeps above that, and a Subpostmaster refuses to rem their excess cash out, it can be the sign of suspicious activity. What if the cash isn't really there…?

1 Pronounced 'onsh.'

JO HAMILTON

South Warnborough is a well-kept, well-to-do sort of place a few miles north of Alton in North East Hampshire. RAF Odiham, a Chinook helicopter base, is just up the road. Jo and David Hamilton have lived in South Warnborough since 1985. The village has a pub, a community-run playground and a community-owned store. It's got its fair share of big houses, but as Jo says, 'many more of us who just get by.'

Jo is a chatty, gentle soul. She is 5'2" tall, loves horses and has a caring nature. She looks out for everyone, and as a result, everyone looks out for her. David is a taciturn but friendly Irishman, who runs his own gardening business. His handshake leaves you in no doubt he can look out for himself.

David and Jo spent most of the nineties running their own haulage business, but as the end of the decade approached, the Hamiltons decided to wind down their company and look for something else.

In 2001, it was put to Jo by the South Warnborough villagers that she might like to take over the ailing community store, which also housed a tiny Post Office counter. Jo agreed. South Warnborough Village Stores is on the busy main road which runs between Odiham and Alton.

In those days, the Subpostmaster at South Warnborough was an elderly gentleman called Alwyn Stacy, who rarely visited the branch. The Post Office counter was managed by another villager, who decided to leave her job in late 2001. Jo reluctantly agreed to take on the Post Office counter whilst managing the shop.

'I never really wanted to do it,' Jo told me. 'It's not my thing. I'm more of a people person.'

Jo and David worked hard to turn South Warnborough Village Stores into a successful business, selling groceries alongside a booming sandwich-making deli. Part of the store became a tearoom, serving drinks and cakes at wooden tables.

Jo remembers that after her predecessor's departure on Christmas Eve 2001, the Post Office sent a trainer to South Warnborough to get her up to speed on Horizon. He arrived on one of the days she was open between Christmas and New Year.

During this period Jo was down to three or four customers a day, most of whom were buying stamps. Seemingly unable to set up dummy transactions on Horizon, the trainer could not show Jo how to deal with other, more complex workflows, including how to prepare and sign off weekly cash accounts. So he tried a different tack.

'He pinned all this stuff on the wall and said, "You put that in that envelope, that in that envelope…" Because it was a bank holiday he said, "I can't show you a balance, but ring the helpdesk." It was complete rubbish.'

Everything else Jo knew about Horizon was learned on the job.

As you might expect for a store in a village with a population which doesn't quite reach 600, the South Warnborough Post Office counter wasn't turning over much. Occasionally, neighbours would drop by with cheques for large-ish sums. Jo remembers a few self-assessment tax payments which could double or treble the weekly turnover in one transaction, but she reckons overall, the counter was shuffling around £2,000 to £3,000 back and forth a week, 'selling stamps and bits and bobs, and paying out pensions.'

Jo knows exactly when things started going wrong. 'I never had any bother with Horizon,' she told me, 'until the chip and pin machine was installed in 2003. Before that, every time I tallied with it, it was fine, plus or minus a few pence.'

Although Jo's training on Horizon was inadequate, it was better than the training she got on the chip and pin machine, which was non-existent. 'A man came in, said, "I've got something for you," set it up and off he went!'

Jo felt like she wasn't in control of the new technology.

'Before chip and pin, it wasn't so bad. You had little piles of dockets. And you had a pension book which you physically tore sheets out of so at the end of the week you could see if you were missing anything. Everything was easy because you had paper, and it all matched. There was always a double-entry so you could always see what was wrong. But once it became chip and pin, no receipts came out. When it went wrong, you couldn't find out what *was* wrong.'

Alwyn Stacy's health deteriorated. In October 2003, shortly before he died, Jo became Postmaster at South Warnborough. Soon after that, things started to go seriously haywire.

On 23 December 2003, after Jo closed at 1pm, she tallied her stock and cash with Horizon. It told her she had a negative discrepancy of £2,032.67.

The run up to Christmas would have meant the counter was busier than usual, but for it to suddenly 'lose' the lower end of a week's average takings was serious.

Jo went home for Christmas, but when she opened up between Christmas and New Year, she called the helpline. Under instruction as to exactly which buttons to press, Jo attempted to clear the discrepancy. Despite following all the advice from the helpline operator, the discrepancy remained. And then things got worse.

During a call to the helpline made on 30 December 2003, Jo was advised to go through another series of button presses on her Horizon screen. Whilst the helpline operator remained on the line, Jo carried out her instructions. Her discrepancy more than doubled, from £2,032.67 to £4,217.07.

Even though Jo's larger discrepancy had been generated thanks to the advice she got from the helpline, Jo was told she was now liable for the new, larger figure.[1] Not having £4,000 spare, she agreed to let the Post Office take the money out of the £450 a month she got as her Subpostmaster salary. From then on, Jo declined to have much faith in the helpline's advice.

While Jo was paying the Post Office this money, further discrepancies arose. Jo called the helpline, but the helpline did not help. No one ever told Jo she might be able to dispute the 'missing' sums. No one ever successfully explained to Jo what might be going wrong and how she might fix it.

'It would just come up with a figure that should be [in the safe and till] at the end of the day, but the money wasn't there,' she told me.

Throughout the early part of 2004, the discrepancies continued to grow. Jo was forced to make further payments from her Subpostmaster salary, which became a serious drain on the business finances. What had at first seemed like a viable opportunity now had a strange cuckoo in the nest, a Horizon terminal demanding ever larger sums of money which Jo didn't have. She began to live with a sense of dread over what figure would appear on her screen when she came to the end of each trading period. The discrepancies grew.

The Post Office's own records show that between December 2003 and her eventual suspension in March 2006, Jo made more than 200 calls

[1] I have seen the balance snapshots Jo printed out and the Horizon helpline call note timings later provided to her which tally exactly.

to the Post Office helpline. In the course of making those calls, Jo had alerted the Post Office to discrepancies she could not explain. Jo says on more than one occasion she was told that there was nothing the helpline could do to help rectify her problem, but if a mistake had been made at the Post Office's end, Jo would receive a transaction correction for the full amount.

By the end of 2004 Jo had dug herself into a financial and psychological hole. She could not keep throwing money she couldn't afford at a problem she did not understand. She was frightened, and alone. One night after cashing up, Jo balanced her account. The discrepancy had leapt again – this time by £8,000.

Jo was crushed. She knew from past experience the act of acknowledging a discrepancy between the cash in her counter and the figure on the Horizon screen would set in motion a chain of events; a process which ended in Jo being made liable for the discrepancy. There was no apparent capacity, or obligation, on the part of the Post Office to investigate the cause.

Jo had run out of money. If she acknowledged the new discrepancy, the Post Office had made it clear through its actions that she would be made liable for it. Jo did not have £8,000, so to accept it would be a conscious act of pushing herself closer to bankruptcy, and the humiliation of losing her livelihood.

If she ignored it – well ... then what?

Maybe she would get a transaction correction the following week correcting the balance and everything would be okay. Maybe it would buy her the time she needed to get her head straight and work out what on earth she was going to do.

Defeated and disheartened, Jo pressed the button which acknowledged Horizon's figures correctly matched the amount of cash being held in her till and safe. She had no idea that what she was doing would be viewed by the Post Office as a criminal offence.

Throughout 2005, Jo signed off Horizon's figures as being an accurate representation of the stock and cash she held in her till and safe. It was not. In fact, the gap kept getting bigger and bigger. She was doing the same thing, at the same time, as Noel Thomas in his Post Office in Anglesey, hundreds of miles away.

Jo describes being in the grip of a giddy sort of madness, trying desperately to find the mistakes which would explain the ever-widening black hole in her accounts. Each day she hoped a mistake would be spotted at the back end of Horizon and the Post Office would send through a transaction correction. Either that or her Horizon terminal would suddenly right itself and show a surplus, cancelling out her debt.

Jo remembers, 'I used to feel sick. Literally, physically sick, every time I went into the Post Office. I thought "one day they're going to come in and audit me and I'm going to be carted off and I don't know what to do." I can remember being absolutely terrified of them coming.'

The South Warnborough branch was now declaring that it was balancing perfectly without any of the problems Jo had been reporting to the helpline over the previous two years. It was also now showing there was a significant amount of cash being held on the premises, contravening Post Office security protocols. The cash wasn't there, but by balancing to zero, Jo was claiming it *was* there. A demand to rem out some or all of that cash back to the Post Office was almost inevitable. If Jo didn't have that cash, she would be rumbled.

Jo explained to David some of what was going on, but didn't fully explain the implications. She knew she was storing up trouble, but felt a way out might present itself if she just kept going. David (and Jo's parents, who part-owned the property) allowed Jo to re-mortgage their house. Jo put £9,000 from the re-mortgage into the Post Office counter safe.

The discrepancy continued climbing towards £30,000.

'I can't tell you what it's like,' she said. 'If you're in that position it's just so scary because I had all the money … and I had this massive lease on the shop. I just didn't know what to do.'

Now in serious difficulties, Jo borrowed £3,000 from a neighbour and friend. That, too, was swallowed up. Jo was at breaking point. She was staying in the shop until midnight several nights a week, trying to make sense of where the money had gone.

In 2006 the Post Office called up. The South Warnborough branch, they noted, was holding tens of thousands of pounds on the premises. This was in contravention of their security policy. Jo was instructed to remit £25,000 in cash, immediately.

After finishing trading for the day, Jo stayed in her shop, going through the reports and receipts over and over again, feeling like she was falling apart. 'I had paperwork all over the office, all over the floor, everything,' she said. 'I was going through them all, going through the previous trading statements and in the end, I just sat down crying.'

Her neighbour saw the light on in the shop and wondered what was going on.

Jo let her neighbour in. 'She said "Whatever is wrong?!" and I just said, "I can't do this any more. I'm *thousands* adrift." '

The two women went through Jo's Horizon receipts. They studied her transactions to see if they could pinpoint how this hole in her accounts had opened up. Between them they could not begin to make sense of the numbers. Jo remembers her neighbour warning her she was on her way to a breakdown if she did not ask for help.

The next morning, Jo did as she was advised. She called the National Federation of Subpostmasters who arranged for the Post Office to conduct an audit at the South Warnborough branch. They also advised her to get a lawyer. When the auditors arrived, Jo explained what had been going on. She was immediately suspended. Then the Post Office security team got involved. Investigators were sent to Jo's house.

'They sat down on the sofa and one of them said, "You've got a large discrepancy – where is it?" and I said, "I've no idea. I've never been able to get to grips with the computer system." And that's when he said, "Well, no one else has ever had problems with Horizon." '

Having listened to her explanations and conducted their investigations, the Post Office charged Jo with theft.

JO'S SENTENCING

In November 2007, on the advice of her barrister, Jo pleaded guilty to false accounting. She agreed to pay the Post Office £36,000 before she was sentenced. In return, the Post Office would drop the theft charge against her.

Jo and David re-mortgaged their home for a second time. This raised £28,000. Appalled at Jo's treatment by the Post Office, the villagers of South Warnborough rallied round. Between them they raised the remaining £8,000 Jo needed to settle with the Post Office and avoid a prosecution for theft.

Jo was scheduled to appear at Winchester Crown Court to be sentenced for false accounting.

At a pre-sentence meeting with a probation officer, Jo was warned she faced the prospect of going to prison. The night before she went to court, Jo packed her bags.

'I was told that I would be 14 days in Holloway so I thought, "I don't care what happens, I'm not wearing someone else's pants!" So I packed 14 pairs of pants into my bag, a toothbrush and toiletries. I can remember zipping it up, feeling like I was going to throw up. But I knew I couldn't escape from it, I had to go through with it.'

Jo went to bed, but couldn't sleep. 'I wondered if the next time I woke up, it would be behind bars.'

On 4 February 2008, the day Jo was sentenced, Winchester Crown Court was packed with well-wishers. The Daily Mail said more than 60 people were present. Jo counted them exactly and came up with 74. There were far too many to fit into the public gallery. The court clerk, sensing trouble was unlikely, invited the genteel crowd into the main well of the court, which is usually reserved for participants in the proceedings.

More than a hundred people had written character references for Jo, including a retired judge. As the hearing progressed, Jo's vicar delivered an impassioned speech. The Reverend Jane Leese told the sentencing judge that Jo 'was more of a vicar' than she was, being 'kind, caring and the centre of the community.' Reverend Leese summed up by asking the judge to bear in mind everything he had heard and seen in court today, because the village 'really loved' Jo.

The judge kept looking between Jo and her supporters. He asked her, with incredulity, 'What have you done?' He said, 'Why are you in my court?'

Jo was given the minimum possible sentence – a 12-month supervision order. She stayed out of prison, but was now a convicted criminal with huge debts and no prospects.

Jo's legal team considered this a success, considering the circumstances. Issy Hogg was Jo's solicitor. 'If Jo had pleaded not guilty, she would have gone to jail,' she told me, matter of factly.

More than a decade later, Jo was making a living from cleaning houses. David was still grafting away in all weathers – hard work for a man in his seventies. The Post Office had robbed the Hamiltons of their future, and a decent retirement.

LEE CASTLETON

Lee Castleton started his career as an electrician, something he put to good use when he joined the RAF as an Aircraftsman in 1987. During the first Gulf War, Lee was attached to 7 Squadron at Odiham working on repairing Chinooks and Tornados which were getting damaged by the amount of sand being sucked into their air intakes. Lee got married, left the RAF in 1996 and spent three years managing a family-owned Costcutter supermarket before trying his hand as a stockbroker. He made a bit of money, but the lifestyle wasn't for him.

So Lee became a Subpostmaster, paying £300,000 to buy a newsagent and its attached residential property (with a mortgage) at Bridlington Post Office on 18 July 2003. Lee worked behind the counter, his wife Lisa-Marie ran the retail side.

'We took over from a couple who were retiring,' Lee told me. 'The shop was looking a little lacklustre but we saw its potential. We were both 35 at the time and prepared to do 18 hours a day – whatever it took to make things a success.'

For the first six months, life was good. The books balanced, footfall was going up and the Castletons were enjoying their new career.

Within twelve months, everything had gone ruinously wrong. Over a nine-week period which began in January 2004, Lee's Horizon terminal went haywire. One week it would show surpluses in the thousands, the next it would show losses in the thousands. The Horizon touchscreen was slow and laggy. Lee was not happy. He called the helpline *ninety-one* times.

'At the outset, they just said, "Oh don't worry, it's just one of those things, you'll have put something in the wrong column, or something will have been inputted incorrectly. It'll all come to light." '

But it didn't. Up to January, Lee had been balancing absolutely perfectly 'to within one or two pence' every week. And then suddenly he was in a world where nothing would add up.

The calls to the helpline continued. 'We battled with the Post Office to give us information. I particularly wanted someone to come out to us and have a look. I didn't see the point in someone sitting in an office looking at pieces of paper or getting the information about my branch from somewhere else. It wasn't going to help me. I needed to see why things were going wrong at my end.'

Lee became frustrated with the Post Office's lack of cooperation.

'My area manager was not interested at all. She had no inclination whatsoever to help. She couldn't get out of the Post Office quick enough when I was trying to tell her about the problems.'

Lee did not suspect his assistant Christine of anything untoward. She had worked for the former owners and been at Bridlington for 16 years. In Lee's words she 'could run the Post Office on her head. She was great.'

The misbalances yo-yoed up and down, but mainly down. Unlike Noel and Jo, Lee was scrupulous in recording what was going on, and never once signed off an incorrect sum.

One week the Bridlington Post Office 'lost' around £3,500. The following week it 'lost' exactly the same amount, almost to the penny. When Lee looked at his printed reports on the 3.5 inch till roll, he thought there was a very good chance the Post Office had failed to park the previous week's discrepancy in the suspense account properly.

Before raising this anomaly with the Post Office, Lee and Christine double-checked their paperwork. Lee went through all the receipts for all the transactions and totalled everything up. The discrepancy was still there. Lee called the helpline. The helpline operator was adamant there was nothing wrong at their end. The new £3,500 discrepancy was real, and unless an error notice came back, it was his debt. Lee approached his area manager. Again, she dismissed his concerns.

Lee's frustration spilled over. He did not believe any of the reassurances he was getting – about the transactions, about his Horizon terminals or the prospect of the misbalancing magically sorting itself out. Realising the situation was getting out of hand and the sums of money supposedly being lost were getting dangerous, Lee demanded a formal intervention.

'I knew that if at least the auditors came into the office, whatever was going on would stop. I think the Post Office people I was speaking to – the helpline, my area manager – were prepared to let what was going on continue for as long as I was prepared to stay open. I think if I'd been £90,000 down they wouldn't have cared. But I knew that if I asked for an audit, at least it would end.'

It did. The auditors came in at 9am the next morning. They took one look at the accounts, one look at the safe and suspended Lee on the spot.

Lee's Post Office was supposedly £22,963.34 down. He says even then, no one explained anything. He remembers the reassuring phrases being thrown at him: 'Oh we'll find out why … we're sure it's just nothing … we'll put someone else in and see if they misbalance, and we'll go from there.'

Lee shifted over to the retail side of the business whilst Lisa-Marie looked after the kids and his line manager installed a new temporary Subpostmaster.[1] Lee says his area manager and the temp seemed very chummy.

The first day the temp was working behind the Post Office counter, she had a negative discrepancy of £240.[2] The following week, on the Thursday morning after cash balancing, the Bridlington Post Office Horizon terminals were both blank. Instead of calling the helpline to find out what was going on, the temp began manually trading without Horizon. She later claimed in court that this was her decision. Her account was not challenged.

Lee is convinced the temp had reported misbalancing problems with Horizon in the branch on the Wednesday evening and had either refused to use it until it was fixed, or the Post Office had told her not to use it until someone had applied a fix. Lee believes that whilst the screens were blank on that Thursday morning a remote fix was being applied. After four hours of paper trading, the system rebooted and the temp began using Horizon again.

From that moment on, Bridlington's mysterious balancing problems ceased. Lee remembers something else about the day the terminals were out of use.

'I'd been up quite early that morning because I was sorting out the newspapers … by this stage I'd handed over the keys to the temp and the Post Office had changed the alarm codes on the counter, so I had no access to the branch at all. I was just getting on with things, humming the tune to Abide With Me.'

The temp arrived for work. She walked past Lee, heading for the Post Office counter.

As she brushed by, she recognised the tune Lee was humming and observed, 'You're going to need all that faith.'

---

1 Regularly referred to as temps, or subs, or subbies.

2 The Post Office later decided Lee was responsible for these losses despite the fact he was already suspended.

Lee's voice cracked on the phone as he repeated the temp's words to me – 'You're going to need all that faith.' Sympathy for his plight was clearly in short supply.

The Post Office told the suspended Lee he had the right to a 'Reasons to Urge' or RTU interview. This terminology tells you everything you need to know about the Post Office's attitude towards its Subpostmasters. An RTU interview required Subpostmasters to 'urge' the Post Office not to sack them. The interview turned into an interrogation.

'They just kept saying, "We want the money. Where have you put it? Where is it?" It was completely different from what they'd been like before. It all became very scripted towards the contract, which I'd never seen…'[1]

Lee told the investigators he had not taken any money. He reiterated his belief that the Horizon system had been malfunctioning.

This put the Post Office in an unusual position. Lee had neither false accounted nor hidden his discrepancies. He had alerted them to the problems the moment they began and tried his best to get them addressed. With no evidence of theft or false accounting, the Post Office was going to have a hard time making any criminal charge stick. Yet there appeared to be a gaping hole in the Bridlington Post Office accounts. How could they recover the £25,000 which Horizon stated was missing?

The Post Office decided to sack Lee and sue him. He was sent a letter stating that under Section 12:12 of his contract he was liable for 'all losses caused through his own negligence, carelessness or error.' And that unless he coughed up the cash, he would be taken to court.

Lee refused to give the Post Office any money, so, true to their word, on 9 June 2005 they raised a civil claim against him at Scarborough County Court. Lee was a member of the National Federation of Retail Newsagents and had access to legal advice through an NFRN insurance policy. Lee's new solicitor told him he had a solid case, and whilst building his defence advised him to counter-claim for defamation of character and loss of income due to his peremptory suspension and subsequent termination.

On 9 February 2006, Lee and his solicitor went to Scarborough for the hearing. Mystifyingly, the Post Office's legal team didn't turn up. The judge dismissed the Post Office's case and awarded Lee the counter-claim.

---

1 When Lee took over Bridlington Post Office he had signed a piece of paper in lieu of a contract. This was common practice.

Lee was feeling good. He had won an important point of principle against the Post Office and a judge had supported his position. But the court victory was short-lived.

After weeks of silence, the Post Office informed Lee they would be seeking to re-raise their claim against him but not – this time – at Scarborough County Court. He was going to be sued at the High Court in London. Unfortunately, Lee's NFRN insurance would not stretch to cover any further legal fees. He took the decision to represent himself. He didn't have much choice.

The cost of taking someone to the High Court is astronomical. Lee's only assets were his business and property. His £300,000 investment in Bridlington Post Office had evaporated on his suspension and he had no income. At the start of proceedings, in December 2006, the judge told the Post Office lawyers that even if they won their case against Lee there was no prospect of retrieving their costs against him. The Post Office informed the judge they were quite aware of this.

Lee put his faith in the justice system and the evidence he had gathered to prove he had done nothing wrong. He was taken apart. At the beginning of the trial, he agreed that when he submitted his branch trading statement to the Post Office he was effectively stating a set of settled accounts, which meant he was legally responsible for their accuracy.

The judge was dismissive of Lee's attempt to claim that his Horizon terminal was playing up. Lee insisted the disputed amount in his suspense account was a phantom discrepancy caused by a misfiring computer system. But without access to the Horizon system's internal data he could not demonstrate it. Having accepted responsibility for the accounts, the onus was on him. Or as the judge said:

> 'Mr Castleton admits that he was an accounting party. The statement of the account, though not its validity, is admitted. Accordingly, the burden of proof lies on Mr Castleton to show that the account is wrong.'

After reading a witness statement provided by Fujitsu, which stated there was no evidence whatsoever of any problem with the Horizon system, the judge ruled:

> 'Since the logic of the system is correct, the conclusion is inescapable

> that the Horizon system was working properly in all material respects, and that the shortfall of £22,963.34 is real, not illusory.'

Lee was ordered to pay the £22,963.34 discrepancy (plus interest) and the Post Office's £321,000 legal costs. He was bankrupted. The Post Office placed a restriction on Lee's family home. If he ever sold the property attached to his branch, they would take their court-endorsed due from the proceeds, which meant he would not be able to afford to buy anywhere else to live. For more than a decade, Lee has been penniless and condemned to living above the source of his ruin. For a while, Lee, his wife and children lived without heating because there was no money to fix their boiler.

The weariness in Lee's voice as he describes what happened to him is heartbreaking. When I first met him, eight years after his court case, I was surprised. Photos I had seen of Lee at the time showed a man in his prime – a smartly-dressed figure with a military bearing. By 2014 I would guess he was around four stone heavier. He moved slowly. All the energy about him was gone.

Lee, to this day, still does not know what went wrong with his Horizon terminal. He received no help as he tried to uncover the source of the problem. He maintains he and his assistant Christine were doing everything right – or at least, nothing different to what they were doing before these wild discrepancies arose. When the figures on his Horizon screen started to depart from reality, Lee didn't false account, he alerted the Post Office. The Post Office's response was to destroy him and then use the High Court judgment against him to bully other Subpostmasters into making good discrepancies.

Lee Castleton's case is a stark illustration of the way the Post Office went about conducting its business. The Subpostmasters Contract (or rather, the Post Office's rather twisted interpretation of it) made it cheaper and easier to pursue individuals and their assets over Horizon discrepancies than spend time and money properly investigating how those discrepancies occurred.

For smaller amounts it was simple – pay up sunshine, or face suspension. Larger discrepancies led to immediate suspension (without pay) and the threat of losing everything.

Those who panicked and either hid their discrepancies or just gave up (like Jo and Noel) were criminally prosecuted. Those who tried to work with the Post Office to get their problems resolved were either sacked (Alan Bates), criminally prosecuted anyway (Kamran Ashraf), or pursued through the civil courts (Lee).

As we saw with Tracy Felstead, mysterious losses were not confined to sub-Post Offices. In 2008 a confidential internal Post Office policy document was circulated to the Post Office's 400 Crown Office managers. It tells them that in the 2007/8 financial year, £2.2m had disappeared from Crown Office branches. This is an extraordinary figure. The document notes the losses are 'having a serious effect on our ability to deliver the … plan to bring us back into profitability by 2011.'

Horizon is not mentioned, except to suggest an occasional loss might be down to 'accountancy error.' The overwhelming tenor of the circular is that staff need to be watched like hawks. It is, of course, entirely possible that back in the noughties hundreds of Crown Office staff *were* somehow losing or trousering vast amounts of cash, but it also should have raised questions over the system which was calculating these losses.

All over the country the Post Office was suspending, sacking and demanding cash from people who weren't in a position to do anything but hand it over or risk losing everything. By the time Lee Castleton had been rinsed at the High Court, the Post Office had successfully prosecuted 363 people and sacked hundreds more. There should have been uproar. Instead, there was silence.

FULL AUTHORITY DIGITAL ENGINE CONTROL

Chinook helicopters are instantly recognisable. They have dual rotor-blades, two noisy Boeing engines and their elongated hulks can be configured to carry up to 50 troops or ten tonnes of cargo, including armoured land rovers. They are workhorses of the sky, and in helicopter terms, absolute beasts. The heavy thud-thud-thud which fills the air when a Chinook approaches is unmistakeable.

The helicopter's connection to the Horizon scandal goes beyond South Warnborough Post Office's proximity to RAF Odiham, and Lee Castleton's Desert Storm experience.

On Friday 2 June 1994, at 5.42pm, a Chinook Mk2 – airframe registration ZD576 – took off from RAF Aldergrove in Northern Ireland, heading towards the west coast of Scotland. There were 25 passengers and four crew on board, led by two experienced special forces pilots. The flight manifest was classified, and shredded on take off. All the passengers were from top level military intelligence, MI5 counter-terrorism or special branch police officers.

Visibility across the North Channel (the short stretch of water between Northern Ireland and the Mull of Kintyre) was good, but conditions around the Mull peninsular, a rounded outcrop of land, with sheer cliffs rising from the sea to a gorse-covered summit, had deteriorated.

The pilots, Flight Lieutenants Jonathan Tapper and Richard Cook, had plotted a change of course into the Chinook's navigation computer before take off. A left turn on the approach to the Mull of Kintyre lighthouse would take them north, around the Mull. If executed properly, they would avoid the worst of the conditions, and continue flying low across the water in good visibility.

The Chinook did not make its intended left turn. The helicopter ploughed into the Mull at a height of 247m, killing everyone on board.

The RAF, and the Air Accidents Investigation Branch concluded that, in the absence of any evidence of technical malfunction, the pilots were probably at fault. They were posthumously found guilty of gross negligence.

The fathers of the dead pilots refused to accept their sons could be to blame for the crash. It went against their character and their years of outstanding service. Mike Tapper and John Cook began a campaign to clear their children's names.

The Chinook Mk2 looked almost identical to its predecessor, the Mk1, but its internal navigation system was very different. Instead of manual controls, a fly-by-wire computer system called Fadec (Full Authority Digital Engine Control) had been installed, which converted the pilots' cockpit manoeuvres into a series of digital instructions to the aircraft's engines and rotors.

Serious concerns about the Mk2 and the Fadec system had been circulating amongst pilots and air crew for some time. An internal MoD document written nine months before the fatal crash described the new software as 'positively dangerous.' When flight ZD576 went down, IT experts and airworthiness assessors at Boscombe Down immediately sent a letter to the MoD and RAF urging them 'in the strongest possible terms' to end operational flights until corrective action was taken. The letter said recommendations over the Fadec software had been 'ignored' and that air crews would be at risk if they continued to fly the helicopter.

In 1997, a leaked report revealed analysis of the Fadec software had uncovered 485 anomalies, including 56 serious 'category one' problems. The company carrying out the analysis had only looked at 20% of the Fadec source code before downing tools and raising the alarm.

The MP for North East Hampshire, James Arbuthnot, took an interest. He had been a junior defence minister in the mid-nineties, and RAF Odiham was in his constituency.

In 1999 Computer Weekly published a lengthy investigation into the Mull of Kintyre crash called 'RAF Justice.' The article detailed serious problems with the Chinooks' Fadec software, but also noted that crucial information about Fadec, Chinooks and specifically Chinook ZD576 had been withheld from accident investigators. Furthermore, when the accident investigators *were* given important information, they failed to interpret it properly.

James Arbuthnot joined the Chinook pilots' families in a push for a full independent inquiry.

For more than a decade, in the face of growing evidence that a miscarriage of justice had taken place, the Ministry of Defence stood by the conclusions of the initial investigation report and chose instead to protect the contractors who had supplied the Chinook's Fadecs.

Finally, in 2011, after an independent review by a retired judge, the initial verdict of gross negligence was set aside. The families of the dead pilots received written apologies and the MoD was lambasted for its long-standing refusal to countenance the possibility that computer software could have had anything to do with the crash.

It may be that on 2 June 1994, two excellent and experienced pilots made a mistake. It's possible they flew their Chinook ZD576 into the side of the Mull of Kintyre, despite having planned to execute a manoeuvre which would take them safely north of the Mull. It is also plausible, thanks to evidence in part uncovered by Computer Weekly, that an IT error may have rendered the aircraft temporarily and catastrophically uncontrollable, resulting in the loss of 29 lives.

Although Computer Weekly's 140-page report on the Chinook disaster isn't credited to a single journalist, the driving force behind it was Tony Collins, who by 2008 was the magazine's editor-in-chief. In 2004, Alan Bates had written to Computer Weekly about the problems he was having with Horizon, but it came to nothing. In early 2008, Lee Castleton sent the magazine an email. Tony read it. Lee wanted help. He'd lost everything at the hands of the Post Office and was certain Horizon was to blame.

Tony called a young staff journalist over, and suggested she start digging. The journalist's name was Rebecca Thomson. Years later I called Rebecca to ask if she would tell me how she broke the Horizon story. It was an illuminating interview.

'Tony passed on Lee's contact details,' she began 'and I gave him a ring. Lee told me his story, which was heartbreaking. It was quite upsetting talking to him because he's such a nice man and he's obviously been broken by this … organisation.'

Rebecca was intrigued.

'He had a young family and he just sounded so downtrodden by it all. When I listened to him, he didn't sound like a crazy, and he had lots of detail – he had his computer log and dates and he just wanted someone to look into his data and see if they could see anything that might have been causing him problems.'

Lee was already talking to other Subpostmasters. 'He gave me names and contact details, so I started calling around,' Rebecca said.

At the same time Rebecca was talking to Lee, the resourceful villagers of South Warnborough were doing some research on Jo Hamilton's behalf. A retired probation officer by the name of Roch Garrard found Alan's Post Office Victims website and saw an article in a Welsh newspaper which covered the prosecution of Noel Thomas. In May 2008, Roch sent a letter to Noel Thomas attaching a Daily Mail article about Jo's conviction. He reflected on the similarities with Noel's situation and told him, 'We believe "something is not right" in the Post Office computer system.'

Roch suggested a telephone call with Noel 'so that we might share information about the difficulties with the Post Office.'

Noel has kept hold of the letter for more than 13 years. He says receiving it was a 'lifeline', with all that implies. Here was someone else, in a different part of the UK, blaming the Horizon computer system for problems they couldn't understand. He was not alone.

The connections began to strengthen. Jo was put in touch with Alan Bates, who also spoke to Rebecca.

'Alan Bates became my main source of contact after a while,' she said. 'Because Lee had so much on his plate I started dealing with Alan, who was very helpful.'

Given the story was not in the public domain, the reputational and legal risks of publishing unproven allegations were high. I asked Rebecca what her biggest concern was.

'Never mentioning Fujitsu. Because they were the ones who might actually sue. Tony said because the Post Office was a publicly-owned company it was very unlikely to sue us. That's what made the story possible to run at all. If it was a private company we were investigating, we couldn't publish, because we couldn't prove anything. All we had was the testimony of the Postmasters and a handful of experts saying, "Yes, this looks suspicious but we have no way of knowing what the actual problems are." '

Rebecca interviewed seven former Subpostmasters for her piece – Lee Castleton, Jo Hamilton, Noel Thomas, Amar Bajaj, Alan Bates, Alan Brown and Julie Ford. All seven blamed Horizon and the Post Office's heavy-handed approach. Rebecca recorded that 'all of the postmasters we spoke to' said the National Federation of Subpostmasters had 'refused to help them investigate their concerns.'

Of the Post Office, Rebecca wrote that it denied receiving 'any complaints from Postmasters, and also denies that any IT-related fault could have caused the systems to show incorrect sums of money owed by some Postmasters.'

The first part of the Post Office's response to Rebecca was untrue because it *had* received complaints from Subpostmasters. Alan Bates started writing letters to the Post Office directly complaining about weaknesses in the Horizon system in 2000. The second part of Post Office's response was also untrue. Alan Brown's story (case study six in Rebecca's piece) was a real systemic computer fault (it later became known as the Callendar Square Incident or Bug) which could and did cause Subpostmasters to be out of pocket.

It was Rebecca's first investigation as a journalist.

'I got very emotionally involved with it,' she said. 'I just felt sorry for them basically. It's quite an affecting story. And I think they were used to people like me asking questions about proof, because they'd been desperate to find proof for themselves. Any documentation they had they were very keen to send to me. I spoke to far more Subpostmasters than the case studies we went with in the end. Some were quite clueless, but some were really switched on.'

I asked what she made of the Post Office's attitude.

'The thing that gets me is that the Post Office should have been looking out for them. I know they weren't actual employees of the Post Office but you kind of assume that a government-run organisation, which is there to provide you with a living … it's just shocking that it could turn around and become so aggressive and could ruin their lives … and how people could end up in these desperate situations by doing comparatively so little.'

Rebecca reflected on a situation which cuts across everything. Why didn't the Post Office want to help?

'Obviously false accounting is wrong. [The Subpostmasters] all turned around and said they knew it was wrong, but they didn't know what else to do. I guess it was that combination of desperation and being put in that position by a company that you automatically would trust because of what it is. It's like the NHS turning on people. Institutionally … it's so … *weird* in a way.'

I asked Rebecca what it was like when, after 12 months of solid work, she got to press the button and publish the story.

'It was obviously exciting. We'd spent a lot of time getting this right, and had really been working up to getting this onto the Today programme or having one of the Sunday papers pick up on it. We genuinely thought it was a great story. But we put it out there and nothing happened.'

There were some follow-up pieces in other trade publications, but the nationals and the broadcast media decided not to touch it. Rebecca was understandably disappointed. What she didn't know was that her investigation would have a long-term impact far beyond anything anyone at Computer Weekly could have expected.

Twelve months or so after her Horizon investigation, Rebecca moved on from Computer Weekly. She spent a couple more years in consumer journalism and then took a job in communications for a large accounting and consultancy firm, which was when I first made contact with her. It led to a strange moment.

On 5 February 2016, Rebecca was exactly a month into her new job. I had tracked her down on Twitter[1] and sent her a message. It said:

> 'Hi Rebecca, just reading your groundbreaking 2009 investigation into Horizon. Could you follow me so I can direct message you?'

This was a public tweet which could be read by anyone. Direct messages are private, but for security reasons two people usually have to be 'following' each other to communicate in this way on Twitter – it's a method of positively opting in to a private conversation. Hence my request.

Rebecca followed me, so we were able to chat to each other in confidence. I asked if she would agree to be interviewed, and two weeks later we spoke on the phone. The conversation did not go the way I expected.

Before I could ask any questions about Rebecca's investigation, she told me that shortly after receiving my public tweet her boss had received a phone call at work from a senior partner within her firm. The partner, who had no idea who Rebecca was, wanted to know if she had been contacted by a journalist with regard to her investigation into Horizon.

Bemused, Rebecca confirmed to her boss she had received a tweet from me and we had gone on to exchange private messages about conducting an interview. Rebecca's boss told her someone claiming to be from the Post Office had contacted the partner to remind him – and Rebecca – that his firm counted the Post Office among its clients. The person claiming to be from the Post Office had apparently suggested Rebecca might like to tread carefully.

An apologetic Rebecca, new in her job, said to me that on the basis of that rather strange conversation at her work, she didn't feel able to talk to me about breaking the Horizon story or her time at Computer Weekly. Our conversation ended shortly thereafter.

I was disturbed by this. The tweet I had initially sent Rebecca was innocuous enough, and that was the only communication between us in the public domain.

I don't mind the Post Office following me on Twitter. I actually asked them to once so I could send a direct message to their Director of Communications. But surely my one public tweet to Rebecca wouldn't provoke anyone in the Post Office to pick up the phone and warn off her

---

1 A social media app and website which allows people to publish short public messages to their followers or specific individuals, or both.

employer. What kind of weirdo would do that?

Rebecca and I stayed in touch. After she left her corporate job and went back to journalism, Rebecca was able to give me the interview which makes up this chapter. She remains something of a hero of mine, for obvious reasons.

TARO NAW

A BBC Wales reporter, Sion Tecwyn, was quick to spot Rebecca's piece in the pages of Computer Weekly. He saw Noel Thomas's name and was intrigued. Sion and Noel knew each other from Noel's time as a county councillor. Sion ran a short TV news piece on BBC Wales Today about Noel's appearance in Computer Weekly's pages. It was framed in the context of an investigation by a respected technical journal which appeared to be calling into question the integrity of the Post Office Horizon system.

The camera operator working with Sion on that news item was called Graham Meggitt. Graham had worked in BBC Wales' current affairs unit with two young journalists called Anna Marie Robinson and Bryn Jones. In 2009 Anna Marie and Bryn were assigned to a half-hour Welsh-language current affairs programme made by the BBC for the S4C channel. It was called Taro Naw.[1]

After Sion's piece about Noel had been broadcast, Graham called Anna Marie and Bryn. As Anna Marie remembers it, Graham said, 'I think there's a really good story here. You should look into it.'

Anna Marie admits, 'Without that, I don't think we would have picked it up, to be honest.'

'Yeah,' adds Bryn, 'because it wasn't a huge story that Sion did – it was just an item buried in the half-hour evening news. It didn't make the headlines. And I don't know if it even appeared online.'

Bryn and Anna Marie took the Horizon story to the editor of Taro Naw. They were given permission to look into this apparent problem with the Post Office computer system. I asked Anna Marie and Bryn to take me through their approach to the story. They told me the first thing they did after being granted time to work on the Horizon story was hit the phones.

'We spent the whole summer ringing people,' enthused Anna Marie. 'We were phone-bashing all over Britain and ended up speaking to people who had no idea about the Computer Weekly article – some of them had no idea there were other people who had been through what they'd been through.'

Bryn: 'Initially we got in touch with the seven who were in Computer

---

1 Pronounced 'tarrow now.'

Weekly. And we spoke to the reporter who wrote the piece … she gave us the numbers of a few people she'd spoken to when she was putting it all together. Those contacts put us in touch with other case studies who hadn't made the published article … we googled … we came across local newspaper stories about Postmasters who'd been prosecuted. People would then hear about the fact we were looking into Horizon and get in touch with us.'

Anna Marie: 'We'd find any stories about Post Offices where there were sudden closures and we'd try to get hold of the Subpostmaster to find out why. Some we'd just send letters to the Post Office address and hope they'd get back to us.'

Bryn: 'And we found someone[2] helpful inside the National Federation of Subpostmasters. He gave us some contacts as well…'

Anna Marie: '… in fact, he became an anonymous contributor to our programme.'

Bryn returned to the Subpostmasters' plight.

'You see, a lot of these people had either been through the court system, or were facing charges, or they'd "lost" ten, twenty thousand pounds and they weren't allowed to talk to us. There was an element of fear there as well. Some of them felt able to talk off the record, but not on the record.'

Adding to the seven case studies in the Computer Weekly article, Bryn and Anna Marie found another 29 Subpostmasters with similar, credible stories to tell, bringing the total to 36.

I asked what it was like putting their investigation together.

Anna Marie: 'It was quite exciting, to be honest. You don't often get to work on a big story like this. We had a very supportive editor who gave us the time. Here in BBC Wales, because there are so few of us, we don't get a lot of time to investigate stuff. But he sort of trusted us, didn't he Bryn?'

Bryn: 'Yeah. If we didn't come up with the goods he still had to fill his half hour, so at the back of your mind you've got to have a plan B.'

Anna Marie: 'And this at the time seemed like it was going to be impossible to broadcast. You're taking on a massive company like the Post Office. But we had so many people saying the same thing.'

---

2 Mark Baker, who you will meet in a few chapters time.

Bryn: 'Yeah it was that feeling of … "hang on. There's something here." '

Anna Marie: 'We worked in a small office and I remember we'd both be on the phone at the same time talking to somebody. And you know when you get goose bumps and shivers … there were a few days when we got quite a few people and I remember we looked at each other whilst on the phone nodding and you could tell from the look we were giving each other I'd found another case study with a now familiar story to tell. It was like magic, but it was like bad magic because these were really sad stories – these people, their lives had been ruined, you know? Ruined…'

Bryn: 'Some of the people we called – they weren't innocent…!'

Anna Marie: 'Yeah – not everybody made the list of 36!'

Bryn: 'We got excited about one, because he was a Welsh speaker … and so we thought, "Oh great!…" '

Anna Marie: 'But when we spoke to him, he said "I'm sorry – I don't fit your bill." '

Bryn: 'He said it was a fair cop!'

Bryn returned to a central theme of this scandal.

Bryn: 'A lot of them thought they were on their own. I'd listen to their story and I'd be able to tell them that actually I'd spoken to two people that same day who'd been through a similar experience.'

Anna Marie: 'They couldn't all be lying and telling us such similar stories.'

Bryn: 'And not knowing each other. Having never heard of other people having suffered in the same way. And it was the same pattern in the way the cases were being prosecuted. This false accounting thing that they were going for with everybody.'

Anna Marie: 'That was an easy way of getting people to admit to a crime.'

Bryn: 'Some of them were still employed by the Post Office, and had paid their own money into the Horizon system. Tens of thousands of pounds in some instances. So they hadn't been taken to court but they were saying, "I don't want to talk on the record, I don't want anything to do with it, but I've lost thousands of pounds." And once so many people start talking to you saying similar things and they've got nothing to gain from talking to you…'

I suggested to Anna Marie and Bryn that finding hard evidence must have been tough.

Anna Marie: 'And we had to do it in Welsh! Our programme is meant to be Welsh with allowance for, say … up to 10% of speech in English. And we only had one case study who spoke Welsh and so we had to persuade our bosses it was worth telling. It was probably one of the most difficult stories I've worked on in 20 years.'

Bryn: 'Also you've got people who've pleaded guilty, or been found guilty. Once you go to the lawyers and say this – you've got a big problem, haven't you? But…'

Anna Marie: 'It was the volume. Because we had 36 people saying the same thing … well, obviously not exactly the same thing, but they all had a similar thread … our lawyer said, "Go for it." '

What did the Post Office say?

Bryn: 'Well the day after the programme went out the Post Office got in contact and asked us for a translation!'

Anna Marie: 'To be honest, before the programme went out I don't think they took us that seriously. We got a paragraph saying Horizon was robust and that the people in our programme had pleaded guilty.'

Bryn: 'They refused to be interviewed about it.'

Anna Marie: 'We were hoping to get an interview … but they obviously weren't that bothered about our programme because they were still prosecuting people years later. The thing that gets me is that these are real people. Actual lives which have been ruined. People who have become ill through stress … contemplating suicide … because they've lost so much, and their reputations have been ruined as well.'

Anna Marie and Bryn's Taro Naw was first broadcast at 9.30pm on Tuesday 8 September 2009. It was presented by Dylan Jones.

During the documentary Noel Thomas' story is told in detail. Then Noel's daughter, Sian, describes getting a phone call from the former South Warnborough Postmaster Jo Hamilton.

'It was an unbelievable feeling,' gushes Sian. 'We were all sat around this table and said, "Oh my gosh! We're not the only ones… There are other people in Britain going through it." '

Although Noel and Jo were in touch, they had never met – so Taro Naw took Noel to South Warnborough Village Stores and filmed the first meeting between the two former Subpostmasters, now both convicted criminals, with similar stories to tell.

'It will be emotional,' we see Sian saying as she packs a suitcase. 'I'm looking forward to hearing her experience so we can compare it to Dad's. We've been fighting hard for the last three years … it's very exciting!'

Jo and Noel are filmed meeting outside Jo's shop and we leave them in South Warnborough Village Stores drinking coffee and wondering how they are going to go about clearing their names.

Meanwhile, back in Wales, the Taro Naw investigative team kicks into action.

Dylan approaches the Post Office to ask if there has been an increase in the number of Postmasters accused of stealing since the Horizon system was rolled out across the country. Despite Taro Naw's Freedom of Information request, the Post Office was unable to retrieve the figures.

The Post Office's standard denial is interesting here, too. Horizon is described as 'dependable', with no 'technological failing.' Indeed, they told Taro Naw that in one court case 'the system was proved to be faultless,'[1] so there was 'no cause for concern.'

The NFSP blithely parroted the Post Office line, telling Taro Naw there was 'no cause for concern.'

Watching the investigation back, the flat denials from the Post Office and the NFSP that anything could be wrong with Horizon stick in the craw – especially as Taro Naw lays out serious and credible evidence, expert opinion and case studies, all of which point to potentially serious flaws with the way the Post Office was going about things.

I asked Bryn and Anna Marie what kind of response the programme got.

Bryn: 'Well to be honest our programme doesn't normally get a huge reaction. Occasionally you'll get an email thanking you for highlighting a story, but we were quite surprised with this one because we got six new cases. People who we hadn't come across before the programme emailed or called us up and said, "That happened to me." Mainly in Wales, but one or two in England as well.'

The 2009 Taro Naw investigation into the Post Office Horizon IT system is an outstanding piece of investigative journalism. Taken with the Computer Weekly piece, there were now two robustly-researched, clear indications that something very wrong was happening to Britain's Subpostmasters. And, crucially, these Subpostmasters were beginning to realise they weren't alone.

---

[1] The court case in which Horizon was 'proved to be faultless', was Lee Castleton's, where Lee was unable to prove Horizon had gone wrong. Not quite the same thing as being proved faultless. For more see the 'Lee Castleton' chapter.

After watching Taro Naw go out, Alan Bates made a decision. He rang round his growing list of aggrieved former Subpostmasters and suggested a meeting.

ALAN MARSHALS THE TROOPS

On Sunday 8 November 2009, two months to the day after the Taro Naw investigation was broadcast, a group of middle-aged convicted criminals met face-to-face for the very first time. Fenny Compton in Warwickshire was chosen for its central location.

Fenny Compton village hall itself was built in 1946, to what looks like a Victorian design. A late twentieth century extension has given it toilets, storage space, a café/breakout area and a large kitchen. It is a tidy, well-organised and quintessentially British community resource – where else would a group of former Subpostmasters meet?

Through the efforts of Alan Bates, Lee Castleton, Jo Hamilton and two other former Subpostmasters – Julian Wilson and Graham Oates – there was a good turnout. Although no formal headcount was made, most agree around 20 to 25 former Subpostmasters attended, many of whom brought a partner or friend, bringing the total number present to around 45. The other significant attendee was Issy Hogg, who drove up from South Warnborough with Jo.

'The main thing I remember about it was just how cold it was,' Jo told me. 'The heating wasn't working and you could see the breath coming out of your mouth, even indoors!'

As the Subpostmasters arrived, the kitchen was put to good use. The electric tea urn was switched on and everyone handed over their sandwiches and cakes so they could be laid out for lunch. Alan's partner, Suzanne, recruited volunteers among the Subpostmasters' partners to find plates and cutlery and organise the distribution of hot drinks.

'I was quite frightened, actually,' remembers Suzanne. 'What we were doing was very against what the Post Office would like us to do.'

The Postmasters filed into the main hall. Everyone kept their coats on.

There was chit-chat and handshaking, but the atmosphere was reserved. Alan pointed to the chairs stacked by the wall and suggested they arrange them into a circle.

'That's something I've always been keen on,' he told me, 'and what I used to do at work. I don't believe in hierarchies in these sorts of things. Putting chairs in a circle is a good leveller. We've tried to do that at every meeting since.'

The attendees took their seats and the room quietened.

Jo Hamilton was sitting separately from Alan and Issy. 'I remember looking round the room at these people, and thinking how we all looked, like we'd been run over by a truck. We were just shattered. Our lives had been ripped off us.'

Alan introduced himself. He asked the Subpostmasters to explain what had happened to them. Karen Wilson, Julian Wilson's wife, remembers it well.

'We went round the room, one by one. Everyone was talking about exactly the same thing – different years, different figures, slightly different actions in court, but the foundations were all the same.'

'The main thing I remember,' says Jo, 'was all of us saying how we'd been told that we were the only ones having problems with Horizon. The Post Office investigators told me I was the only one having problems, and most of the people in the room at Fenny Compton had been told exactly the same thing.'

Suzanne: 'Every time someone spoke, the scenarios seemed to be getting worse and worse. I couldn't believe what people had suffered.'

Issy Hogg was astounded. 'Believe me,' she said, 'I know what a criminal looks like. As I listened to all those people who'd never met, and heard the similarities in their stories and what they went through, I thought, "These people aren't criminals. There's something very seriously wrong here." '

A lot of ground was covered – the methods of the Post Office investigators, the general uselessness of the National Federation of Subpostmasters, the imminent upgrade of Horizon[1] and what might happen to important data still in the system after that.

For Jo, one overriding positive came out of the meeting. 'It was just so important to find out that we weren't alone. That other people had been through almost identical experiences to us.'

Karen concurred. 'We all realised how we all knitted together with the same pattern. We talked about contacting the helpline, what the Post Office had said in court, the Subpostmasters Contract, and the question became, "Well, what do we do now?" '

Issy was only meant to stay for part of the afternoon, but she sat

---

[1] The arrival of Horizon Online in 2010 was being presented as a big shift. Data would be updated at Horizon's back end in real time rather than being stored locally and updated overnight. Its implementation was a disaster.

through the full meeting. Alan told me he deliberately monopolised her time – essentially getting four hours of free legal advice as he worked through the potential options available to the Subpostmasters, trying to push things forward.

Before the meeting concluded, the Subpostmasters agreed they would band together in an attempt to seek redress. Alan was elected chair of the group. Issy would become the point person for all legal queries. Contact details would be collected and circulated. A letter would be drawn up which would be distributed to other Subpostmasters in their local area. Constituency MPs who hadn't already been made aware of the Subpostmasters' plight would be alerted.

Karen remembers, 'I got in the car thinking, "Oh thank God. It's not just us. There are more people out there in the same situation, who've been persecuted in the same way." '

The only thing the group didn't have was a name. A few were discussed. In a post-meeting circular Alan noted there were three options which had not been rejected. They were: Injustice Against Subpostmasters, Victims of Horizon Alliance and Justice for Subpostmasters Alliance.

Among the respondents to Alan's circular, there was a clear favourite.

The Justice for Subpostmasters Alliance was born.

As well as being a key figure in the fight to have the cause of the Mull of Kintyre Chinook crash properly investigated, James Arbuthnot was Jo Hamilton's MP.

James, now Lord, Arbuthnot is an old-school Tory with impeccable pedigree, being a direct descendant of James V and various ancient kings of Scotland. The present-day Lord Arbuthnot received an Eton and Cambridge education, graduating from Trinity College with a law degree. He then became a barrister, before being elected to parliament in 1987, initially sitting as the member for Wanstead and Woodford, then from 1997 to 2015 as the MP for North East Hampshire. He is a friendly, if imposing individual, with a rather tangible sense of propriety about him.

In October 2009, just before the Fenny Compton meeting, Arbuthnot received a letter from a constituent, David Bristow. David had been the Postmaster in the village of Odiham, but was now suspended without pay over a £43,000 discrepancy at his branch. David was 100% certain his problems were down to a malfunctioning Horizon terminal. David mentioned Jo Hamilton's conviction in 2008 and that he was in touch with Alan Bates, whose MP was David Jones.

Arbuthnot wrote to David Jones and Peter Mandelson, who was at the time Secretary of State for Business. He then set up a meeting with David Bristow and Jo Hamilton.

Arbuthnot told me he was 'sceptical' about Jo, for good reason.

'The court process in my experience is pretty thorough, meticulous and generally leans over backwards to avoid convicting people against whom there is no evidence. There's a legal process to follow if you don't get the right result. And anyway, she'd pleaded guilty.'

But Jo was persuasive. 'She was not bowed down by it. She was determined that something had gone wrong and it seemed to her to be unfair. I thought Jo's story sounded like it had something to it.'

Arbuthnot also picked up the phone to the National Federation of Subpostmasters.

'A key official in the Federation was one of my local councillors, a chap called Nippi Singh. He's a friend of mine. I told him that there appeared to be a groundswell of opinion that some Subpostmasters were being wrongly accused of theft.'

Nippi was dismissive. He, along with his superiors at the National

Federation of Subpostmasters, took the same line as the Post Office – there was nothing wrong with Horizon, and anyone who was prosecuted was prosecuted with good reason.

That could have been enough to end the MP's interest in David and Jo's situation. After all, David had no evidence, and Jo had gone through the courts and pleaded guilty. A union rep had given an assurance that there was no issue with Horizon. But by this point Arbuthnot had also taken the time to read the Computer Weekly investigation into Horizon.

'It galvanised me. During the Chinook enquiry, Computer Weekly had been absolutely fantastic, and the fact that they were on Horizon's case gave it, in my mind, credibility.'

In December 2009, David Jones called the Post Office to a meeting at the House of Commons, inviting James Arbuthnot along. During the exploratory meeting, the Post Office representatives insisted Horizon was 'robust.' The MPs smelt a rat and met again four days later. Arbuthnot told Jones, 'I feel a campaign coming on.'

After the 2010 general election, which saw David Cameron installed as prime minister of a coalition government between the Conservatives and the Liberal Democrats, James Arbuthnot wrote an email to all members of parliament explaining he had 'an issue' around Subpostmasters and the Horizon computer system. He asked if anyone else was dealing with similar caseloads.

Arbuthnot told me he was surprised by how many MPs replied. 'It wasn't huge, but it was 20 or so.'

One of the respondents was Oliver Letwin, who attended cabinet meetings and was considered something of a rising star within government at the time. His constituent was Tracey Merritt, a Subpostmaster in Yetminster who had been sacked by the Post Office for losses of just under £12,000. She was being threatened with prosecution. The MPs began to share information.

THE MISRAS

As well as inspiring a half-hour documentary, the creation of the Justice for Subpostmasters Alliance and pushing an influential MP towards the first stirrings of parliamentary action, the May 2009 Computer Weekly investigation put a serious spanner in the works of a criminal trial for theft, which was just about to get underway at Guildford Crown Court. The defendant was Seema Misra, former Subpostmaster at West Byfleet Post Office in Surrey.

Seema was a middle-class Indian from New Delhi. Her partner, Davinder, was also from New Dehli – part of a large, well-to-do Hindu family. By his mid-twenties Davinder had carved out a decent career working in hotel management. He was also looking for a wife. Seema was introduced to Davinder. They married the same year. He was 26, she was 23.

The couple planned to stay and build their lives together in India, but Seema was unsuited to her own North Indian climate. The newly-weds decided to emigrate to England.

Seema went first in 1999, picking up a job in a property consultancy in London, starting as an office junior before shifting into the accounts department. Davinder flew over the same year, joining Seema in her shared house.

Davinder began working in the kitchens of Quaglino's, not far from Piccadilly Circus. It was hard. The pay wasn't good either, but at least both Seema and Davinder had jobs and the ability to support themselves. They lived frugally, which allowed them to put money away.

By 2000 Davinder and Seema (who was now pregnant with the couple's first child) had saved enough to put down a deposit on their first house, a three-bedroom terrace in Finsbury Park. The day after they completed the house purchase, Seema gave birth to her first son, Aditya.

Although the Misras were happy as a family, Davinder wasn't satisfied with how much money he was making. His brother was working in logistics up in Bedfordshire. The pay there was better and the cost of living much lower than London. With Aditya a babe in arms, the Misras let their Finsbury Park house and moved to Luton, where they began renting again. Seema took a job on the staff of Bedfordshire police and Davinder found a job working in the same company as his brother. Seema and Davinder decided that one day they would go into business together.

Eventually the opportunity the Misras had been looking for came up. A dilapidated property with a lock-up shop became available in the village of Caddington, near Luton. The Misras bought it and moved in, fitting out the lock-up and opening for business as a Premier grocery store.

The Misras worked hard to get the business off the ground whilst juggling childcare and the ongoing renovation of the flat above the shop. Their industry was rewarded. The flat was completed and the retail unit began to do well. The Misras were now working for themselves and building a stable family life.

Within a couple of years, the Caddington shop gave the Misras confidence and enough working capital to go for something else. In 2004 Davinder began looking around for a larger shop.

When the West Byfleet Costcutter came up, Davinder wasn't that interested, even though it came with a Post Office counter. The shop was in a retail unit at the base of a modern office block and only available as a leasehold. Owning their own property was important to the Misras.

But once they had thought about the advantages of running a Post Office, they kept coming back to it. The West Byfleet shop was large. It was established. It had staff (which meant the Misras might one day be able to take a holiday) and the Post Office counter came with a Subpostmaster's income of around £60,000. It also meant guaranteed footfall.

The couple started thinking about a move to Surrey.

INSTANT LOSSES

Davinder and his brother contacted the West Byfleet Subpostmaster and asked for more information about taking on the lease. They also asked about the logistics of running a sub-Post Office counter. They liked what they heard.

The Misras came up with a plan. Davinder would run the shop and Seema would apply to become the West Byfleet Subpostmaster.

The Misras made a £200,000 offer to the outgoing Subpostmaster for the shop lease and the Post Office counter. The deal would be financed by the sale of the Misras' shop in Caddington and a £67,000 mortgage.

The offer was provisionally accepted by the leaseholders, as was another offer from a different party. It was down to the Post Office. Seema and another candidate were put forward to become the new West Byfleet Subpostmaster. The Post Office decided they preferred Seema. The Misras were in! To prepare for her new role, in March 2005 Seema was sent on a two-week training course which would teach her how to operate Horizon.

Seema remembers her course starting at 9am every day and finishing around lunchtime. At the end of the two weeks Seema was told she was good to go. She was not tested.

Ideally Seema would have started working at West Byfleet immediately after finishing her course. Unfortunately, between Seema's training and her first day in situ, there was a three-month delay before the property contracts for the shop premises were finalised and completed.

Seema and Davinder finally got their hands on the keys to their new Post Office on 29 June 2005. Seema opened for business as the West Byfleet Subpostmaster the next day. To assist, the Post Office provided her with a trainer, Junaid, who would guide her through her first week.

At the end of the first day's trading, Seema was told by Junaid to request a snapshot balance. Seema pressed the relevant buttons and found her counter was just under £100 down. Junaid could not explain why. He told her she needed to make up the money. When Seema asked why, he told her, 'Balancing is never penny to penny.'

The next day Seema's Post Office counter was down again. Less than £100, but again Junaid could not tell Seema why this had happened. He suggested she take more money out of Davinder's retail till and wait until the end-of-week balancing.

Every day the Post Office opened for the first week of Seema's tenure, the tills were down. At the end of the week, when the balancing was done, she remained down. No transaction corrections were issued by the Post Office. Junaid told Seema a TC could take months to surface. Junaid's week of training was up. Seema never saw him again.

The following week, Seema was given a different Post Office trainer, Michael. Michael seemed a lot more hands-on than Junaid. Michael was concerned Seema was losing money daily and that no one had figured out why. Seema and Michael worked closely during their week together. By the end of it, Seema was £400 down. She appeared to be doing everything right. Yet by the time they rolled the balances over at the end of the second week, no transaction corrections had appeared. Michael finished his training stint, promising to look into the problem. Seema never heard from him again.

Seema raised the issue of her losses with her area manager. The area manager told Seema a transaction correction would probably come back to her, eventually.

She started the next week with no trainer to guide her. Seema's losses continued to grow.

FEAR AND LOATHING IN WEST BYFLEET

Seema and Davinder were worried. Very worried. They'd moved into a new area, committed to a new business, and the accounting system behind their Post Office counter had become a hole into which they were expected to chuck money.

According to the transcript of her trial, Seema made another call to her area manager. She says she told her, 'I can't carry on doing this. I have bought the business to make money, not to lose money. I am losing money day in, day out in the Post Office. Please help me. I can't take this on any more.'

On 5 October 2005 Seema was visited by a Post Office auditor, Keith Noverre, who ran the rule over Seema's accounts and concluded there was a £3,000 discrepancy at the West Byfleet branch. Noverre told Seema to either make good the £3,000 immediately or she would have the money taken out of her salary. The auditor allegedly then told Seema that if she went as much as £500 down in future, she would be sacked. A casual, but chilling reminder of the power the Post Office had over Seema's livelihood and investment. Neither Seema nor the Post Office retain any record of Mr Noverre's comment, but Seema is adamant it is what she was told. It is a crucial point because it informs so many of Seema's subsequent actions, including those which led to her prosecution.

The immediate consequence was a rapidly encroaching atmosphere of paranoia. Seema and Davinder decided the 'losses' must be the fault of their staff.

Seema asked her area manager how she could reorganise the counter so that each individual staff member had responsibility for their own till and stock unit. The area manager didn't know. By 2005, running separate stock units for each member of staff was part of the Post Office's standard operating procedure, but it clearly wasn't happening under the previous regime at the West Byfleet branch. Seema and Davinder attempted the process themselves. In Seema's words 'it created more mess.'

Seema was digging herself a massive hole in plain sight. The area manager put Seema into contact with someone from network support to help Seema convert one master stock unit into four. According to Seema's trial transcript, the first thing the network support manager asked was why she 'wanted to create more trouble' for herself.

Seema persevered and set up her four individual stock units. She also gave each staff member a lockable satchel. After cashing up each night, her employees would put their cash and stock in the satchel, lock it and put it in the safe. Once the system of multiple stock units had been established, Seema's losses, by her estimate, trebled. Things were out of control.

The year turned. As Seema watched closely, she became suspicious of one of her employees. The staff member had been working in the retail part of the shop before the Misras took over. Seema promoted him to work behind the Post Office counter and (as required by the Post Office) trained him herself.

Seema realised all was not as it should be with her new assistant's stock unit. She confronted him. She says he admitted stealing money and told the Misras he would make it good.

Seema and Davinder were both furious and relieved. Furious that her assistant had been stealing, but relieved they appeared to have found the source of the problem.

In February 2006, Seema dismissed her assistant. The discrepancies continued to grow.

Seema continued to raise the numerous problems she was having on a regular basis with her area manager. She also made calls to the Post Office's National Business Centre helpline and the Horizon helpline.

Another counter assistant came under scrutiny. She too appeared to have her hands in the till. In April 2006, she was dismissed. It made no odds. The negative discrepancies got larger.

The Misras were in trouble. Cash was disappearing through their fingers. They had repeatedly been told they were doing nothing wrong, yet when they pointed to their mounting losses, no one from the Post Office seemed to know how to help them.

When it came to resolving financial discrepancies, the Post Office consistently defaulted to the same position: the Misras were contractually obliged to make up the difference between what Horizon said should be in the safe and tills and what was actually there.

The Misras redoubled their efforts. In his first phone call to me, Davinder Misra tearfully related the nights of mounting panic he and Seema experienced, printing off the day's transactions on Horizon's crappy till roll, staying up to 'one … two in the morning', going through the lengths of paper line by line, desperately trying to find some clue as to what might be causing them to lose so much money.

The Misras never did discover the source of their problem. A possible issue with Horizon didn't even cross their minds.

SEEMA LOSES IT

Seema is fuzzy on exactly when she started agreeing monthly Horizon balances which bore no relation to the amount of cash she had behind the counter. She remembers the big jump in discrepancies which came about after introducing individual stock units made it impossible to keep making good with the Misras' own cash.

Although she had experience of working in an accounting department at the beginning of her career, Seema had no formal accountancy qualifications. She didn't know the potential consequences of agreeing a Horizon balance which did not accurately reflect the amount of cash she was holding.

As with all Subpostmasters operating in this period, there was no longer the option to dispute a discrepancy. At the end of each monthly trading period, Seema had two options. She could either 'settle to cash or cheque', which meant she was required to make good the discrepancy with her own cash or a cheque for the relevant amount immediately, or she could 'settle centrally.' By settling centrally, she was acknowledging the 'debt was in her account' but that it hadn't been settled. The Post Office would be alerted to the situation and take steps to recover the 'debt.'

Seema had already been told that any discrepancy larger than £500 would cost her her job.

Seema told me she agreed inaccurate Horizon balances (by pressing 'settle to cash' but without putting any cash into the counter till) in the hope she might run a surplus the next month, or that her discrepancies would be balanced by a transaction correction, or that she would be able to make up the difference by funnelling yet more cash from the retail side of the business into her Post Office accounts.

It was wishful thinking. By April 2006, Seema's losses had reached five figures. Sacking her assistants had made no difference, and the money haemorrhage could no longer be stemmed using the profits from the shop.

In desperation, Seema turned to her sister-in-law, Omika, and asked if she could borrow some money.

Over the course of 2006, Omika loaned Seema £16,000. In court, Omika was asked by the Post Office barrister if she ever queried the purpose of the loans. This led to the following exchange:

'She said there … is a loss in the Post Office and she wanted it for that.'

'Did you ask her whether she had told the Post Office about the loss?'

'I never asked her.'

'Didn't you think it was odd that she had a loss of such a figure?'

'It was not my business. I didn't ask her.'

'But have you ever given £16,000 to anybody else?'

'No, but she is not anybody else. She is my sister-in-law.'

For the Misras, the latter half of 2006 was a spiral of misery. Seema had lost interest in the amount of money she was supposed to owe her counter and, like Noel and Jo before her, just agreed whatever figure Horizon presented at the end of each monthly accounting period. The Misras' only plan for getting out of their situation was to find a buyer for their Post Office, retail business and lease and make good the outstanding discrepancy at their closing audit with funds from the sale of the business. It was a forlorn hope.

During her trial, four years later, Seema was reminded that she could have, at any time, sub-let her Post Office counter to a more experienced temporary Subpostmaster. The new Subpostmaster may have (at the very least) got things back on an even keel. Seema told the court she was not aware this option was available to her until the day she was suspended.

In the latter half of 2006 Seema received two big transaction corrections related to the sale of National Lottery tickets and scratchcards. The Post Office told Seema she must repay more than £23,000 which had been 'lost' since she took over the branch.

The introduction of National Lottery terminals (run by Camelot), their siting (outside the Post Office counter in the retail part of the shop) and the need for Subpostmasters to account for sales and prize handouts through the Horizon terminals created real headaches for experienced hands. Many, due to lack of training, made simple, but expensive mistakes. Others were caught out by the complexities involved and yet more were done for by the theft of activated scratchcards by their own staff and the Camelot reps who delivered them.

The Post Office refused to take any responsibility for the problems Subpostmasters suffered after the introduction of the National Lottery terminals to their counters. Yet by 2012, a major change – known as the 'ping fix' – had been implemented to the way lottery terminals and scratchcards were accounted for, aimed at reducing the likelihood of fraud, and expensive procedural errors.

Seema had no idea what was going on, but she didn't see how she could have made £23,000 worth of mistakes, so she disputed the transaction corrections.[1]

As per Post Office procedure, the TCs were reviewed and the Post Office decided the losses were definitely Seema's fault. The TCs were returned to Seema's branch with a demand she make them good. Seema told the Post Office she did not have the money.

Seema was informed the Post Office would recover the £23,000 owing through her salary. With little option, Seema agreed. In January and February 2007 Seema had £843 docked from her wage packet. In March 2007 it was £654. From April 2007 it was £2,000 a month.

I asked Seema why the Post Office didn't make good its alleged promise to sack her for posting a discrepancy significantly more than £500. Seema does not know. She agrees it doesn't make sense.

By early 2007 Seema had spent six months agreeing incorrect balances on her Horizon terminal. She had reduced the short-term risk of losing her Post Office by completely cutting herself loose from financial reality.

If Seema's counter was still showing regular discrepancies at the time she was hit with the £23,000 transaction correction from problems caused by the lottery, it's hard to see how she wouldn't have been suspended.

Yet because Seema was now agreeing incorrect balances, it looked like she had turned a corner. The calls to the helpline eased up, the complaints to her area manager stopped. Like Jo and Noel before her, Seema had magically transformed herself from a troublesome complainant who couldn't get her counter working properly into a super-efficient Postmaster, with every Horizon trading statement matched exactly by the amount of cash and stock in the branch. In reality, Seema had given up. 'I

---

[1] In Seema's case, the independent investigators tasked with looking at what happened concluded the losses were probably down to a combination of systemic problems, mistakes being made by the Misras and employee theft of activated scratchcards.

In court, much was made of Seema's decision to put these TCs into dispute. The prosecution suggested it demonstrated Seema was aware she could have disputed any of her previous discrepancies rather than just accept or hide them. Seema told me she disputed the National Lottery transaction corrections because she was advised, at the time, that she could.

lost interest, basically,'[2] she said.

The Post Office says it had no idea anything was going wrong in the West Byfleet branch in 2007 because Seema's false accounting masked all the problems. It's true that agreeing incorrect figures makes it difficult to track what might be going wrong in a business, but it is still an odd position to take in the context of Seema's tenure as Postmaster.

Seema had been having problems since day one – 18 months of money apparently disappearing, requests for more training, sacking staff, numerous calls to the helpline, all under threat of being removed from her post. It was while she was agreeing incorrect figures that Seema was hit with a whacking great £23,000 bill which she disputed, was forced to accept, and was now paying off by giving up large chunks of her salary.

Eventually, the inevitable happened. Seema's Post Office, being a large suburban branch with lots of local businesses in the area, took in more money than it paid out, so it was normal for the Post Office to expect regular sums to be 'remmed out'[3] on a weekly basis to the local cash centre.

The moment Seema began – to use a technical term – artificially inflating her cash holdings, she was a hostage to fortune. If Seema pressed a button on Horizon agreeing there was £25,000 in physical cash in her branch, the Post Office was entitled to think it was there. They were equally entitled to request she rem out a portion of that cash, so that her 'onch'[4] sum was not too high. Seema got round the onch problem by borrowing cash from Omika and sending that straight to the Post Office.

Eventually, even with the money she had borrowed from Omika, Seema's cash holdings (as stated to Horizon) began to exceed her onch

---

2 On the witness stand at her trial she tries to explain why:

Seema: 'I didn't do any checks.'
PO barrister: 'Sorry?'
Seema: 'I didn't do any checks to check the actual cash and all that. All I was doing was printing out a snapshot and entering into the system.'
PO barrister: 'Why were you doing that?'
Seema: 'Lost.'
PO barrister: 'By doing that, what were you hoping to achieve?'
Seema: 'Just to make the tills go slowly, slowly, slowly and basically I get rid of the business. I lost interest basically.'

3 See the previous 'Onching And Remming' chapter for a full explanation of this process.

4 As above!

limit, but Seema couldn't remit that extra cash back to the Post Office because she didn't have it.

By the latter half of 2007 the amount of cash Seema was supposedly holding in her branch should have been red-flagged by someone at the Post Office. It was creeping towards £50,000, *way* over what she needed. But for some reason, it wasn't flagged by anyone. Things were about to go horribly wrong.

CRIMINAL CHARGES

On the morning of 14 January 2008 at 8.30am two Post Office auditors, Adrian Norris and Keith Noverre, walked into the West Byfleet Post Office. It was Keith Noverre who had allegedly told Seema during her first audit on 5 October 2005 that if she 'lost' as much as £500 in future, she would be removed from her post.

Neither Seema nor Davinder were present. Seema was in Luton, borrowing yet more money from her sister-in-law, which she intended to put in a rem pouch and send to the Post Office.

The shop had been opened by an employee on the retail side of the branch. At 8.40am one of the Misras' Post Office employees showed up and gave the auditors access to the counter. Then Davinder arrived. He gave the auditors access to the safe.

Seema was called by Davinder and informed that there were Post Office auditors waiting to speak to her. Seema drove back to West Byfleet, arriving shortly after 10am.

The auditors were concerned about the state of the counter. Money, stamps and paperwork weren't where they should be. Seema asked Keith Noverre if he would come into the back office. He did so. In private, Seema told Mr Noverre there was a problem – Horizon's figures would not match the actual amount of cash being held at the branch. Seema expected the discrepancy to be anything between £50,000 and £60,000.

Seema and the auditors went through everything. They completed the trading period up to 9 January 2008. Seema signed off the accounts as being accurate in front of the auditors, even though she had just told them they were not accurate. She told the court at her trial that she did this because she was asked to.

The auditors then looked at the trading period between 10 January and 14 January. They generated a Horizon snapshot, which calculated a discrepancy of £79,000.

Seema was officially cautioned[1] by Adrian Norris. Keith Noverre asked Seema and Davinder to write two separate statements about what had been happening. Seema was told she was welcome to have a solicitor present. She declined.

---

1 Yes, they can do that.

Seema admitted signing off accounts she knew to be false, telling the auditors she was hiding the discrepancy from the Post Office because she was frightened of losing her job. She admitted inflating her cash balance because she was trying to 'save the Post Office, save my business.'

In what must have been a pathetic scene, Seema, in front of the auditors, took £475 out of the retail till and put it towards the £79,000 discrepancy at the Post Office counter.

At 2pm that day Jon Longman, a Post Office security advisor, came to West Byfleet. Mr Longman's job was to investigate any internal crime committed by employees against the Post Office. On his arrival at the branch Seema gave him permission to search the Misras' nearby flat and investigate her bank accounts. Nothing untoward was found.

Seema was then interviewed on the premises in a room above the Post Office. She was again offered the opportunity of having a lawyer present, or a friend. She declined both.

Before the end of the day Seema had been suspended and barred from working at her Post Office counter. To keep the branch open, the auditors arranged for an experienced temporary Subpostmaster to take over. Seema was shifted into the retail side of the shop.

Whilst Seema was in no doubt she was in danger of losing her job, she had no idea what else was coming. As far as she was concerned she was an honest woman with nothing to hide. A Post Office investigation would quickly prove she had not done anything criminal.

The auditors left the Post Office telling Seema they would be in touch. Seema called the NFSP and asked for help.

Seema was invited to an interview with the Post Office in March 2008. On this occasion she was told she was not entitled to have a lawyer present. During this meeting Seema explained her situation, on the record. She was told there was nothing wrong with the Horizon system. Seema was adamant she hadn't stolen any money. She suggested it might be her staff.

In April 2008 Seema received a letter from the Post Office informing her that her contract was going to be terminated. The NFSP rep told her that to avoid being sacked, she should resign, which she did.

On 18 April 2008 Seema's resignation was acknowledged and she was issued with a demand for £77,643.87, payable 'immediately.'

On 1 September 2008 Seema sent the Post Office a cheque for £500.

On 27 November 2008 Seema was summoned to court, charged with

false accounting and the theft of £74,609.84. Her trial was set for 1 June 2009.

SEEMA BLAMES HORIZON

As Seema's trial date of 1 June 2009 approached, various preparatory hearings took place.

After discussions with her solicitor, Seema decided to plead guilty to several false accounting charges. But the theft charge was an altogether different matter. Seema maintained she had not stolen a penny. There was also no evidence of her stealing any money – something she had hoped to prove to the Post Office when she invited them to search her home and check her bank accounts. In the absence of any other rational explanation, she speculated that the missing cash must have been stolen by other members of staff.

The decision to press ahead with the prosecution of Seema for theft was relatively unusual. A false accounting plea and a commitment not to criticise Horizon was usually enough for the Post Office. But Seema was not making any promises about handing over the £74,000 she was adamant she hadn't stolen. This meant the Post Office would likely need a Proceeds of Crime Act (POCA) confiscation order to go after the Misras' cash and property after she was convicted. The Proceeds of Crime Act was introduced in 2002 to allow the authorities to seize the assets of criminals who had stashed away cash or bought themselves nice things with their ill-gotten gains.

Although some judges were content to issue POCA confiscation orders to the Post Office on the strength of a guilty plea for false accounting, more able defence lawyers were wise to this, pointing out that a confiscation order usually required proof of theft, or at the very least, physical evidence of actual proceeds of crime rather than just numbers on a computer screen.

The Post Office did not have any evidence that Seema stole £74,000, but a theft conviction by a jury would make a confiscation order application more likely to succeed.

An email dated 22 May 2009 from the Post Office investigation department to the legal team prosecuting Seema confirms the motive for the theft charge. It reads 'We are some 70 odd thousand pounds light at the moment as I understand it and if we just accept the false accountings it is very difficult for us later to obtain a Confiscation Order and subsequently compensation out of the Confiscation.'

The reply is unambiguous: 'We should not accept the pleas.

Confiscation would ... be a non-starter if we did.'

Three weeks before Seema's trial was due to begin, Computer Weekly published Rebecca Thomson's investigation into Horizon.

The day before her trial, a desperate Seema was searching on the internet. She felt unsupported by her legal team and still could not understand why she, as an innocent woman, was going to be put on trial for theft of money she had not stolen. One of her search queries seemed to return a lifeline.

'I put in something like "Post Office court case help,"' she said, 'and Jo came up!'

A local news website was carrying the story of Jo Hamilton's conviction. Seema could not believe it. Here was someone who looked as if they had been going through the same sort of Horizon nightmares she had been suffering. Seema called Davinder in excitement. They decided to try to contact Jo. Even though the Post Office had long gone, Jo was still working behind the retail counter at South Warnborough Village Stores. South Warnborough Village Stores also just happened to be open on a Sunday, serving afternoon tea. Jo remembers taking Seema's call.

'She kept saying, "You've got to help me. You've got to help me." She was crying and in a terrible state.'

The two women bonded on the phone. Jo told Seema about the journalist from Computer Weekly who had put together an investigation into Horizon. These revelations seemed extraordinary to Seema and Davinder, who believed they were the only ones having problems with Horizon, because that's what the Post Office had told them.

Seema begged Jo for help. Realising how little time was left, Jo ran over the road to Issy's house and told her about Seema. Issy called up the Computer Weekly article on her computer. Jo wanted to know if there was anything that could be done. When Issy later told me about this dramatic moment, she laughed.

'It was the day before the trial. Way too late. There was literally nothing I could do. Seema wasn't even my client. I suggested to Jo that Seema should take a copy of the magazine to court, show it to the judge and ask for an adjournment.'

Jo ran back across the road, called Seema and explained what she had to do. The next day, Seema's barrister approached the trial judge. He respectfully submitted that Seema's legal team weren't prepared to accept the Post Office's assertion that the Horizon computer system was infallible. Their attention had been drawn to a recent article in a specialist magazine which gave credence to the idea that there were potentially serious problems with Horizon, which may have led to the conviction of innocent people.

To Issy's astonishment, the judge granted the adjournment.

Seema immediately dumped her legal team and engaged Issy Hogg's firm, Coomber Rich, as her new solicitors. As well as a new defence team, she would have a new defence. Instead of blaming members of staff for stealing the £74,609.84[1] she was accused of taking, she would raise the possibility of computer error.

Over the summer of 2009, Coomber Rich made an application to engage an independent expert who would find out whether or not the Horizon system *had* been the cause of the errors at the West Byfleet Post Office during Seema's tenure. Legal aid was granted to pay for the expert's time. The possibility of finding some kind of rationale to the Kafka-esque madness of the Misras' situation swam tantalisingly into view. Now, at least, there was hope.

---

[1] Down from the initial £79,000 for reasons which the Post Office never quite explained.

DANGEROUS PRESUMPTIONS

The rules governing the justice system in this country are such that investigators and prosecutors are not allowed to withhold information from the people they are prosecuting, just because it suits their case to do so. They have to hand it over, in a process known as disclosure.

Disclosure, according to the Crown Prosecution Service, 'is an integral part of all stages of the criminal justice process.' Indeed prosecutors are under a strict duty to disclose *everything* in their possession even if it weakens or undermines their case. The CPS says this is 'essential to avoiding miscarriages of justice.'

The collapse of a number of rape prosecutions in the UK over the last five years illustrates the importance of this principle. In one recent example, text messages which may have affected a jury's view of the alleged victim and her alleged assailant's relationship were not given to the defence team. This is not allowed.

To maintain the fiction that Horizon was, to all intents and purposes, faultless, the Post Office had to avoid giving any documentary material to defendants which suggested otherwise. Internally, the Post Office had successfully fostered a cultural belief amongst its staff that Horizon was not capable of being the source of an accounting error. This meant none of them went looking for errors. The Post Office also had a working relationship with Fujitsu which functioned as an echo-chamber. Fujitsu had a vested interest in telling the Post Office that Horizon was working fine and the Post Office had a vested interest in believing it. When individual Subpostmasters jumped up and down loud and long enough about Horizon issues they were having in their branches, Fujitsu would take note, and quietly fix them. The bugs and errors were acknowledged, but only internally, and whilst they were recorded on a Known Error Log, (the 'KEL'), this information never went outside Fujitsu or the Post Office. If it did, there would be written evidence which proved Horizon was not 100% 'robust,' a word which came to characterise the Post Office's defence of its deeply suspect system. The Fujitsu/Post Office echo-chamber maintained that all Horizon problems were caught almost as soon as they arose, and structural or technical fail-safes ensured no Subpostmasters could be held responsible for errors which weren't their fault. It was a belief system that relied on no one looking too closely at what was actually happening.

Where this delusion came into contact with reality, the default inclination was simply to protect corporate interests. The integrity of the justice system was an afterthought.

For example, in August 2009, a Schedule of Sensitive Material was prepared by a Post Office employee acting as Disclosure Officer for one of the 70+ criminal prosecutions of Subpostmasters which took place that year.

A Schedule of Sensitive Material is a very serious document. It allows prosecutors to withhold information from a defendant. There has to be an overwhelming public interest reason not to disclose evidence to a defence team – for instance, a matter of national security.

The item the Post Office Disclosure Officer wished to withhold from the Subpostmaster's defence team was a media article. Given the date of the prosecution, the media article was either the Computer Weekly investigation, or a follow-up piece by another magazine. The schedule stated the article related 'to the integrity of the Horizon system' which the investigator was concerned 'could be used as mitigation' by the defendant.

An attempt to abuse the legal process in this way is almost unthinkable. But it happened, and it wasn't just a badly trained Post Office employee acting alone. Three Court of Appeal judges would later note, 'It does not appear that any action was taken by anyone on behalf of the Post Office to correct the officer's serious error.' It was just the way the Post Office went about prosecuting Subpostmasters.

As well as being able to abuse the legal process through a lack of disclosure, Post Office prosecutors were assisted by a damaging quirk in the law itself.

Section 69 of the Police and Criminal Evidence Act 1984 stated that evidence from all mechanical devices (including computers) was inadmissible without conclusive proof the devices were working properly. This, you might think, makes perfect sense. But it caused a problem.

In the late eighties and early nineties, lawyers defending speeding or drunk drivers hit upon the wheeze of asking police officers if they could demonstrate to the court that their speed guns or breathalysers were working properly at the time they recorded the offences. If they couldn't, PACE Section 69 rendered their evidence inadmissible. By the mid-nineties, Section 69 of PACE was beginning to be seen as a troublesome loophole.

In 1997 the Law Commission published a paper which went into some detail about the use of mechanical and computer evidence in court. It seemed a little too fixated with the effective workings of speedometers, traffic lights and breathalysing devices called 'Intoximeters.' It concluded that the present law is 'unsatisfactory' because of the necessity for prosecutors to 'prove that the computer is reliable.'

'Advances in computer technology' apparently made this so difficult the Law Commission recommended the removal of Section 69 from the PACE Act. As it reasoned (without pointing to any evidence), 'most computer error is … immediately detectable.'

The Law Commission recommended replacing Section 69 with a legal presumption which stated that 'in the absence of evidence to the contrary, the courts will presume that mechanical instruments were in order at the material time.'

For 'mechanical instruments' (like speedometers, traffic lights and Intoximeters), read computers. On the cusp of the twenty-first century, the finest legal minds in the country had decided the complex, sprawling ecosystems of modern IT networks were to be given the same benefit of the doubt as speed guns. It was a decision which reflected the Law Commission's skillset far more than its apparent wisdom.[2]

The new legal presumption turned the burden of proof on its head. Before 1999, prosecutors using computer evidence had to prove beyond reasonable doubt the evidence came from a functioning system. From 1999 – the same year Horizon was rolled out – that option did not exist. If an IT system *seemed to be* working as it should, a defendant would have to prove it wasn't.[3]

For Subpostmasters, this was a disaster. The Post Office was already telling them they were contractually obliged to prove they hadn't made a mistake in order to avoid being held responsible for Horizon-generated

---

[2] When a senior judge, as Lord Hoffmann was, felt able to declare in the same year as the Law Commission's report: 'One needs no expertise in electronics to be able to know whether a computer is working properly', antennae ought to be twitching. (See *DPP v McKeown and Jones*, Hoffman, quoted in 'The Harm That Judges Do', by Paul Marshall).

[3] In 2021, an MP told parliament the world was entering a decade of AI-based computing where 'machine-learning algorithms come to conclusions for reasons even the computer programmer does not understand.' The same year, the Law Commission finally agreed to consider looking at its common law presumption again. At the time of writing, it hadn't.

accounting discrepancies at their branch. Now, if taken to court, they had to *prove* errors in the Horizon system in order to avoid a criminal conviction. Without being given the data – or an appointed IT expert to conduct a proper investigation – they were stuffed.

HARD GOING

The expert appointed by Seema's defence team was Professor Charles McLachlan. Professor McLachlan has worked with computers since the age of 17, when he was engaged to write software analysing the results from a particle accelerator for the UK Atomic Energy Authority. He got an MA in computer science from Cambridge, and from there went on to become the founding partner of a company which delivered software development services (including accounting modules) for SG Warburg and the London International Financial Futures Exchange. By the time Professor McLachlan was engaged by Coomber Rich, he was an elder statesman in the world of financial computer system architecture and had plenty of experience as an expert witness in the civil courts. Seema's case would be his first experience of a criminal trial.

Professor McLachlan went to work, trying to establish if anything had gone wrong with the Horizon software or hardware which could have affected the West Byfleet Post Office. He was entering the fray during the same month – August 2009 – the Post Office had tried its Schedule of Sensitive Material stunt during a different prosecution. Professor McLachlan didn't know it, but his main battle would not be looking for faults in Horizon, but trying to get information out of the Post Office so he could begin to look for faults.

McLachlan is good company, but when he speaks on the record it is with the careful precision of a court-appointed expert witness. 'I was very, very surprised how difficult it was to get disclosure,' he told me. 'My expectation from civil proceedings was judges and third parties were absolutely committed to making disclosure. And in fact, the challenge was usually *over*-disclosure rather than under-disclosure.'

The Post Office seemed determined to avoid giving McLachlan anything, and, mystifyingly, 'the judge didn't have the kind of view that I would have expected about the requirement for disclosure when the defendant's case revolved around the IT system.'

Requests for Horizon's source code and Known Error Log (KEL) were rejected as being too expensive to obtain.

'Fujitsu, on behalf of the Post Office, would send us a file. But that file didn't show all of the error logs. It only showed the transaction data. So if there were any kind of interruption or errors, then they would not be revealed. Just the transactions were there.

'Any of the other information around the system and how it was behaving, wasn't shown, and only when we became aware of that, was that disclosed, so there was no volunteering of stuff or anyone saying, "This would be useful to you. This is important for you to know." '

The Post Office's attitude can be seen from a snotty letter written by their lawyers to Seema's defence team. 'The retrieval of data is not a free service,' it said. 'It is very expensive and depends upon the amount of data which has to be retrieved which is why you are requested to be very precise... Please could you also advise us as to why you consider the data relevant.'

Professor McLachlan's requests to run tests on the West Byfleet system were denied. Requests to look at the Horizon data behind other currently active or recent prosecutions were deemed irrelevant.

'Could Counsel[4] advise,' says another snotty letter, 'how it assists the Defence to know that the prosecution has another undecided case where the reliability of Horizon is in issue.'

Seema's defence team complained to at least two judges during pre-trial hearings that Professor McLachlan simply hadn't been given the access he required.

In February 2010 the Post Office put up a Fujitsu employee, Gareth Jenkins, as their prosecution IT expert. His job was to work with Professor McLachlan to try to find out exactly what was going on at Seema's West Byfleet branch. Despite his position at Fujitsu, Mr Jenkins' legal duty was to the court and the truth. The Post Office had other ideas.

On 15 March 2010, Jarnail Singh, a senior Post Office lawyer, wrote to Mr Jenkins, telling him to call Charles McLachlan and 'arrange a meeting where you can discuss all his reports and his concerns about the Horizon [system] ... deal with it and rebut it ... and then write a detailed report ... preserving the Horizon system.'

Which is exactly what Mr Jenkins did.

---

[4] Counsel is a barrister instructed on a particular case, because that is what they offer. So here the Post Office solicitors are asking Seema's solicitors to ask Seema's barrister a question.

WENDY BUFFREY

Using tried and tested techniques which began with telling confused and frightened people they were the only ones having problems with Horizon, by 2010 the Post Office had turned the criminalisation of its Postmasters into a mini-industry. The blanket denial of IT faults, the bait and switch of theft vs false accounting charges and the vast institutional firepower at its disposal meant that anyone racking up mysterious discrepancies didn't stand a chance, innocent or not.

You either paid up, under duress, or you were suspended. For every prosecution there may have been a dozen sackings, for every sacking there may have been a dozen more Subpostmasters forced to put their own money into the Post Office's coffers. If you could get on top of Horizon and it didn't go wrong for you, life was good. But even successful Subpostmasters were only ever one dodgy balance away from potential ruin.

Wendy Buffrey was Subpostmaster at Up Hatherley Post Office in Cheltenham from 1998 to 2008. She and her husband Doug lived above the shop after buying the property and business from the outgoing Subpostmaster. Together they put tens of thousands of pounds into refurbishing the Post Office fixtures. It wasn't long before they were enjoying life at the centre of the community.

Before Horizon arrived, Wendy had a sobering run-in with the Post Office. In 1999 she was audited. £1,000 was missing from her counter. A couple of days later, a staff member went on holiday to Greece. Wendy hadn't yet done her weekly cashing up and had no idea she was £1,000 down. She was suspended on the spot.

It was only when her staff member failed to return from 'holiday' and remained uncontactable that the Post Office allowed Wendy back in her branch. Wendy and the Post Office came to the conclusion that the missing money was probably in the pocket of the now former staff member. Wendy was reinstated.

But with reference to her contractual responsibility for 'losses of all kinds caused by [her] Assistants,' Wendy was told to pay the missing £1,000 out of her own pocket or lose her job. She told me her treatment on that occasion had a bearing on her actions nine years later.

'When you've ploughed everything you've got into a business and building,' she said, 'and to see how easy it was for them to take it away …

it shook me to my foundations.'

Wendy was given a single day of training on Horizon when it arrived in 2000. She operated it without a problem for eight years. One May afternoon she did a cash and stock balance and was horrified to see her Horizon terminal showing she had an extra £9,000 worth of stamps in stock. Wendy never had anything like £9,000 worth of stamps in her branch and knew this was some kind of error. She reversed the stock out of the balance. In doing so, her Horizon discrepancy doubled to £18,000. When she tried the procedure again, the discrepancy doubled again – to £36,000.

Terrified of trying to do anything else in case the discrepancy doubled again and fearful of being suspended if she reported it, Wendy spent hours going through her transaction receipts. A high value error of this nature should be easy to spot. But Wendy couldn't find anything. She looked again the next morning before the Post Office opened. And again that evening. And again the following day. Nothing. Every waking moment Wendy wasn't actually serving customers she was printing off and ploughing through 3.5 inch strips of records and receipts, stock and cash with a rising sense of panic and disorientation. At the time Doug was very ill. Wendy did not want to burden him with a worry which might turn out to be nothing.

Wendy could not find the source of the mysterious and sudden appearance of £9,000 worth of stock in her accounts, nor why it should double and double again when she tried to reverse it out of the system.

On the Wednesday, which marked the end of her four-weekly trading period, rather than call the helpline, Wendy made what she now describes as 'the single biggest mistake of my life.'

She balanced to zero, which, in the Post Office's eyes, meant she was accepting she had £36,000 worth of stamps on the premises. She didn't. If Wendy was audited, stamps to the value of £36,000 would be found to be 'missing.'

Wendy was in a state. 'I was tired. So tired. And faced with that amount of a loss you stop thinking in a joined-up way.'

Like so many Subpostmasters before her, Wendy hoped a transaction correction would appear days or weeks later, cancelling out this large and inexplicable discrepancy.

'I felt ashamed,' she told me. 'I felt stupid for not finding where the loss was. I'd spent hours and hours – night after night going through the paperwork. And once you've rolled over that one time … if it doesn't come back … you're stuck.'

Wendy believed that if she flagged the problem to the Post Office she would be held liable. She also knew that agreeing an incorrect balance was something she could be suspended for. Her compromise was not to physically sign the account balance receipt which was printed out when she pressed the button to roll over the trading period on the Horizon screen.

Wendy continued looking for the source of her discrepancy. She was 'terrified' of being held liable for a sum she couldn't afford. 'I was so scared. I was so scared I would be labelled a thief.'

The weeks went on, with Wendy feeling 'sick, right in the pit of my stomach' every single day. 'I took out a loan and money on a credit card and tried to right the loss. Every spare penny I had went towards trying to clear the debt, all the time thinking it will be all right and the error will show.'

Wendy developed kidney stones and stress-induced optic neuritis, causing a partial loss of vision.

Over a period of seven months, Wendy pumped £10,000 of her own and borrowed money into the system. There was no transaction correction, and she didn't find the error.

In October 2008, three Post Office auditors knocked at the door. Wendy told them they would find a £26,000 discrepancy. She was suspended on the spot.

The auditors began to check over Wendy's cash and stock, tallying it up with the branch accounts as presented to them in Horizon. They found a £36,000 discrepancy. Wendy refused to agree the auditors' figures and demanded they come back the next day and check everything again. They agreed to do so, and the next day, after a couple of hours behind the counter, the auditors corrected an error they'd made with the girocheques, and realised they had miscounted some cash bundles to the tune of £10,000. There was still a £26,000 discrepancy, but if Wendy had not disputed the initial calculation she would have been liable for the auditors' errors too.

Wendy was presented with her unsigned weekly balances. She says she was 'intimidated' by the auditors into signing them. In doing so she had just put a physical signature on an inaccurate record of her accounts. Although it happened, in Wendy's words, 'under duress', this evidence would be used against her in court.

Four weeks into her suspension, Wendy attended an interview at a sorting office in Swindon. As she considered herself innocent of any crime, she did not take a solicitor. Instead she called the NFSP national office and asked for help, telling them £9,000 worth of stamps had bizarrely appeared in her stock column, which then doubled and doubled again. According to Wendy, the person she spoke to at NFSP HQ told her that because she had been suspended, she was no longer a Subpostmaster and therefore did not qualify for help. Devastated, Wendy approached her regional NFSP rep, Mark Baker. Mark was at that time the NFSP's Executive Officer for that region. He agreed to get involved.

'It was outrageous she was told she couldn't be helped,' he said. 'Of course she was still a Subpostmaster. It was a flagrant breach of the Federation's union rules at the time.'

Mark attended Wendy's Reasons To Urge meeting. Over three hours the Post Office investigators repeatedly asked Wendy where the money was. Wendy replied there was no missing money. It looked to her like some kind of computer error.

Wendy did admit 'changing the account' but 'not to steal.' She was told the investigation would continue and she would likely be called for another interview.

Despite attempts to find out what was going on with her suspension, Wendy received no communication at all from the Post Office until she was summoned for another meeting just before Christmas 2008. She was told she was being terminated.

'I went to that meeting wanting to find out what was going on with the investigation,' Wendy said. 'Where had they got to? Why did the reversal double? Why did those stamps appear like they did? And they still wouldn't admit that the computer system had messed up or anybody else had messed up. They couldn't even tell me how *I'd* messed up.'

Wendy went back to her old job as a technician with the ambulance service, helping to ferry elderly and sick patients around Birmingham. She made plans with her husband to sell their home in order to raise the money the Post Office said she owed. Although they still lived in the property attached to the Post Office and owned the retail premises, Wendy didn't go there any more. The less she thought about it, the better she felt.

In early 2010, after more than a year of silence from the Post Office, Wendy received a summons to court. She was being prosecuted for theft and false accounting. Doug was still off sick. Wendy's mental health began to fall apart.

At first it was tears, stress, anxiety and panic attacks, but then real depression set in.

'I was like a zombie,' she said. 'But I had to work as we had no other income. During the day, I would be happy Wendy, helping people get about, and then I would go home, shut the curtains and lie on my bed, completely empty, looking at the ceiling for hours until I'd get up, go to work and be happy, jolly Wendy again. Day after day after day after day.'

In May 2010, Wendy pleaded not guilty to the charges against her and the case was referred to the Crown Court.

'It was horrendous,' says Wendy. 'I just wanted to screw myself up into a ball and not go out, not do anything. I didn't even want to go to work at that point. But we were still in a situation that I was still trying to pay the loan off. We'd got no other money coming in and Doug wasn't well enough to work.'

They were only just making ends meet and Wendy still had the outstanding demand for £26,000 hanging over her. Hoping the Post Office might drop the criminal charges against her if they were given the money, Doug put the Buffreys' property on the market.

Almost immediately they received a letter from the Post Office's solicitors informing them that they had successfully applied for an order under the Proceeds of Crime Act, freezing both Doug and Wendy's assets.

The Buffreys' solicitor got an agreement from the Post Office which would allow their assets to be unfrozen so they could sell their property, providing all the money from the sale went into the solicitor's account, from which the Post Office could help themselves to £26,000.

Doug found a buyer for their house at a knock down price and secured a smaller property they could move into. On completion day, the sale went ahead and the Post Office took their money. But then something went wrong. Instead of freeing up the remainder of the sale money to allow the Buffreys to buy their new property, the POCA confiscation order remained in place. The property purchase fell through.

By this stage Wendy was in a very fragile state. 'You're just in a bubble. You can't let anything else in to hurt you so you just do what has to be done and you don't let any feelings come into it. You just can't. You just lock it all away.'

The Buffreys were homeless. They moved in with their son, Andrew.

Although the Post Office had now got their hands on Doug and Wendy's cash, they continued to maintain both the theft and false accounting charges against Wendy.

Wendy had pleaded not guilty all the way up to the start of the trial in October 2010. She says she knew she hadn't stolen anything and was not a criminal, but on the day the trial began she was advised by her solicitor that if she pleaded guilty to false accounting, the theft charge would be dropped and she would likely avoid going to jail.

Broken, and traumatised at the prospect of a prison sentence, Wendy agreed.

The guilty plea was entered.

Unbeknownst to Wendy, her friends, family and customers in Up Hatherley had quietly started a letter-writing campaign. Before sentencing at Gloucester Crown Court, the judge was presented with more than 50 character references explaining what an outstanding Postmaster, friend and colleague Wendy was.

In court, the Post Office accepted she was 'not responsible for the actual taking of the money.'

Wendy says the judge told the court this was not an issue of 'larceny' but an extraordinary situation created by Wendy's 'onerous' contract.

According to a contemporaneous BBC report, the judge told Wendy:

'This was a case of false accounting to put off the day that you had to pay a large discrepancy in the Post Office's balance. As your defence barrister put it, you were putting off the "evil day." The offences were committed at a time you were struggling to cope. Pre-sentence reports showed you were a pillar of the community, but because of your [health issues], your problems grew and grew.'

The judge added that because of Wendy's reputation, he suspected she would be 'an asset to the organisers of community payback.'

Wendy was lumped with £1,500 costs and 150 hours community service. The judge, on hearing the Post Office had already been given the £26,000 from the sale of the Buffreys' home, removed the confiscation order which had caused so much anguish.

'When I came out of the court it was as much as I could do to walk back to the car,' Wendy told me. 'It was hard just to put one foot in front of the other. When we finally got home I just sat and cried for hours.'

The day after being sentenced, Wendy received a letter by recorded post. She had been sacked from her job with the ambulance service. She was also told by St John Ambulance (where she volunteered) she was not welcome in the light of her conviction. 'That hit me worse than losing my job,' she says.

Eight weeks after receiving her sentence, Wendy had a complete breakdown. Her personality had changed completely. 'I didn't want to get up. I didn't want to do anything,' she told me.

Wendy made it to her GP. 'I remember the doctor saying to me, "Have you ever had serious thoughts of suicide?" and I can remember saying to him, "If you're saying people don't think about it all the time, then you don't know what you're talking about!" That's … that's how off the edge I was. I was obviously thinking about it all the time and … I thought that was normal.'

Wendy was prescribed amitriptyline, which, after three or four months, helped her turn the corner. She found a job as a cleaner, but she still wasn't right. 'You've lost something from you. It's gone and you know you're not going to get it back.'

Wendy is still at the same cleaning company she started working for in 2011, but has progressed to become a health and safety advisor and trainer.

In 2014 Wendy's son Andrew died, cycling home from work. He hit a pothole and suffered a fatal head injury. 'I haven't been able to grieve him properly,' Wendy told me. 'I don't have that inside me any more.'

FALSE ACCOUNTING AND THE LAW

Clearly, signing off accounts which you know to be incorrect is wrong. But for it to be a criminal offence a) they have to be proper settled accounts and b) there has to be criminal intent.

Jo, Wendy, Noel and Seema were out of their depths, badly supported and fighting to understand a computer system they had no control over. They were all under threat of losing their livelihoods. They were scared and they made mistakes. But were they criminals?

An important part of the law is *mens rea* (literally 'guilty mind') which is all about the concept of criminal intent. It comes from the Latin statement '*actus non facit reum nisi mens sit rea*', which means 'an act does not make a person guilty unless the mind is also guilty.' Differentiating between the criminal act ('*actus reus*') and the criminal intent ('*mens rea*') was developed in English law in the 1600s and remains a key consideration today.

If a defendant can argue there was no criminal intent behind what could be construed as a criminal act it has to be taken into account – unless the offence is a 'strict liability' offence. When it comes to a strict liability offence (for example speeding) it doesn't matter whether there was intent or not. You were over the speed limit – it was an offence.

False accounting is not a strict liability offence. Section 17 of the 1968 Theft Act states:

> '**False Accounting:** Where a person dishonestly, with a view to gain for himself or another or with intent to cause loss to another:
>
> (a) destroys, defaces, conceals or falsifies any account or any record or document made or required for any accounting purpose; or
>
> (b) in furnishing information for any purpose produces or makes use of any account, or any such record or document as aforesaid, which to his knowledge is or may be misleading, false or deceptive in a material particular.'

The key word here is 'dishonestly.' Were the Subpostmasters whose stories you have read so far acting with the purpose of dishonestly intending to gain for themselves, or 'cause loss' to the Post Office? *None* of the

Subpostmasters I know who were prosecuted for false accounting had any financial qualifications. The Post Office never explained that, in their eyes, approving a computer-generated monthly or weekly trading statement was the equivalent of presenting a settled account – a very specific legal process, with very specific legal sanctions if those accounts are presented dishonestly.

Every Subpostmaster I spoke to who signed off accounts they knew to be wrong bitterly regrets their actions. But in each case, the decision was one of desperation, not criminal intent.

Why was this potentially important point never raised by their solicitors? I went back to Issy Hogg, who was Jo Hamilton's solicitor when she was advised to plead guilty in 2008. I asked her why, when someone clearly had no criminal intent, their own lawyer would advise pleading guilty? Issy was adamant.

'When you're fighting theft, and on the face of it the accounts show that the money has gone missing, and the prosecution are offering you false accounting providing you pay the money back, and you can pay the money, well … any solicitor in my shoes would give the same advice. You're going to have to plead to false accounting and avoid prison. No solicitor in those circumstances would not take that option.'

But what about other Subpostmasters who were only charged with false accounting and not theft?

'False accounting is making a false statement to the benefit of yourself or the detriment of another,' Issy replied. 'Clearly, a false statement would be pressing the button on Horizon to say the Subpostmaster was holding more cash than they actually were … so that was the false statement … and on the face of it, it would seem, that it had been to the detriment of the Post Office… If you're trying to say, "I pressed the button in order to buy myself more time to work out what's gone wrong," it could be said that by pressing the button you are being dishonest, because you're saying you've got the money when you haven't. But the critical thing is this "benefit to yourself and detriment to another" and the Post Office were saying at the time, "Well there's our records, we're thirty-six grand down." That's a detriment. And so any solicitor, given that information, is going to give the advice to plead guilty.'

MINISTERIAL COMPLACENCY

At the beginning of 2010 there were several hares running. The story about Horizon and its effect on former Subpostmasters had been broken in the media by Computer Weekly. MPs had summoned the Post Office to parliament to discuss issues being raised by their constituents. The Justice for Subpostmasters Alliance had been formed. Professor McLachlan was angling for important information about the inner workings of the Horizon system to assist Seema Misra's defence against her theft prosecution.

The Post Office had, on the face of it, problems brewing. It had also committed to implementing a new IT contract, which would, in 2010, turn Horizon into Horizon Online. In reality this wasn't much of an upgrade for the system's front-end users. The Horizon software would still be running on Windows NT (which Microsoft stopped supporting in 2004) but instead of keeping data in branches to be uploaded overnight, Horizon Online transactions would take place in real time over ADSL broadband.

This would make the system slightly cheaper to run and allow for the development of the sort of back-end functionality its banking and institutional clients were looking for. And the Post Office needed these clients more than ever. The Royal Mail annual report for the year ending March 2010 made it clear the Post Office's revenue was shrinking rapidly. The riches (and footfall) provided by the Benefits Agency's Post Office Card Account was declining, as more customers decided they wanted their benefits deposited straight into their bank accounts. Government income to the Post Office as a whole was falling, so the Post Office was trying to expand its reach as a financial services provider – selling business insurance, mortgages, issuing credit cards and installing Bank of Ireland-owned cash machines. To succeed at this, the Post Office's retail and reconciliation system – every single link of the Horizon chain – had to be seen as bullet proof by their existing and potential institutional clients.

One of the earliest parliamentary exchanges about the scandal came at the tail end of Labour's 13 years in power. On 14 January 2010, Jacqui Smith asked a question of Pat McFadden, the Postal Affairs Minister at the Department for Business Innovation and Skills (BIS[1]), which technically 'owns' the Post Office on the taxpayer's behalf. Ms Smith stated:

'An increasing number of Subpostmasters face action for the misappropriation of funds that, they believe, is based on shortcomings in the Horizon computer system. Given those numbers,' she continued, 'does my Right Honourable Friend agree that it is time for the Post Office to review those cases and that system so that Subpostmasters can be confident that the computer systems that are put in place are there to support them, not to put their livelihoods at risk?'

McFadden responded, 'I have received representations about that issue from honourable members on behalf of Subpostmasters in their constituencies. The Post Office tells me that it has looked into all those complaints, and says that it has faith in the integrity of the Horizon system. However, I am sure that if there are further complaints, the Post Office will properly examine them, as it should do.'

Ministerial complacency, or inadequacy, or straight up dereliction of duty, has been a hallmark of successive governments since backbench MPs started raising the issue. Over the last 11 years, nine ministers have passed through the same job, blithely repeating mendacious assurances handed to them and, at times, scripted for them by the Post Office. No alarm bells were ringing, no questions were pursued with any rigour. No one rocked the boat. As we will come to see, the lack of government interest in, and oversight of, the Post Office has played a significant part in this scandal.

---

1 Pronounced 'Biz.'

THE ISMAY REPORT

The 2010 rollout of Horizon Online was a disaster. Branches began reporting horrendous problems. One Subpostmaster found himself £1,000 short because a transaction simply disappeared from the system (the helpline operator reported he was 'very anxious'). One reported a cash withdrawal authorised on screen had been recorded within the system as declined, which meant the customer had left with a wad of cash which had not been debited from his account. In this case the honest customer noticed his good fortune and returned the cash. One wonders how many didn't.

Several Subpostmasters reported remming-in figures being doubled up, which meant that Horizon was reporting double the amount of physical cash being accepted onto the premises. This created instant massive negative discrepancies.

Horizon Online was put into 'red alert' by Fujitsu and the rollout was stopped. Years later in court, Fujitsu's Horizon Chief Architect agreed there were 'very serious' problems with the system. At the time, no one at the Post Office or Fujitsu breathed a word – neither to Subpostmasters still in their branches struggling with the system, nor to the defence teams of those who were being prosecuted.

Within the Post Office, at the highest level, problems with Horizon were rinsed in denial. In August 2010, Rod Ismay, the Post Office's Head of Product and Branch Accounting, produced a report which was sent to the Post Office's new Managing Director, Dave Smith. It was circulated to the Post Office's Head of IT, the Heads of its Criminal and Civil law teams and John Scott, the Head of Security.

Mr Ismay listed the growing concern from MPs about Horizon, the media reports and the activity of the Justice for Subpostmasters Alliance. He also noted there were 12 'live' prosecutions where defence teams were 'challenging the integrity of Horizon.'

The legal challenges and campaigners' concerns were dismissed. 'Horizon,' said Mr Ismay, 'is "robust" because it is "founded on its tamperproof logs, its real-time back ups and the absence of 'back doors'".' This was not true, but it was stated without equivocation. Mr Ismay wanted there to be no doubt in his fellow executives' minds. He told his colleagues the Post Office was 'satisfied' all Horizon discrepancies were 'due to theft in branch' and that further review would simply be to 'comfort others.'

It was 'important to be crystal clear,' warned Mr Ismay, 'any investigation would need to be disclosed in court … any perception POL doubts its own systems would mean that all criminal prosecutions would have to be stayed. It would also beg a question for the Court of Appeal over past prosecutions and imprisonments.'

The important notion that a miscarriage of justice might be uncovered by going looking for it seems to have been ignored. If you thought there was the slightest possibility your organisation had been responsible for sending one innocent person to jail, you'd want to know, wouldn't you? Just to be sure?

No investigation took place. The Post Office prosecution machine rolled on.

I got in contact with Dave Smith after Mr Ismay's document came to light, ten years after it was initially sent to him. I wanted to know why Mr Smith didn't order an investigation. Smith told me he did not remember Mr Ismay's report, but pointed to its unequivocal conclusion that Horizon was 'robust.' He said it was a matter of 'personal regret' that Horizon appears to have underpinned 'a number of potentially unsafe convictions.'

He added, 'I am sorry for all those people who have been affected, and I hope that ultimately they are correctly compensated.'

THE TRIAL

After several frustrating months work, Professor McLachlan had developed a good understanding of the way the Horizon system was meant to operate, but was limited by how much the Post Office would give him and what Gareth Jenkins would tell him. When speaking to his Post Office masters, as he did in one email, Jenkins opined, 'It is always difficult to prove there are no errors, particularly over such a long period of time.'

But this was not what the Post Office wanted to hear. Jarnail Singh, the Post Office's senior criminal lawyer, replied to that email with an instruction.

'Find the shortest span of logs, analyse it [and] disprove or rebut what the Defence Expert is saying.'

The judge case-managing Seema's trial could have ordered the Post Office (or Fujitsu) to hand over the information Professor McLachlan was asking for, but the Post Office prosecution team successfully argued McLachlan's information requests were too vague, too expensive and too time-consuming to retrieve.

McLachlan was hunting the needle without being given full access to the haystack. In these conditions, finding out if anything was going wrong with Horizon with specific regard to the West Byfleet Post Office during the period Seema was in charge was going to be difficult, if not impossible.

McLachlan did find an interesting Horizon error on a visit to a branch, demonstrated to him by a Subpostmaster. If the branch held ten traveller's cheques at a value of $100, a stock report printout would show 10 x USD TC 100 with a value of $1,000. If a customer came in and bought a single traveller's cheque with a value of $100, Horizon would show -90 x USD TC 100, which corresponds to a figure of *minus* $9,000. This would only happen if the customer used a debit card.

McLachlan said this Horizon quirk was, 'completely confusing and misleading' and could lead to 'counter staff or Subpostmasters seeking to correct the perceived problem through manual adjustments leading to real discrepancies.'

Jenkins was, according to McLachlan, blasé about it. 'He acknowledges that this is a known feature of Horizon and that the Post Office have not instructed Fujitsu to change the system to produce a meaningful stock report. Jenkins assured me that the Horizon system properly accounted for the traveller's cheques in the end of day process, but I had no opportunity to test whether this was true.'

McLachlan was able to report this bug as an example of Horizon's inherent shakiness, but he was not able to find any evidence of anything demonstrably amiss with Seema's branch during the period she was running it. His expert report, as submitted to the court, was plaintive.

'The Post Office,' wrote McLachlan, 'provided no opportunity to examine the logs of defects, change requests and outstanding known issues for the Horizon system. The Post Office provided no opportunity to understand and review the systems and processes in the Post Office Limited Operating Environment outside Horizon that could give rise to transactions in Horizon.'

McLachlan told the court, 'It was not possible to examine the process for introducing transaction corrections that can give rise to changes in the cash that Horizon records at the branch. It was not possible to examine the processes for Remittances (the movement of cash and stock) into and out of the branch that changes the cash and stock that Horizon records at the branch. It was not possible to examine the processes for revaluing foreign currency which could change the value of cash held at the branch. It was not possible to examine the processes of reconciliation conducted by the Post Office that could give rise to transaction corrections.'

Judges have a responsibility to keep the wheels of the justice system turning, however slowly. After yet another hearing in the summer of 2010, during which more complaints were made by Seema's legal team about the lack of access to information about Horizon, Seema's trial date was shifted into October. The judge at Guildford Crown Court indicated he would need a pretty good reason to postpone it again.

Coincidentally, in September 2010, the month before Seema's trial started, there was a high level meeting between execs from the Post Office's IT, Network and Security departments and several representatives from Fujitsu, including Gareth Jenkins.

The meeting concerned a serious error with Horizon known as the Receipts and Payments Mismatch. The error was affecting branch Subpostmaster accounts and it had been going on for months. Fujitsu, it seemed, had either only just identified it, or only just brought it to the Post Office's attention. The error was not visible to Subpostmasters.

One of the proposed solutions involved diving into the guts of each affected Subpostmaster's accounts and tweaking the sums of money in there to fix the problem.

The minutes of the meeting, on jointly-branded Post Office/Fujitsu headed paper, note this proposed solution 'has significant data integrity concerns' which 'could lead to questions of "tampering" with the branch system and could generate questions around how the discrepancy was caused.'

It also 'could have moral implications of Post Office changing branch data without informing the branch.' Well, indeed.

The minutes demonstrate that the Post Office knew in 2010 that errors affecting Subpostmasters' branch accounts could be generated by Horizon *and* could lie undiscovered, or at least unreported, for months. They also demonstrate the ease with which Fujitsu engineers could access branch accounts. Both of these things could potentially render a prosecution unsafe. It was an essential plank of any criminal prosecution that a) Horizon did not cause accounting errors and b) Subpostmasters were in sole control of their accounts.

Mr Jenkins kept his attendance at this meeting, and the error itself, from Seema's defence team.

In the days leading up to the trial, Seema and Davinder were calm – their lawyers were getting the case together and they were confident.

'We thought everything would be fine,' says Seema. 'We thought it would be all sorted. There was going to be a judge and a jury and everybody would see that it was the Post Office that was wrong and not me.'

On Friday 8 October, three days before Seema's trial was due to start, a Post Office internal memo was sent by Alan Simpson – a member of the security team – to the Head of the Post Office's criminal law team, Rob Wilson. Mr Simpson stated there had been a series of 'incidents' with Horizon, identified by Fujitsu. When Subpostmasters post discrepancies into the local suspense accounts 'these amounts simply disappear.' This is the opposite of the robustness Mr Ismay had asserted two months previously.

Mr Simpson was referring to the Receipts and Payments Mismatch error and alerting one of the most senior lawyers at the Post Office to its existence. This was three days before an important trial where the reliability of Horizon was essential to both the prosecution and defence cases.

Mr Simpson told Mr Wilson, 'My concern is around the proposed solutions, one or more of which may have repercussions in any future prosecutions and on the integrity of the Horizon Online system.'

There is a legal requirement for this sort of information to be disclosed. Seema's lawyers didn't get a sniff of it.

Arriving at Guildford Crown Court on 11 October 2010, Seema wasn't nervous, but she felt strange. She was on trial for theft. But how? She told me it was, as others have described, like an out-of-body experience. 'I still couldn't believe that this was happening to me.'

The trial opened with submissions from Seema's barrister Keith Hadrill, who told the judge that information requested from the Post Office by Professor McLachlan had not been provided to the defence team, because the Post Office deemed it 'too expensive' to retrieve.

Mr Hadrill said this was particularly pertinent because 'the prosecution is by the Post Office. The investigating body is the Post Office and all the material is in possession of the Post Office.' He was pointing out that in a private prosecution, the potential for a massive conflict of interest is baked in.

Mr Hadrill went on to outline a year-long process of delay and obfuscation during which material had been requested and either partially revealed or denied. Then he produced a showstopper.

Gareth Jenkins appeared to have casually mentioned to Professor McLachlan that morning, 'that he has had access to a significant amount of material which we have been requesting and not been given.'

Some of this material related to a now infamous Horizon error known as the Callendar Square Bug.[1] Mr Hadrill told the court it was an example of the inequality of arms they were dealing with. Gareth Jenkins had been allowed access to material by the Post Office which the defence teams had been refused. Hadrill concluded, 'We are deprived of the opportunity to either accept or reject or examine any conclusions which the … expert [Jenkins] has made. They are at an advantage at all stages and we are significantly prejudiced. We have been asking for this material and it was rejected in May.'

Seema's team applied for the trial to be stayed. The judge refused, telling McLachlan and Jenkins to find a room and go through this information to see if the Callendar Square bug was relevant to Seema's trial. This they did, by reviewing the data on Jenkins laptop, agreeing (possibly incorrectly) that it wasn't. Later that afternoon, they returned. With a new

---

[1] First reported, without being named, by Computer Weekly in its 2009 investigation.

revelation.

Mr Hadrill addressed the judge. Whilst the two experts were hunched over Jenkins' laptop, McLachlan had noticed something. 'It is an NT event log.[1] Its existence was never known before today. It clearly had not been declared before today, and Professor McLachlan could not be expected to know the nature of each and every programme as it is created by the experts for Fujitsu.'

The NT event log, it transpired, contained details about Horizon 'failures.' Mr Hadrill said Professor McLachlan would, understandably, like to have the chance to examine this potential vault of information, the existence of which neither the Post Office nor Mr Jenkins had volunteered in more than a year of data requests. The Post Office barrister, Warwick Tatford, invited the judge to take a different view.

'The defence have all the material they need,' he told the court. 'We will make every effort to ensure we try and obtain material Professor McLachlan would like to see, but … we don't anticipate that this should cause a real problem that should delay the trial.'

The judge agreed. The trial was on.

---

1 NT refers to Windows NT, the operating system beneath the Horizon software.

SEEMA IS SENT TO PRISON

Seema admits to being nervous when the trial started. She didn't like being sat on her own in the dock, separated from Davinder and her supporters, one of whom was Jo Hamilton. Another former Subpostmaster had also come down from Preston. Her name was Jackie McDonald. She had been sacked with a Horizon discrepancy of £94,000 and was facing similar charges to Seema.

Davinder was bullish. 'I was fully optimistic because of the level of support from other Subpostmasters and our legal team. There was a lot going on. We had a feeling you know … that God is there, and we are not liars, we didn't steal any money. The jury would see – the Post Office had checked our accounts. We had done nothing wrong.'

The prosecution case was simple. There was a huge discrepancy. Seema had already pleaded guilty to false accounting to cover up the 'loss.' At first she told the Post Office her staff must have taken it. Now she was blaming the computer system, without any evidence. Months of investigation by a leading computer expert had not found a single definite error at the West Byfleet branch. The money was real, it was missing and Seema had taken it.

In his opening speech, the Post Office prosecuting counsel Warwick Tatford told the jury, 'Computer problems should be obvious to the user.' Yet the Post Office knew the Receipts and Payments Mismatch error was not obvious to the user. In fact it was impossible for the user to spot because, when it happened, Horizon informed the user each event had taken place correctly. Mr Tatford told the court that Seema Misra's failure to call the helpline and alert them to any Horizon problems wasn't because she couldn't see those problems, but because those problems didn't exist.

The defence case was that errors in the Horizon IT system had caused the accounting discrepancies. Stark warnings that she would lose her job if the Post Office were to find out about these discrepancies caused Seema to hide them. Staff had stolen money, and she admitted that she hadn't kept on top of things – she could be disorganised – but Seema didn't take any money, and there was nothing to suggest she had. She was innocent of theft.

The trial lasted nine days. Seema took notes throughout, and was frustrated, particularly by some of the Post Office witnesses whose recollections were at odds to hers. 'I was angry, really angry,' she told me. 'If I could remember what happened, why couldn't they?'

For a case which hinged on blaming computer errors for missing money, in a court system which presumes computers are 'in order at the material time' without evidence to the contrary, it was going to be an uphill struggle.

On day five, Professor McLachlan told the court, 'The place that I have got to is that I am unable to exclude system failure of a type that could impact the accounting records at West Byfleet. I cannot make anything stronger than that. I cannot say that I found something that caused that, but I am unable to exclude it.'

Shortly before the trial ended, Seema was told by her doctor she needed to go on medication. The medication was of a sort which could have serious side effects for pregnant women. For peace of mind, she was advised to take a pregnancy test. She did. It was positive. The Misras had been trying to provide a sibling for Aditya for years. But right now?

'It was a complete surprise,' Seema said. 'How could I conceive during what was meant to be the most stressful occasion? How did that happen?!'

After all the witnesses had been cross-examined and the prosecution and defence had once more put their case, the trial finished. On the final day, the judge turned to the jury. On the case against, he told them:

'There is no direct evidence of her taking any money… There is no CCTV evidence. There are no fingerprints or marked bank notes or anything of that kind. There is no evidence of her accumulating cash anywhere else or spending large sums of money or paying off debts, no evidence about her bank accounts at all. Nothing incriminating was found when her home was searched.'

The judge told the jury that the prosecution was asking them to *infer* theft from what they had seen and heard. The jury took a day and a half to come to their conclusion. They decided there was no smoke without fire. Seema was found guilty of theft beyond all reasonable doubt, by a unanimous verdict.

The Post Office was cock-a-hoop. Their senior lawyer, Jarnail Singh, sent round a bizarre and incoherent valedictory email. He crowed to his colleagues:

'After a length trial at Guildford Crown Court commencing on

> the 11th October 2010 when the Jury came to a verdict on the 21st October 2010 when they found the Defendant guilty of theft. The case turned from a relatively straightforward general deficiency case to an unprecedented attack on the Horizon system. We were beset with unparallel degree of disclosure requests by the Defence. Through the hard work of everyone, Counsel Warwick Tatford, Investigation Officer, Jon Longman and through the considerable expertise of Gareth Jenkins of Fujitsu we were able to destroy to the criminal standard of proof (beyond all reasonable doubt) every single suggestion made by the Defence. It is to be hoped the case will set a marker to dissuade other Defendants from jumping on the Horizon bashing bandwagon…'

It did set a marker. Jackie McDonald was not in court to hear the verdict on Seema. When it came through, Jackie was almost paralysed with fear. The thought of going to prison terrified her. Jackie told her legal team she was going to change her plea to guilty. When she was sentenced, the judge at Preston Crown Court gave her 18 months in prison anyway.[2]

On 11 November, Aditya's tenth birthday, Seema was sent to HMP Bronzefield for 15 months.

Davinder watched as she was taken out of court. 'It was so emotional,' he told me. 'To give you an understanding of my cultural background – as an Indian, we don't mess with somebody else's woman. And somebody else was messing with my woman big time – throwing her in a prison. I was helpless. I literally wished I could take a gun and shoot everybody there.'

Seema had a bad time of it. Inmates took drugs in her wing, and some of the younger women had mental disorders and were cutting themselves. Seema could not cope with the prison food, and was in constant fear of being stabbed or attacked. 'I thought I was going to die,' she told me. 'I thought my baby was going to die.' Seema's mental and physical health deteriorated. She developed a serious condition which put her at further risk of losing her baby, the one thing she worried about more than anything else.

---

[2] Less than four years later a retired Court of Appeal judge would examine her prosecution and conclude, like the judge in Seema's case, there was no direct evidence of any theft.

MARK BAKER

One person you will find cropping up throughout this story is Mark Baker, who, since 1988, has been Subpostmaster at Larkhill Post Office in Wiltshire, 'the closest Post Office to Stonehenge,' he told me, proudly, when I went to visit. Mark is a union man, through and through. In 1988 Mark and his wife Erika left the Royal Mail to take over Larkhill Post Office. Mark joined the NFSP and soon rose through the ranks to join the union's executive committee. Unlike most of his union colleagues, Mark had serious concerns about Horizon's rollout in 2000, and what it meant for him and his business.

'I remember complaining to the exec that moving control of our cash ledger onto a computer meant we were no longer in control of our accounts,' he said.

Mark wanted a new Subpostmasters Contract drawn up to reflect this new way of working but he said it was 'quickly poo-poohed' by his fellow exec members 'encouraged by the General Secretary, Colin Baker. There was a kind of, "We must not look a gift horse in the mouth" euphoria about this new piece of kit. It was the future.'

The reports of misbalancing and Postmaster suspensions soon started. Mark admits he was 'ill-equipped' to deal with them, but he didn't get much help.

'My other exec members just shrugged their collective shoulders and scoffed. How could it be the computer? Computers don't make mistakes. The Postmaster must have made a mistake, or worse – they or their staff had stolen the "missing" money.'

Larkhill Post Office is actually part of the Larkhill Army Garrison on Salisbury Plain. Mark had friends in the military who worked in IT. He was also at that time elected as a county councillor for Wiltshire and was appointed a cabinet member. One of his portfolios was IT. 'This put me in contact with all the county IT experts,' he said. 'They explained the various ways in which a computer could lose data and mis-report. An officer friend of mine came to have a look at Horizon in my branch soon after it was installed, to see it for himself.'

Mark's friend was 'underwhelmed' by Horizon. He told the worried Subpostmaster that Horizon was just a networked collection of computer terminals, and as such the network would have a series of administrators, all with certain powers of access to his terminal and his branch.

Mark says his friend, 'confirmed my fear that my cash account was no longer in my control.'

As a Federation member Mark spent quite a bit of time trying to prevent Subpostmasters from being suspended over Horizon discrepancies. If they had already been suspended, he tried to get them reinstated, often by pointing out how Post Office managers had been abusing their (already draconian) powers.

One of the first incontrovertible Horizon faults he looked into involved a Subpostmaster in Yeovil. Julie Ford's terminal was constantly crashing and rebooting, so her son called the helpline. The helpline operator suggested reaching around the back to see if a connector had come out. The son did as he was told and got a massive electric shock. Mice had chewed through the power supply cable.

The remedy was to send out a new cable, which was duly connected. Thereafter, Julie's Horizon terminal would not balance correctly. Yeovil Post Office began to suffer huge, inexplicable discrepancies. Julie Ford was suspended. Julie's Post Office contract manager was Nigel Allen.

Mark says Nigel was, 'an okay bloke, a bit black and white' who, 'certainly wouldn't entertain any criticism of Horizon.' But as far as Mark was concerned the problem in Yeovil was obvious.

'I went to Nigel and said I thought Julie was suffering a loss of data simply because the system was shot to bits,' he said.

Nigel wasn't interested, but Mark challenged him. 'I told him to prove me wrong – completely remove all the kit. Every last vestige. And re-install it.'

Nigel eventually agreed. The hardware was removed, replaced, and re-installed and the terminal went back to balancing perfectly. But it was too late.

'By then Julie had gone bankrupt,' Mark told me. 'She'd been suspended without pay and couldn't meet her bills. Her newspaper supplier took her to court, and that was that. She was bankrupt and wasn't allowed to run a Post Office as a result.'

I asked what happened when Mark took stories like this to the NFSP executive committee.

'They all just laughed. They hadn't a clue what I was talking about. They just wouldn't believe that balancing problems could be caused by technical issues. Because they believed what the Post Office told them about the recovery system.'

I found it extraordinary that NFSP execs would swallow what they were being told.

'There was always an excuse as to why it couldn't be Horizon,' Mark replied. 'They'd say, "We've been told by the Post Office – we've been to meetings with their IT team – and we know that if the computer gets damaged by a power outage, the recovery system will save the transaction." '

Any errors, therefore, had to be the Postmaster's fault.

'With Julie they were saying, "Isn't it all a bit suspicious that she was taken to court by the newspaper supplier? How long had that been going on? Was she stealing the money to keep her head above water?" There were always things to blame other than the kit. That was the attitude from the people I was sat at the top table with.'

I wondered how technically competent these execs were. Mark chuckled at the memory.

'They could barely operate a mobile phone. In fact, Colin Baker didn't have a mobile phone for years. I had to teach George Thomson[1] how to operate one. That's what it was like in those days.'

Mark became frustrated with the NFSP and left after a dispute over the union's support for the Postal Services Act. He joined the CWU in 2011 and became far more vocal about Horizon's inadequacies and the NFSP's failures.

More than one former or serving Subpostmaster has told me they credit Mark with saving their lives. He was, they say, the only person to help out when they were at their very lowest – facing demands from the Post Office for money they could not afford to hand over, and were at risk of losing their businesses, or worse.

---

1 Baker's successor, who took over in 2007, retiring in 2017.

PART 2

A CHANCE TWEET

Seema's conviction and sentence didn't register with me at the time. I was working at BBC Surrey, based (for reasons no one could ever quite explain) on the University of Surrey Stag Hill campus, just a couple of miles up the road from Guildford Crown Court. On 16 November, less than a week after Seema had been sent to prison, I was in my usual seat, presenting the breakfast programme. Towards the end of the show, a tweet from '@SurreyCars' popped up on the studio monitor.

Surrey Cars wished to bid for BBC Surrey's taxi account. Could it do so?

If BBC Surrey *had* a taxi account I would have forwarded the tweet to our station manager and thought no more about it. But we didn't have a taxi account, and I was bored, so I wrote, 'Are you happy to come on air and tell us interesting stories?'

The response came back within a minute. 'I have a story to tell you,' it said. 'Call me.'

I made a note of Surrey Cars' number and called it after the show. Surrey Cars appeared to consist of a single person, whose name was Davinder Misra. I started explaining myself and the fact BBC Surrey didn't have a cab account but Davinder didn't seem bothered. So I asked him about his story.

We spoke for around 40 minutes. At times Davinder's strong Indian accent made him quite hard to understand. He was erratic, but lucid. He explained what had happened to his wife, Seema. He told me she was pregnant. He sobbed a lot. If he was acting, he was a genius. He didn't sound like a genius. He sounded like a genuine person who thought the Post Office and a faulty computer system were responsible for his life falling apart.

During our conversation, Davinder also mentioned an organisation run by someone called Alan, which was about getting justice for Subpostmasters.

Within a few minutes of a quick google search I had found the JFSA website and read the Computer Weekly article. Within an hour I was having my first conversation with Alan Bates.

As well as filling me in on the activities and aims of the JFSA, Alan gave me some context to Seema and Davinder's situation and briefly explained his own. He also said that other than a Computer Weekly article and a Welsh-language piece on S4C, the story had received little or no coverage. Channel 4 News were apparently interested in Seema's case, but lost that interest when she was found guilty.

I put my head round my boss's door and mentioned I might have a story. The next day, after the show, I went to see Davinder.

When I lived in West Byfleet in the 1980s, the unit which housed Seema's former Post Office was a Cullens supermarket. The shop next door was a Woolworths. As a 10-year-old I used to ride my BMX from our house on Dodds Crescent to the West Byfleet Woolies where I would spend hours looking through the racks of vinyl records. Twenty-seven years later, I returned as a knackered local radio presenter, driving a Y-reg VW Polo I bought from an Afghan car dealer in Brentford.

The Woolies was now a Costa. The concrete office block which housed it had not changed. Nor had it aged well.

I bought a coffee and called Davinder. He arrived within two minutes and sat down. He didn't want a drink.

Davinder is a couple of inches shorter than me with thick black hair, dark eyes and a set of eyebrows which are going to be spectacular as he approaches his sixties.

He was intense, but courteous, and grateful I had come by. Over a couple of hours he told me more about what had happened to Seema – occasionally boiling up with anger and raising his voice, which was quite alarming. There were no tangible variations to the story he told me on the phone.

I asked if I could interview him at his house, partly because it would be quieter, but also because I am a nosy hack, and I wanted to see how he was living.

The Misras rented a property on Station Approach, a stone's throw from the Post Office. Davinder lit a cigarette as soon as we left the Costa. Outside he started raising his voice again and became more animated as he remembered more things he wanted to tell me.

Whilst we stood outside, I took a good look at his wife's former Post Office. I asked him to tell me who leased it now and why it was in such a state. Davinder stamped his cigarette into the pavement and stalked towards the entrance. I hesitated.

'C'mon!' he said, marching in.

If Davinder felt remotely self-conscious about barging into a place he no longer ran, he didn't show it. I half-expected us to be confronted and thrown out, but the staff behind the counter were unfazed, whether they knew who he was or not.

In a voice which had again become a little too loud for my liking, Davinder started slagging off the shop and what had happened to it since he left. I wasn't sure this was a politic move, so I steered him back towards the door, telling him I couldn't stay around for long.

The Misras lived above an estate agents. The entrance was up a flight of stairs by the bins round the back. It had a poky little kitchen just off the hall and a huge front room looking out onto Station Road. The curtains were closed. On a sideboard next to the TV, there was a small shrine, as you'd find in most Hindu households. There was a lit candle in front of the shrine and a picture of the Misras, smiling.

Seema had been in prison a week. I don't think housework was Davinder's strongest suit, but he made a fine cup of tea. He showed me some photos of Seema. We moved into the dining room so as not to disturb the Misras' son, Aditya. We sat on a couple of chairs and I got out my microphone and minidisc recorder.

During our interview I asked Davinder if he had seen discrepancies appear on the West Byfleet branch Horizon terminal.

'Yeah. In front of the trainer. He don't have any answer. And then the second time, when the other trainer came there's £500 or something missing and we're like "What's happening?" and even he had no clue what was happening.'

Davinder told me about the problems they had balancing the counter. 'When we did a cash up – how many cheques we had, how much we'd sold – it was not matching at all, so it meant money had gone somewhere. So we told the Post Office, "Call the auditors, please find out what's happening here." And the auditors came … and that's the day we started going towards disaster. They threatened us! They said it had to be right, or next time we'll take the Post Office away.'

But the Misras couldn't get the sums to add up. By this stage of the interview Davinder was distressed and crying, telling me the discrepancies 'just kept going up. We were trying to make it right. We were going out of our minds – 11 o'clock, 12 o'clock at night – we're sitting in the Post Office looking through pieces of paper. We were like a mad people…'

The Misras' faith in everything, the Post Office, the British state, the justice system, even their religion, had been trampled. 'We started doing fasting,' Davinder told me, sniffing. 'We said to our God, "Prove yourself!" Now I don't believe any more in God. I always believed this country was unique, because this country, a small country, could rule all over the world. It was unique. Law is so great … I used to think like this … this … this is like a hell.'

I took the interview home and created a back-up. I thought about Davinder and the story he told me. At no stage did he give me any reason to believe he was making things up. He didn't seem to be a chancer, or have some kind of grand plan to sucker the media into a false story. Whatever the facts of the case, he seemed to genuinely believe Seema was innocent.

His only motivation for speaking to me, as far as I could make out, was a considerable degree of anger and frustration, and a burning sense of injustice at what had happened to his wife.

FIRST BBC COMMISSION

My boss at BBC Surrey was interested in my meeting with Davinder, but she felt it needed a proper going-over before it went anywhere near a transmitter. She suggested I pitch it to Jane French, the editor at Inside Out South in Southampton. Jane had a reputation for being both terrifying and brilliant. I had not worked for her before.

On a story like this, one of the first things any journalist asks is, 'How many people are affected?' I put this question to Alan Bates when we first spoke.

Alan was reluctant to be drawn on a figure. He explained that the number of successful prosecutions the Post Office had made since the introduction of Horizon would also include some people who really were guilty. He said there would also have been a number of unsuccessful prosecutions which could have failed for any number of reasons. He also pointed out that there were dozens, possibly hundreds of Subpostmasters who would have been suspended, sacked and bankrupted for racking up 'losses' on Horizon without being prosecuted. There would also be Subpostmasters still in post, being forced to make good discrepancies to the Post Office out of their own pockets. And there would be more unreported Postmasters voluntarily subsidising discrepancies showing up on Horizon without any formal enforcement action from the Post Office. He eventually guessed the number of Subpostmasters affected by problems with the Horizon system could be in 'the high hundreds, possibly more', but there was absolutely no way of proving it unless they all came forward and all had their cases investigated.

After doing a couple more days' research, and speaking to a very guarded Issy Hogg, I carefully put together a pitch email to Jane French, wondering how long I would have to wait for a reply. Jane got back to me the same day. She liked the story. She was going to put two members of her team on it. If it checked out, I could front the resulting film.

Over the next three months I worked remotely with two BBC producers, Jenny Craddock and Jon Valters. They made first contact with Jo, and Jo put them in contact with David Bristow from Odiham, who was also willing to speak to us.

Like Computer Weekly and Taro Naw, BBC Surrey and Inside Out South didn't have any proof there was anything wrong with the Horizon system, but we had three case studies, all of whom had spotless reputations before they became Subpostmasters, all of whom were telling compelling stories.

After a day's filming in December, I was walking back to the BBC Southampton multi-storey car park, where I had left my car for the day. We'd wrapped filming early and the light was only just beginning to fade. There were a few cars left on my floor, but not many. My phone rang. I didn't recognise the number but answered it anyway. The caller had a measured, baritone voice, with a Midlander's flattened vowels, and what he told me stopped me in my tracks.

Michael Rudkin was a former Subpostmaster who used to be a big cheese at the NFSP. In fact, he'd been Chair of the Negotiating Committee,[1] the inner circle of the Fed's Executive. Michael had been given my number by Alan Bates, and he wanted to tell me what had happened to him. I was polite, but may have sounded a little impatient at first, as I was hoping to beat the rush hour traffic out of Southampton. I soon forgot about that.

Over the next half hour Michael told me about his Post Office in Ibstock, his rise to prominence within the NFSP and his abrupt fall from grace. Seen as a trusted pair of hands, on 19 August 2008 he was asked to visit Fujitsu HQ by the Post Office to discuss various Horizon issues, including the way branches were being asked to handle foreign exchange cash, a big bone of contention at the time.

Rudkin was met at Fujitsu reception by a friendly chap called Martin Rolfe, who signed him in, gave him a guest pass and took him on a little tour of the building. This concluded at Rolfe's own office space. Martin introduced Michael to one of his colleagues, who didn't take well to a Fed exec being in his place of work. 'He was rude and rather negative,' said Michael. Martin engineered a swift exit.

'He said, "Let's get out of here. Come with me, Michael." As though I was his long lost friend.'

The two men went through several secure doors which needed a pin-pad entry code. As they did so, they discussed some of the issues Rudkin wanted to raise around problems with bureau de change and accounting for foreign cash.

They went downstairs and ended up in the doorway of what Rudkin

---

1 So called because it negotiated Postmaster remuneration with the Post Office.

describes as 'a boiler room. A subterranean office. All their gubbins – the air conditioning, the central heating was in that room.'

In what sounds like some kind of bizarre dream, Rudkin told me that alongside the machinery in this boiler room, there were two desks, with two Horizon terminals sitting on them. The terminals were recognisably the same as the terminals Rudkin had in his own Post Office – that is, exactly the same hardware you'd find on a Post Office counter top – and they were running the same software. Four men in office-wear were present. Rolfe introduced them as 'The Covert Operations Team.' As soon as the men clocked the arrival of visitors, three of them left. They were not friendly as they did so. One remained sitting at a terminal. Rolfe gestured towards the unattended Horizon terminal and said, 'This is one of the offices we have a problem with.' The man who had left the terminal in a hurry was still logged on.

Rudkin said Rolfe was showing him the branch's figures and told him, 'This is the live system.' Rudkin asked what he meant – could the figures be adjusted in real time on the system?

According to Rudkin, Rolfe 'made an alteration on screen to demonstrate to me that he could do that. He then reversed the transaction and he made a joke about reversing the transaction, otherwise the office would not balance.'

Rudkin challenged him. 'I said, "Have you just altered the bureau de change figures in that branch?" and he said "Yeah."'

Rudkin was aghast. 'I said to him, "For years, we've been told that you do not have remote access into Post Office branch accounts."'

Rolfe seemed to think it was a bit of a joke. Rudkin didn't, asking in that rather intimidating baritone, 'What *the fuck* is going on here?'

Rudkin told me he could not be escorted out of the building quickly enough.

Sitting on a concrete ledge in a cold and now deserted car park, I could not quite believe what I was hearing. Then came the kicker.

The day after his visit to Bracknell, Michael was woken at his home in Ibstock at 8.30am by a man standing at the end of his bed. He was a Post Office auditor. 'You've got a shortage of £44,000,' said the auditor. 'You're suspended.'

Rudkin was stunned. 'It's been noted, Michael,' continued the auditor, 'you spend far too much time on Federation business. If you want your office back, you've got to step down from the Federation.'

As I listened, Rudkin began to detail exactly how his life slowly began to fall apart from that moment. It was an almost fantastical story which involved his wife being prosecuted and convicted for false accounting, a Confiscation Order placed on his land and property and a further attempt to pin non-existent 'losses' on him, which led to the termination of his contract. The Post Office had stolen his assets, his good name and in the months since her conviction, his wife Susan's mental health had deteriorated to the point she was considered a serious suicide risk. Susan was prescribed diazepam – which Michael and his son were having to ensure she took – to keep her calm.

I thanked Michael for his call, and explained that it was unlikely we would want to interview him for our Inside Out South piece as he was outside our patch. We agreed to stay in touch.

Within the space of a month, I had gone from not really thinking much about the Post Office to hearing multiple examples of behaviour which, *if it was true*, pointed to a powerful government-owned organisation which seemed to have gone completely rogue.

I related Michael Rudkin's tale to the Inside Out South team. They were astounded, but also agreed that as Michael was out of our patch, we wouldn't consider it for our existing investigation. Jon and Jenny told me they had been looking at the numbers of people affected. By this stage they had found and watched the 2009 Taro Naw programme. Again the question was, 'How many people had become alleged victims of the Horizon computer system? How big was this?'

Jon went to the Post Office and asked them directly how many prosecutions, suspensions and dismissals they'd initiated over the previous ten years. The response was terse. The Post Office press office was 'not able to provide the information' he asked for.

Without numbers or evidence, we sought a political overview. The Post Office had installed Horizon in every Post Office branch in the country, and it was successfully processing millions of transactions every day. There was no concrete evidence in the public domain to suggest it was faulty. Yet stories of genuine problems told by credible people were emerging everywhere. There was a formal campaign group, for goodness' sake!

As both Jo Hamilton and David Bristow were his constituents, we filmed an interview with James Arbuthnot. He spoke on camera in his measured, diffident way, telling us he was 'very concerned' about the number of cases, adding, 'The Post Office has been pretty hard-nosed in the way they have taken these cases to court. Now that's tough for these people who have been faced with a new computer system, which they've been struggling to master, and I think they need to think again and be more sympathetic.'

Arbuthnot's careful contribution to our piece might seem underwhelming nearly ten years on, but to even get him on camera was a big deal for us. He was a former government minister and a Tory grandee. Just by apparently suggesting there *might* be something in the claims being made by Seema, Jo and David (two of whom, don't forget, were convicted criminals), Arbuthnot was sending out a signal.

Although we didn't interview him, Alan Bates helped considerably. He put us on to a law firm he was working with – Shoosmiths, based in Basingstoke. Shoosmiths told us they had 55 cases lined up and were looking to launch a no-win no-fee class action[1] against the Post Office. The Shoosmiths partner we interviewed on camera, Amanda Glover, echoed something I would come to hear, time and again:

'Once you've met these individuals, what you do find is that they are all very good citizens. They all come with the same story, they wanted to be part of the community. They're very believable, and when you've got such numbers it has to be more than coincidence that this is happening to such a large number – right across the country.'

The Post Office refused to put anyone up for interview. In fact, their lawyers sent Jane French a letter, which I briefly read but can't remember much about. There was also a long press statement which included the line, 'The Post Office Horizon system is absolutely accurate and reliable.'

We finally broadcast our investigation on 7 February 2011, taking over the BBC Surrey Breakfast Show in the morning to interview Jo Hamilton and Issy Hogg live, and then broadcasting the Inside Out film in the evening.

Watching the programme at his home in Reading that night was a former Fujitsu engineer called Richard Roll.

---

1 In English law, this is actually called a Group Litigation. Class action is more readily understood, hence my use of it, but there is a technical difference. Generally in the US 'class action' is used to mean a type of representative action, i.e. an action brought on behalf of all members of a defined class, who don't need to do anything to be part of it. However, a Group Litigation Order only binds the claimants who specifically sign up to it.

THE WHISTLEBLOWER

Richard Roll's professional career started in the Royal Air Force, where he became an avionics technician working on Nimrod planes and, you guessed it, Chinooks. Whilst in the RAF he was taught machine code. Richard left the RAF in 1989 and spent the nineties first in robotics and then IT. He joined Fujitsu in 2001 as a third tier technical support operator for Horizon.

The third tier unit, known as the Software Support Centre, or SSC, was based on the sixth floor of Fujitsu's unlovely corporate headquarters in Bracknell. It was a secure area, comprising some 30 to 40 staff. Some were testers, some worked in Windows NT, and some were UNIX experts. UNIX is the language of Horizon's servers and these folk were grand wizards of code. Richard's specialism was ASCII (pronounced 'Askey', as in Arthur), a method of encoding alphabetical characters into binary which allowed him to insert instructions into the Horizon operating system.

Subpostmasters would only reach third tier support when their Horizon issues had been deemed unsolvable by the second tier team. Second tier operators were based in various call centres around the country. They had reasonable technical knowledge, but they were some way from the third tier cadre in terms of ability and access.

When it came to Horizon, third tier support were extremely capable, and to all intents and purposes, a law unto themselves. They had one mission – to keep the Horizon network going by any means necessary.

This meant on-the-go repairs, updates, patches, bug fixes and sometimes complete coding rewrites. The scale of the network, the infrastructure it was using, the number of different products it was processing and the coding errors inadvertently programmed into the system meant this was a full time shift operation. Bug fixes or patches would be written, tested and rolled out across 40,000 machines overnight, or at weekends when the terminals were not in use. System errors which risked bringing the entire network to a standstill were given high priority, but patches for a minor bug, maybe only arising in a few known circumstances, could take six to eight months to schedule, before being rolled into the Post Office estate.

It was common practice for these specialist Fujitsu engineers in

Bracknell to take control of Subpostmasters' individual Horizon terminals and remotely investigate a problem. This could be done without any identifying login trail. The usual practice was to tell a Subpostmaster to leave an unwell terminal alone but switched on, so an engineer could dive in and start making remote investigations/fixes. Sometimes the team didn't feel the need to ask permission – if a terminal was switched on, and not being used, or it was out of hours, they'd just get to work on it.

If a problem needed deep-level examination, third tier support could clone a Subpostmaster's Horizon terminal and download its contents onto the hardware at Bracknell. Here the code could be worked on, fixed and uploaded back into a Subpostmaster's branch overnight.

Richard found it a tough – at times punishing – environment. The scale and complexity of Horizon and its inherent shakiness meant there was a lot to do. Spotting and fixing problems before they triggered a fine under the service level agreement Fujitsu had with the Post Office[2] could save thousands, sometimes tens of thousands of pounds. The system of financial penalties for service breakdowns meant Fujitsu did not have an incentive to keep the Post Office fully informed about every problem as it manifested itself.

Richard's team was under pressure. When he worked there, Fujitsu UK was not the all-conquering tech behemoth it is today. Without the Horizon contract, Richard felt that Fujitsu UK might be in deep trouble. The relationship with the Post Office therefore had to be protected at all costs.

And this is what rankled. The Subpostmasters who were calling in the problems and whose livelihoods depended on Horizon functioning properly, did not appear to feature much in Fujitsu's corporate thinking. The *Post Office* was the client, not the Subpostmasters, and Horizon was the golden goose. So long as Horizon gave the appearance of functioning as it should, the client was going to be happy. What they didn't know, couldn't hurt them.

The other side of the service level agreement was that whilst the Post Office were entitled to (sometimes large) payments for service interruptions, if they wanted information from Fujitsu, it would cost *them* money. They had a certain quota of requests which came with the contract but

---

[2] A contract, or series of contracts and agreements which have never been made public.

any requests above that number triggered a fee. Subpostmasters with a discrepancy were not entitled to any investigation. The Post Office could ask Fujitsu to investigate a branch discrepancy if it wanted to, but a finite number of 'free' requests made them reluctant unless it was in their interests to do so.

Even if the Post Office did ask Fujitsu to investigate a problem, Fujitsu had no imperative or incentive to find one. As the courts would later rule, this meant bugs and errors could be misdiagnosed, ignored or quietly fixed without the Post Office or Subpostmasters being any wiser.

The contractual environment created a dangerous situation. It was cheaper and easier for all concerned to blame a Subpostmaster (and then go after them for a discrepancy with threats), rather than spend time and money digging into allegedly dodgy code.

Richard eventually got out, fed up dealing with angry and upset Subpostmasters, and fed up with Fujitsu's work culture. He retrained as a chiropractor and set up a practice in Reading. On 7 February 2011, as Richard sat eating his dinner, he watched Seema, Jo and David's story being told, and he resolved to do something.

TRYING TO GET TRACTION

The viewer response to our Inside Out piece was eye-opening. Normally when you put a film together, it goes out into the ether, and that's it – job done, everyone goes home. This was different. I was being forwarded emails sent to the team at Inside Out. One said:

> 'I am currently being sued for the loss of £186,000 plus four years' interest. My nightmare began when the Post Office audit team arrived at our village store in April 2007 to carry out a check on the Horizon system and within a short period of time they asked me to account for a deficit of £186,000 which of course I could not do... I am being forced to apply for bankruptcy because after a traumatic four year legal battle I am unable to pay back the money.'

The next said:

> 'I am another victim of the Post Office Horizon system. I lost my business and income overnight, and lost my investment in the business after ten years as Postmaster, with no redress. Post Office refused to help me and accused me of the theft of more than £30,000, which 'went missing.' I had to pay to them 'back.' It nearly financially ruined me, and I am still in financial and health recovery. I did not steal the money. I believe their system is flawed, or it is too easy for operators to make mistakes, or they have insufficient checks built into it. Although I identified a number of instances where I thought something had gone wrong they refused to look into them.'

Another wrote:

> 'I was taken to court by the Post Office and sentenced to prison for false accounting. The amount owing to the Post Office changed at every court hearing but the last amount was £51,000. In court the judge asked if the money was stolen. The Post Office did not say yes I stole the money, but by saying money was in the Post Office when it was not, false accounting was the charge. One day I lost £6,000, according to the system. I do think the Horizon system has lots of

> flaws. And I find it hard to understand why they can accuse people but don't look into the system. They have ruined many people's lives including my own. I'm sure there are many more Subpostmasters like myself out there.'

And another…

> 'I am an ex-Subpostmistress, who was also prosecuted for false accounting, and have been through hell, debt and disbelief for almost six years. I would very much like to talk to the people involved, and my heart goes out to the others. Several Postmasters joke about the black hole that money seems to disappear into, leaving you having to make good unexplained shortages! I even had ex-employers standing up for me in court, that couldn't believe what was happening, the Post Office was the worst company I have ever worked for. The training is abysmal, and the support non-existent… I knew I was innocent of dishonesty, and I never stole any money, but I now have a conviction for false accounting, debts, a destroyed reputation, a wrecked family, asthma, and a long recovery from emotional trauma… Fifty-five of us can't all be wrong, but I thought I was the only one.'

And another…

> 'I am a former Subpostmistress with 24 years' experience who has been at the receiving end of the Horizon System. My problems began in October 2009 when my office was relocated into a Portacabin whilst my shop and office were rebuilt. The first balance after moving was short by £388, the next on 6 December 2009 was short by £3,500 …, the next balance on 6 January 2010, which followed a period with bad snow conditions, my daughter's wedding, Christmas, New Year and more bad snow (when the Office was only open for two and a half weeks) was £9,000 short… At this point I rang Horizon and demanded that they compare their logs with mine since they appeared to differ. I was dismissed with the words, "Sorry, we've checked the nodes. They're working. This is your problem…" I was very angry and told Horizon and everyone else at Post Office that I had printed out the logs and would not

accept that my office had lost this money until they had compared the logs they had with mine. I was ignored ... I continued to ring the helpline. By this stage we were almost on first name terms, but still nothing was done. An auditor was sent out to sit and watch me while I worked, to see if I was doing anything wrong. At the end of a morning, the office was £200 short and all he could offer was that I might be keying in items too fast for the computer.'

And yet another...

> 'I am one of the Subpostmasters that this has happened to, and you brought out how awful it is, and how we feel. So frustrated and so sick with worry. What really makes me annoyed is that the Post Office has evidently bullied these people into GIVING the monies that the Post Office says they owe. I have refused to do this.'

And finally...

> 'This happened to me about one year ago. I reported discrepancies and then the auditors arrived. I was found to be £23,000 approx out. After a serious accident I had already had a nervous breakdown and this caused me to relapse into depression. I knew I had done nothing wrong but I could not prove it and I do not believe the Post Office could be bothered to look for it. In the end my parents paid the debt. My mental state at the time was fragile... I eventually lost the Post Office and in the end I could no longer afford to run the business.'

From the Post Office, we didn't hear a word.

Guessing at the population density of our patch there might be, at *most*, a thousand Subpostmasters in our area. If a hundred of them were watching BBC1 at 7.30pm on a Monday night and of them, seven wrote in to say they had suffered Horizon discrepancies ... how many more victims were there who hadn't written in, or heard about the programme?

We knew around twenty aggrieved Subpostmasters met up in Fenny Compton. Taro Naw said they spoke to more than thirty people claiming mysterious discrepancies. Shoosmiths told us they were dealing with 55 former Subpostmasters at the time of our broadcast. The fact we had apparently found seven new victims in less than seven days suggested there could well be many more. Alan's guess that the numbers of affected people could be in the 'high hundreds' seemed potentially credible.

The one thing which connected these people was that they were suffering severe financial hardship (or worse) because of their dealings with the Post Office. The fundamental problem appeared to be the Post Office's assumption that Horizon was an incorruptible source of perfect financial accuracy.

In the days that followed the programme's transmission I decided to put my energy into trying to get some traction for the story.

I uploaded the Inside Out film to my blog, sent my first email to Private Eye and alerted various news editors working at some of the BBC's national outlets, attempting to interest them in the story.

I forwarded the viewer correspondence (with permission) to the Justice for Subpostmasters Alliance and, where requested, Amanda Glover at Shoosmiths. Amanda emailed back to say eight new former Subpostmasters had come forward to her within a week of the programme going out.

Something very serious was going on.

Less than two months after our broadcast, the Post Office's auditors Ernst and Young were invited to run their eyes over their client's business. In August 2010 Rod Ismay had told the Post Office board about Horizon's 'tamper proof logs, its real time back ups and the absence of "back doors."' Ernst and Young took a different view.

'Our audit work,' it stated in a letter to the Post Office management, 'has again identified weaknesses mainly relating to the control environment operated by POL's third party IT suppliers' (i.e. Fujitsu).

It noted users of the Credence system, which recorded data going in and out of Subpostmaster accounts, 'have the access rights to create and amend reports, including those which may be relied upon for audit evidence. These users can change report design, and processing without documented request, test or approval.'

Furthermore, no one knew who the users were, as 'there are three generic administrator accounts without specific users assigned to these accounts,' and 'the process for requesting and granting user access rights to Credence does not maintain documentation to record evidence of request or approval of access rights.'

Ernst and Young were directly contradicting the Ismay report, spelling out to the Post Office not only the existence of back doors in Horizon, but that they were swinging open for untraceable users to waltz through.

The auditor's letter recommended the Post Office get a grip of how its IT security was being managed. It suggested that when it came to wandering into the Horizon system and having a little tinker, the ability 'to make such changes should be limited to authorised individuals.'

My initial attempts to find anyone willing to take the Post Office story on failed. I probably could have been more assiduous in pushing it, but I was getting distracted by my day job at the radio station and the imminent arrival of our third child. One saving grace was the blog post I put up about the story which contained a complete transcript of the TV piece and a link to it on YouTube.

I left the blog post open to comments, and one commenter, 'Joanne from Bolton', wrote:

> 'I too am in court over allegedly taking £3,545. I am not a Postmistress but a counter clerk who worked on their own behind the counter.... [It] started when my Horizon system went down and the new system [Horizon Online] was ready to be installed. For ten years I have done this job and never had a problem. I have followed the Post Office ways and suddenly I am accused. The good thing about this item is I don't feel alone and I know others can relate to what is happening to me, but it is staff as well that can be accused, not just Postmasters.'

There was something about this post I found deeply affecting. I got the feeling the poor woman had no idea how much her life would change for the worse if she ended up with a criminal conviction.

A few months later I got an email from a Subpostmaster called John Dickson, who had seen my blog post.

He wrote:

> 'We have run a Post Office for 16 years, 13 down in Essex and three years in Pleasley, Mansfield. Last October 14th we had an audit and were told there was nearly £24,000 missing. We were aware of some money missing but nowhere near that amount. I was suspended and I am actually in court on charges of false accounting tomorrow. They were prosecuting my wife as well, because we always did the balance together, but the barrister said because she had never signed any of the paperwork they hadn't got a case against her. Eventually they were persuaded to drop the case against her as long as I plead guilty. The Post Office have also put

a charge on our mortgage for the missing amount although they are not prosecuting us for theft as they had no evidence. The Post Office did a taped interview with us individually, and two copies were made, one sent to their solicitors and one kept as a working copy. When our solicitor asked for a copy of the tape, Post Office had lost it.

'I did resign because I felt it was better that I resigned than be sacked, but then we were not allowed to sell the Post Office as it was, we could only sell it as a 'local'[1] which meant the salary dropped about £1,000 per month and thus making not a viable business. The Post Office has now been relocated round the corner and we are trying to sell the house and retail space, not with much luck. The bank is not going to hold out much longer and so we could be dealing with repossession.

'It is disgusting how they can walk all over Subpostmasters, completely destroying their lives, and seem to be allowed to get away with it.'

I emailed John the next day, and we spoke after he'd been to court. He'd pleaded guilty and was awaiting sentencing. His helplessness was heartbreaking. When the Post Office started legal action against him, he hadn't realised other people were in similar predicaments. I felt both angry and guilty. For the lack of better awareness, even after a high profile case like Seema's, Subpostmasters were being steamrollered into criminal convictions. Their union wouldn't help them and the legal system didn't seem willing or able to stop it. If the media couldn't shine a proper light on this story, it was going to keep happening. I started trying again to find someone at the BBC who might take an interest.

Around the same time I spoke to John, there was a fortuitous meeting in Oxfordshire. James Arbuthnot found himself at an Anglo-American defence and public policy conference in the grounds of Ditchley country house. Alice Perkins was there. Perkins was a high-flying civil servant,

---

1 A 'Local' is a type of Post Office branch introduced in 2010. It offers fewer transactions to the public than a larger branch and this is reflected in the lower income levels to the Postmaster, a sort of Post Office 'Lite.'

who had just been announced as the new Chairman of the Post Office. Arbuthnot knew and respected Perkins from the period they had worked together at the Ministry of Defence. He approached her and told her straight out, 'There's an issue with the Horizon system.'

Perkins suggested they meet, once she had got her feet under the Post Office Chairman's desk.

The next development came from Shoosmiths, who in August 2011 began firing off pre-action letters of claim[2] to the Post Office. The first detailed the case of Julian Wilson. Julian was a founding member of the Justice for Subpostmasters Alliance. He had been prosecuted over a £27,000 discrepancy at his Post Office in his adopted village of Astwood Bank, just south of Redditch. Julian was told by Post Office investigators he was the only Postmaster having problems with Horizon. He was charged with theft and false accounting.

In June 2009, the Post Office offered to drop the theft charge if Julian accepted the charge of false accounting. Acting on the advice of his barrister, who told him it was his best chance of staying out of prison, Julian pleaded guilty and was sentenced to 300 hours of community service at Worcester Crown Court.

Bruised and humiliated by his experience, Julian began to do some research. He was soon in touch with Alan Bates.

I would get to know Julian and his devoted wife Karen quite well over the next five years. Julian was the designated media spokesperson for the JFSA. I used to look forward to our conversations. He was a friendly soul with a lovely Hampshire burr to his voice – think of the cricket commentator, John Arlott. In fact, Julian loved his cricket, and was a popular member of the Astwood Bank Cricket Club, whose members loyally stuck by him after his prosecution.

Julian told me how, in the five years leading up to his suspension, he suffered a series of Horizon losses at his branch. He was at first told it

---

2 A pre-action letter of claim is a necessary step before commencing legal action against an individual or organisation. The letter should include the basis on which the claim is made, a summary of the facts, what the claimant wants from the defendant, and if money, how the amount is calculated. The recipient has (depending on the complexity of the claim) between 14 days and three months to respond. The reply should include confirmation as to whether the claim is accepted and, if it is not accepted, the reasons why, together with an explanation as to which facts and parts of the claim are disputed and whether the defendant is making a counterclaim as well as providing details of any counterclaim.

would sort itself out, then he was told he was liable. Julian repeatedly sought help from the Post Office helpline but got nowhere. He wrote to Head Office, threatening to shut his branch until someone came out to help him. He was threatened with breach of contract. The losses grew. He wrote to his MP and the Chairman of the Post Office, but received no help. Unable to keep throwing money into his branch accounts, Julian kept track of the growing discrepancies, but did not acknowledge them on Horizon. In September 2008, the auditors walked in. Julian told them exactly how much they would find 'missing' – £27,811.98. The auditors agreed with his figure and he was suspended on the spot.

Just before Christmas the same year, without warning, the Post Office served a confiscation order on the Wilsons' assets. Their bank accounts were frozen, and a charge was put on their family home. When Julian rang the person who had signed the confiscation order at the Post Office to ask how they were going to live, the reply was: 'Live off the money you've stolen.'

Shoosmiths' letter to the Post Office fleshed out the detail of Julian's story, stating, 'Mr Wilson was warned of the prospect of criminal proceedings and going to jail, even though his bank statements demonstrated that he had not misappropriated the shortfall.'

Shoosmiths warned, 'It is denied that ... Post Office Ltd had grounds to prosecute Mr Wilson.'

The Post Office was put on notice it was being sued for breach of contract, negligence and misrepresentation.

On 3 August 2011 I sent another email to Private Eye. I had been a subscriber to the magazine for more than a decade, and must have picked up my first copy as a schoolboy. Over the course of the 1990s and 2000s the Eye had chronicled one publicly-financed IT disaster after another. I was convinced that if I could get the Post Office story away it would take off. Or at least, take root. My first attempt to contact the Eye was via an email to its generic 'Strobes' editorial address. This time I decided to call and see if there was a specific person I should get in touch with. I was told there wasn't, but was assured that if I did send another email to 'Strobes' it would definitely get read. I didn't feel hopeful, but to my delight I soon got a personal response from the Eye staffer Richard Brooks. We had a chat. I told him everything I knew and gave him everything I had.

On 28 September 2011 the first Private Eye piece about the Post Office Horizon IT scandal appeared as the lead item in the magazine's *In*

The Back section.[1]

I was ready for the story to explode. It didn't.

[1] This was the beginning of Private Eye's ten-year campaign to keep this story in the, er, public eye. Due to the magazine's house style, Richard did not get a byline on his work on this story for nine years. He deserves a huge amount of recognition for his work on this story, and I will be forever grateful to him for the few occasions he invited me to work in the Eye offices and attend a couple of their legendary lunches.

CULTURAL BLINDNESS

Still the Post Office prosecution machine rolled on. In 2010 there were 55 successful criminalisations where Horizon evidence was essential to the prosecution. In 2011 there were 44. The same year, the Post Office's shiny new Horizon Online system suffered two serious haemorrhages, which were bad enough to make the national news. In July it lost access to all its pin-pad machines, and in December the terminals in 4,000 branches temporarily ceased to function.

On 12 January 2012, there was a Post Office board meeting. Les Owen, a non-executive director, had read the article in Private Eye. He wanted assurance there was no substance to it. The Post Office's General Counsel,[2] Susan Crichton, told him that Subpostmasters were indeed challenging the integrity of the Horizon system, but it had been audited by Royal Mail Group Internal Audit with the reports viewed by Deloitte. Furthermore, she told him, the Post Office 'has also won every criminal prosecution in which it has used evidence based on the Horizon system's integrity.' Mr Owen appeared satisfied. In reality, the Post Office was abusing its legal powers in order to convict people, and then using the fact of those convictions as an endorsement of its activities.

During 2012 (which saw 50 Horizon-related convictions), James Arbuthnot became more active. In February he organised a meeting with the JFSA and Shoosmiths at Portcullis House, the Palace of Westminster's steampunk gothic alter-ego, which squats in the shadow of Big Ben on the northern bank of the Thames. Several MPs attended, as did Issy Hogg, three representatives from Shoosmiths and a number of former Subpostmasters, led, as ever, by Alan Bates.

Fully briefed, Arbuthnot was able to outline his concerns to Alice Perkins and Alwen Lyons, the Post Office's Company Secretary, at a smaller meeting in his office at the House of Commons in March. The two execs seemed responsive to his concerns.

That same month, Horizon fell over again, paralysing the entire network for several hours, leaving Subpostmasters unable to process a single transaction. The Consumer Focus watchdog was not amused, telling the

---

2 The top in-house lawyer in any company.

BBC, 'We are concerned that this is the fourth major service interruption in the Post Office's electronic systems in nine months.'

An internal briefing note written the same month acknowledged the growing media interest in Horizon (and the Post Office's pursuit of Subpostmasters who fell foul of it), but the Post Office's 'Chief Architect' Peter Stanley was unequivocal. 'There is nothing,' he told his fellow execs, 'which would give concern regarding the integrity of the Horizon Online system.'

Nothing?

Simon Baker was a senior project manager at the Post Office at the time. He remains one of the few people within the organisation who has ever spoken to me, let alone agreed to go on the record. He is a bright, articulate sort with a background in IT.

Baker told me until Alice Perkins arrived, most people within the Post Office thought the campaigning Subpostmasters' case was, in his words, 'without merit.' Up to that point, the strategy for dealing with them had been one of minimal engagement. Baker told me that within the Post Office, they simply didn't talk about Horizon problems. 'We shut down the conversation and we were doing it quite successfully.'

According to Baker, Perkins' approach was different. 'I remember Alice coming in saying, "We really need to sort this out and get to the truth." The feeling was this was only a couple of months work.'

There was a lot going on at the Post Office at the time. The business was in the process of being carved out of the Royal Mail Group, so the parcels and letter delivery side could be privatised. Paula Vennells had just been promoted from within to become the Post Office's first ever chief executive. Her job was to stop the Post Office from being a drain on the exchequer.

On paper, Vennells was the perfect choice. She joined the Post Office in 2007 as Group Network Director, after a career working for big, customer-facing companies. She began as a graduate trainee at Unilever, then moved to L'Oreal, Dixons, Argos and finally, Whitbread. On her decision to take a public-sector post, Vennells told the Daily Telegraph:

> 'I felt I'd done the rounds in terms of big corporate jobs and saw something in the Post Office that was bigger and deeper, maybe it was something about giving back. If you work for the Post Office you can't just focus on the commercial side by itself, it's about

> community too. People care desperately for the Post Office. Very often it's the Subpostmaster or mistress that notices that an elderly customer hasn't turned up recently and finds out what's happened to them.'

Vennells' emphasis on community suggests there was a moral and possibly even spiritual motivation behind her decision to join the Post Office. This chimed with her faith. The Reverend Vennells is a non-stipendiary Church of England vicar, once telling a business conference how she took 'biblical inspiration from the young King Solomon, who showed humility in asking God for a wise and understanding heart, so that he could rule his people with justice.'[3]

With Vennells' appointment as chief executive, David Cameron's government handed the Post Office a £1.34bn grant, payable over several years, to complete a process called Network Transformation. Whilst this sounded potentially revolutionary, it boiled down to giving some branches a makeover, closing others, cancelling the payment of most Subpostmaster salaries and leaving the ageing Horizon kit exactly where it was. In return for chucking hundreds of millions of quid at the Post Office in the short term, the government required it to become operationally profitable by 2020.

Vennells embraced the challenge. Unfortunately for her, the Post Office was stuffed to the gills with plodders. Many had started as posties or counter clerks and worked their way up into middle-management. By keeping their heads down for 20 or 30 years, these employees were rewarded for their loyalty with jobs they didn't really have the capacity for. New blood was required, with fresh ideas and experience of the commercial world. Simon Baker was a good example.

Another bright young thing who joined the Post Office shortly after Paula Vennells became chief executive was Colin. Colin was brought in to help shake up the approach to communications and marketing. It didn't take long before he became concerned about the Post Office's approach to the issues around Horizon. Several years later we got in touch. In 2020, I met Colin for a drink, checked his bona fides and went over the events

---

3 Taken from a Faith in Business profile of Paula Vennells which reviews her speech to the 2017 Faith in Business Conference at Ridley Hall. The page was mysteriously deleted in 2020, but you can still find it on the excellent Wayback Machine website.

he described several times in a number of subsequent conversations. Marketing people can be good fun, and Colin is good fun, but the picture he paints of life at the Post Office is deeply at odds with the image the Post Office likes to project.

Colin came forward because of the serious ethical concerns he has about what he witnessed during his time at the Post Office. Colin is not his real name.

Colin told me when he first arrived at the Post Office, 'The lines seemed to be drawn between the Post Office lifers and the new folk. The lifers had an impressive loyalty and Post Office was the only employment many had known. One guy told me he was "virtually unemployable anywhere else" and that "Post Office is who I am." If you wanted to belong and fit in, you had to put the future of the Post Office first. If that meant turning a blind eye – or worse – that's what people would do.'

Colin says Paula Vennells recognised this. 'She set up a lot of training events for the senior leadership team, to try to improve the performance of people who were there, but it was pushing water uphill. Trying to change some of these people … they said to me, "People like you will come and go, but I'll still be here in ten years." And I think that's how they saw Paula as well.'

The other downside to an insular culture, over-promotion and a lack of fresh thinking was the Post Office employees' emotional and financial dependency on 'the business.' There were plenty of people within the organisation whose identity was bound up in the Post Office's own self-image. They saw the Post Office as virtuous, so they were virtuous for working at the Post Office. Criticism of the Post Office was therefore a direct attack on their own personal integrity.

Colin said it was strange to be around. 'The main thing everyone said at the Post Office, was that, "We are Britain's most trusted organisation." ' At senior management level, Colin found this obsession both weird and dangerous.

He described it to me as 'a sort of lifebuoy which became a cage. It stops you from making sensible decisions. It leads to cultural blindness.'

Colin had seen media reports about Horizon and the problems Subpostmasters had been having, but once he was on the inside, he realised that bringing it up was not the done thing.

'It was a really strange situation. It was one of those things where everyone knew what was going on, but very few people spoke about it.'

Under Paula Vennells, Colin told me meeting the government's 2020 objective 'became the relentless focus of an organisation unused to having to think too much about commerciality. Whilst it was clearly vital to support the objective, the cultural impact was significant. Anything that could get in the way of "2020" as it became known, was logged as a risk to be managed and minimised carefully.'

Horizon, and the campaign by the JFSA, was a risk to be managed. According to Simon Baker, Alice Perkins informed Vennells it was also a problem which could not be ignored. Vennells, Baker told me, was 'not very happy about it.'

But Perkins won out. In May 2012, the Post Office Chairman and Chief Executive invited James Arbuthnot and Oliver Letwin over to discuss Horizon. The MPs trooped across London to the Post Office's former headquarters in Old Street.

The occasion appears to have been productive. Letwin and Arbuthnot were given a briefing note, which stated:

'Although we recognize that Horizon is not perfect – no computer system is – it has been audited by internal and external teams, it has also been tested in the courts.' The note continues to the conclusion there is 'no evidence' any problems have been found 'of the nature suggested by JFSA.'[4]

Arbuthnot remembers Vennells and Perkins, 'were clear that they believed their systems worked well, but they were equally clear that they wanted and needed to find a way through that would solve the problem to the satisfaction of everyone.'

Perkins and Vennells suggested the Post Office appoint a team of independent forensic accountants to have a proper look at their IT and business processes. Arbuthnot and Letwin thought this was a very good idea.

Within three months, Second Sight were on the scene.

---

[4] This was a substantial shift in position from the public statement given to the BBC, just 15 months previously, which asserted Horizon's 'absolute' accuracy and reliability.

SECOND SIGHT GET HIRED

The process for appointing Second Sight as investigators was unusual. They were not exactly household names. In fact the only reason they were in the frame was because the Post Office General Counsel, Susan Crichton, had worked with Second Sight's Managing Director Ron Warmington at GE Capital, the financial services arm of General Electric.

I have come to know Ron Warmington well over the years. He is an ebullient and vastly experienced forensic accountant with a penchant for driving vintage Bentleys. Before setting up Second Sight, Ron was the global head of fraud investigation at Citibank. He had spent his career catching corporate criminals and either setting up, operating or investigating other people's security structures within large organisations. Second Sight was effectively a consultancy he ran with fellow director Ian Henderson. It had no institutional shareholders and no conflicts of interest.

Susan Crichton knew Ron well enough to be confident he would do a thorough job. She suggested he pitched for the contract.

A beauty parade whittled the potential candidates down to two – Deloitte and Second Sight. Deloitte wanted hundreds of thousands of pounds to conduct the investigation, Second Sight wanted tens of thousands. Simon Baker felt the brand *imprimatur* Deloitte would bring to the process tipped the balance in their favour. On the other hand, Paula Vennells was not in the mood to spend hundreds of thousands of pounds on an investigation which most of her advisors were convinced would simply confirm exactly what they already knew. Second Sight were much cheaper.

'I had no confidence that Ron and Ian understood the intricacies of mainframe computers,' said Simon, 'but their instincts as investigators were good. They knew how to detect something that wasn't working and chase it down.'

Ron and Ian were wheeled in to Post Office towers. But the Post Office had to first convince Ron the job was worth doing.

'I made it very clear,' said Ron, 'that I wasn't remotely interested in doing the work unless they were as committed as I was to seeking the truth. I said, "Are you interested in seeking the truth or do you want to carry out a whitewash? What do you want?" '

According to Ron, Perkins and Vennells immediately and

enthusiastically made it clear that getting to the bottom of the matter was why they were there. Ron didn't like this.

'I said, "Hang on a minute. You said that too quickly. If this goes against you, this could seriously damage your brand and perhaps even undermine your business model." '

Vennells and Perkins once more asserted that they wanted 'the truth at all costs.'

Second Sight got the gig.

Although Second Sight would be contracted to the Post Office, James Arbuthnot was insistent they should be deemed acceptable by the MPs who had been pushing for an investigation. With the Post Office's agreement, Ron Warmington and Ian Henderson were summoned to a meeting at Portcullis House. James Arbuthnot hosted. Oliver Letwin and their fellow MPs, Andrew Bridgen and Mike Wood, were present. The mood was, I am told, 'deeply suspicious.'

Ron and Ian were subjected to a grilling, but their assurances satisfied MPs as to their integrity and independence. Arbuthnot says,

'We were all very impressed. It was clear that they knew what they were talking about and they weren't going to be brow-beaten by the Post Office, or for that matter, by us. They would just get on and do a professional job.'

Andrew Bridgen remained unhappy with the contractual arrangement. He wanted Second Sight to be appointed and paid by the Cabinet Office. But the Cabinet Office wasn't interested. Arbuthnot set out the reality to Mr Bridgen, telling him, 'Unless you've got some other brilliant source of money – who else is going to do it?'

After the meeting Arbuthnot rang Alan Bates. Bates was understandably insistent that *he* should now get a look at the whites of Second Sight's eyes before endorsing the investigation.

The JFSA had, by this stage, been bolstered by the arrival of Kay Linnell, a forensic accountant who, like Issy Hogg, just so happened to live in the same village as Jo Hamilton.

Kay was starting to take a keen interest in the JFSA's cause and seemed to click well with Alan Bates. She was a powerful ally for the JFSA to have. Kay is a qualified arbitrator and mediator, expert determiner and fraud investigator who knows her way around civil and criminal courts both as an expert witness and litigation support specialist. I've met Kay a few times. She doesn't mince her words.

Kay travelled with Alan to London to meet Ron and Ian at James Arbuthnot's office. She deliberately turned the experience into an interrogation.

'I think I was a bit fierce,' said Kay. 'My concern at that time was that they'd do a surface investigation and bury the issues. They had to prove to me that they would do an independent review and report back everything they had found.'

'She went for the jugular,' says Ron, 'and essentially doubted our competence and doubted whether we were going to be "seeking the truth," as we said we were.'

Ron and Ian assured Kay they knew what they were doing, and that they would take the complaints of the campaigning Subpostmasters very seriously. Once she had finished her cross-examination, Kay was satisfied. Second Sight received the JFSA's stamp of approval.

To complete the loop, Kay and Alan went to meet Paula Vennells. By now well-versed in the misery suffered by several dozen Subpostmasters at the hands of the Post Office, Kay and Alan weren't necessarily expecting Vennells to display King Solomon's wise and understanding heart, but a bit of acknowledgment would have been nice.

According to Kay, the Reverend Vennells was uninterested. 'The attitude ... was, "It's history and we need to focus on building the future." ' Kay thought Vennells' lack of engagement was 'callous.'

Although empathy might have been in short supply, Paula Vennells exuded corporate propriety. In a final letter confirming that Second Sight had been appointed to the approval of all, Vennells re-affirmed to James Arbuthnot that, 'Alice and I intend total transparency.' At the same time, she cautioned him against issuing a press release to announce Second Sight's appointment, suggesting it would 'not be without risk both in terms of human sensitivities and reputational distortions.'

The BBC's social affairs correspondent Matt Prodger got wind of it anyway. Prodger published a piece on the BBC website, quoting Seema Misra ('I'm no thief, I never was. I haven't taken a single penny from the Post Office. I put money *in* the Post Office.'). He also spoke to a still grumbling Andrew Bridgen, who told him, 'It is important that this whole review should be beyond reproach and conducted at arm's length from the Post Office.'

Forced by Prodger into saying something publicly, the Post Office insisted it had 'no hesitation in agreeing to an external review of these few individual cases that have been raised with us by a number of MPs,' adding it continued to have 'absolute confidence' in Horizon and the 'robustness and integrity of its branch accounting processes.'

Second Sight got to work.

THE FLAT DENIAL

Ron and Ian were given the names of thirteen Subpostmasters, including Seema Misra, Tracey Merritt and Jo Hamilton. They were formally instructed to 'consider and to advise on whether there are any systemic issues and/or concerns with the "Horizon" system.'

Their instructions also stated they should deliver a report containing their 'expert and reasoned opinion' in the 'light of the evidence seen.'

Ron started by asking Susan Crichton for the Post Office's general file on Horizon problems. The Post Office didn't have one.

This, thought Ron, was odd. 'As a lead investigator, as head of investigations, where three or more cases looked pretty similar, I'd always have a general file and put an investigator in charge of the whole caboodle,' he told me.

It seems the Post Office preferred to see each individual case as isolated, and was making no effort to draw together potential common themes. So Ron started building a general file from scratch.

At the outset, Ron and Ian told me they fully expected to find a few wrong-uns, a few incompetents, or 'scatty' Subpostmasters, and a few where something might have happened which wasn't the Subpostmaster's fault. But the starting point was *not* the Horizon programming data.

'Even with the small sample of Subpostmasters we had,' said Ron, 'we were looking at all sorts of different ranges of dates. In many cases the Subpostmasters didn't know within a month – certainly not within an hour or day – when something went wrong.'

Horizon is a vast, complex system running on millions of lines of code. Every time a patch or update was rolled out into the network, the system changed slightly. This (as you know from The Subpostmasters' Bind chapter earlier in this book), happened at the rate of once a week, creating around 20,000 different versions of Horizon over its lifetime. Trying to find a line of bad code in a specific version of Horizon could take weeks. Not knowing which version of Horizon you were meant to be looking at made it almost impossible.

Ron and Ian decided instead that they – led by the Subpostmasters – would examine the Post Office's internal operational processes, the interfaces between Horizon and other companies' IT systems (such as Camelot, the Bank of Ireland, the Co-Op, various energy companies and the LINK system for processing credit and debit cards), Horizon's power supply and telecommunications equipment, Subpostmaster training, the actions needed to balance the accounts at the end of each trading period, transaction corrections and the helpline. Importantly, the company would also examine the Post Office's audit and investigative processes, scrutinising how they assisted Subpostmasters who called for help *and* how they went about providing the information which could lead to a Subpostmaster being prosecuted or, in Lee Castleton's case, sued.

The investigators got going. The division of labour was fairly straightforward. As a rule, Ron travelled the country speaking to Subpostmasters, and Ian Henderson liaised with the Post Office to gather the relevant information. The two men went on a Horizon training course to get a feel for what it was like to use the system, and they started digging into interview recordings.

Progress was slow. The lack of a general case file was frustrating. Second Sight had to seek information from various different Post Office departments, some of which were more efficient than others. Frustratingly, some important evidence had been destroyed or was lost.

Nonetheless, the Post Office team assigned to assist Second Sight, which included both Simon Baker and the Post Office's then 'Head of Partnerships' Angela van den Bogerd, appeared helpful and to be acting with the total transparency promised by Paula Vennells.

Baker told me that's exactly how it was. 'Really my role was just to give Second Sight anything they asked for or anything I thought would be interesting to them. I had no manager, no one telling me what to do or what not to do. I would just take them as much as I could.'

Ian Henderson spent a week working out of Susan Crichton's office, sitting next to Jarnail Singh. Crichton, as far as Henderson could make out, was just not engaged.

'I hesitate to use the word insignificant but that's the word that springs to mind. I don't remember having any significant meetings with her in terms of what we were doing.'

Jarnail Singh was another matter altogether. Henderson couldn't make head nor tail of him.

'My God. He was on another bloody planet! He was mired in the Post Office culture. I felt like he'd lost the ability to think critically and actually stand back and look at evidence objectively.'

Nonetheless Henderson was given complete access to the Post Office's prosecution files on the thirteen initial case studies. Whole tranches of documents which had never been properly examined before were being handed over by the Post Office team.

The JFSA began to lobby for more case studies to be examined than the original thirteen. The Post Office agreed, sending a document to every branch in the country inviting any Subpostmaster (or their assistants, or Post Office staff, or their contractors) to 'raise concerns regarding Horizon, and feel comfortable about doing so.'

This document was important. It explained the Post Office was committed to 'the highest standards of corporate governance, openness, probity and accountability' and the process for raising concerns contained the important and unequivocal statement: 'Second Sight will be entitled to request information related to a concern from Post Office Limited, and if Post Office Limited holds that information, Post Office Limited will provide it to Second Sight.'

No ifs, no buts. If we have it, we will hand it over.

To deal with the extra workload Second Sight took on a number of experienced investigators and a lawyer.

Michael Rudkin's story was now in the frame. At the invitation of Fujitsu on 13 September 2012, Henderson made his way to their Bracknell HQ for a nose round and a chat with the Horizon team. Henderson found there was an appreciable number of *Post Office* staff working on the Horizon system at Fujitsu, but no one within Post Office senior management seemed to know whose responsibility they were, or what they were doing. He also met Gareth Jenkins.

'He was with two colleagues,' Henderson remembered. 'We chatted for at least an hour. The purpose of the meeting was to give me an overview of Horizon, from a technical perspective. One of the issues that came up was remote access.'

Jenkins confirmed to Henderson that remote access to the Horizon system was a given – wondering at first if Henderson's inquiry was a joke.

'He said, "Well of course we've got remote access. We couldn't do our job without it." '

Jenkins then explained to Henderson how he could log in as a Subpostmaster, take control of a terminal and download a clone of a machine to work on, exactly what Richard Roll had been doing in the same building from 2001 to 2004.

'He was very open,' Henderson said, 'and very willing to go on the record. I didn't regard him as hiding anything. For us, he was the turning point in getting to the truth.'

The two men stayed in touch through Simon Baker. On request, Jenkins volunteered information about two serious Horizon errors which Baker passed on to Second Sight.

When it came to the merits of the campaigners' cases, Ron and Ian developed a system. They gathered as much hard evidence as possible, either themselves or through their investigators. Then Ron would argue each individual Subpostmaster's case whilst Ian attempted to demolish it. Having had a good row over the evidence, its reliability and what it meant, the pair would piece together what they agreed they were left with, and then go and seek some more evidence. The Second Sight team was determined to establish the facts of what really happened in every case, and where they couldn't, they would only report on what *might* have happened if there was a very good reason to.

Henderson thought things were going extremely well, until a strange moment at Post Office HQ, five days after his visit to Fujitsu. By this stage Second Sight were having bi-weekly meetings with various Post Office execs. On this occasion, Henderson met Susan Crichton and Simon Baker.[1] After the meeting, he wandered into the corridor where he bumped into Lesley Sewell, the Post Office's Chief Information Officer and Alwen Lyons, the Company Secretary. Lyons had joined the Post Office in 1984 as a graduate trainee and was, in Henderson's words, a 'furiously loyal, old-fashioned company retainer.' Her father was a Subpostmaster from the East End of London who had risen to become General Secretary of the National Federation of Subpostmasters. Lyons was the living embodiment of the Post Office culture, and had the ear of the board.

The three got chatting. Henderson mentioned what Gareth Jenkins had told him about remote access. 'Instantly, Alwen Lyons said, "No that's completely wrong. There is no question of remote access. It's impossible. We know it can't happen."'

Henderson admits being momentarily thrown. This was, in his words, a 'conflict of evidence.' Instead of asking if Lyons was suggesting a Horizon system architect at Fujitsu was living in cloud-cuckoo land, Henderson let the two women change the subject. He subsequently told me his normal practice when faced with a situation like this was to seek

---

[1] At 11.30am on Tuesday 18 September in Room 1112, according to Ian's diary.

further evidence before challenging what he was being told. But the force of Alwen Lyons' response left him in no doubt there was something going on.

'I remember thinking "Christ. If we push this, we're going to get sacked." It was that serious. I think that was when Jenkins' cards were marked, and he was regarded as potentially dangerous.'

Alwen Lyons' flat denial to Ian Henderson about remote access was not unique. Colin, my contact in the marketing team, remembers something similar happening at a meeting he attended. He describes it as his first ethical 'red flag':

'I was in a room with a group of Post Office colleagues discussing the Horizon problem. A member of staff from Fujitsu was present and he openly admitted it was possible for him to access the systems in the Post Office branches. I looked around at my colleagues expecting to see shocked looks but it was almost as if no one else heard what I heard. And then there was a discussion about, "Well – how are we going to deal with this?" '

Colin described himself as 'speechless.' He told me he sat there trying to make sense of what on earth was going on.

'When I asked a colleague about it afterwards, expressing concern, he said something to the effect of, "Oh he only meant theoretically." I probed further but he was part of the loyal old-guard and was reluctant to say anymore. I asked around several people in different departments and whilst few would openly speak about it, only the new-ish colleagues were willing to admit they'd heard the same thing, and couldn't understand what was going on.'

Second Sight's investigation rolled into 2013. Henderson's chance conversation with Alwen Lyons seemed to him to be the beginning of a sea change in the Post Office's helpfulness. In his words, they became 'concerned about controlling the flow of evidence relating to what was going on within Fujitsu, limiting or preventing our access to emails and the investigative work that we wanted to do.'

Whilst on the face of it the Post Office continued to be cooperative, it was taking a lot longer to get the information Second Sight were requesting. That said, the main problems were visible in plain sight.

With every tape he listened to, Ron's concerns about the Post Office security team grew.

'They were consistently saying, "I want to know what you did with the money. You've stolen the money." It sounded like the behaviour of people I would have fired within a week of hiring them. It was thuggish behaviour.'

Many interviews were conducted after Subpostmasters with large discrepancies had been suspended without pay. Ron heard the desperation in their voices.

'One said, "I've got Christmas coming up. How am I going to pay for food for the children?" and the investigator's response was, "Well, you can use the money that you've stolen from us."' Ron describes this as, 'completely unprofessional, and atypical of the behaviour of a properly qualified, competent company investigator.'

Ron found the attitude of the Post Office security team bizarre, especially when they might be dealing with a Subpostmaster who had many years' unblemished service and who had never had a shortfall of more than £300 before. 'Why would you treat a person like that as a fraud suspect?' he said. 'Or, worse – as a suspected thief? That was abhorrent to me.'

When Second Sight were appointed, the MPs they spoke to made it clear that the priority was finding out whether there was any evidence of unsafe prosecutions. As Ron looked at what the Post Office were doing he began to develop profound misgivings.

Normally if a company wants to recover assets from fraudulent activity it will go via the civil courts. Prosecuting someone through the criminal courts for the purposes of asset recovery could be an abuse of process. But the Post Office was using private criminal prosecutions, and according to Ron, it was 'pretty obvious that the Post Office investigation approach was designed around asset recovery rather than seeking the truth. It was all about recovering money, which was pretty bloody awful as far as I was concerned, and it just didn't comply with anything I'd ever come across before.'

On the issue of Horizon failures causing accounting errors – the cry which had been going up from Subpostmasters since the system was rolled out – Ron was beginning to see clear evidence of problems, and not just the two big software errors mentioned to them by Gareth Jenkins.

He said they became 'deeply suspicious' that telecommunication and power interrupts as well as hardware failures at the front end 'were probably working together to bring about mysterious shortfalls.'

One such example was known as a 'one-sided transaction.' A customer could buy three thousand pounds' worth of premium bonds. These would be registered on the Horizon system, allowing the Subpostmaster to complete the transaction. The transaction would go through to the systems at National Savings and Investments which would send the premium bonds to the customer, but a telecommunications blip could stop the transaction reaching the customer's bank. This would generate a £3,000 shortfall in the Post Office branch, and in Ron's words, 'a very happy customer.'

The Post Office was insistent that any failure like this at the back-end would be picked up and corrected via a transaction correction. They also claimed that if there were power failures, then Subpostmasters (assuming they followed the correct recovery procedures, as directed by the Horizon terminal), would not be out of pocket.

This did not wash with Ron. He asked the Post Office:

'These instructions, these recovery procedures, appear on a screen which might be dead. How do you know the messages that you say the Postmaster is clumsily failing to adhere to aren't actually invisible to him in the first place?'

Ron and Ian began to hear a phrase which would be regularly repeated to them by the Post Office for most of the next two years, 'We do not understand.'

'It drove me to distraction,' said Ron, who is in no doubt it was deliberate, legalistic obtuseness, designed to avoid giving the Second Sight team any useful information.

The more Subpostmasters the Second Sight team spoke to, the more issues came to light. The more issues came to light, the harder it seemed to get any answers.

THE INTERIM REPORT

By February 2013, the MPs who had been waiting for more than six months for information on their constituents' cases got restless. James Arbuthnot called Ian Henderson, who told him they were thinking of putting together a thematic report dealing with some of the common issues connecting the individual Subpostmaster cases. Arbuthnot's group of MPs scheduled a meeting at Portcullis House on 25 March and asked both Henderson and Warmington along to give them an update.

A week before the meeting took place, Alice Perkins called James Arbuthnot to express her dismay. She told him the Post Office was very concerned that Second Sight should be voicing any opinion, let alone a preliminary one to which the Post Office had no right of reply. Arbuthnot invited her to attend the meeting with MPs, but she refused. It was the first sign to Arbuthnot that the Post Office was worried about the conclusions Second Sight were drawing.

In May, Ron and Ian began to circulate some of their preliminary conclusions to the JFSA and the Post Office, seeking final comments from all parties before publishing what they would call an Interim Report. The Post Office started to become difficult. Ron Warmington wrote to James Arbuthnot, bemoaning the smokescreen which had been blowing in as their investigation progressed.

'We have consistently and clearly asked for short, easy-to-understand, honest and complete answers to the assertions that we have put forward,' Warmington told the MP. 'What we are getting are highly technical, multi-page responses that will appear to many to have been crafted so as to avoid actually giving any answers to those assertions and allegations at all.'

Speculating as to *why* they were encountering this gradual change in behaviour, Ron wrote, 'They probably fear it will be career death to concede any failings whatsoever.'

Second Sight were also under pressure from Subpostmasters. The JFSA wanted Second Sight to say that Horizon was not fit for purpose. Ron remembers having several conversations with Alan Bates.

'He was pleading with us, almost on bended knees, to use the phrase "systemic failings" or "systemic problems" with Horizon. We refused. We said our definition of a systemic failing was something that manifests itself right across the entire network. We were happy Horizon mainly worked well.'

As the final version of Second Sight's Interim Report evolved, it became clear to the Post Office board that their investigators were going to detail some fault-lines in the Post Office's processes. What to do about it became a matter of paramount importance.

Colin was working with the team organising the public response to the report. 'At the time there was a complete belief that there could be no findings other than what was expected, which was that there were no issues with Horizon.'

By this stage Colin was feeling really uncomfortable with the 'official version of the truth' and the whole approach around Horizon. He began to ask questions. Shortly afterwards another red flag went up. Colin was having a casual conversation with a senior member of the Post Office operations team. As they were chatting, Colin asked him if he thought it was a coincidence so many of their Subpostmasters were criminals. The ops team member told Colin that Subpostmasters were a specific class of people: 'failed coppers and retired publicans' who were 'all on the take.'

Colin felt this glib reply was the 'mentality' which gave people at the Post Office 'permission to believe what they needed to believe to carry on in the way they did.'

In June, Ron and Ian began to circulate drafts of their Interim Report to relevant Post Office departments and execs to give them the opportunity to comment on or challenge their conclusions.

Far from confirming everything was hunky dory, it looked as if Second Sight were proposing to criticise the Post Office's training, support, investigation and basic treatment of Subpostmasters. The two bugs Gareth Jenkins revealed via Simon Baker were also given due prominence.

The report's impending publication caused a flurry of high level activity at the Post Office. Most company boards meet once a month, or once every two months. On 24 June, the Post Office held the first of six full Board meetings which took place over the course of *five weeks*. Second Sight were not informed about any of this.

Ron and Ian began to come under direct pressure from the Post Office to water down their criticisms and language. On 3 July Ron Warmington wrote to Janet Walker, James Arbuthnot's Chief of Staff, telling her he and Ian had been 'summoned' to a 4pm meeting with Paula Vennells with a warning that Second Sight had been told the Post Office wanted 'a substantial change to the scope either of the (virtually finalised) Interim Report or even of the entire Investigation. I'm pre-advised that we are to cut the report back to only 'bottomed-out SOFTWARE-related issues." '

Ron was livid. He told Janet it might be 'a resignation matter.'

James Arbuthnot called Ian Henderson just before the Vennells summit to reassure him he had spoken to Vennells and Alwen Lyons and had a separate phone conversation with Jo Swinson, the Minister for Postal Affairs at the Business, Innovation and Skills Department. The upshot was that he and the MPs had Second Sight's back, and they must stick to their agreed brief.

Ron and Ian went into the meeting with Vennells sufficiently emboldened, and drew lines around the report they were not prepared to cross.

On 7 July, Alan Bates pronounced himself satisfied with the contents of the report, though he later told me that having seen all the pre-release versions, it had been 'reviewed and reviewed and reviewed by the Post Office until they had reviewed it flat.'

On 8 July 2013, over eight jargon-free pages, the Interim Report was finally published. It contained Second Sight's expert, reasoned and independent opinion on the problems at the Post Office.

In the headline fight over whether Horizon did or didn't work, there was no clear conclusion. 'In the course of our extensive discussions with POL over the last 12 months,' it read, 'POL has disclosed to Second Sight that, in 2011 and 2012, it had discovered "defects" in Horizon Online that had impacted 76 branches.'

These were the two major bugs disclosed by Gareth Jenkins, one of which was the Receipts and Payments Mismatch. Looking at Horizon as a whole, Second Sight concluded, 'We have so far found no evidence of system wide (systemic) problems with the Horizon software.'

The Interim Report also revealed a level of corporate dysfunction that perhaps, at that stage, was too large for anyone to properly grasp. Second Sight had a lot to say about the Post Office's culture of bureaucratic intransigence, and its unwillingness to engage properly with the issues affecting Subpostmasters, for instance:

> 'Second Sight has asked POL to deliver ... responses ... that addressed the spirit, as well as the letter, of the Subpostmasters' complaints; and that were backed by evidence. Whilst the responses received from POL can be seen to be thorough, they are long and highly technical... In some cases, they present counter-assertions, based on Standard Operating Procedures and Controls, rather than

> tangible evidence of what actually happened.'

The Post Office's heavy-handed investigation goons are also critiqued. The language is polite, but the implication is devastating.

> 'When POL does investigate cases, there is often a focus on "asset recovery solutions" without first establishing the underlying root cause of the problem. This is also an example of a missed opportunity to be in a much better position to resolve problems and to benefit from process improvements.'

The report concludes:

> 'Had POL investigated more of the "mysterious shortages" and problems reported to it [by its own Subpostmasters] with the thoroughness that it has investigated those reported to it by Second Sight, POL would have been in a much better position to resolve the matters raised, and would also have benefited from process improvements.'

In other words – if you'd done a proper investigation when your Subpostmasters raised these issues in the first place, not only would you have helped the individual Subpostmasters, you'd have a far more robust and efficient system.

Appended to the eight page report were four 'spot reviews' which looked at a selection of anonymised individual cases. One of them, 'Spot Review SR05,' described a Subpostmaster who, on a visit to Fujitsu headquarters on 19 August 2008, witnessed a member of staff remotely changing the figures in a Subpostmaster's branch account. The account was, of course, Michael Rudkin's – the caller who spooked me with his remarkable tale in the BBC Southampton car park.

Second Sight had managed to confirm that there were Post Office employees working at Fujitsu HQ in Bracknell and that there was a basement room running what it called 'test' versions of Horizon, but the Post Office denied these terminals were connected to the live system. This was in stark contrast to Rudkin's recollection that his host had specifically told him the system was live.

The Post Office flatly denied that any of its employees in the Fujitsu building in 2008 had 'access to the back-office accounting system.'

Second Sight noted this was a 'conflict of evidence' and their enquiries were continuing.

Matt Prodger from the BBC was quick to react to the Interim Report's revelation about the two software bugs. He produced a series of TV, radio and news pieces across the day. The Post Office's response to the BBC set up their line of defence for the next few years, pointing out Second Sight had been clear Horizon contained no *systemic* errors. The Post Office told Prodger, 'The Horizon computer system and its supporting processes function effectively across our network.'

James Arbuthnot issued a press release which was as warm in its praise for the Post Office as it was for the JFSA and Second Sight.

'I am impressed with the way the Post Office has behaved on this matter,' he stated. 'Since the first approach from our group of MPs, it has acted with forthrightness and transparency and has agreed both to support and fund the investigations. It clearly wants to get to the bottom of what has gone wrong. I want to put on record my thanks to senior staff who have made this happen.'

The report was formally launched at an event at the House of Commons. Various MPs, Shoosmiths, Alan Bates, Kay Linnell and observers from Jo Swinson's office and the Post Office were present. Arbuthnot spoke, calling the report 'a good one' but 'only a step along the way.' Second Sight took questions.

The next day, Jo Swinson made a statement to the House, telling MPs new processes and better training would be implemented as a result of the report, but 'there is no evidence to suggest that any convictions would have been different had these processes and training systems been in place.' This is patently untrue. There was plenty of evidence in the report which made it obvious the Post Office's prosecution strategy was at least potentially suspect, but Swinson and the government either didn't see it or didn't want to see it.

Swinson also steered her colleagues away from suspicions about the Horizon system itself, telling them, 'The report mentions a couple of bugs in the Horizon system, which the Post Office proactively found and rectified … [but] … what it has found to be lacking in Horizon is not the software, but the support and other issues around the software.'

On behalf of the government, Swinson announced the Post Office would set up a working party to complete the review of cases started by Second Sight. This would be attended by the JFSA and Second Sight, and have an independent chair.

Within days of the report landing, the Post Office stopped the prosecution of three Subpostmasters, Sue Knight, Tom Brown and Kym Wyllie. Alan Bates called this 'the first demonstration that we have seen that the Post Office are serious about resolving these issues.'

In reality, the cover-up was just about to begin.

THE CLARKE ADVICE

As the Interim Report was being finalised, without informing Second Sight, the JFSA or James Arbuthnot's group of MPs, the Post Office approached Cartwright King, the solicitors who worked with the Post Office on the criminal prosecution of Subpostmasters. Cartwright King's senior criminal barrister, Simon Clarke, was instructed to write a formal piece of advice about Gareth Jenkins.

Clarke read a draft of Second Sight's report and took on board the gravity of the situation. The Interim Report seemed to flatly contradict what he and his colleagues had been told by the Post Office about the safety and security of the Horizon system.

The next day Simon Clarke and his colleague Martin Smith held a teleconference with Gareth Jenkins, who gaily told them he was the source of the information about the bugs in Second Sight's report.

Clarke demanded more information from the Post Office, before writing what is now known as the Clarke Advice, delivered to the Post Office a week after the official launch of the Interim Report. This document was kept hidden by the Post Office until it was eventually disclosed to an eagle-eyed lawyer at the Court of Appeal more than seven years later.

The Clarke Advice considered five occasions on which Gareth Jenkins had given evidence to the courts in the prosecution of Subpostmasters. The five instances were all in 2012 or 2013, chosen by Clarke because they 'both represent recent examples of the evidence being given in support of Post Office prosecutions by Jenkins and highlight the situation as asserted by him *after* it became known that there were defects in Horizon which materially affected the presentation of data and the provision of false balance figures.'

In his advice, Simon Clarke analyses Jenkins' awareness of bugs in Horizon and contrasts them with his witness statements to the courts. He notes that in his witness statements, 'Jenkins is attesting to the then integrity and robust nature of Horizon – there is nothing wrong with the system. Unfortunately, that was not the case.'

Clarke concludes that Jenkins, 'failed to disclose material known to him but which undermines his expert opinion. This failure is in plain breach of his duty as an expert witness.'

Jenkins' failure, according to Clarke, puts the Post Office 'in breach of their duty as a prosecutor', warning, 'there are a number of now convicted defendants to whom the existence of bugs should have been disclosed but was not.'

In other words, lads, you may have some unsafe convictions on your hands.

Clarke recommended a 'review of all Post Office prosecutions.' The Post Office took this to mean 'all prosecutions since 2010' and instigated what became known as the Cartwright King Sift Review.

The decision to focus purely on post-2010 cases was because, according to the Post Office, 'the bugs known of at that stage were believed only to apply to Horizon Online rather than Legacy Horizon, and 1 January 2010 was the earliest date on which Horizon Online was migrated into all Post Office branches.'

Legacy Horizon is a term adopted by the Post Office to describe the original Horizon – Clint's 'bag of shit.' The lack of curiosity about Legacy Horizon can only be for one of two reasons. Either the Post Office believed Horizon Online was such a bad upgrade it was worse than Legacy Horizon, or it was hesitant to look too closely at Legacy Horizon for fear of what it might find. Whilst the former beggars belief, the latter is unforgivable.

The Cartwright King Sift Review was kept secret from MPs and campaigners.

Now, at least, firmly aware that knowledge of Horizon bugs had a potential material impact on the Post Office's responsibilities to the criminal courts, a weekly teleconference between Post Office execs, Fujitsu and Cartwright King was established. This was also not disclosed to MPs and campaigners. Ongoing problems with Horizon would be discussed, and the lawyers would assess whether or not disclosure to an individual Subpostmaster's defence team was necessary, or indeed, whether a prosecution should go ahead. The level of paranoia within the Post Office about the information being circulated was such that John Scott, the Post Office's Head of Security, ordered that notes taken at the meeting should be destroyed. Emails were deleted and paper notes were shredded.

Scott's instruction evidently caused consternation among some members of the Post Office legal team. Jarnail Singh approached Simon Clarke's colleague Martin Smith for clarification, using his now familiar word soup:

'Martin – I know Simon is advising on disclosure. As discussed can he look into the common myth that emails, written communications etc.. meetings. If its produced its then available for disclosure. If it?s not then technically it isn?t? Possible true of civil cases NOT CRIMINAL CASES?'

On receiving and deciphering the request, Clarke typed out a second Advice. This one warned:

'The duty to record and retain material cannot be abrogated. To do so would amount to a breach of the law. A decision-based failure to record and retain material … where it is taken partly or wholly in order to avoid future disclosure obligations, may well amount to a conspiracy to pervert the course of justice.'

There appears to have been some internal nervousness at Cartwright King about the tenor of Clarke's opinion and how it would go down with their clients. Clarke's colleague Andy Cash forwarded it to Susan Crichton with an obsequious cover note.

'I am sure you will appreciate,' wrote Cash, 'that the advice is sent as part of our brief to … protect the reputation of the Post Office. It is fully accepted that you may wish to take a second opinion on the views expressed.'

Crichton was alarmed. She wrote back to Cash telling him she was 'deeply concerned' that 'there may have been an attempt to destroy documentary material.' Two months later the Post Office issued an internal protocol relating to information retention for those involved with the weekly teleconference. It said:

'We will in future collect and retain any and all information which might suggest that Horizon Online may not be working as it should, or that our training and back-up systems are less than we would wish.'

The protocol went on to state:

'Defendants are entitled to this information where it meets the test for disclosure and we would not wish to be associated with any wrongful conviction.'

It is not known whether John Scott was disciplined for issuing the instruction to destroy documents. All we know is that shortly after the internal protocol was issued, Susan Crichton left the Post Office. John Scott remained Head of Security until 2016.

The Cartwright King Sift Review took several months to conclude. It looked at 308 prosecutions and applied a disclosure test formulated specifically for the exercise by leading criminal barrister Brian Altman QC,[1] which was written in October 2013. This involved asking if the information which Second Sight had brought to light should be disclosed to Subpostmasters who had been prosecuted by the Post Office. Cartwright King concluded, from the parameters set by Altman, that 26 convicted Subpostmasters should be contacted.

At last, evidence of potential unsafe convictions had finally come to light. This should have immediately been communicated to the JFSA and campaigning MPs. Instead, the Post Office chose to keep the existence and conclusions of the Sift Review secret and continued for years to explicitly deny there had been any miscarriages of justice due to the Horizon computer system, and the Post Office's enforcement of the Subpostmasters Contract.

---

1 Queen's Counsel, a senior barrister recognised as an expert in their legal field. A QC will often take the lead on highly complex cases which demand greater experience and expertise. QCs are often known as 'silks' because when they are appointed, they have the right to wear a silk gown.

THE DETICA REPORT

Second Sight and Simon Clarke were not the only independent observers to take one look at the Post Office and see it was in a complete mess.

In April, as Second Sight's Interim Report was being prepared, a company owned by BAE Systems called Detica NetReveal was brought in to examine the Post Office's fraud repellency, business processes and IT.

The report, delivered in October 2013, is highly critical. Several of Second Sight's recommendations 'resonate strongly' with the report's authors, not least the 'habitual desire to assign responsibility to an individual rather than to conduct root cause analysis.'

The authors go on to list just how bad things are within the network, noting the Post Office's 'insecure systems and processes', 'inconsistent audits', 'lack of robust controls and records', accompanied by 'inadequate processes and documentation.'

Alarmingly, Detica note that Post Office auditors are incentivised by the number of branches they fail, effectively 'rewarding interventions solely based on the failure of a SPMRs[2] career, home and livelihood.' This, the report notes, is 'likely to be a contributory factor behind the blame culture identified by Second Sight.'

The authors then turn their attention to the Horizon system, which they seem to view as something of a basket case. Due to the inability of Horizon to talk to one of the Post Office's key stock ordering systems ('Galaxy') it seems the Post Office has no idea whether the stock it is sending its branches is being sold, 'nor the stock levels of each branch.'

'Product codes for items in Galaxy and Horizon are different in each system,' states the report, 'meaning it is not possible to identify all products individually end to end.' Detica found it 'was not possible to either match the two systems or ascertain whether any team in the Post Office had been tasked with or had succeeded in doing this.'

When Detica did attempt a closer look at Galaxy, 'this was challenging as the computers which had access to the system were sufficiently antiquated that they could not accept a USB port device.'

It wasn't just stock the Post Office struggled with. Detica found 'the

---

2 Common shorthand in a lot of Post Office and court documents for Subpostmaster. Sometimes shortened still further to SPM or even SP.

Post Office is not able to account fully for the whereabouts of significant values of cash in the network.'

This was down to a litany of poor processes where cash was taken in and out of the system multiple times for multiple reasons. The processes were reliant on manual interventions from Post Office staff and Subpostmasters to keep track of it. The report explained, 'the only cash data visible to central operational teams, including the Fraud Analysis team is the branch level (not denomination level) generated cash figures… This data is overwritten each day, therefore teams that rely on this information need to extract manually each working day.'

Horizon's incompatibility with the Post Office's cash machine network was another issue. Detica note 'losses from ATMs have been one of the major concerns of the Post Office during 2012/2013 … two branches recently audited … showed shortfalls where in each case the cause was attributed to not understanding how the ATM operates. Both SPMRs claimed that the only training received in how to use the ATM was provided by the installation engineer.'

Detica gave 40 recommendations for changing the Post Office's processes, fraud detection capacity and IT. It concluded 'some re-design' of Horizon was of 'critical importance' for the Post Office and hoped its report would 'underline the urgency with which the Post Office needs to adapt its business practices and technology.'

As the Detica report authors note with some frustration, 'The assumption that activities should be performed in the same way as they have always been done has been prevalent … the disconnect between current practice and what is required is striking.'

Whilst Second Sight's findings were published, the Detica report was kept secret. In fact, Second Sight were not told it had been commissioned, were never spoken to by the report's authors, nor were they shown its contents when it was handed to Susan Crichton, Lesley Sewell and other members of the Post Office board.

Within the space of a few months in the latter half of 2013, the Post Office had been told by three teams of experts it had duff business processes, duff IT and needed to examine its entire prosecution and asset-recovery strategy.

How would it respond?

THE MEDIATION SCHEME

Whilst the secret CK Sift Review was ongoing, the Post Office kept up its public-facing show of willingness to cooperate with MPs and the JFSA. At the end of August 2013, nearly two months after the publication of the Interim Report, the Post Office launched Jo Swinson's promised review of the cases Second Sight had begun to investigate. It was called the 'Initial Complaint Review and Mediation Scheme,' which became known more simply as the Mediation Scheme.

It is tempting in retrospect to see the Mediation Scheme as a complete waste of time and money. Many applicants now describe it as such. It eventually collapsed in acrimony, but the scheme would come to serve a useful purpose. At the start, all was well.

'I naïvely thought this was wrapping up,' Simon Baker told me. 'As long as we continued to be transparent and settle any grievances *and* give the Subpostmasters financial compensation, within a few months we'd have an agreement everyone could live with. That's how I thought things were going to pan out.'

The idea behind the scheme was to create a space for Subpostmasters with a grievance to sit down with a Post Office negotiator, in the presence of a qualified mediator, and try to get *somewhere.* Mediation gives participants the opportunity to say what they want without prejudicing themselves or any future legal action. Everything is confidential, but nothing is binding unless both parties come to an agreement. The job of a mediator is to allow free and frank discussion, establish trust and common ground, and then grope towards some kind of resolution. Successful mediations can end in confidential agreements, often involving a cash settlement. If there is no resolution, the parties can walk away.

The Mediation Scheme would be funded entirely by the Post Office. The scheme would be overseen by a Working Group comprising the JFSA, Second Sight and the Post Office itself. The Working Group would be chaired by Sir Anthony Hooper, a retired Court of Appeal judge.

Although the number and seniority of Post Office execs on the Working Group would change, the nominated point person would be Angela van den Bogerd, newly-promoted to the post of Programme Director for the Branch Support Programme.

The failure to secure any parliamentary representation on the Working

Group was not, at the time, seen as a problem. MPs were happy to believe the Post Office were acting in good faith. In fact, James Arbuthnot turned up on the Post Office's Mediation Scheme press release, stating:

'I am very pleased indeed with the Working Group's proposed process. To my mind, it represents the very best chance all parties … have of ensuring the best outcome for everyone. It is fair, thorough, and independent.'

The scheme was open to serving or former Subpostmasters, or their managers or assistants or Crown Office counter clerks who might have a grievance against the Post Office. The eligibility criteria made it absolutely clear it was open to those who might already have 'a police caution or have been subject to a criminal prosecution or conviction.'

To get on the scheme, a Subpostmaster had to have suffered 'a financial loss or unfair treatment that you believe you have suffered as a result of the Horizon system or any associated issues.'

The hoops which required jumping through before anyone got to mediation were as follows: once accepted on to the scheme, an applicant would be assigned a professional advisor, paid for by the Post Office, who would help the Subpostmaster put together a 'Case Questionnaire Response' (CQR). This would tell the story from the Subpostmaster's perspective. If accepted, the case would be sent to the Post Office, who would produce a 'Post Office Investigation Report' (POIR). Using the CQR and POIR Second Sight would then investigate, asking for more information as required, before producing its 'Case Review Report' (CRR) which would make a recommendation as to whether mediation between the Post Office and the applicant should take place.

Mediation in the architecture of this particular scheme was only expected (and funded) to last one day. An agreement to go to mediation simply meant nothing more than a commitment to sitting in a room for a few hours and having a chat. If both parties approached the scheme with the right mindset and expectations, it could, it was hoped, lead to closure for some of the applicants, if not all.

All serving Subpostmasters were made aware of their options. The JFSA also spread the word through its network of former Subpostmasters. By the time the application window for the scheme closed in November 2013, 150 people had come forward. They included Seema Misra, Lee Castleton, Jo Hamilton, Julian Wilson, Michael Rudkin, Jackie McDonald, Scott Darlington, Noel Thomas and, of course, Alan Bates.

Of the 150 applicants, ten had been jailed and at least 30 had been successfully prosecuted by the Post Office. Other applicants had been prosecuted but were either found not guilty or the charges against them were dropped. The alleged offences were mainly fraud, false accounting or theft. Some had been pursued through the civil courts.

Many had been suspended, almost all had been forced out of their jobs. At least one person had had a total mental breakdown resulting in them being held in a secure hospital.

One applicant was Gina Griffiths, widow of Martin Griffiths.

MARTIN GRIFFITHS

Martin Griffiths was a well loved family man. In 2008 he was running Hope Farm Road sub-Post Office in Great Sutton near Ellesmere Port in Cheshire. He had been Subpostmaster there for 13 years. Martin ran the Post Office counter and his wife Gina bossed the retail side of their busy shop. Outside work, Martin was a popular club cricketer, playing for the Boughton Hall team in Chester. He was also dedicated to his business – the first person to arrive in the morning and the last to leave at night.

During his tenure at Hope Farm Road, Martin managed the transition from pen-and-paper book-keeping to the Horizon system. Martin and Gina built the business up and were doing well, taking home around £50,000 a year. Unlike many Postmasters who live in properties adjoining or above the shop, Martin and Gina had managed to buy a separate family home in Guilden Sutton. Every working day, Martin made the short drive down the A41 to Great Sutton to be there for his customers.

In 2009, the problems with Horizon began. Martin's income had allowed him to swallow losses at his counter in the past (and some had been considerable), but now large, inexplicable discrepancies showed up on his computer screen. First thousands, then tens of thousands of pounds went missing. Martin could not find out what was causing it.

At first Martin thought it might be a member of staff. He kept his eyes open for cash going missing. Were the losses happening when one particular employee was on shift?

This atmosphere of suspicion continued for more than a year, but Martin could not find any evidence of any employee with their hands in the till.

Rather than declare a false balance, as other Subpostmasters had done, Martin acknowledged his discrepancies to the Post Office. Their response was uncompromising. Horizon was functioning perfectly. Its figures were correct. Martin was not running his Post Office properly. He would have to make good his losses.

Martin was a proud man, but there was a vulnerability about him. He didn't want to trouble his family with any financial worries, so at first he didn't tell them what was happening. He made good the losses with cheques, and by taking money from his savings. As Subpostmaster, Martin saw it as his responsibility to make good the discrepancies *and* discover their source.

The stress began to take its toll. As Martin fought to make sense of the losses he could not explain, his personality and state of mind started to deteriorate. He had been outgoing and sociable, but during this period he began to change. Instead of coming back from a long day at work and being his normal garrulous self, he'd sit and brood in the family front room.

In 2011, Martin was audited. He had a £23,000 discrepancy. The Post Office suspended him. A temporary Subpostmaster was installed. This was another blow to Martin's self-esteem.

After three months, Martin got his job back, but the losses continued to escalate, and Martin seemed unable to stop them.

The deteriorating financial situation also affected Martin's relationship with Gina and his friends. Martin used to go to his local cricket club and stand on the pavilion balcony with a pint in his hand, nattering away to friends and clubmates. But now on match days he would just sit, quietly watching the game. Other than visits to the cricket club, he stopped going out at all.

Between January 2012 and October 2013 another £57,000 went 'missing' from Hope Farm Road. Martin did what he could to find the money to make good the discrepancies. The Griffiths' savings accounts were emptied, poured down a widening electronic plughole. Martin turned to his parents. They gave Martin money from their life savings. It was swallowed up.

The situation was desperate. The Griffiths could not understand why Horizon was continually showing these horrendous discrepancies. Under the terms of his contract, Martin was not entitled to any investigative help from the Post Office. He was repeatedly told to make good the losses and sharpen up his branch-management skills or face the termination of his contract.

On 2 May 2013, whilst Martin was dealing with a regular Royal Mail collection, two balaclava-clad men burst into the Post Office. One had a sledgehammer, the other a crowbar. Martin was standing at the open armoured door of his Post Office counter, preparing to hand over a large bag of parcels. As the men ran towards him, Martin tried to retreat behind the safety of the counter but his arm was grabbed by a robber who brought the crowbar down hard on Martin's hand. The robber got into the secure area.

Martin was told that if he didn't hand over the contents of the safe he would be beaten to a pulp. Martin complied. The robbers left with around £54,000 in cash.

Martin was already fragile from the depressive state he'd fallen into. Now he was right on the edge.

The next day, a Post Office investigator came by to assess what had happened. Despite Martin's ordeal, the investigator showed little sympathy.

Within days, one of the robbers had been arrested. £15,000 in cash was recovered by the police and returned to the Post Office. £39,000 remained unaccounted for.

Martin was interviewed by a Post Office investigator again. This time he was pushed on the details of what happened during the robbery, until the investigator had what he needed. During his interview Martin acknowledged his security door had been open – something a lot of Subpostmasters did when handing over parcels for collection. This was a technical failure to properly secure his counter. This breach of the often unrealistic Post Office security procedures would likely make Martin liable for at least some of the cash that was stolen. The investigator left.

Two months later, Martin was sent a letter informing him that due to his failure to manage the discrepancies at his branch and his failure to settle them in good time he was being sacked, still owing thousands of pounds to the Post Office. He would be ejected from Hope Farm Road on 3 October 2013.

On 17 July 2013, Martin received another letter from the Post Office. They had decided he was responsible for £7,500 of the missing £39,000 stolen during the robbery. He was told to send the Post Office a cheque.

Martin was already broken. This was the final straw.

On 2 September 2013, a week or so after the investigator's visit, Martin turned 59. On his birthday his son Matt came over with a card and present.

Matt told me he found his father sitting placidly in his usual armchair. Martin took his gifts calmly and said, 'Thanks son. Give us a hug.' Matt did so. Martin held him for a moment and quietly said, 'This will probably be the last birthday you see me.'

Matt was too stunned to respond coherently. His dad was clearly in a depressive state, something by now his family, wife and GP had recognised, and were doing what they could to help him.

On Friday 19 September 2013 Martin had his last contact with the

Post Office. It was an appeal against Martin's culpability for the money which was taken from his branch during the robbery. The Post Office maintained he had been partly responsible for the stolen cash.

On the morning of Monday 23 September 2013, Martin got ready for work as usual. Although the branch wasn't due to open until 9am, Martin had got into the habit of leaving before 8am to make the 20 minute drive from Guilden Sutton to Hope Farm Road. Once inside the branch, Martin would sit behind the counter trying to get to grips with what was happening to his Post Office. On 23 September, Martin left at 7.30am. Gina was due to follow at 8.30am.

When Gina arrived for her 9am shift, the shop was still locked. Martin was not there. Gina called her son in a panic. In 18 years of being a Subpostmaster, Martin had never once failed to open up on time. On the phone to Matt, Gina kept saying, 'I know something's wrong. I know something's wrong. I know something's wrong.'

Matt tried to calm her down and said he'd be straight round. Whilst Matt was driving over to Hope Farm Road, Gina called again. She'd heard a news report about a man being hit by a bus on the A41 – the route that Martin drove to work. Matt remembers her saying over and over,

'I know it's your dad. I know it's your dad. *I know it's your dad.*'

It was. That morning, whilst driving down the A41, Martin had pulled over in a lay-by. He sat there for an hour, then he got out of his car and deliberately stepped into the path of an oncoming bus.

Martin was taken to Aintree Hospital. The police found Martin's ID and contacted the family. Matt was taken to hospital by his grandad. They both went to Martin's bedside and found him lying in an induced coma, covered in blood.

Alongside his ID, the police had found a note in which Martin apologised to Gina and his family and told them he loved them.

Three weeks after he was hit by the bus, Martin's brain died. The decision was taken to switch off his life support machine.

On 11 October 2013, Martin's family gathered round his hospital bed and watched him slip away.

They made a public statement, which was printed in the Chester Chronicle. It read:

> 'Martin, who lived his whole life in Chester, was known as a keen sportsman – playing football, tennis and cricket. He was closely linked to Chester Boughton Hall Cricket Club and Chester

> Nomads Football Club. Aged 59, he leaves behind his wife Gina, children Matthew and Lauren and parents Doreen and Keith. He was loved by all and will be greatly missed.'

The coroner at Martin's inquest returned a verdict of suicide.

Word of Martin's death spread quickly through the Subpostmaster community. Alan Bates contacted Gina and told her what he was involved with, explaining the Mediation Scheme and what it hoped to achieve. With the grieving family's permission, Alan helped Gina join the Mediation Scheme on Martin's behalf.

I spoke to Matt just a couple of years after his father's death. He told me about the processes he went through when thinking about what happened.

'I felt I should have done more,' he told me. 'At the time I went round the house and tried to have conversations with him, but he wouldn't say anything. I would leave the house frustrated. I shouldn't have done that. I should have been there. I should have maybe forced him to sell the Post Office quicker, get him out of there.'

Matt believes 'without doubt' the way the Post Office hounded his father over the last four years of his life was the main contributory factor to Martin's depression and eventual suicide.

MOP AND BUCKET

For the campaigning Subpostmasters, many of whom had waited years to get some kind of recognition for what they were going through, the Mediation Scheme was a small chink of light at the end of a very long tunnel. The independent experts who had found clear evidence Horizon was fallible were now going to properly examine their cases, and the Post Office had committed themselves to listening to the Subpostmasters' complaints.

On top of investigating each individual Subpostmaster's situation, Second Sight continued their investigation into Horizon as a system by analysing information from the Post Office and the disaffected applicants.

This meant Second Sight would be able to take a fuller view of Horizon's reliability and fitness for purpose, whilst also doing some groundwork for the Post Office and each applicant's advisors when it came to discussing the parameters for mediation.

James Arbuthnot was chuffed as chips. 'The Mediation Scheme was a huge step. I was delighted,' he told me.

I asked him how the Post Office was persuaded to set up such a scheme and pay for it.

'They didn't want to,' he replied. 'But it was obvious from the Interim Report that they hadn't got to the bottom of it, which was what the whole process was designed to achieve. Second Sight were saying there were indications that things had been systemically wrong, at least in terms of the support systems, if not the computer software. So there was more work to be done.'

Around this time Shoosmiths and the JFSA parted company, dropping the legal claim against the Post Office in the process. The firm had grown its number of potential claimants from 55 to around 100, including Jo Hamilton and Seema Misra, but things had not progressed since 2012's initial letters-before-action. Although I have heard multiple reasons for the relationship dissolving, it seems the main factor was money. Shoosmiths couldn't get the right insurers on board to cover the cost of a class action. If they went to court and failed, Shoosmiths would be liable for their own and most of the Post Office's costs. These could stretch into millions. Plus, there was the unappetising (and very likely) prospect of being counter-sued by the Post Office.

I asked Shoosmiths why the relationship ended. They replied, 'At the time of our involvement, we had completed investigations on behalf of a number of clients. Our involvement concluded when the results were submitted under the Post Office's Mediation Scheme.'

When I asked for clarification, I was told no further explanation would be forthcoming.

Shoosmiths' withdrawal meant the JFSA's attempts to hold the Post Office to account through the courts would have to wait a few years. At the time, it didn't seem that big a deal, largely because there was another show in town: a scheme backed by MPs and the JFSA, paid for by the Post Office, aimed at addressing past misdeeds.

Everything was set fair. The JFSA, Sir Anthony Hooper, Second Sight and the Post Office got down to business. The Mediation Scheme was a strictly confidential process, something all parties were intent on respecting, at least, at first.

Simon Baker set up and attended the first Working Group meeting. He was pleased with the atmosphere. 'It went really well!' he told me. 'There was a lot of emotional scar tissue, quite honestly, in people like Alan, but I came out thinking this is going to work. We can give these people support.'

Simon left the Post Office to join the National Grid at the end of September 2013. By coincidence, shortly afterwards, the wheels began to come off.

Even as applications to join the Mediation Scheme were being received during the autumn of 2013, the Post Office's apparent initial interest in making the process a success seemed to evaporate.

Post Office representatives at the Working Group began to take a strict legalistic approach to everything. Working Group meetings, which were supposed to be conducted in a spirit of procedural cooperation, became attritional.

Second Sight's requests for information either took weeks to process, or were refused on grounds of being too expensive to obtain, or legally privileged.[1]

Kay Linnell puts the turning point down to the departure of Susan

---

[1] A communication between a lawyer and their client is considered 'privileged.' This means it cannot be revealed to anyone unless the client says otherwise (known as 'waiving privilege'). This includes a court, or parliament.

Crichton in November 2013 and the arrival of a new Post Office general counsel, Chris Aujard.

It is still not clear why Crichton chose to leave when she did – perhaps she fancied a change, or saw what was coming and decided to walk away. Her departure was discussed at a Post Office board meeting in September 2013. The Post Office has provided me with minutes of all its 2013 board meetings from 24 June onwards. Unfortunately, they are so heavily redacted it's impossible to get any sense of what was really going on.

Crichton's replacement as general counsel was an 'interim' appointment, which might suggest he was brought in by the Post Office board to do a specific job. Chris Aujard has not responded to my request for an interview, but an insight into his thought process appeared shortly after he left the Post Office in 2015. General Counsel magazine ran an article about corporate crisis-handling. It was called 'Keep Calm and Call Counsel.' Aujard is the star interviewee, but the Post Office isn't mentioned at all. It is a revealing read.

'The bigger the corporation,' hoots the article's anonymous author, 'the more likely the crisis... What they don't see is the general counsel busy behind the scenes with the mop and bucket.'

It goes on, 'There's no hard and fast rule as to who takes the lead in a crisis, of course. The clean-up team will depend on the nature of the emergency and company protocols, not to mention the judgement of the CEO. But usually, says veteran general counsel Chris Aujard, "at some point, no matter where the crisis enters the organisation, the GC gets involved."'

In the article, Aujard comes on strong as the go-to man in a crisis, especially when the executives around him are flapping like loose sails:

'They tend to go down the route of denial,' he says. '"This can't be happening, you've got it wrong, everyone's got it wrong." They might go through the process of grudging acceptance: "Well, ok, maybe there is something in it."'

Aujard warms to his theme. 'There's a skill that general counsel typically have, which is to turn around to the C-suite[2] and say, "Look, this is not something that you should push to one side and deal with tomorrow. This is today's issue and it's pressingly urgent – and by the way, it could

[2] Executives with 'Chief' in their title hence 'C'-suite – Chief Executive, Chief Finance Officer, Chief Technical Officer etc.

cost some of you your jobs." '

Self-preservation. Always a way to motivate people. But what about the public-facing response to a crisis? How does Aujard recommend addressing that?

'You can't send stuff out saying, "It's all our fault, terribly sorry, we'll pay you any compensation you ask for!" '

Of course not.

With Aujard's arrival in 2013, there was a clear perception in some quarters that the aims and emphasis of the Mediation Scheme changed. According to Kay Linnell, Aujard made 'everything an argument – access to records, responses to requests and a dogged insistence that they should continue destroying accounting and other information after a six year period in accordance with their in-house policy.'

Linnell watched as the Post Office turned the scheme into a 'bottom-protecting exercise.'

Ron Warmington puts it more strongly. 'Open warfare began. It was pretty clear Aujard had either been instructed or was just naturally-minded to treat us like idiots, kick us in the long grass and close the process down. We saw a marked change from "seek the truth … just ask and you will be given" to an antagonistic refusal to cooperate.'

Everything became interminable. And once more, it came down to disclosure.

'Where the Post Office were unable or unwilling to help,' said Sir Anthony Hooper, 'was with documentation which might have shown that there was something wrong with Horizon.'

Ron and Ian heard a familiar phrase return with increasing regularity.

'No matter how simple a question we asked,' Ron told me, 'the response was invariably, "We don't understand. We don't understand what you are talking about." We were tearing our hair out and saying, "Well, this isn't difficult to understand. Why can't you understand that?!" '

By way of example, getting the Post Office to acknowledge the existence of their own internal suspense accounts (rather than the ones which used to exist in branches before 2005) took forever.

'Aujard and Angela van den Bogerd said, "We don't have suspense accounts," ' remembers Ron. 'I said, "Well of course you have suspense accounts. You have relationships with about 60 other clients: Bank of Ireland, DWP, NS&I, etc etc etc, and unless by some miracle of finance that I've never come across before, you are going to have differences between what's in your books in relation to your client and what's in their books in relation to their counterparts. Otherwise the two sets of books get hopelessly out of whack and nobody knows who owes what to whom. So you will have suspense accounts."'

After ten months of to-ing and fro-ing, the Post Office acknowledged it had suspense accounts. Second Sight found that the unclaimed money parked in the suspense accounts – hundreds of thousands of pounds – would sit around for a set period, after which it would be banked as profit. But the Post Office didn't want to talk about that (and still doesn't).

The delays in getting basic data, and the Post Office's apparent view that each piece of information it produced should be supplied with glacial reluctance, nearly strangled the whole process.

Ron admitted he was almost at the point of resigning. 'You have to understand my background as an investigator was one of having worked in huge corporations that had an appetite to seek the truth first and to work out the consequences of the truth much later. So that if there was evidence that something had been messed up by the corporation itself there was very little focus given as to what the outcome would be for the corporation. It was never the case that one would alter the investigative thoroughness or the findings for fear that the implications for the company itself would be negative.'

For Kay it wasn't just the sudden change of approach, it was the attitude which came with it. 'The Post Office was arrogant and in denial that any employee of Post Office or anyone associated with the Horizon system could ever have made a single error.'

Sir Anthony Hooper was concerned. Although hired as an independent chair, he could not help but step back and make his own assessment of the Post Office's prosecution decisions. He described it to me like this: 'If there was a substantial loss in a branch of five or ten thousand pounds or more, there had to be one of three reasons. One – a fault in Horizon. Two – some sort of clerical error. Three – theft.'

Sir Anthony felt a clerical error of that scale would likely be picked up. 'So for the big losses, it was either theft or Horizon. And as I pointed out to senior management at the Post Office, it was very difficult to see how it could be theft.'

Sir Anthony's reasoning is firstly that Postmasters had to be of good character when they were employed, which made them far less susceptible than most to crimes of dishonesty. Also, stealing money from the Post Office was 'a very short-sighted thing to do, because under the Post

Office contract, they were immediately liable for the loss.' This is a point that has been raised repeatedly by Postmasters, their advisors and MPs for years. It seems obvious. As Sir Anthony said, 'If I decide to steal, I'm usually going to steal from someone who can't immediately recover the money from me.'[1]

Whilst the Working Group was overseeing the Mediation Scheme, the Cartwright King Sift Review was being carried out, in parallel, in secret. I asked Sir Anthony (a retired Court of Appeal Criminal Division judge, let's not forget) if he was told by the Post Office that a review into its prosecutions was happening whilst he was employed by them.

'I have no memory of ever being told,' he said. 'And I should have been told.'

[1] The counter-argument to this, and one widely used by Post Office staff, is that easy access to tempting sums of cash can be a corrupting influence for someone who might be running a struggling business.

WAR OF ATTRITION

James Arbuthnot was not party to the Post Office's new strategy of obfuscation and denial. He wasn't a member of the Working Group, but he soon got to hear how difficult the Post Office was becoming. He sought reassurance from Paula Vennells. He didn't get any.

'I would go to the Post Office, or have Paula Vennells or Alice Perkins into meetings at my room in parliament to try and move things along, and I would be told they were trying to stay clear of the process because it's meant to be an independent investigation,' he told me.

As a result, a scheme which all parties initially thought would take a matter of weeks to complete made little or no progress in 2013 at all. Even by spring 2014 none of the 146 applicants who were accepted onto the scheme had got anywhere close to actual mediation – though Second Sight were making progress on their wider investigation.

In this new spirit of attrition, the reports produced by the Post Office about applicants to the scheme became exercises in self-justification. In each case the Post Office was at pains to deny it had ever made an incorrect decision. Time and again, the blame for an individual Subpostmaster's woes was laid squarely at her or his own feet.

Kay Linnell thought the Post Office strategy was transparent. They wanted to 'get rid of all the complainants and by whatever means protect the Post Office perception of their own reputation as Persil white.'

Nonetheless, documents were emerging which were building an evidenced picture of legally as well as morally unacceptable behaviour. Kay told me it became apparent to her that the Post Office used 'bullying tactics', and that Subpostmasters had to 'toe the line or face criminal prosecution.'

According to Kay, criminal prosecution 'was used as a threat and executed without any underlying investigation, proper review or understanding of CPS guidelines – in one case we reviewed, an in-house Post Office lawyer had marked a file as "insufficient evidence to prosecute." Then a few days later that lawyer filled in a "prosecute this person" form. This was an absolute abuse of the right to bring prosecutions. If the CPS had been involved those prosecutions would never have taken place.'

I have heard several Postmasters suggest in retrospect that the Post Office's behaviour in changing its position on the Mediation Scheme was part of a cunning plan. They believe that in the face of credible evidence and genuine concerns, the Post Office agreed to set up a scheme (which they owned, financed and controlled) in order to tie up the applicants, the JFSA and Second Sight with minutiae and misplaced activity. That way everything could be dragged out for as long as possible, distracting the Subpostmasters from a potential legal action, and sapping their will.

Colin from Marketing disagrees. He remembers the incredulity amongst his colleagues when one of the first Case Review Reports into an applicant's case came through. 'It was clear Second Sight believed there was an issue and there could have been an unsafe conviction. No one on our side could believe it. Everyone was like … "*What?!*" Then they produced a couple more. And they were coming up the same.'

The internal reaction was one of deep concern. Not for the Subpostmasters, naturally, but for the Post Office's reputation.

Colin watched this with interest. 'What was crazy about the Post Office was that there was almost this mentality of refusing to admit that there *is* a problem. It's almost like an alcoholic being in a denial that they are an alcoholic. It really was that sort of mentality.'

Things took a darker turn. Instead of confronting the issue, the Post Office retreated further into corporate denial, and got nasty.

Colin says, 'It became clear we needed to "switch" and start discrediting Second Sight. And that's what began to happen. Post Office began to discredit the people we had hired by saying things like … they're "too old", or it's been too long since they did a job like this, or they're not up to the job. And that was purely because the Post Office did not like the conclusions that Second Sight were coming to.'

COMPLETE BREAKDOWN

As 2014 dragged on, the Post Office became more aggressive in challenging Second Sight. The arrangement by which the independent investigators would be the sole arbiter of whether a case was suitable for mediation was put into dispute. On being presented with a Case Review Report, the Post Office began demanding Second Sight's recommendations should go to a vote. The JFSA would get one vote, the Post Office another. As chair, Sir Anthony Hooper would have the casting vote.

Alan Bates was livid. He felt Second Sight's investigators, being both independent and thorough, were best placed to decide whether or not a case should go to mediation.

Debating the merits of an applicant's case at Working Group level would require a lengthy examination of Second Sight's methods, a re-examination of the Post Office's position, and a defence by the JFSA of each applicant's case. Unlike Second Sight and the Post Office, the JFSA had no detailed knowledge of each case – as far as they saw it, they were on the Working Group to oversee process. Alan Bates felt being asked to take responsibility for representing each applicant at Working Group level was completely unfair, especially as the Post Office, tooled up with litigation lawyers, could spend as much money as they wanted preparing their case against a Second Sight recommendation if they felt that letting it go to mediation was not in their interests. The professional advisors assisting the Subpostmasters were not permitted to bill the Post Office for any more than £1,500 of their time. Any work beyond that either had to be funded by the applicant or offered *pro bono*[2] by the advisor. As it was, several professional advisors had already worked many hours for free to help applicants put their initial CQRs together.

By May 2014 I would describe the sunniest of my sources as pragmatically pessimistic. Those among them who had been trying to work with the Post Office to make the mediation process a success were spitting feathers. One furious respondent picked up the phone and gave me their view of what was going on, stating with great vehemence that they had 'never come across an organisation with lower levels of morality than the

[2] Short for '*pro bono publico*', literally 'for the public good', but nowadays taken to mean: 'for free.'

Post Office.'

It's entirely possible the Post Office were trying to provoke the JFSA into throwing in the towel. This would allow the Post Office to play the injured party to MPs and the media, and paint the JFSA as stroppy campaigners. Ron Warmington told me he was feeling frustrated enough to walk, but James Arbuthnot persuaded him not to. Alan and Kay weren't going anywhere, either. They knew every internal document extracted from the Post Office had value.

Throughout the first half of 2014 I stayed in touch with as many well-informed people as I could. It seemed to me that a publicly-funded organisation, which (at the very least) had a case to answer about the possibility it had illegitimately pursued and prosecuted dozens of people, was now doing everything it could to sabotage its own independent investigation and Mediation Scheme. Aside from questions about miscarriages of justice, what about the misuse of public funds?

Whilst the former point was going to be difficult to prove without hard evidence – and at that stage no documents were leaking out of the process – the latter point started to feel like it was self-evident. Guessing I might be able to get at least one or two of my fulminating sources to go on the record, I wondered if the waste-of-public-money angle might interest Panorama. I mentioned it to Jane French at Inside Out South.

Jane pointed me in the direction of the executive producer of the Northern Ireland Panorama unit, Andy Head. Andy was an Inside Out South alumnus. Jane gave me his details and he kindly took my call. I explained the story. Andy liked it, but was non-committal. We agreed to stay in touch.

THE BRIEFING REPORTS

By the middle of 2014, the MPs wanted to know what was going on. Despite the off-the-record concerns which must have reached his ears as well as mine, James Arbuthnot seemed to be taking the Post Office's word on trust. He was still in regular communication with Paula Vennells and getting full assurances from her. On 15 July, Arbuthnot sent an email to other MPs in the Post Office parliamentary group. In the email, he tried to explain why there was nothing to tell them.

'I had hoped,' he wrote, 'we might schedule a meeting before summer during which the Post Office might offer us an update on how the Mediation Scheme is progressing. To this end I have been in correspondence with Paula Vennells, the Chief Executive, to see what might be arranged. It appears that not a great deal can be added to what was said in our last meeting. The Mediation Scheme is progressing, but at a slower pace than any of us would have liked.'

Arbuthnot told his colleagues that Paula Vennells was not giving much away. 'She has reiterated to me that the integrity of the Mediation Scheme requires that confidentiality of cases be respected. In her letter to me she has also said that individual case details may not be shared with us at any point, including at the end of the Scheme.'

If he got the sense he might be being played, he didn't show it, finishing his email, 'I would like to believe that at the end of the Scheme we will be presented with a report which shows why and how we got to the stage where hundreds of individuals were (and still are) coming forward with their concerns and their often harrowing stories. I do believe that the Mediation Scheme has a good chance of righting things, but we shall all need clarity as to what happened and why, and how it is being put right.'

In an attempt to break the Working Group deadlock and show some progress, Sir Anthony Hooper asked Second Sight to produce an update to their 2013 Interim Report. In July and August 2014, Briefing Reports 1 and 2 were delivered.

Briefing Report 1 shed a little more light on some of the issues raised by the Interim Report, but those MPs who hadn't been following the Mediation Scheme as closely as James Arbuthnot could be forgiven for wondering what on earth Second Sight had been doing for 12 months. The language of the report is too delicate to touch on the hostilities going on behind closed doors. The most interesting paragraph addressed the issue of remote access to branch accounts.

'Post Office,' the report stated, 'has confirmed that it is their understanding that it is not, and never has been, possible for anyone to access Branch Data and amend live transactional or stock data without the knowledge of the Subpostmaster or their staff.'

This latest Post Office denial was interesting because it turned on the word 'understanding.' The Post Office *understands* remote access is not possible, but we are not told what it bases its understanding on.

Although Briefing Report 1 was largely written by Ron and Ian and didn't deviate much in tone or content from 2013's Interim Report, the Post Office refused to publish the document or make it available to journalists. As the report itself was not contentious (there were no more references to software errors, for example), it went largely unremarked by anyone outside the Mediation Scheme.

Briefing Report 2 was another matter entirely. Not just because of what it contained, but the way the Post Office chose to deal with it.

Like the Interim Report, Second Sight's second Briefing Report rattles around various aspects of the Post Office's systems and alights on areas of concern. Of the Subpostmasters Contract it says:

'We have been told by many Applicants that they were not given a copy of the 114-page Standard Contract until long after they had committed to purchase their sub-Post Office, or long after they had started work as a Subpostmaster, or even at all.'

Bearing in mind the Subpostmasters Contract formed the basis of action over liability for losses, this was perturbing.

Second Sight noted that many applicants said they only had small discrepancies before Horizon was installed. After Horizon came along, they found themselves having to cope with multi-thousand pound discrepancies.

On Subpostmaster training it comments:

'Many Applicants have reported in their CQRs that they received fewer than two days' training and were simply handed Operating Manuals for self-study and to train their counter staff.'

As far as the helpline was concerned, Second Sight reported:

'A frequently recurring response by the helpline, relating to shortfalls, is said to have been: 'Don't worry about it, it will sort itself out…' Many Applicants have reported that problems did not sort themselves out, nor was any indication given by the helpline as to how long they should wait before realising that a problem that had not sorted itself out would probably not now do so, nor how they were supposed to balance the books during the intervening period.'

Alan Bates' original complaint – that Subpostmasters simply didn't have the tools to properly interrogate their own accounts – was also confirmed in the report.

'Post Office,' it says, 'may hold Subpostmasters accountable for shortages that they are unable to fully investigate due to a lack of access to data. A Subpostmaster has very limited options in these circumstances and often has to make good losses even where the underlying root cause has not been established or understood.'

Second Sight reported that this lack of access to information escalated once a Subpostmaster had been suspended:

'Their ability to investigate transactional discrepancies, or to defend themselves against allegations made by Post Office, were often thwarted because, following their suspension (usually on the day of an audit) they were, as a matter of Post Office policy, denied access to the branch... Post Office investigators also removed records, often including personal documents such as diaries... Applicants have also reported that, despite their requests, they never regained access to any of the records they needed to prove their innocence.'

Troubling stuff. As were the conclusions about Horizon's ageing hardware and the way faulty equipment was replaced:

'This process is referred to as "kit swapouts" and principally involves the replacement of broken units with reconditioned ones. Reports of several reconditioned components or units being tried, and failing, before a working one is found, are not unusual. Many Applicants believe that faulty equipment could be responsible for otherwise unidentified shortages. Post Office's position on this is that it cannot happen.'

The most damning section was saved till last. It was about the Post Office's investigation team, which Second Sight said, 'has, in many cases, failed to identify the underlying root cause of shortfalls prior to initiating civil recovery action or criminal proceedings.'

This wasn't down to isolated lapses. The report said:

'Almost all the Professional Advisors assert that there was inadequate investigation prior to suspension (without pay); termination; or civil/criminal action.'

Second Sight were clearly drilling into the concerns MPs and the JFSA had been raising for years and essentially concluding they were correct. Briefing Report 2 spells it out:

'Post Office's investigators seem to have defaulted to seeking evidence that would support a charge of False Accounting, rather than carrying out an investigation into the root cause of any suspected problems.'

Finally, confirming Charles McLachlan's experience of talking to a Post Office investigator, Second Sight made it as plain as day that no one was looking properly at the IT.

The report states: 'Post Office's instructions to (and training of) its investigators seems to have disregarded the possibility that the Horizon system could be in any way relevant to their investigations.'

The alarm bells were now ringing loudly and clearly. Briefing Report 2 was sent to the Working Group, scheme applicants, their advisors and their MPs. The Post Office again refused to release to journalists what it insisted was a confidential document. Inevitably it was leaked, and there was a small flurry of media activity. I put a note on my blog, Private Eye ran their first article in a year, Radio 4's PM programme covered it, as did BBC North East and the BBC News website.

On 27 August, six days after the report landed, Angela van den Bogerd sent a letter to every applicant stating Second Sight's Briefing Report 2 was 'not endorsed by Post Office.'

Van den Bogerd told applicants the Post Office 'believes that the Report is inaccurate in important areas, that there is no clear statement of the evidence upon which many of the opinions expressed in the Report are based, and that it includes matters which are beyond the scope of the Scheme and/or Second Sight's professional expertise.'

To show just how much it wanted to disavow its own independent investigators, the Post Office produced a 61-page 'Reply' to Second Sight's Briefing Report 2, nearly three times the length of the document it tried to rubbish. The Reply clearly wanted to be a damning evisceration of Second Sight's work. Instead it comes across like a clumsy legalistic moan. It starts by developing the themes outlined in Angela van den Bogerd's letter – that Second Sight's conclusions are not conclusive enough. Then it states where Second Sight do offer an opinion, they are either not qualified to make it, or if they *are* qualified, they shouldn't be making them because they are outside the scheme's scope.

The Post Office had spent the previous 12 months giving applicants the runaround by displaying a sluggish reluctance to hand over documents and process Second Sight's requests for evidence. Now it was using Second Sight's inability to reach evidenced conclusions due to being given the runaround as a stick to beat them with.

The Reply is particularly dismissive of the problems Subpostmasters raised regarding cash machines,[1] stating, 'The Report suggests that Applicants also found it difficult to account for cash being dispensed from ATMs. Little evidence is presented to support this view … there is no evidence to support the Report's view that the ATM accounting procedure was too complex.'

It concludes problems with ATMs and the support the Post Office gives its Subpostmasters to operate them 'has not been shown to be a thematic issue.'

Less than a year previously, the secret Detica report stated that 'losses from ATMs have been one of the major concerns of the Post Office.' Hmm.

The report and its rebuttal, kindly sent to me by a number of sources, meant I finally had documentary evidence to corroborate everything I had been hearing for most of 2014 – there had been a massive dust-up between the Post Office and its own investigators. It was time to try to get another film made.

---

1 Also known as Automated Teller Machines, or ATMs.

INSIDE OUT SOUTH THE SEQUEL

I took what I knew back to Jane French at Inside Out, giving her a blow-by-blow account of the previous few months' machinations.

The top line felt pretty strong: a publicly-owned institution stood accused of conspiring to criminalise or sack dozens of innocent people. Now it was spending hundreds of thousands of pounds on a wide-ranging investigation it was simultaneously trying to sabotage.

Despite our problems with access to the Subpostmasters on the Mediation Scheme, Jane agreed it made sense to commission a new film. This time, she wondered, instead of making it specific to the South region, we might be able to get buy-in from other Inside Out regions by offering to produce several versions of the same film, using case studies relevant to their own region.

Jane assigned her assistant editor, Jane Goddard, as film-maker, and detailed one of the team's young staff producers, Tim Robinson, to help me with research. I knew Jane Goddard well – she would get involved in the film as we moved towards putting together a shooting schedule, but Tim was an unknown quantity. He'd been seconded to Inside Out from the BBC South newsroom and was still in his twenties, making me feel ancient. It was the first time I'd been given an opportunity to work closely with any other journalist on the Post Office story. I hoped we would hit it off.

We went for lunch. Over a baked potato in the BBC South staff canteen, I explained the bare bones of the current and historical situation. Tim quickly grasped its significance and seemed enthusiastic about getting stuck in. Neither of us had any idea what the next three months would do to us.

Jane French decided that revisiting the Post Office story would make a good start to the new series of Inside Out in January 2015. I wasn't sure this was a good idea. I was worried a canny newspaper journalist would get a sniff of what was happening and scoop us. The Briefing Report 2 rebuttal, like the initial report, had gone to every applicant on the scheme, their MPs and the JFSA. I figured it would be in the hands of other hacks who might be beavering away somewhere readying a big exclusive. After all, this was a massive story, right?

Tim was a godsend. He had the ability to find and recognise key evidential details and then call them to mind, at will. He dived straight in and started making calls.

With Jane French's permission, I approached Matt Prodger to see if he would be interested in getting BBC network news involved. I thought this could become a collaborative project, with the investigation driven by Inside Out in the South, but made fully national by the buy-in from other regions and the involvement of network news.

If we got everything aligned, we could co-ordinate our schedule so Matt would have enough material to put the story out nationally on the day the Inside Out investigations were broadcast. He would get a strong news line and the regional Inside Out output would get a huge plug. Everybody wins. Matt was receptive to the idea.

Keen to make sure we hadn't missed anything important, Tim and I started amassing all the published material we could find on the Post Office story.

Tim decided to try to find at least one person in every BBC TV region who:

- was on the Mediation Scheme
- had a compelling story to tell
- would be prepared to go on camera

But we had a problem. All the Subpostmasters we contacted had promised not to talk to any journalists whilst the Mediation Scheme was ongoing. Seema was not answering my calls and Jo said she would have to refer any decision about talking to me to Alan Bates.

I gave Alan a call. I was expecting him to refuse point blank to allow any Subpostmasters to deal with me until the mediation process was over, but I could not have been more wrong. He suggested a meeting.

MEETING ALAN BATES

I felt I had got to know Alan reasonably well over the four years we'd been in contact, but I hadn't met him face-to-face. He lives in North Wales, which is a five-hour drive from where I live in Surrey. If he'd been willing to let me point a camera at him, I might have had an excuse to come and find him sooner. He hadn't, so we didn't.

On 7 October 2014, we finally met in the café at Dobbies Garden Centre just off the A5 at Shrewsbury. Tim drove us up from Southampton in BBC South's shiny white stake-out van, which was dubbed the Mystery Machine.

When we arrived, Alan was sitting at a table with two other people. As we approached, he rose to introduce us to Mohamed and Rubbina Shaheen, a careworn middle-aged couple with their own appalling story to tell. Rubbina and Mohamed had run the Greenfields Post Office in Shrewsbury. Rubbina was the nominated Subpostmaster. Their nightmare began in 2009, and it followed the usual unexplained discrepancy, suspension, sacking and criminal prosecution pathway, but Rubbina's story was particularly awful.

Eleven days after Seema was sent to prison in 2010, Rubbina appeared at Shrewsbury Crown Court. She had originally been charged with theft and false accounting. Internal records show Post Office lawyers wrote with annoyance that she had employed solicitors 'who have jumped on the Horizon bandwagon.' The same document goes on to state it is 'absolutely vital' they 'win' their case against her because 'failure could bring the whole of the Royal Mail system down.'

Rubbina accepted the plea bargain offered by the Post Office prosecutors. In exchange for a guilty plea to false accounting the Post Office dropped the theft charge. Despite pleading guilty to false accounting, Rubbina was sent to prison for 12 months. Whilst Rubbina was being prosecuted, their home was repossessed by their bank and sold at auction. On Rubbina's release, the couple spent six weeks sleeping in a van. A good 'win' for the Post Office.

A kindly neighbour found Rubbina and Mohamed and let them use the facilities in his home whilst they were struggling to get back on their feet. Eventually they found a roof over their heads, and when I met them, they were attempting to rebuild their lives. Rubbina had a kindly, empathetic manner and Mohamed, with his chunky cardigan, checked shirt and neatly clipped moustache, was a true gentleman. It was almost impossible to imagine them living like vagrants. They were the embodiment of respectable, personable citizens in late middle-age. As I spoke to them I did start to wonder why Asian Subpostmasters seemed to be getting far more punitive sentences than their white counterparts.[1] What possible benefit could have been gained by putting Rubbina in prison?

We chatted over a cup of tea. I found Rubbina and Mohamed to be really good company and was delighted they had come to meet us, but I was still equally keen to use Alan's time to grill him about the politics of the Mediation Scheme.

Tim sensed this, and suggested he took Rubbina and Mohamed to a separate table to hear more about their story.

Alan and I settled down to talk. I explained that I fully understood his reluctance to say anything on the record for fear of further scuppering the Mediation Scheme, but it was clear from what I had been hearing since the beginning of the year (now confirmed by the Post Office's rebuttal) that the Post Office was at loggerheads with Second Sight.

I explained that this was a huge story, but if no one from the Post Office, Second Sight or the JFSA was prepared to talk about it, it was going to be very difficult to tell on television.

There was also the looming problem of applicant confidentiality agreements. Individual Postmasters weren't yet bound by confidentiality, but if they signed up to a settlement agreement, they might be.

I was concerned that applicants who might be free to talk in limited circumstances whilst awaiting mediation could find themselves signing a wider gagging agreement as part of any mediated compensation payment. This might stop them from talking about their experiences.

Alan gave a hollow chuckle. 'The way things are going,' he said, 'I would be surprised if any applicants get a satisfactory mediation, let alone compensation.'

Knowing how much trust JFSA members put in Alan and how much influence he had over them, I wondered if he might be able to help us out. Not just by relaxing his 'no journalists' contact rule, but by putting us

---

1 A suspicion which has continued to grow. I have not yet been able to properly investigate this in any quantifiable way, but from my anecdotal experience, non-white Subpostmasters generally seem to have received harsher sentences than their white counterparts for similar crimes. It is an area requiring proper academic investigation.

in touch with Mediation Scheme applicants whose stories could give our investigation even bigger impact.

I started suggesting a few names. I had got to hear about Martin Griffiths' terrible situation and wondered if his family would speak. I was also interested in Tom Brown and Sue Knight – two Subpostmasters from opposite ends of the country whose prosecutions had been dropped immediately following the Interim Report's publication. At that time neither of us had any idea about the Clarke Advice or the Cartwright King Sift Review.

I plugged away, pointing out how much individual Subpostmasters valued journalists highlighting their stories and scrutinising what the Post Office had put them through. And of course, I renewed my pitch to get Alan on camera. I'd seen the 2009 Taro Naw documentary and told him how good an interviewee he was.

Alan listened politely, then reached into his bag. 'Here,' he said. 'I've got something for you.'

Alan produced a dictaphone. 'I've been contacted by someone who used to work at Fujitsu. He got in touch with me through the JFSA website. I'll play you our conversation, but you can't have it.'

'Can I take notes?' I asked.

'Sure,' he said.

I wished I had shorthand. Alan was enjoying giving me the big reveal, but as he was about to switch the machine on, he suddenly looked defensive.

'I maybe didn't ask him all the sort of questions I should. I was probably trying not to scare him off and…'

I assured Alan I would not judge his interviewing technique. He pressed play and I started scribbling.

Alan's correspondent described working at Fujitsu in Bracknell between 2001 and 2004. He had been third tier support for the Horizon system and he wanted to help. It was my first, albeit indirect, contact with Richard Roll.

The recording ended. Alan put his recorder away and gave me a 'what-do-you-think-of-that?' face.

'What's his name?' I asked.

'I'm not telling you,' Alan replied. 'I'm saving that for when you get a Panorama.'

Great, I thought.

By the time we finished our tea and cake at Dobbies I still wasn't quite sure why Alan had called the meeting. He didn't pass on any documentation, and if he wanted to he could quite easily have played the whistle-blower audio to me down the phone. Maybe he just wanted to check me and Tim out before agreeing to anything.

Within a couple of days, Alan came good. He put us in contact with Sue Knight and he also gave us the number of a former Subpostmaster called Pam Stubbs who ran the Barkham Post Office near Reading. Both said they would be happy to do an interview. Sue lived on The Lizard in Cornwall. Featuring her in our film meant we might be able to get some buy-in from BBC South West.

Whilst I was making plans to do some filming in Berkshire and Cornwall, Tim spoke to former NFSP executive member-turned CWU Subpostmaster rep, Mark Baker. Mark gave Tim the details of a serving Subpostmaster, Steve Phillips, from a small town called Nelson, near Caerphilly in South Wales. Steve had a discrepancy of just over £18,000. The Post Office had sent him a letter demanding he settle the discrepancy out of his own pocket. Steve was refusing on the grounds it was almost certainly Horizon playing up.

Before going to see Pam Stubbs, I gave her a call.

PAM STUBBS

Between August 1999 and June 2010, Pam Stubbs was Subpostmaster in Barkham, a village almost completely subsumed by the town of Wokingham in Berkshire.

Pam was a grammar school girl with a talent for sport. She went to the Chelsea College of Physical Education in Eastbourne and had in a previous career been a PE teacher. She is a doughty, no-nonsense sort.

From 1987 to 1999 Pam ran the retail side of Barkham Post Office with her Subpostmaster husband Martin, a former manager at the Bank of England. Pam and Martin bought the Post Office when Martin took early retirement. He'd served at the Bank for more than 25 years and was ready for a change.

Running the Post Office was a culture shock for the Stubbs. Martin was from dashing officer-class stock (his father was a fighter pilot) and she had spent 18 years teaching in a convent; but they both felt running a Post Office was a rather romantic way to spend their mid-life together.

The Post Office they inherited wasn't doing well, so Pam and Martin put their backs into making it a going concern. It involved a huge amount of work and very early mornings, but they turned the retail operation round and the business thrived. Pam and Martin were natural pillars of the community. They joined Bearwood Lakes golf club. Martin was elected a county councillor.

All was going well until Martin was diagnosed with stomach cancer in the autumn of 1998. He died 11 months later. Pam was devastated. She could have thrown in the towel and moved away, but she didn't want to go somewhere nobody knew him. She made the decision to stay and keep the shop and Post Office going.

Pam was made Postmaster on 4 August 1999, the day after Martin died. Nothing would be the same after losing the love of her life, but Pam worked through her grief. She knew how to run the Post Office counter, she knew her customers and she knew her husband would have been thrilled at the way she picked up the reins.

Pam was a brilliant Subpostmaster. The business continued to go from strength to strength. A lot of local companies used the Barkham Post Office for depositing money and shipping their products to customers. Like her husband, Pam was a natural at book-keeping, and when

Horizon arrived in 2000, she was looking forward to seeing what it could do.

Unfortunately, the engineers who installed Horizon, rewiring Pam's fuse board in the process, did not do their jobs properly. Pam's counter, shop and home all began to suffer regular power outages. One day Pam had 36 power cuts, requiring a Horizon reboot every time. Her branch account balance began to fluctuate. Pam, who had balanced to the penny pretty much every week, was now facing a £1,000 shortfall in her accounts. She called the Post Office. Initially, they refused to send anyone out to look at the problem. Eventually, someone called Frank Manning arranged for an electrician to go to Barkham. The electrician reported back saying there were problems, but before these were revealed to Pam, Mr Manning went on a site visit himself.

Afterwards, Manning wrote an email to his colleagues, telling them he was 'too scared to accept a cup of tea in case the Horizon system crashed 'cos the electricity supply is still a live (excuse the pun) issue… The balances are a mess … I worry that something like 25 reboots in one day is having an effect overall … she [Pam] keeps getting promises of attention – but nothing is actually being done now to clear up the problem.'

To make things crystal clear, Manning uses bold type to state in his email '**It is Horizon related** – the problems have only arisen since install and the postmistress is now barking, and rightly so in my view.'

Mr Manning's colleague replied the following day. 'Can you confirm,' she wrote, 'that the office have had an independent electrician visit it and that the problems are due to the electrics input by Horizon?'

'Yes and yes,' replied Manning.

Pam was not told about this exchange and received no further help from the Post Office which simply insisted there was nothing amiss with Horizon and that her £1,000 discrepancy was a debt to be paid.

Pam eventually resolved the problem by contacting her electricity company and telling them she thought there might be something wrong with the supply coming into the building. An engineer was dispatched. He detached her meter, tested it and wired everything back up to Pam's fuse board. The power fluctuations disappeared and everything ran smoothly thereafter. Pam was still saddled with a £1,000 discrepancy, which she reluctantly paid out.

Thereafter, Pam and her assistants operated the two Horizon terminals at Barkham Post Office without a problem for eight years. Occasionally she would be a few quid down or a few quid up, but it was never a large amount.

In 2009, Pam marked a decade of running the Barkham Post Office without Martin. She took stock.

Pam was, by this stage, a district councillor and chair of Barkham Parish Council. Money was coming in and things were going well, but Pam felt it was time to retire. She decided to sell the retail business and pass on the title of Subpostmaster to a deserving successor.

But there was a problem. Whilst trade was good, the Barkham Post Office building itself wasn't in good nick. Although it had a great location (on the main Bearwood Road about a mile outside Wokingham), Pam's house wasn't very modern, and Pam felt the shop itself was poky and old-fashioned.

Before selling the business, Pam got an architect in and applied for permission to flatten the original building and build a new one, complete with decent living premises above it.

Pam spoke to the Post Office about her plans. They agreed the proposal, and to ensure business continuity once Pam's building work had begun, they came to an arrangement.

The Post Office would source and deliver (at Pam's expense) a Portacabin, which would be placed on the car-parking apron in front of Pam's Post Office. The Portacabin would become the new, temporary, Barkham Post Office. Pam would sell a few retail essentials (as space allowed) and at the back, behind a secure, glass-fronted counter, there would be a single operational Horizon terminal.

The move from the old shop to the Portacabin was scheduled for October 2009. A security team was booked by the Post Office to help Pam shift the cash out of her safe into a new temporary safe (supplied by the Post Office, again at Pam's expense) which would go in the Portacabin.

Despite their promises, on the allotted day, no one from the Post Office was present to help Pam make the move. When it became apparent no security team was going to turn up, Pam had to shift the cash herself using her builders as protection.

No instructions were given, nor was any training provided with the new safe. Pam was not made aware it had an automatic time lock. Once the cash had been put in the safe, Pam struggled to get it out.

The engineers from Fujitsu arrived to relocate the Horizon terminal. This was done with little ceremony and no testing, other than to establish a network connection.

From the day Pam moved in to the Portacabin and opened for business, her Horizon terminal started throwing up problems. After the first two weeks' trading Pam's accounts were showing a negative discrepancy of £400. At the end of the next trading period there was £2,500 cash 'missing.'

Pam was aghast. Unable to find out what had gone wrong, she called the helpline. Pam was told it would sort itself out, but if she wanted to balance the books she would need to put her own money into the till. She did so.

December 2009 brought a pretty fierce drop in temperature, and whilst Pam did her best to keep her Post Office open, the snow and cold kept customers away. Pam found herself closing early or not opening the Portacabin Post Office at all. Between Christmas and New Year, when trade is quiet anyway, Pam shut up shop completely to enjoy the holiday period and attend her daughter's wedding.

As Pam did the accounts on 6 January, she found herself with a cash discrepancy of more than £9,000.

'At that point,' she said, 'I just freaked. I had been calling the helpline the whole time. There was no way that money could have gone.'

Pam was advised to settle centrally. This meant she was legally accepting the accounts showing on Horizon were correct and if the Post Office decided the discrepancy was her responsibility, she would be liable for it.

Pam thought the source of the discrepancy was pretty obvious. After eight years of perfectly normal operation, the Horizon terminal which had been transferred from her branch to the Portacabin was playing up. To her detriment.

Yet she kept being told it was her shortage and her problem. As far as the Post Office and Fujitsu were concerned, there was nothing wrong with Horizon.

Eventually Pam spoke to a helpful lady at the Post Office who told her that she could dispute her discrepancy. Pam thought this was exactly what she was doing, but apparently without stating explicitly that she wanted to take things to a formal dispute, it wouldn't happen. Pam put her discrepancy into formal dispute.

Pam re-opened her Portacabin after the Christmas break and continued to trade into January 2010.

At the end of January 2010, Pam did another balance. She was a further £26,000 down. She called the Post Office helpline. She drew their attention to the fact she had bagged up and 'remmed out' £26,000 for return to a Post Office cash centre on 5 January. She had the Horizon printed receipt, and the sum had been confirmed as being received by the cash centre. The Post Office referred Pam to the Horizon helpline. Her call was escalated. The Horizon back-end had no record of the transaction. The helpline operator asked for the transaction number on Pam's receipt. She gave it to them. Eventually the Horizon team found the rem out. Pam's £26,000 'debt' was cancelled by a transaction correction (and never raised or acknowledged by the Post Office again), but there was still January's discrepancy of £9,000.

One of the quirks of Horizon at the time was that unless a printed receipt for some transactions was positively requested by the operator, it wasn't produced. Subpostmasters could, however, request a print-out of all transactions going back over a specific period of time, which Pam did, ending up with a box 'the size of a small suitcase' filled with rolls of 3.5 inch wide Horizon printer paper. This detailed every single transaction from 17 November 2009, which she divided into weekly bundles.

'At the time,' she said, 'I didn't know what I was going to do with them because it looked like so much jumbled rubbish. But when it was quiet, after my daughter had got married and gone away on honeymoon, I just sat down and went through them slowly, looking at the receipts to see what they showed.'

Using the overnight balance as a starting point Pam noted any cash deposits or any cash withdrawals during that day which were £50 or over. She also noted the value of any rems in or rems out. Then she would look at the balance at the end of the following day to see how closely it matched the manual calculations she had been making. They were never going to tally exactly because Pam chose not to look at small cash transactions, card payments, stamp purchases and so on, but Pam found that even using her rather crude method, every single day she was trading between 17 November and the end of January, her figures were within 'spitting distance' of the overnight cash figures reported by Horizon. This demonstrated to Pam that there was simply 'no opportunity for £9,000 cash to go missing.'

Behind the counter, during opening hours, Pam started positively requesting a receipt for every transaction she made. She completed regular daily balance snapshots where she would manually count the cash and stock at her branch and then request Horizon deliver an electronic balance. This was the best way to try to narrow the window during which a discrepancy could be generated without being noticed.

Pam also made the next accounting period a short one. Instead of waiting to the end of the month, Pam totted everything up on 13 February. A further £8,000 had disappeared. Pam was extremely distressed.

In the next trading period, Horizon reported a cash surplus of £155. At the end of the next, a loss of nearly £1,000.

Pam says by this stage she was on first name terms with a woman at the helpline who seemed determined to do what she could to help her, but who was essentially powerless. She kept referring Pam's problems further up the line for further investigation, but Pam got nothing back.

Eventually Pam's contract manager, Nigel Allen, ordered a Post Office auditor into the branch. On 19 May 2010, Rajinder Gahir spent the morning in Pam's Portacabin. He watched as she made a cash declaration at 9am. Mr Gahir then witnessed every transaction Pam did for four hours, sitting on a stool next to her in the cramped space behind the Horizon terminal so he could see exactly what buttons she was pressing and in which order. At 1pm he watched Pam make another cash declaration. She was £190 down.

Mr Gahir had no explanation for this. 'He'd watched me. And he said, "Oh no, this can't happen." But it had. I said, "There are ten sessions in a week and if the same thing happened in ten sessions, that's a couple of thousand pounds." '

Gahir wondered if perhaps Pam was pressing the touchscreen's buttons 'too quickly', and promised to report this theory to Mr Allen for further investigation. Pam heard nothing more about this theory. If it was investigated, Pam wasn't told about any conclusion.

On 15 May Pam's trading statement showed a £5,000 'loss' on top of the £17,000 she already had in dispute.

Pam kept going back to the paper receipts. 'I asked continually if the Horizon people could check their data with mine. This was absolutely refused. Right from 6 January onwards, they would not do it. It was apparently impossible. It couldn't be done. The mantra was "Horizon is correct. You're wrong. There's no point in checking it because it's your fault." '

I asked Pam what the Post Office thought was going on.

'They thought someone was stealing the money. Or that I was making such massive errors ... say someone was paying in £5,000 and I was only recording £1,000. But customers tend to notice if you make that kind of mistake.'

I asked if anyone could be stealing the money.

'Well, I had one counter assistant [but] she would rather have shot herself than take any money. Whatever was going on had nothing to do with her. I checked her work. I basically kept a tight hold on the cash so I knew what should be there.'

The Post Office sent another auditor to do a full 'audit.' Pam explained how it worked.

'They do all their figures on their own laptop, and then at the end of it they say, "These are the figures that we have. All we have to do now is put them on your terminal and they will come up with the same figures, but they will now be on your Horizon terminal." He did exactly that and it came up different. I was a further £386.86 shorter on Horizon than I was according to his laptop. And he said, "No – that's wrong. The figures have to be the same because I've inputted them on my laptop. All I've done is transfer them to your terminal." Well … he and I spent nearly four hours re-inputting his figures with me checking. Then with both of us inputting the figures and double checking and it still came up with this £386.86 difference between the total on his laptop and my Horizon terminal. And he said, "You're just going to have to accept the Horizon figures." And I thought, "Why?"'

When Pam's audit report came through, the unexplained £386.86 loss was described on the ledger as 'adjustments out of office.'

'They just accepted it. They said, "Oh it was an error." They didn't say whose error, or what the error was. It was just an error. Which was then tacked on to the amount I supposedly owed.'

In her reserved manner, Pam told me she was getting 'more than a little cross' by this stage.

'All my customers knew about it, because I was in a tiny little space in the Portacabin. There's nowhere to hide. And when you're behind the counter in tears, your customers can see you.'

The stand-off continued. Eventually a letter arrived from the Post Office. 'It quoted Section 12:12 in my contract which stated I was responsible for any losses. I dug out my contract and read Section 12. It said I was responsible for losses caused by my negligence. And I had yet to see single bit of proof from the Post Office that I had been negligent.'

Pam wrote back asking the Post Office to demonstrate her negligence.

'I said, "Just show me where I wasn't following procedure. Show me."

And they have never done it.'

She persevered. 'I had called Nigel Allen on day one. And I was calling him again and again, but the message came back, "Nigel Allen does not get involved in balance issues." I offered to send him a copy of the summary of my overnight cash figures from my transaction logs. And he sent back another message saying it was "not his area of expertise." All I got was several letters from him quoting Section 12:12 of the contract.'

Eventually, Nigel Allen *did* call Pam and told her to start doing cash declarations (that is, totting up how much money and stock she held in her branch and tallying it against Horizon's figures) three times a day. If Pam was more than £50 out on any declaration, she should contact him.

'So I rang him up three times a day. Because it was more than £50 out three times a day.'

On 8 June an auditor turned up unannounced at Pam's Portacabin. Pam asked if he had come to do another audit.

'Yes,' he said. 'A closing audit.'

Pam was declared £28,000 short of cash. She was suspended on the spot. She never worked for the Post Office again.

The Barkham Portacabin was closed for two weeks, but it was not powered down. Pam is convinced during this period her Horizon terminal was fixed remotely.

A new temporary Subpostmaster was installed in the Portacabin. He balanced to zero every night without a problem.

When the building work on Pam's new house and shop was finished the Horizon terminal was shifted back behind her purpose-built counter.

'The Fujitsu engineers came the day before and powered the Horizon terminal down. They did a series of checks while they were powering it down. The Subby [temporary Subpostmaster] was told not to touch it. They came back again on the day it was moved and did more checks. They moved it into the new Post Office, powered it up, did more checks, tested it and again told the Subby not to touch it again until the next day. Then they came in the next day, did further checks and only then told him he could use it.'

As Pam watched the fuss that was being made of the Horizon terminal transfer into what was no longer her Post Office she struck up a conversation with one of the Fujitsu engineers. He was part of the team who moved the Horizon terminal out to the Portacabin. Pam vaguely knew him from previous visits he had made to Barkham to replace faulty

Horizon components before her troubles began.

'I said to him, "This is a bit different to what happened last October when we moved out, isn't it?" '

According to Pam, the engineer replied, 'Well – I didn't say this, and I can't say it, because I want to keep my job – but they discovered that moving terminals about without proper safeguards was causing faults.'

Pam did not take the engineer's name and didn't want to escalate the conversation because she didn't want the engineer to lose his job. But it further corroborated the evidence of her own eyes.

Whilst the Post Office was being moved from the Portacabin into the new premises, Pam also managed to rescue some important paperwork.

'I saw the temporary Subpostmaster carrying boxes of Post Office material out of the Post Office to the bins. I said, "What are you doing?!" and he actually said, "The Post Office have told me to throw away anything that doesn't relate to me and my time here." So they were telling him to throw away all of the weekly reports, and all of the trading statements which had been generated during the period the Post Office was being run from the Portacabin. And I thought, "This is ridiculous! You're meant to keep those for two years!" You have to. You're obligated to. So I said, "Do you mind if I have those?" and he said, "No – please take them." '

They didn't help. Like so many suspended Subpostmasters before her, Pam was left in limbo, running the retail side of her business, waiting for the Post Office to do something.

The Post Office continued to maintain its position that neither it nor Horizon was to blame for Pam's discrepancies. Pam maintained she had done nothing wrong and no one had provided any evidence to suggest she had.

'I was called for an interview with the Post Office investigation unit in January 2011 and I was required to go to our local Crown Office and be interviewed by their local fraud investigator. We talked for hours. I was allowed to take somebody with me, so I took a friend from the parish council who was also a professor of computing.'

The investigator was sent away with a flea in his ear.

Pam was not informed of the outcome of the interview – which was that there was no fraud and no action should be taken – until many years later. From the Post Office at the time, she heard nothing at all.

The stand-off continued until Pam realised she was never going to be reinstated. She started making plans to sell the business early. In order to do this Pam had to hand in her notice. The business was eventually sold in April 2011. The Post Office presented her with a final bill of £36,000 plus interest. Pam refused to give them a penny, saying it remained in dispute. She did not hear from the Post Office again until she applied to the Mediation Scheme.

Pam had no idea there were other Subpostmasters in a similar situation until her accountant handed her a local newspaper cutting which wrote up BBC Inside Out South's broadcast in February 2011. Pam was the author of one of the emails we received in response to the programme, which is how she had been put in touch with the JFSA.

By the time I spoke to her in late 2014, Pam was one of the few people to have actually completed her mediation process, and she had a lot to say about it.

Pam had not false accounted. She had not been sacked. She had not been sued. She did not have a criminal conviction. It was self-evident she had been treated very badly.

Pam had also collected huge volumes of paperwork. Documentary evidence of both missing transactions and inexplicable entries in her Horizon account which could not possibly have been her fault.

Tim and I parked the Mystery Machine on Pam's sloping drive at her house in Barkham, just a few minutes walk from her former Post Office. It was a cold and dark November afternoon. We were greeted at the door by two noisy dogs. They were hushed away and soon Pam, Tim and I were sitting in her front room having a cup of tea. Pam patiently took us through the episode whereby Horizon 'lost' £26,000 she had remmed out.

Despite being a tiny Post Office, even when she was in the Portacabin, Pam always had a cash surplus. Barkham is quite a well-to-do location and there wasn't much to pay out in the way of cash benefits. Pam also had several business customers, who liked and trusted her. They would give her their daily cash takings which could amount to tens of thousands of pounds a week. As a result Pam insisted the Post Office arrange twice-weekly cash collections to ensure she was never holding too much money in her safe.

On 5 January 2010 Pam bagged up £26,000 into two separate pouches (the maximum allowed in each pouch was £25,000), ready for the CashCo man. Pam ran through the remming out procedure on Horizon. First she told Horizon what was going to be in each pouch. Horizon printed out four receipts – two receipts per pouch. The four letter Horizon code for this sequence of actions is known as ROST (Rem Out STandby).

Each of the four receipts was signed. Each pouch had a signed receipt placed inside it. The remaining two receipts were retained by Pam. When the cash was counted and placed inside the pouches Pam sealed them. Once sealed, they are nominally tamper-proof.

When the man from CashCo arrived, Pam told Horizon the pouches were about to be dispatched. The four letter code for this sequence of actions is RODP (Rem Out DisPatched). Horizon printed one sticky, barcoded label for each pouch. The barcoded labels were stuck to the pouches.

The CashCo man used his barcode scanner to scan the barcodes on each pouch. This confirmed his receipt of the pouches. Pam used her barcode scanner to scan the CashCo man's ID card barcode and the barcodes on the pouches. Horizon printed two receipts. These confirmed the rem out, or RODP. Horizon should, at this point, have taken £26,000 off Pam's cash balance. The CashCo man and Pam signed each receipt and retained one each. Pam found and showed us the physical Horizon receipt for this transaction.

The following week, with more cash in the safe needing to be taken off the premises, Pam prepared two new pouches for dispatch. When the CashCo man arrived she set up an RODP on Horizon. But instead of printing off two barcode stickers for the two pouches Pam was about to rem out, Horizon printed off four stickers with four barcodes on. The latter two barcodes corresponded to the two pouches which Pam was about to rem out. The first two barcodes corresponded to the pouches which were prepared and remmed out the previous week. According to Horizon, the pouches, and therefore the cash, were still in the Barkham Post Office safe awaiting dispatch. If Pam were to be audited at that moment, there would be a £26,000 loss at her branch – the difference between the sum Horizon thought she should be holding and the actual amount of cash on the premises.

Pam was stunned. She showed the CashCo man the receipt she and his colleague had signed the previous week, confirming the rem out. He accepted this was evidence that the money has already been remmed out. Later that day, CashCo confirmed they received the £26,000 on the Friday it was dispatched.

Yet Horizon thought the £26,000 was still in the Barkham Post Office safe.

As we know, this episode came to a sensible conclusion. Once Pam informed the Post Office of the Horizon error and they received confirmation from CashCo that the cash had indeed been remmed out and received, Pam was sent a transaction correction which manually changed her balance to acknowledge the remming out of the £26,000. But no one ever explained to Pam how or why it had or could have happened.

Pam also showed us another interesting photocopy which had been thrown up by a disclosure request she made during the mediation process. It was taken from an internal Post Office email discussion.

On 13 September 2010, during the long period after her suspension when Pam had no idea what was going on, Pam's contract manager, Nigel Allen, emailed Mark Dinsdale at the Post Office investigations team, pushing for the heavy mob.

'Mrs Stubbs … is alleging that her losses of 28k+ are due to problems with the Horizon system after it was relocated into a Portacabin last October whilst the branch was being renovated… Given the fact that we have not experienced similar losses with the temporary SPMR who was appointed after Mrs Stubbs was suspended and the same Horizon kit is being used, shouldn't we be asking her some very searching questions under caution?'

Mark Dinsdale replied:

'This is quickly turning into a bit of a problem… I don't know why we were never approached to deal with this as a criminal investigation in the first instance, perhaps it was felt that it wasn't at the time. The auditor supposedly witnessed all transactions for half a day and witnessed Horizon being short, thereby corroborating her account and also now a potential witness for her… This now leaves us in a very difficult situation. With the SPMR writing letters to Dave Smith [the Post Office Managing Director at the time], her MP and no doubt countless other people, this is high profile. She has also joined the SPMR's fight to question the integrity of Horizon. As it stands no investigation has taken place by us, various interventions have probably complicated this, yet because it is a question of Horizon integrity we can't simply ignore it, or drop it, but probably have some difficult questions ahead of us in terms of why has it taken so long for us to consider this criminal if this is the course of action we take.'

Dinsdale was bemoaning the fact that the Post Office support team had sent anyone in to help Pam, because all it did was corroborate her account. This, in his view, was clearly a bad thing. He seemed to be telling Mr Allen that if no one had tried to help Pam, but instead had informed him, he would have been able to start a criminal investigation earlier and the Post Office would be in a much stronger position to prosecute – the preferred method of getting back their 'missing' £28,000.

The note about it being a high profile case suggested Dinsdale thought it was going to be much harder for the Post Office to isolate Pam and pick her off. Notice a discussion about actual evidence of theft is entirely absent.

Did the Post Office *ever* consider that Pam could be right and Horizon could be the problem? The answer comes in an email lower down the chain, Nigel Allen told another Post Office employee, Andrew Winn, that 'according to Fujitsu there are no software issues at the branch,' to which Andrew Winn replied, 'It may be worth getting something in writing from Fujitsu' to that effect. No further queries. So that's that.

Unable to prosecute without any evidence and hindered by a potential Post Office employee who would probably support Pam's assertions that she was doing nothing wrong, the Post Office decided to leave Pam in limbo: suspended, accused of breaking her contract and facing demands for a sum which eventually (and again, mystifyingly) rose to £36,000.

We drank Pam's tea, watched her hunt about for relevant bits of paperwork and became more engrossed with everything she told us. Once we had finished hearing the true awfulness of Pam's suspension and departure from the Post Office we asked about her experience of the Mediation Scheme. Until this point, what actually happened on the scheme had been shrouded in secrecy. Alan Bates, Working Group member and co-architect of the scheme, was not formally notified of the outcome of any mediation, and the campaigning Subpostmasters we knew well were still reluctant to talk on the record because they hadn't got close to being mediated.

Now we were sitting in front of someone who had been through the whole process.

In Pam's view it was a total sham.

'The lady from CEDR[1] was very good,' Pam told us. 'She did try to keep absolutely neutral on both sides. But she rang the Post Office the day before we were due to meet. And she asked the Post Office mediation representative what authority they would have when they came to negotiate. And she said their answer was "None." They said, "We have no authority to do anything." '

Pam paused to sip her tea. 'And the lady from CEDR was horrified, because the whole point of mediation is that you are trying to create a situation where you can agree a resolution. So she told them to jolly well go away and get some authority and not come to the mediation meeting without it.'

I asked Pam to describe what talking to the Post Office face-to-face was like.

---

[1] The mediator. CEDR stands for Centre for Effective Dispute Resolution. The acronym is pronounced 'See-dur.'

'It was … well … they were so dismissive of everything I had to say. They wouldn't even let me read to the end of my opening statement.'

Tim and I filmed a short interview with Pam, thanked her for her time and said our goodbyes. It was dark by the time we left and there was a wintry rain coming down. The Barkham road was busy with commuter traffic. We fired up the Mystery Machine and joined the flow. The next day, at Inside Out South's base in Southampton we explained what we had to our colleagues. The two Janes suggested Tim and I pitch the story to The One Show, BBC1's wildly successful prime-time magazine programme. A hastily arranged visit to London went well enough for The One Show executive editor Sandy Smith to commission and fund two films about the Post Office Horizon story. One would explain the background, the other would explain the recent, crazy developments.

MPS BREAK COVER

In parliament, the MPs who had been content to let the Mediation Scheme play out were obviously alarmed to receive the Post Office's letter disavowing Second Sight's second briefing report. For some it would be the first real sense that things were going badly wrong. The more active MPs were being given extra information by a number of sources, including their own constituents. James Arbuthnot was worried enough to call a summit.

On 17 November 2014, a group led by James Arbuthnot, Andrew Bridgen, Oliver Letwin and Mike Wood were met by a four-strong delegation from the Post Office: Paula Vennells, Mark Davies (the Post Office's Director of Communications), Chris Aujard and Angela van den Bogerd. Alan Bates was also present. He had addressed the MPs before Vennells and her team arrived. Bates painted a bleak picture – the Post Office was refusing to release documents to Second Sight, it was refusing to allow convicted claimants to go forward to mediation (despite the terms of the Mediation Scheme expressly accepting convicted claimants) and it was insisting the Working Group should be involved in deciding which cases went through to mediation.

James Arbuthnot remembers Chris Aujard and Angela van den Bogerd being the most vocal of the Post Office representatives. He told me Paula Vennells 'sat quietly, almost subserviently, by' – strange behaviour for a chief executive. In fact, Arbuthnot says Vennells appeared to be 'embarrassed that Angela van den Bogerd and Chris Aujard were undermining the entire basis of the discussions we had been having for more than two years.'

It was, of course, open to Vennells to step in and say something, but, according to Arbuthnot, she chose to remain almost mute.

'She knew what she was doing to Second Sight,' Andrew Bridgen told me, 'and there's only one reason for that. We were watching an arm of government ... attempting a cover-up. I completely despised her.'

The occasion was not a happy one. Bates and the MPs repeatedly raised their concerns, but the Post Office would not be moved on the issue of convicted claimants. The issue of trying to force all decisions about mediation through the Working Group was the only area Vennells appeared to give any ground. She said she would take the MPs' request away and consider it.

'I walked out of the room,' said Bridgen, 'and I was genuinely angry. I felt that there was no way forward. The relationship had completely broken down.'

A week later Vennells wrote to Arbuthnot and told him she had considered the request to allow convicted claimants to progress to mediation and had decided to refuse it. This was the final straw. On 28 November Arbuthnot called together his core group MPs for another meeting. They decided enough was enough.

Arbuthnot went to see the Speaker of the House of Commons to secure an adjournment debate. He then prepared a press release and emailed his parliamentary group of MPs. Arbuthnot told them the Post Office was 'neither allowing the Mediation Scheme to proceed as it was designed to nor doing what they said they would' and he had 'lost faith in the Post Office Board's commitment to a fair resolution.'

The MPs sent out a press release on 8 December with quotes from the core group. Huw Irranca-Davies told the media, 'The mediation process has failed even those Subpostmasters who were originally included.'

Mike Wood added 'We are all shocked that the Post Office seems not to want to get to the bottom of all this.'

Andrew Bridgen said 'MPs have been working with the Post Office for two years now in the belief that they would work towards a solution to this issue. It would appear that this belief is increasingly looking misplaced.'

Arbuthnot was teed up for BBC Radio 4's Today programme. For more than three decades, Today has been the UK establishment's talking shop. Pretty much everyone who is anyone tunes in. On 9 December, its listeners heard a pre-recorded phone interview with Jo Hamilton, followed by a live interview with James Arbuthnot. Arbuthnot did not hold back, telling the presenter John Humphrys the Post Office were 'trying to sabotage' the Mediation Scheme.

'They're doing this in secret,' he said. 'They're trying to bar from mediation 90% of the Subpostmasters for whom it was set up. They're arguing, for example, that those who, like Jo Hamilton, pleaded guilty to false accounting, shouldn't have the Mediation Scheme available to them, despite having agreed expressly with MPs that those who had pleaded guilty to false accounting *should* have it available to them.'

Humphrys then turned his attention to the Post Office's Mark Davies. It remains the only broadcast interview any Post Office executive has ever given on the subject of the Horizon scandal. Davies told Humphrys the Post Office rejected Arbuthnot's claims 'outright.'

'What did he say that was wrong?' wondered Humphrys.

'Well, I think,' blustered Davies, 'to go back to the original setting up of this inquiry, we as the Post Office, take our responsibilities to our people, extremely seriously…'

'What did he say that was wrong?' repeated Humphrys.

Davies came across as evasive, hiding behind the 'confidentiality' of the Mediation Scheme. The discussion was inconclusive, but it was now on the record.

The same day Arbuthnot appeared on Today, the law firm Edwin Coe announced it was working with the JFSA to consider taking the Post Office to court. Edwin Coe partner, David Greene, said in his press release:

'Many of the Subpostmasters have lost everything. We are now exploring their options to bring this to a speedy conclusion and achieve the justice the Subpostmasters deserve.'

A gargantuan filming and editing effort, sparked by a tip-off to Tim from Huw Irranca-Davies on 1 December, meant our first One Show film was ready to go the same evening. I travelled up to London and watched our report go out, sitting on the famous One Show sofa next to a bemused John Cleese. I then spent the most nerve-wracking two minutes of my life giving more context to the story live on prime-time television. After a straight week of working 12 to 14 hour days I was more than a little concerned I would either blurt out some howler or simply be unable to string a sentence together. Thankfully, the occasion passed off without incident, and Sandy suggested we schedule our second One Show film to go out on the same day as James Arbuthnot's Westminster Hall adjournment debate, which had been scheduled for 17 December.

THE WESTMINSTER HALL DEBATE

The debate at the Houses of Parliament was my first proper visit to the Palace of Westminster in over 15 years. It is like entering a nineteenth century time capsule. Particulars are checked, humourless white-tied stewards order you about, and every moment you spend on the premises is designed to make you feel unwelcome. There are Members of Parliament and Very Much Non-Members of Parliament, and we in the latter group are clearly there on sufferance.

I joined the queue outside the debate room, standing on the stone steps in the corner of Westminster Hall. Mark Baker from the CWU was there. So was Alan Bates. Alan saw Mark and turned his back on him. Alan won't talk to Mark as he used to be an NFSP rep, so it was all a bit awkward, but by standing in between them and chatting to one before turning 180 degrees and chatting to the other, I was able to pick up some useful information, not least that the JFSA was due to have another group meeting in Kineton village hall in Warwickshire, not far from Fenny Compton. I also discovered there were moves afoot to request an inquiry into the Mediation Scheme by the Business, Innovation and Skills (BIS) Select Committee, 'some time in the New Year.'

The debate itself was revealing. It began with a speech from James Arbuthnot who told the House that 'the way in which the Post Office has treated Subpostmasters and members of parliament who have expressed concern about the matter is so worrying, and to my mind shocking.'

Various individual cases were raised by the MPs present and various theories as to how and why Horizon might be going wrong were also aired, but the main thrust of the debate was the disbelief at the way the Post Office had acted, both towards its own Subpostmasters and then towards MPs.

Here are a few choice excerpts.

> **James Arbuthnot MP**: '[The Mediation Scheme] is a sham... The Post Office has ... broken its word to members of parliament in so many different respects that it is frankly bewildering. There are many ways to describe it, but I think the best is to say that the Post Office has been duplicitous. It has spent public money on a Mediation Scheme that it has set out to sabotage.'

Andrew Bridgen MP: 'The way in which Post Office senior management have dealt with our Working Group of MPs has been extremely high-handed ... if Post Office management speak to Cabinet members and senior members of parliament in the way they do, the way they treat their Subpostmasters must be feudal.'

Mike Wood MP: 'We met the five senior managers of Post Office Ltd – the chair of the board, the chief executive, the chief technical officer and two others – who said, "We cannot conceive of there being failings in our Horizon system." I asked all five of them about that. First, that makes us wonder which planet they live on. Secondly, we know that if the organisation operates from the premise that, uniquely, it has a computer system with which there are no problems and can be no problems, that explains its behaviour further down the line. Its investigation department should be renamed, because it has never done an investigation since it was set up. When problems are found, eventually it goes to the individual Postmasters and Postmistresses and says, "There is a problem here. Patently, it is not our system – it's faultless – so it must be you."'

Ian Murray MP: 'The more it goes on, the more we will hear of Subpostmasters ending up in prison or declaring guilt for something that they have not done in order to avoid a custodial sentence. That is not how justice works in this country and it is not how justice should be seen to be working.'

Kevan Jones MP: 'People's lives have been ruined – decent, honest and hard-working people. That is just not fair. If it happened in any other area of life, it would be a national scandal. It is a national scandal.'

Albert Owen MP: 'The Post Office encouraged people to commit false accounting, and then it penalised them in the hardest way possible – by taking their livelihoods and reputations from them and destroying their standing in the proud communities we represent.'

James Arbuthnot MP: 'The Post Office ... is undermining and

> belittling the work of the forensic accountants whom it chose… The Post Office is trying to close down the Mediation Scheme… The Post Office has no intention of getting to the bottom of what went wrong. Documents have been destroyed.'

As well as piling into the Post Office for its behaviour, Arbuthnot also used the occasion to demand an investigation by the Criminal Cases Review Commission. The CCRC is a public body, set up in 1997, with a statutory mandate to put right miscarriages of justice. Anyone with a criminal conviction can apply, and if the CCRC's commissioners believe a conviction has a 'realistic possibility' of being quashed, it can refer it back to the relevant court.[1]

When an adjournment debate is called, the relevant minister is required to attend, listen to MPs and finish up by stating the government's position. Jo Swinson, still the Minister for Postal Affairs, gave her response. Her contribution was to reveal that she had written to Sir Anthony Hooper and he had written back to say that he couldn't tell her anything because the scheme was confidential.

An exasperated Kevan Jones almost yelled at her, 'You're the minister. *Do* something!'

Swinson replied that in response to the situation being described by MPs, 'What I would normally propose doing is to get a team of forensic accountants to go through every scenario and to have the report looked at by someone independent, such as a former Court of Appeal judge… That is why Second Sight, the team of forensic accountants, has been employed and why we have someone of the calibre of Sir Anthony Hooper to oversee the process.'

The government was clearly telling MPs it was relying on Second Sight's investigation and Sir Anthony Hooper's chairmanship to get to the truth.

After the debate finished Tim and I got a taxi to Broadcasting House to watch our second film go out on The One Show. This featured Steve Phillips in Nelson, the Postmaster Mark Baker put us in touch with. We

---

1 Convictions at magistrates' courts can be overturned at a Crown Court. Crown Court convictions must be quashed at the Court of Appeal. Once a referral by the CCRC has been made to the courts, it is then for each court to decide whether to quash the convictions. The original prosecuting authority can resist the appeals if it wishes to.

also had a sequence where we invited a number of Subpostmasters back to Fenny Compton to have them recreate that famous first JFSA meeting in 2009. Alan declined to take part, but Lee Castleton, Jo Hamilton, Issy Hogg, Rubbina Shaheen, Michael Rudkin, Noel Thomas, Sue Knight and Julian Wilson all came along. During The One Show I delivered my live contextual sofa chat around a clip of the Westminster Hall debate, sitting next to a bemused Greg Davies, Michael Ball and Victoria Wood. It's a strange programme.

GINA'S ULTIMATUM

Just before the adjournment debate, on 4 December 2014, the Post Office finished its Mediation Scheme investigation (POIR) into Martin Griffiths.

Given the sensitivity of the situation, Martin's parents and Gina, Martin's widow, had made it clear to the Post Office they wanted Alan Bates to be copied in on all documentation relating to Martin's case. This was agreed by the Mediation Scheme Working Group.

In their POIR report, the Post Office maintained their claim that there was nothing wrong with the Horizon terminal at Hope Farm Road. There was also no apology for the manner in which Martin was deemed part-culpable for the robbery at his branch.

The report was sent to Second Sight, who would use it and Martin's Case Questionnaire Review to give their independent, evidenced opinion on what had happened at Hope Farm Road. Again, given the sensitivity of the situation, it had been agreed that the Post Office's POIR would be sent to Gina as soon as it had been completed. For some reason the Post Office chose to sit on it for seven weeks.

On 22 January 2015, the Post Office sent Gina their POIR on Martin. Despite the Working Group agreement that Alan Bates should be kept informed about the Griffiths case, the Post Office failed to give a copy of their POIR to Alan or let him know it would soon be in Gina's hands.

On 23 January 2015, *the same day* Gina received the report, the Post Office called her. Gina was offered a sum of money. To get it, she would have to leave the Mediation Scheme and sign a non-disclosure agreement. The offer expired that day.

Gina had a matter of hours to read the Post Office report into what happened at Hope Farm Road and make a decision. She did not know whether Second Sight's report, which still was not finished, would corroborate or take issue with the Post Office version of events.

Under considerable pressure, without alerting Alan, Gina accepted the Post Office's offer.

Later that month, Second Sight finished their investigation into what happened at Hope Farm Road. They handed it to the Post Office.

On 5 February 2015, all documentation pertaining to Martin Griffiths was removed from the Working Group's shared drives, save for a signed statement from Gina Griffiths saying she had withdrawn from the Mediation Scheme. This was the first Alan Bates knew about it.

The Second Sight Case Review Report cleared Martin of any serious wrongdoing with regard to the alarming discrepancies at his branch. Second Sight also found the decision to make him culpable for cash lost during the May 2013 robbery was 'unfair.'

PETE MURRAY

Martin Griffiths' eventual successor at Hope Farm Road was Pete Murray, who I have come to know well. Pete already had a Post Office in Wallasey which he was running without difficulty. In October 2014 he was invited to take on Hope Farm Road as a second Post Office. No one told him about his predecessor's problems or that he had taken his own life. Within a few weeks of assuming control of the Hope Farm Road branch, Pete suffered unresolved Horizon discrepancies. Despite reporting everything, making good where he could afford to, and persistently asking for help, he got nothing but demands for cash. Pete had £23,000 taken by the Post Office in monthly instalments from his Postmasters' salary. He then received threats demanding direct payment of a further £35,000 despite the Post Office 'never showing or telling me what I have done wrong.'

Pete told me he didn't false account and always declared his discrepancies. He tried to get assistance from the Post Office helpline, his contract manager and the 'agents' accounting team.' Once, in desperation, he left a message on the Post Office Head of Security's voicemail.

The man who called back identified himself as the Post Office's Deputy Head of Security. According to Pete, 'He just told me repeatedly, "Don't trust your staff." He said it over and over again.'

On 1 November 2018, both Pete's branches were subjected to a surprise 'audit.' Further discrepancies totalling £2,000 were found. Pete was suspended without pay from both his branches, including the problem-free branch in Wallasey. Just before the busiest and most profitable time of the year, Pete was left without an income. Five days before Christmas, he suffered a stress-related stroke. Mark Baker got involved. Pete credits Mark with saving him from ruin, and stopping him from making a similar decision to Martin Griffiths.

In 2019, with help from Mark, Pete was reinstated by the Post Office, but they continued to hold him liable for what was now a £37,000 discrepancy. The Post Office arranged for a BT engineer to visit the Hope Farm Road branch to check the broadband line which connected the Horizon terminals in the branch with the rest of the Post Office network. The engineer arrived on 12 August 2019. Soon she had called a colleague in to help. They were there for four hours. In an email to the Post Office describing their visit, Pete said,

'When I asked if it was a new or an old issue which they had found, the man told me that they had found two major faults, one could be new, but one was older, and this is basically verifying faults which I have been trying to report to POL for the last few years, but have always fallen on deaf ears.'

Pete described the BT engineers' findings as 'vital evidence and perhaps a major clue into some of the problems' with the Horizon system in his branch. He requested the Post Office send him the BT engineers' documentation. The Post Office did not reply. On 29 August, Pete sent another email.

'This is just a quick note to remind you that I would like to get a copy of BT repairs report for the day they came to investigate and repair the connection to my branch … the BT engineer who came to fix my line in that office explained to me that we didn't have a good connection – given that the previous owner of the business took his own life as a direct result of the broken system, this is extremely serious.'

Pete has still never seen the BT engineers' report about the problems they found and fixed at his branch. In 2021 he signed a settlement agreement with the Post Office and got out of his Hope Farm Road and Wallasey branches for good.

REGIONAL VARIATIONS

As well as the fire and fury, the Westminster Hall debate had produced some concrete figures from the government about the Mediation Scheme. Of the 146 accepted applications, ten were sorted without investigation and two resolved after a preliminary inquiry. Of the remaining 134 cases, 24 had been recommended for mediation by Second Sight and according to Jo Swinson the Post Office had only refused to mediate with two of the 24 cases. This left 110 cases still outstanding, more than a year after the scheme's application window had closed.

Now the MPs had made their feelings about the Post Office's behaviour abundantly clear, the Post Office had a choice. It could make peace overtures, or it could enter a period of menacing denialism which, to any rational observer, was completely unhinged. It chose to do the latter.

On 17 January 2015, the Post Office circulated a response document to the Westminster Hall debate. It had the same moany tone as its rebuttal to Second Sight's Briefing Report 2, though this time there was an added sense of wounded pride as the Post Office implicitly asked the reader to wonder if the MPs who had been so vocal before Christmas had perhaps made fools of themselves.

The Post Office said, 'During the debate, the Scheme's scope and Post Office's approach to it were called into question. The Scheme was described as a "sham" and Post Office was accused of bad faith and of undermining its own Scheme. Post Office does not accept this.'

It then lists everything it has done to help the campaigning Subpostmasters ('instigated an independent review of the Horizon System by Second Sight; established the Scheme in collaboration with JFSA and Second Sight; provided funding for Scheme Applicants to obtain professional advice in articulating their complaints against Post Office; established a 20 strong team dedicated to re-investigate every case in full; produced over 130 investigation reports on individual cases in the Scheme; provided Second Sight with thousands of pages of information to inform their investigation…').

The Post Office concluded that 'after two and half years of investigation and independent review, the facts are that Post Office has found no evidence, nor has any been advanced by either an Applicant or Second Sight, which suggests that Horizon does not accurately record and store branch transaction data or that it is not working as it should.'

On Sunday 18 January, Alan Bates held his JFSA group meeting in Kineton. I begged Alan to let me come along, so I might be able to get some footage for our scheduled Inside Out films. He agreed. There were more than 60 former Subpostmasters present. It was good to meet so many of them.

Addressing the meeting, Alan explained the JFSA had spent more than a year watching their initial hopes for the Mediation Scheme disappear into a procedural swamp created by the Post Office. Now, it was time to fight back. Alan explained the legal situation. Although the Mediation Scheme had been drifting on a disaster course for some time, it was still generating useful information. No matter how much the Post Office was trying to frustrate the process, there was still a process, creating a channel through which important documents were trickling.

Compared to the situation a couple of years previously, the JFSA and its Subpostmasters were now in possession of documentary evidence. It wasn't everything they needed by any means, but it was something. Alan had been having conversations with lawyers who felt the documents still coming to light could help persuade insurers to underwrite a legal action. If the JFSA got insurance, they wouldn't have to ask the claimants to put up any money to get on board.

Alan asked the meeting to vote on taking legal action against the Post Office. It was agreed unanimously.

Over the next couple of weeks Tim and I made Inside Out films on the Post Office story for BBC South, BBC West, BBC South West, BBC East Midlands, BBC West Midlands and BBC North East and Cumbria. Each film highlighted Subpostmasters from each region who were willing to go on camera and tell their stories. They were Rachel Williams, Tracey Merritt, Julian and Karen Wilson, Noel Thomas, Pam Stubbs, Steve Philips, Jo Hamilton, Michael and Susan Rudkin, Peter Holmes and Sue Knight.

For me, the most affecting Subpostmaster is in the BBC North East film. Peter Holmes was a former police officer. He had a soft Geordie accent and exuded a quiet decency. His police career was one of selfless public service – he even made the newspapers in 1967 when he was shot by a robber whilst trying to stop a bank raid.

On leaving the force, Peter worked as a hotelier for 19 years before becoming the manager of Jesmond Post Office in Newcastle. He started having problems with Horizon and his cash discrepancies grew. Peter asked the Post Office for help and got none he could make sense of. He began to agree Horizon's figures in the hope his problems would sort themselves out. They didn't. The discrepancies reached £46,000. Peter called for help again. The Post Office sent in the auditors. Peter was sacked and prosecuted for theft and false accounting.

'There was no evidence produced, apart from the evidence of the computer,' he told us on camera, 'and I think the computer was wrong. But we wouldn't have the information on hand to be able to argue against the figures produced by the computer. The computer is … God to these guys. They're the judge, the jury and the executioner. And that's the way you felt – done down all the time.'

Peter was facing a hefty jail sentence.

'Ex-policemen don't like to go prison…' he said, pointedly, 'so … the advice from my legal team was to plead guilty to the false accounting – it being the lesser charge, and the Post Office will then drop the theft charge. That was what they told my barrister, just the day before we were going to court.'

Peter reluctantly pleaded guilty. In court the judge drew attention to Peter's good character:

'You had a respectable record in the police force and working in various businesses,' he said. 'It's very sad to see you in court, you are highly spoken of by colleagues and friends and what you did was totally out of character.'

Peter was convicted in 2010. He was 68 years old. He was a thoroughly trustworthy member of society. He in turn trusted the Post Office, and when it tried to ruin him, he turned to the justice system, which threw him to the wolves. Peter agreed Horizon figures that were not correct, and it was his decision to plead guilty, but *there was no evidence of theft* – so why was he charged with it?

It didn't occur to Peter to find out if anyone else was having problems with Horizon until after he was convicted. In fact, he told us, it didn't occur to him even then.

'One of the friends who came to court with me, as a character witness, God bless her, went home after the court, [she went] straight on the computer and rang me up. "Peter – just type into Google, 'Post Office problems' and stand back and see the response" and there was page after page of this stuff!'

A full five years after his conviction, the bewildered-looking ex-copper tells the BBC:

'I can fully say I'm not guilty. It's just the damn computer.'

Peter died of a brain tumour before he could see his conviction quashed.

THE GEORGE THOMSON SHOW

In January 2015, the Business, Innovation and Skills Select Committee announced its intention to hold an inquiry into the Post Office Mediation Scheme. There are more than 30 parliamentary select committees, populated by backbench MPs drawn from various parties. Select committees don't have much power, but they can exert influence. Their oral evidence sessions are broadcast live, and they publish as much as possible of the written evidence they receive.

As part of the Mediation Scheme inquiry, representatives of the Post Office, the CWU, the NFSP, the JFSA and Second Sight were asked to attend an oral evidence session on Tuesday 3 February in the Wilson Room at Portcullis House. Further letters were sent to everyone involved in the Mediation Scheme, asking for written submissions.

Paula Vennells and Angela van den Bogerd agreed to be questioned by MPs. Four days before the evidence session, Vennells was sent a list of questions by the BIS committee, one of which was:

'Is it possible to access the system remotely? We are told it is.'

This prompted Vennells to send an email to her colleagues about remote access to the Horizon system. She asked her Director of Communications Mark Davies and her Chief Information Officer Lesley Sewell to investigate, telling them of her response to MPs, 'I need to say no it is not possible and we are sure of this.'

Lesley Sewell had been told by Second Sight's Ian Henderson more than two years previously that remote access was possible. At the time Alwen Lyons had flatly contradicted him.

Is it possible that by 2015 Paula Vennells still hadn't properly informed herself of the situation? Had the Post Office's Chief Information Officer spent the last two years *not* finding out the answer to that burningly important question and *not* making sure the Post Office board had the full picture? When it came to the Post Office, remote access was becoming a fault line down which actual concepts of reality were disappearing.

Eventually, just over a dozen people were involved in the email chain shaping an answer that responded to Vennells' 'need' to tell MPs remote access was not possible. It concluded, 'There is no functionality (by design) for transactions to be edited or amended.'

On the day the Select Committee was due to meet (at 9.30am sharp),

James Arbuthnot's terrifyingly efficient Chief of Staff, Janet Walker, met me at 9am outside the main entrance to Portcullis House. Janet took one look at the security queues before marching me round to a staff entrance at the rear of the building and bundling me in the back way.

Having only ever watched select committee hearings on television, I asked Janet to fill me in on the protocol. 'You'll have to wait outside the Wilson Room until about twenty-five past nine,' she pronounced. 'The MPs have a preparatory meeting, then the witnesses and public are invited in.'

At 9.15am, the scenes outside the Wilson Room were even more awkward than in Westminster Hall just before Christmas. About 20 people were standing by the public door (MPs have separate entrances to these meeting rooms) in little groups, doing everything they could to avoid eye contact with the other little groups. No one wanted to be overheard, but standing and looking at each other in silence would be even more weird, so conversations were being carried out very, very quietly.

I made a beeline for Paula Vennells. She was surrounded by flunkies. I shouldered my way through, presented myself directly to her, and held out my hand. I kept my voice low, as that seemed to be the thing to do.

'Hello,' I said. 'I'm Nick Wallis from the BBC. I've been covering the Horizon story.'

'Hello,' she said, offering the limpest shake. It was like holding a damp rag.

'I've been trying to get an interview with you for some time,' I said. 'Is there any chance we can actually make that happen?'

Vennells looked like she'd rather drink a cup of cold sick.

'Mmm,' she replied. 'You'll need to go through the press office.'

'That's what I've been trying to do for several years now.'

She looked at me but didn't say anything.

'Do you think next time I ask, you could see your way to agreeing? It would be an opportunity to get the Post Office's perspective across.'

Vennells gave an imperceptible nod.

Conversation over, I withdrew from her protective circle, and then introduced myself to Ian Henderson from Second Sight. This proved a more fruitful contact. We swapped numbers.

At 9.25am we filed into the Wilson Room. The MPs on the Select Committee were arraigned in a horseshoe, facing the witnesses. The Chair was Adrian Bailey MP.

The first evidence session was attended by Alan Bates and Kay Linnell from the JFSA, Andy Furey and Mark Baker from the CWU and George Thomson, General Secretary of the National Federation of Subpostmasters. Thomson is a working-class Glaswegian whose sharp accent and throaty vocal delivery cut through the air like a buzzsaw.

During the first session, Thomson gave a masterclass in bravura bullshit. He tried to dominate the panel (despite being the least qualified to speak), and used every opportunity to deliver an unequivocal defence of the Horizon system.

'It has performed exceptionally robustly,' he volunteered, in response to the MPs' first question of the session. 'Systemically, it is very strong. However, there are one or two issues where money went missing and Postmasters have felt that it had to be Horizon, while in a lot of cases it could have been errors or, in fact, members of staff misappropriating money.'

Thomson took the MPs' second question too, leaning back comfortably in his chair, and speaking with the authority of a man who had seen all this before.

'If a Subpostmaster happens to end up being £30,000 short – I made this point to Pat McFadden many years ago when he was Post Office Minister – they think, "Well, I know that I never took that money, so it has to be a Horizon mistake." That is the Postmaster's point of view. However, a member of staff could have misappropriated the money or actually done the transaction wrong... Subpostmasters sometimes think that the problem has to be the Horizon system when in effect it was mistakes by members of staff or misappropriation.'

Through force of personality and brass neck, Thomson grabbed the initiative and established himself as the panel's straight-talking go-to guy. The fact he was spouting nonsense didn't matter. He could now start dropping diversionary bombs, basically doing anything he could to undermine the direction of the inquiry.

Thomson's tactics made things difficult for the committee. I suspect the first session was designed to give the MPs enough ammunition to throw at the Post Office and Paula Vennells, who were up next, but they were being derailed. Unions are supposed to stand up for their members. On that morning George Thomson spun the Post Office line far more effectively than any Post Office exec could. This was partly because he was a far better speaker than Paula Vennells or Angela van den Bogerd, but also because his position as General Secretary of the National Federation of Subpostmasters gave him third party authority.

Thomson finished one answer by waving around a Post Office Horizon training manual.

'I have brought along an original Royal Mail migration pack to show you. Every Postmaster in Britain in 2000 and 2001 had one, and this is mine because I was a Postmaster then. This was full of training materials, so from day one the Post Office has taken this extremely seriously.'

Adrian Bailey began to smell something.

'I cannot see the contents of that pack,' he said, 'but I must admit that if someone handed me that and told me that it was my training, I might run a mile. Perhaps I could bring in Alan, because I can see that he is shaking his head.'

Alan Bates' loathing of the NFSP knows no bounds. He made his first point eloquently.

'I was also involved with the training at that point when the system came in, and I was a Subpostmaster then. I had one and a half days' training, my staff had one day's training and I believe that the regional people who worked for the Post Office had two and half days' training. I, too, received a 500-page pack to take away and learn how to use the system afterwards. That is how it was dropped on everyone. I had five members of staff who did training at that session. One of them had never even turned on a computer before, but she did a day's training and then she was certified as being sound and correct and fine to use the system at the end of one day. It was madness; she had no idea what she was doing. Staff were just abandoned.'

Kay Linnell came across as an interesting character. Her first contribution was to note that the Subpostmasters Contract made no concessions to the massive changes caused by the arrival of Horizon.

'When the Post Office moved to a computerised system,' she said, 'they did not amend the contract between the Subpostmasters and the Post Office. The individual Subpostmaster remained totally responsible for all gains and losses, but they were no longer able to check each and every transaction because there were no [paper] slips.'

Mark Baker won instant credibility by telling the committee he was the only member of the panel who was still a serving Subpostmaster. The MPs leaned in. Mark's first point was that the Post Office did nothing to help people having problems.

'Mr Thomson alluded to human error. There will always be human error when humans interact with computers. However, what has been systemic and consistent throughout Horizon's life is the failure to recognise that parts of the infrastructure could be to blame for some of these discrepancies occurring. The Post Office failed to recognise that they needed to drill down into each and every kind of discrepancy … it was not supporting the postmasters … or looking into their cases.'

Baker also explained to the committee the difficulty of being legally and financially responsible for a computer system he could not control.

'Training is generally received by serving Subpostmasters through the form of manuals. We call them Branch Focuses. They arrive every week and we read them to receive training and instructions on how to operate certain transactions. They are hopeless. My wife prepared a 54-page dossier, randomly taking one month's selection of Focuses and highlighting all the misinformation and errors contained within them, which she sent to the board of directors. She did not get a single reply from any director. The file was passed on to a functionary further down the line, who made a hopeless job of trying to explain everything my wife was trying to point out. [My wife] was trying to point out that we are reliant on receiving the correct instructions in order to be able to operate Horizon and perform the transactions, and the people who are telling us how to do it cannot even get it right.'

Yet for every opinion or statement of fact made by Kay Linnell, the CWU or Alan Bates, George Thomson countered it with the idea that this was meaningless fuss, making the blanket assertion that on Horizon, the Post Office has 'done nothing wrong.'

Alan Bates was initially calm, but lost his temper when Thomson claimed that losses only appeared to happen in Subpostmaster-controlled branches and not Crown Offices. Bates jumped in.

'One of the few documents that has come to light in all of this,' he said, 'is a 2007-08 internal report from the Post Office, which showed that the Crown Offices lost £2.2 million across their counters that year. So Crown Offices do lose money.'

He perhaps should have left it there, but continued angrily, 'The reason why the JFSA was set up was that the Federation refused to support Subpostmasters in any cases about Horizon – it never once supported people in court cases or anything like that… It is really frustrating to have to sit here listening to somebody who is meant to be representing Subpostmasters. It is like they are in a paid position in the Post Office.'

Adrian Bailey slapped him down.

'Can you talk just about the issues? It is not about personalities.'

Alan retreated, and Thomson's assertion lay unchallenged by the MPs. Kay Linnell spoke up, instinctively filling the slightly awkward silence with a point of her own.

'The only thing I would add is that Horizon is the entire system, not just the information technology… I would like you to ask the Post Office in the next session what adjustments it has made to correct the errors it has found. There obviously were errors, because there have been corrections.'

Bailey was curt. 'Believe you me, we will cover all the angles. We do not need panellists to tell us what to ask.'

Thomson was loving this. He was quite aware that every second he was talking diverted attention from Alan, Kay, Andy and Mark. The more Thomson drew fire, the less information MPs would hear from people who knew what they were talking about.

Thomson went on to tell the committee the Mediation Scheme was very effective, despite not having any NFSP members as applicants or NFSP officials working on it. He suggested that some of the Subpostmasters on it were dishonest and 'chancing their luck' and warned MPs that the JFSA's complaints were in danger of 'creating a cottage industry that damages the brand.'

He dismissed Alan Bates' suggestion the government should take the Second Sight investigation and Mediation Scheme out of the Post Office's control (without explaining why he thought it was a bad idea) and he belittled Subpostmasters having problems, inferring they were either on the take or incompetent. Then he took pains to single out one Subpostmaster by name, making defamatory allegations about what had been going on at his branch. Thomson could do this because he knew full well he was protected by parliamentary privilege.[1] The committee chair called Thomson's attempt to throw mud in this way 'totally out of order.'

[1] Parliamentary privilege is slightly different from legal privilege. It means you can, more or less, say what you like in a parliamentary setting and not get sued.

PAULA VENNELLS SPEAKS

After the George Thomson show we came to the second session of the Select Committee hearing. Finally, and for the first time, Paula Vennells was going to say something in public about Horizon.

There were three people on the second panel. Vennells sat in the middle with Angela van den Bogerd on her right. Ian Henderson from Second Sight took a seat to their left.

Vennells had clearly decided she was there to demonstrate her profound concern for the Mediation Scheme applicants whilst pushing the point about the thousands of Subpostmasters who weren't having problems with Horizon and the millions of people up and down the country who loved the Post Office. Both Vennells and van den Bogerd were keen to highlight the 'branch user forum' which they had set up in the light of Second Sight's Interim Report. The branch user forum allowed serving Subpostmasters to feed back problems they were having with Horizon and other branch procedures.

When Ian Henderson spoke, it was to offer a recurring lament about the Mediation Scheme and the Post Office's failure to disclose information to Second Sight. As far as he was concerned the Post Office was failing to do what it had promised MPs and Subpostmasters that it would do. This reached farcical levels in a discussion about emails.[2]

Ian Henderson: 'One issue we have been looking at relates to the Fujitsu office in Bracknell. We first requested documents relating to that in February 2013 – almost two years ago. We have still not been provided with those documents. We are very concerned about the operation of the suspense account by Post Office. We have been asking for that information since July last year.'

Adrian Bailey: [to Paula Vennells] 'Can you explain why this is so? Do you accept the comments that have just been made?'

[2] Forgive me for reproducing large chunks of dialogue over the course of this chapter, but its Pinter-esque nature reveals the alternate reality the two Post Office execs were living in. For extra cognitive dissonance, try reading it out loud.

Angela van den Bogerd: 'May I respond?... We did provide the emails requested to Second Sight, a whole year's worth of emails actually, but Second Sight have since asked us for another year's worth of emails.'

Ian Henderson: 'Can I come back on that? Unfortunately, the emails that were provided were for the wrong year. We were investigating a specific incident in 2008 and the year's worth of emails that we were given related to 2009. Therefore, it was not surprising that we said, "We have asked for 2008, please provide it." We have still not had that.'

Adrian Bailey: 'That seems an amazing error on your part, when I think of what Subpostmasters go through if they make an error. It is such a basic error for the Post Office to make.'

Angela van den Bogerd: 'We provided what we were asked for at the time, so, clearly, there must have been some misunderstanding. We would not have pulled a year's worth of emails for a wrong year.'

Adrian Bailey: 'I want to follow this through. Could you provide the evidence to this Committee that you provided a response to the actual question and that it was not an error?'

Angela van den Bogerd: 'Certainly.'

Nadhim Zahawi MP: 'Mr Henderson, did you ask for the emails from 2008?'

Ian Henderson: 'Yes, we did.'

Nadhim Zahawi: 'And you were provided with 2009 instead?'

Ian Henderson: 'We were provided with 2009. We were told at the time that with the first batch there were some technology issues relating to the provision of the 2008 emails. Two years down the line, we still don't have those.'

Nadhim Zahawi: 'You are saying that you actually asked for the correct ones, and you still don't have those?'

Ian Henderson: 'Yes.'

Far more serious was the discussion about evidence of criminal wrongdoing. Nadhim Zahawi did a great job on trying to pin the Post Office down on this.

Ian Henderson: 'When this scheme first started we were given full access to [the Post Office's legal and prosecution] files. Again, presumably on legal advice, that access has been extremely restricted. We feel that this is a very severe constraint on our ability to conduct an independent investigation into what has happened.'

Nadhim Zahawi: 'When did the policy change?'

Ian Henderson: 'We have never been told formally that the policy has changed. When we were first appointed, we were told that the principle behind what we were doing was to seek the truth, irrespective of the consequences. We could look at anything that we felt, as an independent investigator, was necessary to conduct our investigation. Unsurprisingly, with cases that came into the early part of the scheme that involved a criminal prosecution, we were provided with full access to a small number of files. As further cases were accepted into the scheme, we unsurprisingly asked for full access to those legal files. Responses were to the effect, "Under no circumstances are we going to give you access to those files. You are entitled to the public documents that would normally be available to the defendant if the case had gone to trial." We felt it was necessary for us to review the internal legal files, looking at the depth of any investigation that had happened and possibly even legal advice relating to the prosecution.'

Nadhim Zahawi: 'Paula, why don't you hand those files over? What is the problem?'

Paula Vennells: 'The point I want to pick up first, if I may...'

Nadhim Zahawi: 'No, answer my question. Why will you not give Ian Henderson those files?'

Paula Vennells: 'As far as I am aware, Mr Zahawi, we have shared whatever information was appropriate on every single individual.'

Nadhim Zahawi: 'That is not what Ian Henderson is saying.'

Paula Vennells: 'It is the first time, personally, that I have heard that. I am happy to go away and have a look.'

Nadhim Zahawi: 'He has said that under no circumstances could he be given those files. That is what you have just told me. Is that right?'

Ian Henderson: 'We have not been given those files.'

Nadhim Zahawi: 'You have been told by Paula's organisation that under no circumstances could you be given those files. Is that right or wrong?'

Paula Vennells: 'Who told you that, Ian?'

Ian Henderson: 'It came up at one of the Working Group meetings, at which you and I were present.'

[Pregnant silence].

Angela van den Bogerd: 'I do not recall that conversation.'

Nadhim Zahawi: 'This sounds like a shambles to me. You came in here and opened by saying the system was working beautifully. You now realise why you are in front of the Committee.'

Paula Vennells: 'Ian said – he is quite right – that the reason we set up this Mediation Scheme was to get to the truth about this system. The system itself is working very well.'

Nadhim Zahawi: 'But you have been obstructive. We are hearing from Ian that your organisation has been obstructive to his independent work. Is that right or wrong?'

Paula Vennells: 'It is wrong. We have provided for every single case detailed, thorough, independent investigation. They run to pages and pages of reports. There are on average 80 pieces of evidence…'

Nadhim Zahawi: 'Let me stop you here. We have just heard from Ian Henderson, who is independent, that you have not provided the prosecution files that they think they should look at. They need your files, not just what is publicly available. They need that information. Will you provide it? Yes or no?'

Paula Vennells: 'Mr Zahawi, you have just heard that it is the first time I have heard that piece of information.'

Nadhim Zahawi: 'I am simply asking for a commitment from you. You are the head of the organisation. Will you provide it? Yes or no? Give me a simple answer.'

Paula Vennells: 'Mr Henderson is a forensic accountant. He is not a qualified legal individual. Neither am I.'

Nadhim Zahawi: 'I am simply asking whether you will provide it – yes or no?'

Paula Vennells: 'I am not prepared on behalf of the Post Office to give…'

Nadhim Zahawi: 'Right. I have got my answer. You will not provide it.'

Paula Vennells: 'No, you have not got your answer. You have not heard a yes or a no. I am simply saying that at the moment I am not able to answer your question.'

Nadhim Zahawi: 'Why?'

Paula Vennells: 'Because I do not know the details of the situation.'

Nadhim Zahawi: 'You used to provide the information and you have stopped providing it. Will you provide it going forward? Yes or no?'

Paula Vennells: 'I am not aware that we stopped what we provided previously. Angela has been involved daily for the last two years. She sits on the Working Group alongside Ian at Second Sight. If there is a misunderstanding, I am happy to…'

Nadhim Zahawi: 'Angela, will you provide it? If your CEO cannot answer, will you provide the prosecution files as requested by Ian Henderson?'

Angela van den Bogerd: 'Mr Zahawi, as Ian said, we have previously provided them, and we have provided the information necessary for those investigations as a pack. So there are thousands of pieces of information already provided to Second Sight.'

Nadhim Zahawi: 'But we have heard already that he has been obstructed from getting the legal files that you use internally, which he used to get before. That is what I have heard. Will you now commit to providing those files going forward?'

Angela van den Bogerd: 'We provided them to Second Sight early in the investigation.'

Nadhim Zahawi: 'Will you provide them?'

Angela van den Bogerd: 'Just let me finish, please. We have been working with Second Sight over the last few weeks to get to an understanding of what we need to provide. We are working through those, and information has been flowing.'

Nadhim Zahawi: 'So you do not understand what you need to provide?'

Angela van den Bogerd: 'We have been providing what we agreed we would provide at the outset. In some cases, Second Sight have concluded their investigation on that basis. What has been asked in the last few weeks is for access to further information that we were not providing under the agreement that we had.'

Nadhim Zahawi: 'What he is asking you for – there is no wriggle room – is to provide the prosecution files going forward. Will you commit to doing that? That is all I am asking.'

Angela van den Bogerd: 'What I am saying is that we have already been exchanging that information over the last few weeks.'

Nadhim Zahawi: 'So you have been providing them?'

Angela van den Bogerd: 'We have been providing that over the last few weeks.'

Nadhim Zahawi: 'Is that right, Mr Henderson?'

Ian Henderson: 'No, it is not, I am sorry to say.'

The session developed a circular rhythm. The MPs would ask a question which Paula Vennells would answer with something irrelevant. They would press her to give the answer to the actual question and it would turn out she either didn't know the answer, possibly knew the answer but wouldn't give it, or decided she needed to take some offline advice before answering the question on the record. The question would then be picked up by Angela van den Bogerd who would do what she could to satisfy MPs with a non-answer and finally Ian Henderson would either answer the question or raise a different point of concern he felt was important, which the MPs would then bat back to the Post Office. At one point, committee member Brian Binley MP brought the conversation back to the legal advice they had been given about handing information to Second Sight.

Brian Binley: 'I asked a very specific question about whether you had been given legal advice not to show certain pieces of information within your organisation. You said no, you had not. You intimated a few moments ago that, in fact, the reason that you are not giving or may not have given matters because it was Data Protection Act. That would be legal advice. I put the question to you again: have you had legal advice not to show papers that have been requested of you?'

Paula Vennells: 'Mr Binley, I have just tried to explain to you. I do not…'

Brian Binley: 'Clearly unsatisfactory. I have just asked you a question. Will you please answer for the record?'

Paula Vennells: 'Personally I have not had legal advice on that.'

Brian Binley: 'I did not say personally. Come on, you are the head of a big organisation.'

Paula Vennells: 'Yes, and I have just explained to you that, on my right, we have been saying that we have sharing information and, on the left, we have…'

Brian Binley: 'It is not about sharing information. I asked you a specific question. You mentioned the Data Protection Act, a matter of legality. I am, therefore, putting the question again. Have you been given legal advice not to give over certain papers – yes or no?'

Angela van den Bogerd: 'We do not take specific advice on data protection for this particular matter. As an organisation, we comply with data protection all the time.'

Brian Binley: 'It is applied by many people in many different ways, mostly without any legal foundation whatsoever. I don't want your nonsense, frankly, because I am hearing too much of it, so let's be clear on this: have you been given legal advice not to hand these papers over – yes or no?'

Angela van den Bogerd: 'So with the issue of data protection, yes, we would need to redact information. That is not nonsense, Mr Binley.'

Brian Binley: 'Forgive me, I have been around long enough to know how many people hide behind the Data Protection Act. Everybody in this room knows that, too, so let's talk about facts. I asked you a question and you haven't given me a straight answer, so I will draw my own conclusions.'

Ian Henderson: 'Chairman, may I add something by way of clarification? It is the general counsel of Post Office, to whom I have spoken, who said that he is not prepared to disclose to us the full legal files. I do not know to what extent he gave the same answer and advice to the chief executive of the Post Office.'

Brian Binley: 'Thank you, Mr Henderson.'

Towards the end of the session Ian Henderson put on public record his concerns about the Post Office's woeful investigation function and apparent abuse of legal process. He told the committee:

'We are very concerned about the prosecution cases. We have seen no evidence that the Post Office's own investigators were ever trained or prepared to consider that Horizon was at fault. That was never a factor that was taken into account in any of the investigations by Post Office that we have looked at ... because we think that there have been prosecutions brought by the Post Office where there has been inadequate investigation and inadequate evidence to support some of the charges brought against defendants ... a common tactic employed by the Post Office, or lawyers acting on its behalf, is to bring charges for both false accounting, which is a relatively easy charge to prove, and theft; then, as a bargaining point ... a plea-bargain, almost ... before trial, they drop the charge for theft on the basis that, first, the defendant will probably avoid a custodial sentence and, secondly, the evidence is much simpler. When we have looked at the evidence made available to us – bear in mind that I have been an expert witness for the Crown Prosecution Service, instructed by the CPS on fraud cases... I have not been satisfied that there is sufficient evidence to support a charge for theft. You can imagine the consequences that flow from that.'

Here was an independent investigator giving evidence to a parliamentary inquiry that a publicly-owned company run by the person sitting next to him had brought criminal prosecutions without sufficient evidence, and that miscarriages of justice had very possibly occurred.

Paula Vennells simply denied it. She told the committee:

'We are a business that genuinely cares about the people who work for us. If there had been any miscarriages of justice, it would have

> been really important to me and the Post Office that we surfaced those. As the investigations have gone through, so far we have no evidence of that.'

The Post Office's written evidence to the committee doubles down on this point. It says:

> 'Post Office is under an absolute duty to disclose any evidence that might undermine a prosecution case or support the case of a defendant... To date no such evidence has been provided.'

I have pored over both the above paragraphs many times. By 2015 the Cartwright King Sift Review had been completed and 26 potentially unsafe prosecutions had been 'surfaced.' It is, I suppose, entirely possible that both the Post Office and Ms Vennells could argue they were talking in strict terms only about applicants to the mediation scheme. So when they stated that they had not uncovered any evidence of miscarriages of justice, they meant (but did not add), 'amongst members of the mediation scheme.' What parliament did not hear about was evidence of *other* miscarriages of justice the Post Office *had* uncovered.

As with Second Sight's Briefing Report and the Westminster Hall debate, after the Select Committee hearing, the Post Office produced yet another rebuttal document, disparaging Second Sight, Alan Bates and Mark Baker's contribution to the oral evidence session. This was submitted as supplementary written evidence to the inquiry. In it, the Post Office first asserts it is 'not seeking to frustrate the work of Second Sight through inappropriate control of information. As part of its investigation, Post Office provides all the information it holds relevant to the case.'

This was not true.

The submission stated Horizon 'third party interfaces', such as cash machines and National Lottery products, 'do not cause problems.'

As per the Detica report, this was also not true.

'The Committee was told that power cuts or telecommunications interruptions have caused errors in branches' accounts. This is not the case.'

Tell that to Pam Stubbs.

Other written submissions to the inquiry were illuminating. Howe and Co were a firm of solicitors who had been helping Subpostmasters make their way through the Mediation Scheme. Despite dealing with the majority of applicants, by February 2015, they had only got a single applicant as far as actual mediation. I have already quoted what they had to say about the quality of the Post Office's audit processes,[1] but with regard to the scheme as a whole, Howe and Co told the inquiry that the Post Office was not 'engaging in this process with the intention of determining the truth or arriving at just settlements but is instead focussed purely on corporate defence.'

In succinct terms, Howe and Co put their finger on the button of why the Mediation Scheme was failing:

'The starting point of every single case is that there is an asserted discrepancy between the balances of cash and stock on Horizon and those in the branch. The only way of identifying this is by performing a formal reconciliation between the Horizon Reports and the actual balances on hand in the branch. POL has ignored all requests to provide any of the reconciliations relating to any of our clients.'

Howe and Co pointed out these reconciliations are at 'the heart of every single case' and 'without these fundamental documents it is literally impossible to know without doubt whether there was any difference between the branch and Horizon at all, or that the difference asserted by POL equates to the actual difference between Horizon and the branch.'

The inquiry hearing was a landmark. It pushed yet more evidence of dysfunctionality and corporate backsliding right into the open. Second Sight had directly contradicted the Post Office's position and cast doubt on the credibility of the Post Office's criminal investigations. I thought it was dynamite, but there was no media reaction at all.

Ian Henderson simply went back to working with Ron Warmington and their team of investigators on delivering a final briefing report into Horizon, marking nearly three years work. This, I was assured, would be far more damning than the three[2] reports they had already delivered.

Aside from the formal parliamentary proceedings, which had obviously thrown up a huge amount of useful, on-the-record information, a buzz and chatter amongst Subpostmasters had started up again. Many of them had either been mediated, refused for mediation or were finding the process so torturous that they'd given up. As a result, I was starting to get a lot of emails and calls from the Subpostmasters who, for most of 2014,

---

1 See the 'Going In Hard' chapter.

2 1) Interim Report – 8 July 2013; 2) Briefing Report Part 1 – 25 July 2014; 3) Briefing Report Part 2 – 21 August 2014.

hadn't been able or willing to get in touch.

As well as keeping Jane French and The One Show execs informed about what was going on, I got back in touch with Andy Head at Panorama. I also made contact with Andy Verity, the BBC's economics correspondent. Matt Prodger had left the BBC in January 2015 and there wasn't anyone I could speak to inside BBC Newsgathering with a detailed knowledge of the Horizon story. I knew Andy from when I used to read the news on his Wake Up to Money programme on 5 Live. Although he held a slightly different brief to Matt Prodger, I was sure he'd see the value of the story.

On 7 March 2015, Alan Bates posted a short update on the JFSA website:

'A regular request from individuals in the group is to enquire as to whether or not you should attend mediation meetings. The simple answer is that it is your decision. However we are aware that some meetings are taking place, and we only hear back from a percentage of those who have attended and those comments are mainly about how disastrous the meetings have been.'

Bates recommended that anyone who was invited to attend mediation should delay their decision until Second Sight delivered their final report.

WORKING GROUP DISSOLVES

On 10 March 2015, before Second Sight could deliver their promised report, the Post Office terminated the Working Group with immediate effect. Second Sight were given a month's notice and told to deliver their final report within that timeframe. They were also ordered to return or destroy all the documents pertaining to their investigation. The Post Office also posted their own Final Report on their website and confirmed that Second Sight's independent report, when it was finalised, would be kept confidential. They finally, formally announced that any applicant in the Mediation Scheme with a criminal conviction could go whistle.

'Having completed all its investigations,' it said, 'the Post Office has now decided to put forward for mediation all cases remaining in the Scheme except those that have been subject to a previous court ruling. This will accelerate the conclusion of the Scheme in the interests of Applicants and ensure that commitments made to Applicants at the outset are met.'

This final act of sabotage sent the MPs into apoplexy. James Arbuthnot had agreed to support the scheme because he was assured Jo Hamilton would be allowed to take part. Now, 18 months down the line, he was explicitly being told that because of her false accounting conviction, she couldn't. It was a humiliation.

On 11 March, James Arbuthnot stood up at Prime Minister's Questions in the House of Commons and asked:

'Is my right honourable friend aware that in connection with the Post Office Mediation Scheme, the Post Office has just sacked the independent investigator, Second Sight, and told it to destroy all its papers? Does he agree that it is essential that Second Sight's second report should not be suppressed, but should be supplied to Subpostmasters and MPs?'

David Cameron replied:

'The Business Committee is currently taking evidence on this issue, and it should be given all the relevant information. The government should not interfere with the independent mediation process, but I will ask the Business Secretary to write to my right honourable friend about his concern and to ensure that the Business Committee can do its job properly.'

Within hours of James Arbuthnot asking his question, Mark Davies, the Post Office communications director circulated a memo to journalists:

> 'In his intervention Mr Arbuthnot suggested that we had "sacked" the firm of forensic accountants which has been involved in reviewing complaints within the Scheme and went on to suggest that we had ordered them to destroy documents. I can confirm that we have given Second Sight notice in respect of their contract. However, Second Sight were engaged specifically to provide a number of services to the Working Group on this matter. Since the Working Group has now been closed it is not altogether surprising that we are now bringing those now outdated arrangements to an end during the notice period…
>
> 'As to the point on the destruction of documents, no documents relating to the Scheme are being destroyed. Post Office has repeatedly said it will not destroy information relating to the Scheme. Second Sight will have copies of information produced in relation to the Scheme and are required to return those documents to Post Office or confirm they have destroyed them when they have completed their work.
>
> 'Any suggestion that the Post Office is seeking to "suppress" the forthcoming Second Sight report is simply incorrect … the report is confidential to the parties to the mediation and it will not, therefore, be generally available.
>
> 'Regrettably, Mr Arbuthnot omitted to balance his intervention by noting that Post Office, far from suppressing information, published its own 187 page report detailing progress on the Scheme so far and announced that it will mediate all remaining cases in the Scheme, save for those which have already been subject to a court ruling.
>
> 'None of this was reported… Should reporting today focus on Mr Arbuthnot's claims, I trust that the position as set out above will be fully reflected.'

Davies needn't have worried. Far too little of anything to do with the Mediation Scheme was being reported by anyone. The latest developments were too procedural for The One Show. Now Matt Prodger had gone, no one at the BBC appeared to be watching the story. Computer Weekly and Private Eye were plugging away, but that was more or less it.

I asked Alan Bates what was going to happen next. He didn't know.

The same day James Arbuthnot asked his question of David Cameron, I had a coffee with Andy Verity at Broadcasting House. Whilst I was filling him in on the story, Andy spotted Jonathan Coffey, a Panorama producer, working at a nearby table. Andy introduced me to Jonathan and we swapped email addresses.

On 12 March Alan posted the following on the JFSA website:

'As of the time of writing, the current situation which all of you should now be aware of is that Post Office has taken the decision to close down the Working Group of the Initial Complaint Review and Mediation Scheme. It has also, as those of you who saw Prime Minister's Questions in the Commons yesterday (11 March) would have seen, sacked Second Sight, the independent investigators.

'When Post Office first notified us of their decision on Tuesday morning (10 March), I wrote … to the Minister, and as yet have not received a reply.'

In the midst of all this excitement the BIS Select Committee inquiry concluded. The chair of the committee, Adrian Bailey, sent a two page letter (dated 17 March) to Vince Cable, the Business Secretary.

The letter spoke of 'concerns' about the Post Office, not least that 'the Mediation Scheme is not operating in the manner envisaged.'

Bailey also noted James Arbuthnot's intervention on 11 March at Prime Minister's Questions with particular reference to the destruction of documents, but overall the letter was disappointingly wet. It concluded:

'We understand some of the cases being considered may be complex. I hope that, with your influence being brought to bear on the Post Office, the cases at hand may be directed towards a constructive resolution.'

The political process was beginning to fizzle out. Once again, the campaigning Subpostmasters and their MPs had come up against the same problem Alan Bates had found when trying to engage ministers during the previous decade.

Sir Vince Cable was Secretary of State at BIS from 2010 to 2015. He was happy to be interviewed for this book about the Horizon scandal. Over Zoom, he told me the subject never crossed his desk whilst he was in charge.

'We had a big issue with the Post Office. We wanted to stop the wide-scale involuntary closures of Post Offices and we fought for money for it. We got over a billion quid and that launched the transformation programme and my role was meeting Alice Perkins and Paula Vennells from time to time, just to check the programme was proceeding.'

Cable says neither Vennells nor Perkins raised the Horizon issue at any time during his tenure. I told him it was definitely raised by MPs to Jo Swinson who seemed to have basically parroted whatever the Post Office told her department.

'Well – I have spoken to Jo recently,' Cable told me, 'just to try and go back over our records of what happened. I think the point that has been lost in all of this is that the Post Office was very much an arm's length body. BIS had a representative on the board, but it wasn't something that was micro-managed by government.'

I asked if this was a structural failure. Shareholders are meant to hold companies to account, but the government's arm's length arrangement allowed ministers to turn a blind eye.

'The argument in favour is that companies are free to make business decisions which would be misdirected if politicians were trying to micro-manage them, but the downside is that you don't have the degree of oversight. Commercialisation in this case led to serious things happening which we weren't aware of until too late.'

I asked if Jo Swinson had expressed any regret for swallowing the Post Office line and regurgitating it to outraged MPs in the House of Commons.

Cable replied, 'We all regret that this terrible injustice has happened, but I don't think she can be blamed. Either the people at the Post Office were acting in good faith and they believed what the machines were telling them, and as a result a horrible mistake was made. Or they were covering up the fact an error had been made and they were pursuing people and sending them to prison, which is a dreadful scandal if it happened … there's no way ministers could have second guessed which of those was actually going on.'

When I spoke to Colin in 2020, I asked if there was this alleged distance between government and the Post Office. Colin candidly contradicted the official 'arm's length' relationship ministers and the government seem so keen to describe.

Colin told me Jo Swinson was meeting Post Office people regularly.

'Post Office and government were working very closely together. When my colleagues gave the Minister an answer to a question she didn't like, she would push back – she wouldn't just say, "Okay I'm going to have to front that out" – she would kick and scream.'

Writing years later, the barrister Paul Marshall looked into the ministerial statements around the collapse of the Mediation Scheme. He picked up on Jo Swinson's reply to the furious MPs at the Westminster Hall debate in 2014. At the time, Swinson told MPs that if she had been made aware of concerns about the Post Office Horizon system, she would 'get a team of forensic accountants to go through every scenario and to have the report looked at by someone independent, such as a former Court of Appeal judge,' implying there wasn't much more she could do.

Marshall asked, 'Given what the minister had told parliament on 17 December 2014, is it plausible that the Post Office sacked Second Sight without briefing the government, as its owner, on the reason for it doing so?… Assuming the Post Office did brief the government on those reasons… If the Post Office gave a truthful explanation to the government, that would make the government complicit in a six year cover-up.'

Jo Swinson has consistently ignored all requests for an interview about what she knew and the decisions she took as a result. She appears content to let her old boss vouch for her.

SECOND SIGHT'S FINAL REPORT

On 9 April 2015, almost a month to the day after the Working Group was euthanised, Second Sight handed the Post Office their final report. Bafflingly, it was given exactly the same name as the document which had appeared in August the previous year – Briefing Report 2. According to Second Sight this was because the August 2014 report was a 'living document.' The 2015 version was intended to be the final version of Briefing Report 2. The decision to give two different documents produced eight months apart exactly the same name has caused minor befuddlement ever since. To reduce any ongoing confusion I have called the final Second Sight report the 'April 2015 report' or just 'Final Report.'

Before sending Second Sight's Final Report to anyone, the Post Office put together another point-by-point rebuttal. Again, this was longer than the report it was trying to rebut. Both documents were sent on 16 April to Subpostmasters and their Mediation Scheme advisors with dire warnings about confidentiality.

I got hold of the Second Sight final report four days later and published it on my blog. Its conclusions followed the trend established in the 2013 Interim Report, but they had hardened up considerably. The most striking conclusion was that Second Sight could not categorically state Horizon was fit for purpose, stating:

'For the Horizon System to be considered fully "fit for purpose" for all users, it would, in our opinion, need to accurately record and process, with a high degree of error repellency, the full range of products and services offered by Post Office, whilst providing a clear transactional audit trail allowing easy investigation of any problems and errors that arise. The cases that we have reviewed demonstrate that this design objective has not always been achieved.'

Second Sight moved from the concerns expressed in 2013 and 2014 about the Post Office's investigators to a certainty they were not doing their job properly.

'We have established,' said the report, 'that Post Office's investigators have, in many cases, failed to identify the underlying root causes of shortfalls prior to the initiation of civil recovery action or criminal proceedings.'

On the flat denials issued to parliament about remote access, Second

Sight were clear:

'Our current, evidence-based opinion is that Fujitsu/Post Office, did have and may well still have the ability to directly alter branch records without the knowledge of the Subpostmaster.'

With regard to the question as to whether there had been miscarriages of justice, Second Sight were very careful, stating:

'We are aware of cases where criminal charges have been brought which appear to have been motivated primarily by Post Office's desire to recover losses. In some cases, those criminal charges do not seem to have been supported by the necessary degree of evidence and have been dropped prior to trial, often as part of an agreement to accept a guilty plea to a charge of false accounting, so long as the defendant agreed to repay all of the missing funds.

'We have also been told of agreements whereby no mention was to be made in court, by the defendant, of any criticism of the Horizon system.

'We remain concerned that some of these decisions to prosecute may have been contrary to the Code for Crown Prosecutors with which Post Office, as a private prosecutor, is required to comply. In order to investigate this matter we had requested access to the complete legal files held by Post Office in a number of cases. Post Office has stated that this subject is outside the scope of our investigation. We strongly disagree with this view.'

This was explosive stuff, far stronger than the interim conclusions reached in 2013, but no one was listening. Parliament had been dissolved in preparation for the 2015 general election, and the Post Office managed to kill the story by refusing to comment publicly, whilst hyperactively doing everything it could to suppress and limit any journalistic interest behind the scenes. Second Sight were contracted to the Post Office and therefore couldn't say anything, and Alan's unwillingness to be interviewed meant there was no media focal point for the JFSA's campaign.

After I posted the Final Report on my blog, Neil Tweedie from the Daily Mail got in touch. He was putting together a piece on the scandal and we had a good chat. Neil's article appeared across a double page spread in the Daily Mail on 25 April headlined: 'Decent lives destroyed by the Post Office.' In the piece, Tweedie interviewed three Subpostmasters who had all suffered in almost identical ways to the many Subpostmasters I was now familiar with.

Julie Carter had remained under threat of prosecution since 2009 after £60,000 went missing from her Post Office in Newcastle-upon-Tyne.

She blamed problems with Horizon, but was accused of fraud, losing her job and house. She was living in a council flat and was confined to a wheelchair with multiple sclerosis, a condition her husband Kevin believes had been made worse by the stress of what the Post Office did to her. 'You could not print what I think about those people,' he says in Tweedie's piece. 'I wouldn't buy a stamp from them if I could avoid it. I hate them, despise them.'

Sarah Burgess-Boyde was similarly ruined. Despite having her own struggles with Horizon (during a thunderstorm the system malfunctioned and credited her branch with £250,000-worth of stamps it didn't have), she turned around a failing sub-Post Office in Newcastle. Then the discrepancies began.

'As soon as I knew there was a problem I told them. I ended up with a £40,000 anomaly.' She was suspended in 2009, sacked and prosecuted for theft.

The case collapsed on the second day of the trial when the Post Office offered no evidence, but the damage was done. Sarah required counselling for depression and had not worked since her suspension.

She told Tweedie, 'My life will never be the same again. The truth is, the people running the Post Office are terrified that their brand will become toxic if they admit something is wrong.'

The final case study was a Subpostmaster called Jim Withers, who ran the Cromer Post Office in Norfolk. Tweedie described Withers raiding his savings and selling his car, shovelling money into Horizon to try to balance his discrepancies.

Jim told the Mail, 'I rang the helpline and they said, "Don't worry, it will sort itself out"... One time, the woman at the call centre told us what to do, we did it and it doubled the loss! The woman said, "Don't worry about it" again and put the phone down.'

Jim was ruined. He lost his home, his business and was living in rented accommodation.

Tweedie spells it out. 'The scandal surrounding Horizon quite likely represents one of the most widespread miscarriages of justice in the UK this century... Yet, the Post Office – one of the last bastions of nationalisation – has used millions of pounds of taxpayers' money to pursue people through the courts and silence criticism via an army of expensive lawyers, while continuing to deny to parliament that there was ever anything amiss.'

TWISTING THE KNIFE

On 14 May, after the general election which obliterated the Liberal Democrats and confirmed the Conservatives in power, Alan Bates sent a circular to JFSA members. He told them the Post Office had 'got rid of the Working Group because of the questions Post Office were not prepared to answer at meetings, which had the added bonus of removing a very senior and highly respected judge from seeing the paperwork that was emerging.'

Bates confirmed the mediation meetings which had taken place to date were largely pointless:

'We are being told by Applicants that these meetings are worse than disastrous as Post Office does not understand what a mediation meeting is all about, and is treating it as an opportunity to blame individuals, pointing out it is all their fault (where have you heard that before?)'

Bates said that due to 'conditions the Post Office has created' the JFSA no longer considered the Mediation Scheme fit for purpose and was recommending all applicants should now defer attending any mediation meetings 'until such time as a true and honest scheme is in operation, and no longer an exercise in highly paid lawyers dancing on the head of a pin.'

The JFSA founder encouraged his members to go back to parliament, telling them, 'Now there has been a change in government we all need to revisit our MPs and inform them of the latest developments.'

This was especially important as James Arbuthnot had stood down as an MP at the general election, which meant someone was going to have to take up the leadership role on the Horizon scandal in the Commons.

It was interesting Alan's note did not mention Edwin Coe, the legal firm he had joined forces with back in December. Nor was there any mention of the Criminal Cases Review Commission, despite the commission having publicly acknowledged (at James Arbuthnot's urging) they were looking into the Subpostmasters' plight.

In fact, the idea of any legal action was entirely absent from the email. I assumed the relationship with Edwin Coe had evaporated. Pinning the JFSA's hopes on a government-funded independent inquiry into the Post Office seemed unlikely – the government had no interest in creating negative headlines for the Post Office. The lack of public awareness of the scandal meant there was no pressure on ministers to do anything.

Having been told they were excluded from the Mediation Scheme, many of the Subpostmasters who had been criminalised were at a loss for what to do next. They had invested so much hope in the scheme, and after nearly two years of waiting for their chance to sit down and discuss what went wrong with the Post Office, they were now being told the Post Office wanted nothing to do with them.

Tracy Felstead suffered more than most.

'When I got that letter it felt like they'd won again,' she told me. 'They stabbed you again and they've twisted the knife. It messed me up.'

Tracy's participation in the Mediation Scheme had brought to the surface some long-suppressed trauma. The Post Office's cruel dismissal of her case had a direct effect on her mental health. Tracy's anxiety, which she had successfully medicated for more than a decade, got worse. 'I felt like I had no life… My attacks got worse. If I saw a police car or prison van I would start to panic. If I heard a song on the radio from the time [I was being prosecuted] I would have to switch it off or get away. I started to not eat… It became too much. I couldn't cope any more. I kind of … lost me.'

A PANORAMA IS BORN

I eventually managed to persuade Andy Head the Horizon story would make a good Panorama. He called with a proposition. One of their reporters, John Sweeney, was working on a film neither of them had much enthusiasm for. It was scheduled to go out in June. It might be the commissioners in London would agree to take John off the film if there was something which could slot into its place.

The Horizon story was ideal. Andy explained it meant John would be the presenter of the film, but I would get to work on it as a producer.

Any regret I had at not being able to front the programme was more than overshadowed by knowing Panorama would be bringing its guns to bear on the story. I was also intrigued by the prospect of working with one of the BBC's highest-profile investigative journalists. John had a track record of fearless reporting and was famous for his Scientologist-provoked YouTube meltdown. The first thing he said to me was, 'Bloody good story, this. I like it.' Then he told me about his experience of doorstepping[1] Vladimir Putin.

I was introduced by phone on 28 April to the film's director and senior producer, Matt Bardo. Matt is ridiculously intelligent, sociopathically hard-working and good fun to be around.

My first production meeting with John and Matt was over coffee and biscuits at The Heights, a bar on the fifth floor of the St George's Hotel, just outside Broadcasting House.

John used to be lampooned as 'the foghorn-voiced John Sweeney' in Private Eye. He certainly seemed incapable of talking quietly.

We weren't discussing the story in anything but the broadest terms and the place was virtually deserted, but I felt uncomfortable. I kept my voice down, hoping that everyone would follow suit. They didn't.

When Panorama contracted me, both Matt and Andy had given me an informal, but quite thorough briefing on the programme's data-handling protocols, which were strict, for good reason. Yet here we were in a quiet public bar, potentially about to discuss a sensitive investigation, VERY

---

[1] An occasionally dangerous journalistic tradition of approaching someone who has been avoiding more formal routes of enquiry and asking them questions they don't want to answer. The verb 'to doorstep' comes from the most frequent location chosen for these confrontations. Nowadays they often happen in more neutral environments.

LOUDLY.

I went along with this until two TV producer types came and sat down at the table next to ours. They opened their laptops and started working away in silence. If I were them, I would not only be earwigging our conversation, I would be live-tweeting it, too. As John bellowed away, and Matt made polite conversation about the work I had done on the Post Office to date, I started to feel faintly paranoid. My responses to Matt and John became so vague and non-committal I could tell they thought I might be some kind of idiot. Eventually, whilst Matt was talking, I wrote John a note suggesting that this was not perhaps the best environment to be discussing our plans.

John read it quietly and passed it on to Matt. 'Shall we go the pub?' he intoned, loudly, and stood up. 'I fancy a pint.'

The rest of the meeting, at the noisy Yorkshire Grey on Langham Street, was a success.

I found John to be a hearty, cackling, attention-seeking industry survivor, who takes a childish delight in his own achievements and excessive bad language. This, though, is John's Initial Impression Persona, which he seems to maintain for his own amusement. Spend any time in his company and he soon shows you an endearingly open and vulnerable side. John has an enthusiasm for life, a willingness to send himself up and best of all, he enjoys ruffling feathers.

On 29 April, Computer Weekly published confirmation that the Criminal Cases Review Commission would be looking into potential miscarriages of justice in relation to the number of Subpostmasters who had been prosecuted by the Post Office.

The Panorama was very much Matt's investigation (led, ultimately, by Andy), but I had strong ideas about the way it should be going, as did John. Whilst I wanted to be as committed as possible to the making of the film, I was only contracted to work three days a week, as I still had to fit my One Show and Channel 5 commitments around it. This meant I wasn't full time, and, crucially, I wasn't in Northern Ireland, which was where most of the research and all of the editing was being done.

At the Northern Ireland office Conor Spackman was the team's in-house document cruncher – a man of few, but often very well-placed, words. The final addition to the team was Tim Robinson, who had been sprung from BBC South to join Conor as a researcher.

Tim had been an essential part of the production team for The One

Show Post Office commissions and it was good to know he was on board, though his first task wasn't quite what he expected.

'I was pretty fired up,' he told me afterwards, 'looking forward to getting my teeth stuck into some serious investigative journalism. On my first day Matt, Andy and John were in the office. I was handed a picture of a red 1973 GPO motorcycle. "We want you to find us one of these" said Matt. I thought, "Oh. Okay…" '

Tim did good. After failing to spring a pristine model kept at the British Postal Museum, Tim was put on to the Post Office Vehicle Owners club. Tim explained himself to the club secretary and an email was sent to the general membership. Red gold was struck. A gentleman in Kent had recently bought a working 1970 GPO motorbike (made by Puch) and given it a lick of paint. Tim gave him a call.

'The owner said he had no immediate plans for it, so it was sitting, unused, in his garage. He was prepared to loan it to Panorama for a nominal fee, providing we didn't kill it.'

Tim hired a van, drove to Kent and was given a lesson on how to start and ride the motorbike by the owner, which Tim recorded on his phone's video camera. Tim then drove the van and bike to Caversham, home of BBC Monitoring until 2018. Caversham House is a re-purposed stately home on the edge of Reading, complete with a quarter mile-long driveway. Tim parked his van in the Caversham car park and unloaded the bike. Using the video he had recorded on his phone, Tim taught himself to ride the Puch by pootling up and down the drive, knowing he would have to teach John Sweeney what to do when they met the following day.

When John was informed about his filming wheels, he told everyone he would be absolutely fine, as he'd once hired and ridden an almost identical Puch motorbike in Vietnam. This was duly entered onto the BBC risk assessment form. What John didn't mention was that within a few hours of riding the bike in Vietnam, he'd fallen off and broken his arm.

Tim drove the bike up to Cambridgeshire where John and I were filming an interview with Seema Misra's expert witness, Charles McLachlan. The initial encounter between John and his ride was not promising. The Puch seemed unaccustomed to dealing with someone of John's dimensions. It also seemed to misfire and splutter to a halt far too often. Although we got some great shots of the Puch breaking down with John eventually kicking it out of frustration, this was not really what we wanted it to do.

Tim called the owner, who admitted he had put non-recommended fuel in the tank because it 'smelled better.' That evening Tim took the bike home and, using YouTube videos, taught himself how to drain an engine and mix the perfect two-stroke formula.

After that, the GPO bike ran like a dream. Our camera operator for the film was Joe Cooper. Joe tapped up a farmer he knew in Hampshire, who had a private road running through his land. With the road closed, Joe filmed some excellent drone shots of John steaming along on two wheels in the early evening sun. John grew to love the bike and christened it The Beast. As well as sailing majestically through the fields of Hampshire, John rode it in Cambridgeshire, Surrey, London and several dozen times around the roundabouts adjacent to the Fujitsu building in Berkshire, all without incident.

The bright red custom GPO Puch, with John's wobbly frame on top, became the visual motif which strung our film together.

RICHARD ROLL

Almost as soon as the Panorama commission was confirmed I called Alan Bates and told him.

'Oh,' said Alan. There was a pause. 'Good.'

It gave me no small amount of professional satisfaction to ask Alan if, now I had secured a Panorama, he would give me the name and number of the former Fujitsu employee he had let me listen to at Dobbies Garden Centre.

I also asked Alan if he would stop playing silly buggers and agree to be interviewed.

'Has Paula Vennells agreed to be interviewed?' he replied.

I told him I would be surprised if she thought she could duck a Panorama. I then reiterated my polite suggestion that whether or not Paula Vennells took part, it would be nice if Alan, as the head of a national campaigning organisation, felt able to go on camera to explain the Post Office Horizon story from the JFSA's perspective.

Alan said he'd think about an interview, and agreed to pass on the whistleblower's details. Alan hadn't spoken to him since he played me the tape in October 2014.

At last, I was going to make contact with Richard Roll. As soon as I got off the phone to Alan, I tried calling Richard on the landline Alan had given me. It didn't work. Heart sinking, I sent Richard a speculative email suggesting we have a chat. A few days later, to my eternal gratitude, Richard replied saying he was quite happy to meet up. This we did, at The Leathern Bottle pub in Wokingham on Sunday 10 May 2015.

I arrived early as I wanted to pick a table with some privacy. Wokingham isn't far from Bracknell and Fujitsu is a big local employer. The Leathern Bottle is a vast split-level pub, full of nooks and crannies. That evening it was virtually empty.

Richard arrived punctually. The first thing he did was tell me he had Asperger Syndrome.[1] He apologised in case he appeared socially awkward

---

[1] According to the Autism Speaks website, Asperger's generally involves typical to strong verbal language skills and intellectual ability, difficulty with social interactions, restricted interests and a desire for sameness. It can also include remarkable focus and persistence, aptitude for recognising patterns and attention to detail.

or wasn't that good at small talk. I apologised for my lack of technical knowledge and said I hoped we'd be able to understand each other. He smiled. I relaxed.

I put my recorder on the table. Over two pints of lime and soda, Richard told me that when he saw the 2011 Inside Out broadcast, he realised he had some insider knowledge and might be able to help. After the programme, Richard had googled around and found the Justice for Subpostmasters Alliance website. He emailed Alan Bates and they ended up having the recorded chat which Alan played to me at the Shrewsbury Dobbies in 2014.

From the outset of our conversation, it was a given that glitches, bugs and system failures were part and parcel of any computer network. I asked Richard if Horizon was any different from any other computer system.

'Yes,' he said, immediately. I asked why.

'I'd say there was nothing else like it. The size of it. The complexity of it all. What you were being asked to do.'

I asked whether the scale and ambition of the Horizon system made it more susceptible to code errors and problems.

'The bigger, more complex the thing,' he replied, 'the more likely [errors] happen. Because if you've got one chance in a thousand, multiplied by 20,000, then suddenly you're creating a certainty. On a smaller system it would be easier to find the bugs.'

Richard also explained a certain amount of sloppiness with the protocols around fixes during his time at Fujitsu.

'Testing had been cut back … at times a patch would be released and it would all be cleared up and then someone would, on the development side, use an old bit of code to develop a new bit and they hadn't applied the patches to it. So when the new bit came out, six months later, and that update is released, you've suddenly got the bug you fixed last year. So you've got to go through the whole process again.'

Even once the work had been done, there could be delays. 'You can find a bug very quickly and the code to fix it, but now you've got to schedule it in and all that time you've got a problem. You're working every night trying to pick up all the code and all the transactions that have failed so you can shoehorn them through and not meet any financial implications.'

Richard's department saved Fujitsu so much money by fixing problems before the client noticed them, they won a company-wide President's award.

'There were times when we could say, "We've saved this company £1.5m today by fixing a bug to get payments through to avoid contract fines," ' he told me.

It was an enlightening discussion which raised several serious questions. I asked Richard straight up if there was any doubt in his mind that some Subpostmasters had been put at a material disadvantage by errors within the Horizon system.

'No,' he said instantly. 'No doubt at all.'

I asked if he could remember any specific instance – names, dates, locations, nature – of a problem he was involved in fixing. He grimaced.

'I'm sorry, I knew you were going to ask me this and I was racking my brains before we met up. I can't. It was 11 years ago.'

Richard told me he was basing his assertion that Postmasters had been financially disadvantaged by errors in Horizon code on knowing how easily it could happen. Given what was going on, given the scale of the system and the nature of the problems they were dealing with, the probability a Subpostmaster would be left out of pocket by a Horizon error was, in his view, inevitable.

I asked about the likelihood this could have happened to multiple Subpostmasters – dozens, possibly hundreds.

'Given there were 18,000 Post Offices when I was at Fujitsu and the sort of problems we were dealing with all the time… Yeah. Sounds reasonable.'

Before we parted, we discussed the possibility of Richard taking part in a filmed interview. He was up for it. I also asked him about the allegation made by Michael Rudkin, the Subpostmaster who believed he had seen a manual intervention on the live Horizon system being demonstrated to him at Fujitsu HQ.

I asked if Richard knew of any Horizon terminals being located in the basement of the Fujitsu building.

He could not help. I asked him if he could give me any examples of specific, systemic problems with Horizon – something the Post Office were denying existed. Richard explained what became known as the transaction code mismatch error.

'Different companies would be given an ID. So Barclays Bank might be 1234 and you might have a transaction code 56789. That might be taking money out or something. However there could be a company, say,

British Gas, whose number might be 123, and they might have a transaction code 456789. So when it came in you had that same number. You didn't know whether it was British Gas or Barclays Bank. Somebody had to sit down and decipher which one it was.'

'Manually?'

'Yeah.'

'Why was this not sorted out with a patch or a piece of code?'

'There was nothing you could do about it because they'd already given the numbers out to these companies … running with this in all different places. They were never going to change. So there was no way you could differentiate when this data came in. I don't know how that finished. It may be that they worked out a way of getting it to say – okay that must be a gas payment transaction … but then if you had a glitch there at some point, you might find that somebody's bank account had had money taken out of it … or money put in or something…'

After our meeting I wrote up a rough transcript of our conversation and reported it to Matt Bardo. Matt arranged to meet Richard at home to go through all his proof of employment documents and other bona fides. During this meeting Matt gave Richard another grilling about his position and job role at Fujitsu.

Having established Richard was a credible enough source to be interviewed, we put him in front of a camera for the John Sweeney treatment. Relevant parts of the interview were isolated and we took them back to Richard so he could help us ensure we knew exactly what he meant when he said them.

The next job was to find some way of corroborating what Richard was saying with someone who understood programming and Horizon to the same level he did. We did this by setting up a meeting between Richard and an independent expert who had knowledge of Horizon architecture, the history of Horizon through the courts and computer systems of similar scale. The Panorama team sat in on the meeting. Over two hours, Richard was grilled by the independent expert who, after some fairly intensive questioning, pronounced himself satisfied that Richard was a credible interviewee, and that the transaction code mismatch problem was feasible and real. The programmer, who also works as an expert witness for the courts, was also certain that the activities of Richard, his colleagues and successors should have been disclosed by the Post Office on all the occasions its prosecutors asserted that Horizon was robust.

We had a scoop in the can.

At least, we were pretty sure we did, but before we could transmit the Roll Revelations we needed to go back to the Post Office and understand their position. Extensive discussions about the appropriate way to do this resulted in a recorded, on-the-record, *off*-camera 'briefing chat' between Matt Bardo and three Post Office execs; Angela van den Bogerd, Patrick Bourke from the Public Affairs team and Mark Davies, the Director of Communications. Matt asked them about remote access – the sort described by Richard Roll. The execs denied it was possible. Matt, being a thorough sort, asked:

'So it is not now, and never has been possible, for anybody, from Post Office or Fujitsu to interfere with transactions without the clear knowledge of the Subpostmaster?'

The reply came back. 'It is 100% true to say we can't change, alter or modify existing transaction data, so the integrity is 100% preserved.'

Matt double-double-checked, 'And that's true now, and has been for the duration of the system?'

The answer, an unequivocal, 'Yes.'

This was incorrect.

TROUBLE AT THE POST OFFICE

Richard was extremely important because he opened a window onto the reality of keeping Europe's largest non-military computer network functioning on a day-to-day basis, but his involvement finished in 2004. We needed to speak to someone who could give us an inside track on the recent parliamentary fireworks and the Mediation Scheme.

After a lot of to-ing and fro-ing – largely down to their contractual obligations to the Post Office – Second Sight agreed to give us an interview. Between them, Ron and Ian decided Ian would be the best interviewee.

We eventually decided on Jo Hamilton, Seema Misra and Noel Thomas, and we tried, oh we tried, to get Paula Vennells on to the programme. She wouldn't consent to an interview. Neither, then, would Alan Bates.

To give us some pictures, we found a helpful Subpostmaster willing to let us use his Post Office to get some good shots of Horizon in action, and, as the interviewees were being lined up, Conor and Tim scoured the documents we had been given access to by various sources. They were looking for new, important information, and they found it.

By the time the Panorama finally went to air on 17 August 2015, the programme was able to reveal:

1) An internal Post Office document which concluded that Noel Thomas' discrepancies were probably caused by 'operational errors.' Noel had been prosecuted and sent to prison.
2) The Receipts and Payments Mismatch Bug and the meeting just before Seema's trial to discuss it.
3) That after looking into Jo Hamilton's case, the Post Office's own criminal investigator wrote a report saying he could find 'no evidence of theft' at South Warnborough Post Office. Yet Jo was still charged with theft.

The programme also strengthened the commonly-held suspicion that slapping theft charges on Subpostmasters who had large discrepancies was nothing to do with evidence but a tactic to secure convictions. One document revealed a discussion about the best approach for securing a Proceeds of Crime Act order against a Subpostmaster. It read:

'I am never confident with false accounting charges … the theft charge makes life so much easier.'

During his interview for the programme, James Arbuthnot called on Paula Vennells to resign and said the Post Office's behaviour was 'disgusting', an 'abuse of power' and 'one of the most shocking things that I came across while I was a member of parliament – I'm still utterly shocked by it.'

Ian Henderson, who had been investigating the Post Office up close for almost three years, accused his paymasters of 'institutional ... blindness.'

The night Trouble At The Post Office was broadcast I went on The One Show to plug it. A piece of fortuitous summer scheduling meant that Panorama went out directly after The One Show at 7.30pm. At the end of my sofa chat with Matt and Alex I told the viewers that if they were interested in watching the programme all they had to do was stay exactly where they were and do nothing. The best possible call to action.

With my slot over and the rest of The One Show still happening I slipped out of the studio and nipped round the corner to The George pub on Great Portland Street. I bought myself a pint, put my headphones on and watched Trouble At The Post Office go out on my laptop. The next day I was told we got three million viewers. Not quite The One Show, but not bad for a Panorama.

The Post Office immediately issued a complaint to the BBC, calling our broadcast 'partial, selective and misleading.'

The National Federation of Subpostmasters, which we hadn't even mentioned, told Subpostmasters:

'The NFSP has not received calls from Subpostmasters querying Horizon and alleging systemic failings. If there were a widespread problem, our Subpostmasters would have made us aware of it. As a result, we have no choice but to conclude that Horizon is a fundamentally sound and safe system.'

A few days after the broadcast, I called Alan Bates.

'What did you think?'

'Well,' he said. 'I was disappointed you didn't mention the JFSA.'

I explained that had he participated in the film we would have mentioned the JFSA. Probably more than once.

'So, what's next?' I asked.

'We'll see,' he replied.

JUST OUTCOMES

Always a man to keep his cards close to his chest, whilst I had been helping pull the Panorama together, Alan was working with Kay Linnell to progress their plan to take the Post Office to court.

Kay and Alan also ensured the Criminal Cases Review Commission was properly prepped to receive applications from former Subpostmasters.

Usually, the CCRC will only get involved once an applicant has already had an appeal direct to the relevant court turned down. It can, however, consider cases in 'exceptional circumstances.' The CCRC clearly considered the Subpostmasters' cases to be exceptional – in March 2015 it supplied the JFSA with an FAQ specifically to help former Subpostmasters with criminal convictions come forward.

Being solely a criminal process, the CCRC's deliberations could run parallel to any action Alan and Kay brought at the High Court, which mainly concerns itself with civil (that is, non-criminal) matters. The problem was getting a civil action off the ground. Bringing a case of this nature to the High Court would be ruinously expensive and there would be no legal aid[1]. Alan and his Subpostmasters were a resourceful bunch, but they did not have the millions of pounds they needed to fund the case, nor did they have many super-rich friends. Alan and Kay would therefore have to look for external funding, which, in Kay's words, was 'a nightmare.'

The JFSA had two routes open to them. They could either try to find a firm of solicitors rich and committed enough to take on the cost of funding the prep for the case – involving investigation costs for dozens, or even hundreds of individual claimants, instructing barristers, and getting something called after-the-event insurance. This insures you against being counter-sued and/or legal costs if a judgment goes against you. For obvious reasons, after-the-event insurance can come with punishingly high premiums, especially if there is a decent possibility you will lose your case.

---

[1] Legal aid is the provision of financial assistance to those who are unable to afford legal representation. In 2009, Britain spent £2bn on legal aid, more per capita than any other country in the world. The UK government's austerity policy (introduced in 2010) and the 2012 Legal Aid, Sentencing and Punishment of Offenders Act removed access to legal aid for most people aiming to navigate the civil courts.

'Or,' said Kay, 'you find a solicitor at the same time as you find after-the-event insurance with chambers who are prepared to risk a bit, with funders who are prepared to put money down on the table to finance you to get to the first trial. It actually took Alan and I less than a year to do that, and I think that's pretty good going.'

It *was* pretty good going. In short order, over the latter half of 2015, the JFSA persuaded a firm of solicitors called Freeths, a litigation funder called Therium and a team of barristers from Henderson Chambers to take on their case. And they got their after-the-event insurance.

The risks were huge. The Post Office pretends it is a stand-alone business, independent from, but just happening to be owned by, the government. The reality is very different. As a business, the Post Office cannot go bust, because no government will let it. The political and social repercussions would far outweigh the cost of keeping it afloat. This allows the Post Office to defy corporate gravity. It can make decisions with far fewer consequences than similarly capitalised real-world businesses, because it has no existential risks. The quid pro quo is that the government has to approve every major piece of Post Office expenditure.

On a practical level, this means two things:

- The Post Office has potentially limitless funds to throw at something it wants to make go away, for example a pesky legal claim;
- The government controls the Post Office's decision-making, because it controls the Post Office's access to funding.

As well as its financial firepower and access to state resources, the Post Office had not lost a single significant legal challenge over the reliability of Horizon, nor was there much incontrovertible evidential material in the public domain which suggested any systemic problems (even though Second Sight's final report had pointedly failed to sign Horizon off as fit for purpose).

There was another issue which would have to be considered before any forensic investigation of the Horizon system – the Subpostmasters Contract. Whilst all of us have a reasonable amount of protection when it comes to the contracts we sign as individuals (for instance under the Consumer Rights Act), very little protection exists against unfairness in English law for business deals. Business owners are expected to do their own legal due diligence on any contract they sign. If they consider a contract to be unfair it is up to them to either negotiate better terms, or walk away. If a Postmaster – a small business agent – signed a document agreeing to be held liable for all financial discrepancies at their branch (due to their carelessness, negligence or error), then they were liable, especially if those discrepancies were part of accounts they had agreed were settled accounts. Persuading a judge that this contract was unfair would take phenomenal legal acumen.

James Hartley is a litigation specialist at Freeths. He comes across as a thoughtful, serious person. When I asked what made him decide to take the JFSA's case on, I was expecting a strategic or tactical answer. Instead I got a philosophical one.

'We took a step back and thought, "What is the just outcome from all of this?" – and the more we read into it the more we realised the only just outcome could possibly be in favour of the Postmasters.'

When I asked the same question of Patrick Green, the dashing QC from Henderson Chambers who led the claimants' team of barristers, he gave an equally surprising, but very un-philosophical instant answer: 'Richard Roll!'

If the former Fujitsu man's tales of diving into Subpostmaster accounts to fix things without their knowledge were true, there was a potential crack in the Post Office's hitherto bullet-proof armour. According to Green, Roll's testimony 'made a fundamental difference.'

But whistleblowers and thoughts of just outcomes will only get you so far. You need cold hard cash, which is where Therium came in.

Litigation funding is a strange business. It was considered unlawful until well into this century under the ancient concept of 'champerty,' which stopped third parties profiting from court actions in which they had no legitimate interest. Reforms introduced by Lord Justice Jackson in 2013 (as a way of trying to keep a lid on the costs of taking legal action) quietly set these issues aside, almost instantly creating a market.

Based on the no-win, no-fee principle, litigation funding involves gambling large amounts of other people's money (which may have been provided by a hedge fund or shareholders) on the outcome of a case. If the funder loses the case it is backing, it loses its investors millions. If the funder wins, it takes a multiple of its stake – a 'success fee' – from any settlement or award.

A commonly used multiple is 3 to 1 (in other words, a £3 return for every £1 risked on the case). Litigation funders don't tend to get out of bed unless there is at least £10m of recoverable damages on the table. This reflects the risk involved, plus the amount of time and expense that goes into deciding which cases to back. All prospective funders have their own teams of lawyers who will pore over the merits of a case and take a good look at the legal teams proposing to fight it. Competence, a clear strategy and a strong track record are essential.

Litigation funders accept they won't win every case, so when they win, they want to be sure they will win big, in order to offset their losses.

In February 2016, Alan called. This was a rarity in itself, and he was certainly the most animated I'd heard him in a long time.

'We've got it. We've got funding,' he said.

'What does that mean?' I asked.

'I've got the money to take the Post Office to court.'

I asked how much.

'There's no limit.'

I was flabbergasted. 'You've secured *unlimited* funds?'

'Yep.'

Alan explained the next steps. Freeths would file a claim against the Post Office with his name on it and then they would seek a Group Litigation Order (GLO) from the High Court to turn it into a class action.[1]

In April 2016, *Bates v Post Office* was duly filed. A couple of months later, submitting enough documentation to suggest Bates was not an isolated case, Freeths applied for a GLO. I was told a presiding judge would be appointed in the autumn of 2016. The date got pushed back to 2017.

Whilst the wheels of justice were slowly cranking up once more, I called round some of the Subpostmasters I'd got to know quite well. This was partly to see how they were, and partly to get the latest gossip. A lot were obviously despondent about the outcome of the Mediation Scheme, having pinned their hopes on it for so long. The JFSA had now been campaigning for six years. Many of its members had been living with criminal convictions in straightened financial circumstances that really made them fear for the future. People were getting old. Sadly, in August 2016, Julian Wilson, the former Astwood Bank Subpostmaster, ran out of road.

---

1 Which, to stop annoying the lawyers and pedants reading this, I will henceforth call by its proper name – a Group Litigation. For the technical difference between a US class action and an English Group Litigation, see the footnote on page 177 in the 'First BBC Commission' chapter, or the glossary.

JULIAN WILSON

I interviewed Julian in December 2014 for the second One Show film we made during the gathering at the village hall in Fenny Compton. Julian's wife Karen stood alongside him with tears streaming down her face as Julian explained in his measured, careful way how problems with the computer system at their Post Office caused their lives to fall apart.

After years of campaigning alongside Alan, Julian was accepted onto the Mediation Scheme, only to be told that as a convicted criminal, the Post Office would not mediate with him.

Karen believes the stress of what Julian went through during the Mediation Scheme gave him type 2 diabetes, and reports his doctor acknowledging Julian's health was beginning to wane because of the pressure he was under.

'He became more insular,' Karen said. 'Doing 300 hours' community service cleaning graves in a high visibility jacket wrecked his self-esteem and confidence.'

In all the years I knew him I never made a film specifically about Julian. I just used to ring him for a chat, to get an alternative perspective on what was happening with the Horizon story and get his opinion of how things were going.

'Hello Nick…' he'd say every time I called up. 'What can I do for you?'

That question was Julian's attitude in a nutshell. It was all about what he could do for me. He never once asked me to do anything for him. He would always take the call and always help where he could. Then he would ask after my kids and my work and always end the conversation by saying, 'Call me any time, Nick. Any time you like.'

Julian found he had cancer towards the end of 2015.

When I was told about Julian's diagnosis I didn't immediately pick up the phone. I called him the following April to chat about the JFSA's High Court claim. Julian was fresh out of surgery and preparing for another bout of chemotherapy. I'd heard things were touch and go, but his voice sounded strong.

'Don't worry,' he told me, cheerily. 'I'm on the mend. I'm feeling better. Things are going to be alright.'

We spoke about Julian's determination to see his name cleared and the latest on the various legal obstacles he and the JFSA were facing. There was never a trace of bitterness in his voice. Julian accepted things with great patience even though he was still in danger of losing his house because the Post Office had a charge on his property.

Given the GLO could provide the peg for another film, I felt Julian's situation could be used to highlight how long everything was taking and that, for some, time was running out. Julian agreed it made sense. He had no qualms about appearing on camera, even though he might not be looking his best.

Over the summer, Julian's health deteriorated. On 16 August I received an email from Julian's brother, Mike. Mike had never contacted me before. The message said:

'Nick I just thought I would let you know that my brother Julian Wilson who is one of the Subpostmasters wronged by Post Office is seriously ill with liver cancer at his home in Redditch. It looks alas as if it might be terminal. Just thought I would let you know as you both met and he always appreciated what you were doing.'

I realise now Mike was giving me a chance to call Julian and say goodbye. I missed it. Julian died on 22 August 2016.

Mike wrote to Paula Vennells shortly after Julian died, informing her of his beloved brother's death. He told her Julian's death was due 'in no small part by the seven years of stress he suffered as one of the Subpostmasters who have all been wronged terribly as a result of the Post Office negligence.' Understandably emotional, he told Vennells she would 'no doubt' be in court herself in the future, adding, 'I would take great pleasure if you were to go to prison together with all your accomplices.'

Ms Vennells did not respond, leaving her 'correspondence manager' to send the Post Office's condolences.

GROUP LITIGATION GRANTED

The first open court hearing of *Bates v Post Office* was not scheduled until 26 January 2017. It was set to formalise the GLO arrangements. I was only made aware of the hearing two days before it happened. I alerted Sandy Smith at The One Show. He suggested that after spending the day in court I should get in a cab and go straight to The One Show studios at Broadcasting House and explain to the nation what had happened whilst perched next to yet another bewildered celebrity, live on the famous sofa.

I was thrilled but nervous. I had basically got The One Show to commission three minutes of prime time television from me on trust. Other than the fact of it happening, nothing had been put into the public domain about the Subpostmasters' litigation. Knowing how dull legal argument can be, and often is, I hoped that by the scheduled end of the hearing I had something to say.

I arrived at the Royal Courts of Justice at 9.30am, got through security and made my way up the main block's eastern stairs to Court 4. Alan, Kay and the Freeths team were already lurking outside. We shook hands and I explained the situation with The One Show. James Hartley, who had been politely resistant to giving me any information for a full eight months, could not have been more friendly or helpful. Kay Linnell was very forthcoming on the expected course of the day's events and Alan almost seemed pleased to see me. The whole group was quite jolly, which, given what they were about to go through, and how much was at stake, surprised me.

Patrick Green soon bowled up, as did the Post Office legal team. I was the only journalist present. I positioned myself at the back of court as the lawyers took their seats. At the appointed hour, the usher yelled: 'Court rise!'

We did. The judge, Senior Master Fontaine, walked to her place. We bowed. She bowed. We all sat down.

The first thing I found out was that there were already 198 claimants, the vast majority of whom were former Subpostmasters (the rest being either Crown Post Office employees or sub-Post Office assistants). This was up from the 150 who applied to the Mediation Scheme. The total sum being sought in damages was not confirmed as it had not been calculated. The particulars of each individual claim had yet to be finalised, but I had been assured outside court the final figure could run into tens of millions of pounds.

The granting of the GLO was uncontested – but the basis on which it should proceed was the subject of much debate. The Post Office lawyers had a number of ideas about this, which led the Master at one stage to wonder aloud why they and their client had agreed to a GLO at all.

It wasn't long before my concerns about having something to tell The One Show fell away.

During the morning session Patrick Green quoted from the Post Office's post-broadcast response to the 2015 Panorama programme (in which the Post Office accused the BBC of being 'partial, selective and misleading'). Mr Green drew the court's attention to the section of the response which stated:

'There is … no evidence of transactions recorded by branches being altered through "remote access" to the system. Transactions as they are recorded by branches cannot be edited, and the Panorama programme did not show anything that contradicts this.'

Mr Green told Master Fontaine, 'It is absolutely clear that they are saying that transactions cannot be edited remotely. And that turns out to be untrue because they have now admitted that there are four ways in which those transactions can be remotely changed.'

Oh *have they* now?

Green turned to a legal submission prepared by the Post Office for the litigation. He read it to the court.

'A balancing transaction can add a transaction to the branches' accounts but it cannot edit or delete other data in those accounts. Balancing transactions only exist within Horizon Online, not the old version of Horizon, and have only been in use since around 2010. Their uses logged within the system is extremely rare. As far as Post Office is currently aware, balancing transaction has only been used once to correct a single branch's accounts.'

Green continued:

'Database and server access and edit permission is provided within strict controls, including logging user access, to a small controlled number of specialist Fujitsu, not Post Office, administrators. As far as we're currently aware privileged administrator access has not been used to alter branch transaction data. We are seeking further assistance from Fujitsu on this point.'

Master Fontaine raised an eyebrow in the direction of the Post Office

QC, Anthony de Garr Robinson. Mr de Garr Robinson got to his feet and stated that the years of repeated denials about third party remote access to Horizon were 'a matter of enormous regret.'

He noted the Post Office's Panorama response was 'written by people who thought it was correct. The Horizon system is a very complicated system. It involves lots of departments … both in Fujitsu and in the Post Office. And the people who are responsible for the correspondence didn't know that, in fact, there were these two other routes.'

I started bashing away on my laptop at the back of court. This was extraordinary. The Post Office was now accepting (albeit in an extremely limited way) that its denials to Panorama were wrong because the people involved in making those denials did not know a fundamental truth about a massive bone of contention consistently raised by the media, Subpostmasters and MPs.

I was reminded of the phone-hacking scandal which engulfed the British newspaper, The News of the World. Before being jailed, the newspaper's former editor, Andy Coulson, persistently claimed he did not know his journalists were hacking celebrities' phones, despite evidence it was rife. This led to the suggestion[1] he was either 'complicit in crime, or he was one of the most incompetent Fleet Street editors of modern times.' Could so many Post Office execs be that staggeringly incompetent, or were they complicit in something darker?

On top of the remote access revelation, an important decision was made – the GLO could remain open to new claimants until July. Freeths would fund an advertising campaign with a view to bolstering the claimant numbers beyond the 198 already gathered. These could be former or existing Subpostmasters, employees of Subpostmasters or Crown Office employees.

The hearing went long into the afternoon. Full day court sessions don't usually stretch beyond 4.30pm. The One Show had booked me a cab for 4.45pm. This would take me straight to the studio at Broadcasting House for rehearsal.

By 4.30pm the proceedings seemed to be nearing an end, but I didn't want to leave in case I missed something important. I texted my producer with key lines from the day and asked her to keep my cab waiting outside.

---

1 By the politician Chris Huhne, later sent to jail himself for perverting the course of justice over a speeding fine.

The wrangling eventually concluded at 5.30pm. The One Show was on air at 7pm. I threw a few hurried goodbyes at Alan and his legal team and almost ran out of court, along the corridor and down the stone steps into the massive Victorian gothic hall of the Royal Courts of Justice. No one else was about. Even the court staff and security team at reception had gone home. Struggling with my heavy laptop bag, I half-jogged, half-limped towards the pairs of giant wooden doors at the courts' main entrance. Depending on traffic, getting to Broadcasting House and rehearsing everything before the programme went to air could prove tricky. The later I left it, the more likely the show's director would find something else to fill his three currently unrehearsed minutes.

I was in the annoying position of having what, in Post Office Horizon scandal terms, was a huge scoop, but I was in serious danger of losing my slot.

When I got to the Royal Courts of Justice's main entrance, which is set in a whopping great porch at the southern end of the Great Hall, I realised just how infrequently courts were expected to sit late. Both sets of doors were already locked, each with a padlocked six-foot metal bar across them. I shook the brass door handles – partly in frustration, and partly because I was hoping a security guard might appear out of the gloom and ask what I thought I was doing.

I waited a second. Nothing. I was going to have to find another way out, if there was one. I ran back into the deserted hall. Looking at the countless doors and arches which spun off into the darkness, I had a brief and somewhat farcical notion of being trapped in a Harry Potter movie. I tried to guess which arch or doorway was most likely to lead to an exit.

I was close to making a decision which might see me lost in a rabbit warren of corridors and staircases when I was saved by the noise of high heels clacking on flagstones. Tracking east to west along the corridor behind the large northern arch of the Great Hall was a smartly-dressed woman carrying a briefcase. Guessing she might be a lawyer familiar with the building, I ran the length of the hall, calling after her. She very kindly stopped as I gabbled a question at her about exits. The smartly-dressed lady didn't seem 100% sure of where she was going, but within two minutes we had found our way into a courtyard and were marching towards a security hut and some large metal gates. I shouted my thanks and ran towards the Strand, hoping my cab hadn't disappeared.

It hadn't. The traffic was at its usual crawl, but I was able to use the time in transit to formulate my thoughts, write a draft script and call through to the production office to discuss exactly what I'd be doing once I got to Broadcasting House.

In the end it all worked out. Six hours of court proceedings were condensed into three minutes of live sofa chat with Matt Baker and Angela Scanlon, and we were able to incorporate a short statement from the Post Office (welcoming 'the progress made today') into the conversation. The bemused celebrity on this occasion was Reggie Yates.

On watching the broadcast that evening, a concerned serving Subpostmaster wrote to the Post Office Chairman alerting him to the issues I had raised on the sofa. Donna Gilhooly, the Chairman and Chief Executive's 'Correspondence Manager' wrote back telling the Subpostmaster it was 'disappointing' The One Show had 'incorrectly characterised the discussions' which had taken place in court. Remote access was apparently only 'very briefly touched on' and it 'has not yet been the subject of proper evidence or argument.' It was therefore 'regrettable that the BBC's summary of the issue was inaccurate.'

It bloody wasn't inaccurate. And given I am under a legal responsibility to report court proceedings accurately and fairly, I would have been in contempt of court and unlikely to find any more work as a journalist again if what I said *was* inaccurate. Grr.

PART 3

LARGE COMMERCIAL DEALS

Numbers matter in a GLO. Each claimant has a value attached to their case. Once the value of all the cases is totted up, the funders can see what they might be in for if they win, and the viability of progressing the case can be assessed. If each client is seeking £500,000, ten claimants can win a maximum of £5m. If your litigation is going to cost £20m to fight, it's a non-starter. A hundred claimants with the same average claim could win £50m, which is getting interesting. Find a *thousand* claimants looking for £500,000 each and suddenly you've got a potential winnings pot of £500m. Obviously, every individual case is different – as it was with the Subpostmasters. Some had been forced to hand over thousands of pounds to the Post Office, but managed to keep their jobs and businesses. They would only likely claim that strict financial loss back (with interest). Others were sacked, suspended and prosecuted, losing their homes, savings and suffering (for example) future earnings loss, reputational damage and stress-related health problems. Each of these could be apportioned a value, and for some Subpostmasters, the total ran into millions.

The JFSA had until the end of July 2017 to find more Subpostmasters willing to join their litigation. There was no financial commitment, and no liability, just an agreement to be represented by Freeths and bound by the terms of any outcome. Word went out across the Subpostmasters' networks. Adverts were placed in newspapers. Hundreds of Subpostmasters, Post Office managers and counter assistants came forward before the deadline. Some were still serving, most were retired or had been sacked. Once they had been assessed for suitability the final number of claimants topped out at 589.[2] Of these, 61 had criminal convictions. This doubled the number of contested convictions anyone had previously been aware of.

James Hartley found it jarring to switch between thinking about the business end of the litigation whilst listening to the Subpostmasters' heartbreaking stories.

'These cases have to be large commercial deals,' he told me. 'We're talking about tens of millions of pounds – there's no other way of doing

2 Several claimants pulled out over the course of the litigation, bringing the final total to 555.

it, but we would constantly be having conversations with Subpostmasters who were understandably focused on their own situation. Their lives had been ruined. Their reputations had been completely demolished. They had virtually nothing. The enormous contrast between those two perspectives was always striking. And harrowing. Whenever they tell the stories of what happened to them, the shock never goes away, however many stories you hear.'

Hartley and his team were focused and determined. 'The overriding memory I have is the gravity of the whole thing we were embarking on, because of the human tragedy, coupled with the massive financial numbers we were talking about in terms of having to launch into this legal battle. It was pretty serious stuff.'

There followed weeks of intense work by the Freeths solicitors, taking statements from every claimant, preparing the lead witness cases, and arguing the toss with the Post Office's legal team over what seemed like absolutely everything.

Once the Group Litigation Order had been formally secured, a managing judge was appointed. *Bates and Others v Post Office Ltd*, to give the case its full title, was put in the hands of Sir Peter Fraser. Mr Justice Fraser is a former Royal Marine who spent most of his career as a barrister dealing with multimillion pound commercial disputes at the Technology and Construction Courts in England, Hong Kong, China, South Africa, Sweden, France, Bermuda, Dubai and Oman. It was a job which would keep most people busy enough, but within 12 years of finishing his pupillage Fraser also found time to develop his interest in criminal law by sitting as a Crown Court judge. In his spare time he is an Iron Man triathlete. Given his expertise in construction, natural authority and favoured recreational pursuit, it was almost inevitable that Fraser would end up with the nickname 'the Iron Judge.' It fits. One of his peers describes him as 'conspicuously able.'

The first thing Fraser had to do was stamp his authority on the litigation. His first judgment, issued in November 2017, was made in response to an application by the Post Office to delay the first trial. The judgment is essentially a 21-paragraph bollocking. Fraser recorded that between them, the parties were:

- 'failing to respond to proposed directions for two months'
- 'failing to lodge required documents with the court'
- 'failing to lodge documents in good time'

- 'threatening pointless interlocutory[3] skirmishes'
- 'refusing to disclose obviously relevant documents'

Ah, disclosure again. As a reminder, one of the obligations of civil and criminal legal proceedings is that documents considered relevant to a case must be shared between the parties on request. If Party A has a document that Party B thinks will help them, Party B can demand to see it. Party A must then either surrender that document or come up with a good reason as to why they shouldn't. 'Because it might damage our position' is *not* acceptable, but lack of relevance is. Lawyers can therefore spend weeks arguing over the nature and scope of disclosure requests (as they did, at length, before Seema Misra's trial). Complex cases involve thousands, sometimes hundreds of thousands of documents, all of which have to be read, assessed, cross-referenced and filed. Initial tranches of disclosure can lead to more disclosure requests, which then get contested again. If Party B thinks a document is essential and Party A is determined not to disclose it, a judge can make a decision in either party's favour, but as this comes with costs and consequences, it is a last resort. Although the principle behind disclosure is fairness, it can easily be weaponised in an adversarial system.

Kathleen Donnelly was one of the barristers from Henderson Chambers working closely with the claimants. She felt the Post Office were trying to game them.

'It is obvious that the Post Office had a strategy to withhold material until they were forced to produce it. This caused delay, disruption and ran up costs. We only received significant documents after a battle and were left with little time to review them, sometimes just days before a witness was cross-examined. It was exasperating.'

Fraser was incensed at what he called the 'leisurely' and 'dilatory' attitude displayed by both parties in getting the litigation anywhere near its first trial. The Post Office lawyers didn't think there needed to be any trial until 2019 at the earliest. Fraser called this 'unacceptable' and fixed a date for November 2018. The day after this was agreed, the Post Office's leading counsel, Anthony de Garr Robinson QC, told the court he was

[3] If the parties involved in a litigation cannot resolve a procedural or legal point during the preparation for a trial, one or both of them might approach the court seeking an order from the managing judge. Interlocutory (literally to speak between, or interrupt) applications can lead to interlocutory hearings, which are expensive and time-consuming. They can divert, delay and unnecessarily increase costs.

not available, so could the first trial be punted into 2019 anyway?

With a possible element of judicial steam coming out of his ears, Fraser 'declined' this application and laid down the law. 'The delay until November 2018 is more than enough as it is… All of the many claimants, and the defendant, need resolution of the matters in issue… A fundamental change of attitude by the legal advisors involved in this group litigation is required. A failure to heed this warning will result in draconian costs orders.'

The parties were on notice.

CROWDFUNDING

In terms of scale and the resources required to deal with it, between 2017 and 2019 *Bates v Post Office* was the biggest litigation going through the civil courts in England. The work required to get everything in shape in time for the first trial was head-spinning.

The first big battle was over the structure of the trial itself. Torturous negotiations produced a 19-page list of 23 disputed areas relating to the correct interpretation of the Subpostmasters Contract. These became known as the Common Issues, which were posed as questions for the judge to decide.

There was a huge burden on the Postmasters' legal team, who had to wade through the disclosed documents, witness statements and reams and reams of contract law to put together a strategy which would deliver a persuasive case. It was, according to Kathleen Donnelly, a stressful time.

'We were not sleeping well, we were not eating well, and we basically lived in chambers. It was a difficult case. We knew what we thought had gone on, but we had to convince the judge, and a lot of the legal points were really, really difficult. But we were in good spirits. As a team, the more the pressure mounted, the better we worked together. Everything the Post Office threw at us made us more determined.'

Six former Postmasters from the 500+ claimants were chosen as lead witnesses. Appropriately, as lead claimant, Alan Bates would be first into the witness box. I asked James Hartley what the point of having witnesses was, given the trial was about deciding the meaning and fairness of various iterations of a contract. Hartley explained the need to have 'tangible examples' of how the contract impacted on people in real life.

As well as claimant witnesses, the Post Office would also put forward more than a dozen of their own staff from various departments within the organisation. These defence witnesses could describe their interactions with Postmasters, which, again, would show how the wording of the Subpostmasters Contract (in its various iterations over the period Horizon was in use) was interpreted on the ground.

In June 2018, the JFSA and Freeths held final meetings for the claimants to update them on progress and prep them for November's trial. Freeths even circulated a Frequently Asked Questions document explaining the dress and behaviour expected of claimants, should they wish to attend court. Jo Hamilton was counting the days to the start of the first trial.

'You felt nervous, excited ... we were all talking to each other on the phone and there was a real feeling of eager anticipation. But we didn't realise the battle that was coming and how epic the whole thing was.'

Despite the enormity of the litigation, *Bates v Post Office* generated little or no media interest. Recriminations over the decision to leave the EU were playing out as a grand drama across the political spectrum. Theresa May's Brexit deal, the Withdrawal Agreement, the Northern Ireland backstop *et al* were taking up a lot of bandwidth. Remaining minutes of airtime were filled with slightly more 'grabby' subjects like the Beast from the East, the Thai cave rescue of a group of young footballers, Harry and Meghan getting married and Prince Louis being born. A complicated-sounding legal dispute over an employment contract by former Subpostmasters (a job title which itself needs explaining to most people) was not the sort of story to excite broadcast news editors, especially when the four week-long first trial was not even going to produce a 'winner.'

Twenty or thirty years ago, *Bates v Post Office* would have had at least one dedicated agency reporter sitting through every open court date, churning out copy designed to catch a news editor's eye. Nowadays, big civil and criminal cases can have periods when there is not a single journalist in court. Yes – we'll be sent along to mark the first day, report on star witnesses, summing ups, verdicts and sentencing, but it's a genuine rarity to be assigned to a long case for its duration.

My experience of hearing the admission about remote access in January 2017 had brought home the value of sitting through a potentially unpromising day of legal argument. Outside that one day in court, the Post Office had so far refused to give up any of its secrets without a serious fight. I was concerned that during the trial, a game-changing revelation could surface and then sink away unreported if there were no journalists around to drag it into the public domain.

My problem was money. As a freelance hack, I had spent a precarious few years living hand-to-mouth and had no reserves. The good years just about subsidised the thin ones and 2018 had been annoyingly thin. No news organisation could justify paying me to be there, and I just wasn't in a financial position to sit in court unpaid for a whole month.

Inspired by the superb book Beyond Contempt, which detailed Peter Jukes' crowdfunded reporting of the News International phone-hacking trial at the Old Bailey, I wondered if there was any way I might be able to try something similar. After looking at various options, I settled on a Kickstarter campaign. Kickstarter is an 'all-or-nothing' crowdfunding platform. Supporters make pledges and give the Kickstarter website their account details. If you don't reach your target, your supporters' money stays in their accounts, and everyone walks away. If I failed to reach my target there would be no hassle or fallout, and at least I could say I tried.

I worked out the minimum I needed to cover the first trial at a modest loss, which was about £3,000. Then I built a website called PostOfficeTrial.com.[1] On 31 August I pressed the button on a six-week crowdfunding campaign – hustling hard on social media and begging every friend, family member and contact I had to stump up some cash and spread the word.

The same day I launched my crowdfunder, the Criminal Cases Review Commission, which had been looking at more than two dozen Subpostmaster cases for more than three years, issued a bizarre letter. 'Apart from a small number of points of clarification,' it told applicants, 'the investigation phase of the CCRC's review is complete. We are now in a position to move into the decision-making phase of the cases this autumn.'

I was astonished. I knew that civil and criminal law ran along separate tracks, but could it be possible the CCRC was proposing to *ignore* the wealth of evidence that was surely going to come out of the litigation? Was it somehow inadmissible to its criminal deliberations?

I assumed either the CCRC already had enough to refer the Subpostmaster applicants to the Court of Appeal, or it was legally unable to consider any evidence which the litigation was going to produce. There was, of course, the insane possibility the CCRC was just about to tell its Subpostmaster applicants there was *not* enough evidence to quash their convictions days before a month-long trial which would almost certainly reveal valuable information directly or indirectly relevant to their cases.

To my unending delight (and gratitude to the people who put their hands in their pockets), my crowdfunding campaign worked. In nine days I was more than double funded. I was elated. With careful management, I might be able to attend both the Common Issues trial *and* the Horizon

---

1 Which I have continued to maintain since 2018, documenting this scandal, thanks to the generosity of many hundreds of people.

trial, which was scheduled for early 2019.

Shortly before the Common Issues trial began, the Post Office threw another spanner in the works. It issued a strikeout application, objecting to some of the witness evidence the claimants were intending to use in court. More of Alan's supposedly unlimited funds were going to be drained dealing with this latest development. The Post Office seemed determined to make the litigation as expensive as possible.

EXTREMELY AGGRESSIVE LITIGATION

Judgment number 2 in *Bates v Post Office* deals with the strikeout application, which was heard on 10 October 2018, less than a month before the first trial was due to begin.

The Post Office had taken a look at the witness statements of the six lead claimants and decided they weren't relevant because they described events which had nothing to do with the witnesses' contracts, were too subjective and weren't relevant to the area of law which the first trial was examining.

Mr Justice Fraser dismissed the Post Office's application, positing a suspicion it was 'simply attempting to restrict evidence for public relations reasons.'

The judge recorded that in the 17 months which had passed since the group litigation was formally adopted:

'The legal advisors for the parties regularly give the appearance of taking turns to outdo their opponents in terms of lack of cooperation … it appears to me that extremely aggressive litigation tactics are being used in these proceedings… It is both very expensive, and entirely counter-productive.'

Just how expensive is revealed in the judgment. The JFSA and the Post Office had spent £10m between them before either trial had begun!

Fraser concluded, 'No judge ever knows (and should never speculate) about what is going on in the background to any litigation, particularly complex litigation such as this. However, this application regrettably falls into a pattern that has, in my judgement, clearly emerged over the last year at least. Attempts are being made to outmanoeuvre one another in the litigation, and tactical steps have led to constant interlocutory strife.'

'This,' he orders, 'simply must stop.'

Although convention might have prevented Mr Justice Fraser from speculating on what was going on in the background to the litigation, it was obvious to everyone else. The Post Office were using their unlimited resources to drag everything out as expensively as possible, obstructing the claimants' access to information whilst draining their cash.

The strategy was explained in a meeting held on 26 September 2018. The Post Office's Chief Financial Officer, Alisdair Cameron, was holding court with a number of union officials. Five other senior Post Office executives were present. Andy Furey, from the Communication Workers Union, asked Cameron about the cost of compensating Subpostmasters if the Post Office lost the GLO. According to Furey, Cameron was 'candid' in his response.

'He bragged that the Post Office's pockets were deeper than the JFSA, who had to secure financial backing, and the Post Office would win by virtue of being able to find the money to make the litigation process onerous, time-consuming and difficult at every step of the way.'

Furey says Cameron allegedly[2] told him that litigation funders were 'hard-nosed business people' who might make a strong initial play, but 'would not hesitate to pull out at any point when victory wasn't guaranteed or looking unlikely.' According to Furey, Cameron explained to those present that the litigation funders 'would quickly cut their losses and move on to fresh pastures when the costs started to mount or spiral, coupled with increasingly longer timescales than ideal. He basically said that these investors were mercenaries and had no aim other than making money. They were looking for a quick and healthy return on their investment and when this wasn't looking likely they would withdraw financial support. The case would collapse through lack of funding and legal resources.'

Furey says none of the other Post Office executives present stepped in to correct this view of their organisation's approach to the litigation. The union man has no doubts about what he was being told.

'The very clear impression we were left with was – irrespective of the merits of the case – the Post Office would be able to play a longer game due to unlimited financial resources to defend itself, allied to legal tactics designed to increase costs, which the JFSA couldn't match. At the time I was certain that we were hearing exactly the strategic plan to beat the JFSA and that the senior leaders of the Post Office were not perturbed by the prospect of losing, as they didn't believe the JFSA would be able to sustain the legal challenge.'

The Post Office has since called Furey's recollection a 'mischaracterisation.' Furey told me, if required, he is prepared to put what he heard and witnessed into a sworn affidavit. Just a few months later, Mr Justice Fraser effectively confirmed Alisdair Cameron's comments and the claimants' suspicions by stating the Post Office 'has appeared determined to

---

2 And, as it turned out in Therium's case, wholly incorrectly.

make this litigation, and therefore resolution of this intractable dispute, as difficult and expensive as it can.'

FIRST TRIAL BEGINS

The Rolls Building, off Fetter Lane in central London, is a very different beast to the Royal Courts of Justice and, in its own way, just as annoying. It is named in a nod to the office of the Master of the Rolls, the second most senior position in the England and Wales judiciary after the Lord Chief Justice.

Whilst the RCJ is all sprawling gothic splendour, competing with the likes of Westminster Abbey, the National Gallery and the British Museum for architectural overkill and impracticality, the Rolls Building was completed in 2011. From the outside it therefore looks exactly the same as every other twenty-first century city centre office block. It houses the High Court's Chancery Division, the Commercial and Admiralty Court and the Technology and Construction Court. The Rolls Building is described as the largest specialist centre for the resolution of financial, business and property litigation anywhere in the world. Over the course of 13 months I came to loathe it.

From its uninspiring corporate exterior, to the hopelessly inadequate facilities (which seem designed-in, as a punishment for the humans forced to use it), the Rolls Building has one message, and that message is, 'I don't like you.'

There are three floors of 31 courtrooms, 11 hearing rooms and 55 consultation rooms, into which lawyers and their clients can sweep importantly during breaks in proceedings.

The interior is coloured various shades of corporate brown and the overall atmosphere is deadening. This, the Rolls Building announces, is where the *business* of justice is administered. You can keep the stodgy theatricality of the Royal Courts of Justice – we are here to *work*.

To be fair, the chairs are comfy. You are never that far from a plug socket (a serious problem in the RCJ, which was designed during an era when the most technologically advanced source of power was steam) and the courtroom acoustics aren't too bad. Overall, though, it is not a welcoming environment. And there's no press room.

The *Bates v Post Office* Common Issues trial was to be conducted over 16 days in one of the Rolls Building's three mega courts. It started on 7 November 2018.

At a few minutes past midnight, on the day proceedings were due to begin, Sue Knight and her husband Nigel left their home in St Keverne in Cornwall, and climbed into their ageing Citröen. They drove for five hours in the darkness to Basingstoke in Hampshire. Once parked up, they bought themselves some breakfast and paid £50 each for a peak-time return train ticket to London.

Sue later told me, 'My tummy was rolling all the way! There was a lot of anticipation. I was thinking, "Is this really happening?!" Hopefully this was going to be the beginning of the end. People were going to believe us. Sometimes you lose belief in yourself... And it was happening. It was going to happen.'

Sue and Nigel got to the Rolls Building with time to spare, so they could meet and have a coffee with some of their fellow claimants who had also come along to mark the beginning of the trial. Karen Wilson travelled down from the Midlands wearing her late husband Julian's tie as a scarf. She showed me the urn containing his ashes in her bag. 'I don't want him to be a victim,' she said. 'I don't want people to think the Post Office killed him. But what they did contributed to his death. He should have been enjoying his retirement.'

Tracey Merritt, Scott Darlington, Jasvinder Barang, Teju Adedayo and Jo Hamilton were also bobbing around outside. Jo was buzzing.

'It was so exciting for us to be there and for it to kick off!' she remembered. 'All the years of fighting and we'd actually managed to secure the funding and get the blooming thing into court, despite the Post Office trying to derail it goodness knows how many times.'

Shortly after 10am we began to queue for security. Although we were surrounded by lawyers in wigs and gowns working on other cases, Mr Justice Fraser had decided legal costume for the *Bates v Post Office* litigation would be unnecessary. He had also apparently declared he did not wish to see a single piece of paper in his courtroom. This meant there would be no porters wheeling boxes of files into Court 26 each morning. Instead, all the paperwork would be uploaded onto searchable custom-designed courtroom software called Opus. Documents would be read from screens by both parties, the judge and witnesses. The litigation would also be served by real-time speech transcription from two stenographers who sat in court directly below the judge's bench. One stenographer would bash out what she heard as it was being said, the other would smooth over typos and correct any homophones. The results would appear on more custom screens positioned in front of the judge, witness box and leading counsel. This allowed the active participants to go over the exact wording of anything that was said at any stage during the day – something which might be used to clarify a point made during the course of live proceedings.

There are three good reasons for a journalist to attend court.

The first is obvious – you can write down what is being said and report it.

The second is that if you hear a document being discussed during proceedings which sounds like it might be interesting, you can request it from the parties. This is usually a tedious process because the parties are not obliged to hand it over, but the courts in England and Wales have decided that in the interests of open justice, a journalist asking for a document referred to in court should usually be given it, unless there is a good reason not to. This potentially creates a pathway for getting confidential information into the public domain whether the parties like it or not. If a journalist *isn't* in court to witness a document being used in evidence, something big enough to hang a Panorama on can be mentioned once and then disappear for good, without anyone requesting to see it.

The third reason to be in court is relationship-building. Getting to know claimants, defendants, solicitors, barristers, clerks, stenographers and ushers is a lot easier if you are exchanging pleasantries and literally rubbing shoulders with them as you file into court every day. Contacts provide off-the-record tips and guidance which can sometimes point you in the direction of hard, publishable information. Alternatively, they can provide helpful and accurate context to something which might have happened or been said.

For some reason, the Rolls Building's courtrooms were designed without press benches, which means journalists have no reserved seating. There is nothing for those who use shorthand to lean on, other than their knees. Not that there was any difficulty finding somewhere to sit in Court 26. Its dimensions feel only slightly smaller than an Olympic swimming pool and it can easily accommodate a couple of hundred people. Unfortunately, it has a ceiling lower than any equivalent-sized room I've been in, other than a multi-storey car park. The judge's elevated bench runs across the long, wide, northern side of the court, with the clerk seated directly below the judge, next to the stenographers. In the middle of the court, separated by a short aisle, are three rows of bench desks for each party's lawyers. Every place with a desk has its own computer screen, linked to the Opus software. Behind the lawyers' desks, stretching across the long back wall and encroaching round the corners into both sides of the court, are two rows of around 150 individual seats. These are for witnesses, journalists and members of the public, and seemed available to use ad hoc.[3]

The courtroom's main architectural feature is a giant, round concrete pillar right in the middle of the court towards its rear. It was of obvious structural importance, but it ruined many of the sight lines for those of us in the cheap seats.

We filed in and began to settle. The visiting claimants sat behind their legal teams. Various Post Office staff, including Angela van den Bogerd and the Post Office witnesses sat behind theirs. Kay and Alan had places on the rear row of bench desks alongside the legal assistants and trainee solicitors in the Freeths team. This gave them the advantage of having their own screens to follow the action.

I decided that if I was to have a chance of building any kind of rapport with the Post Office solicitors I should go and sit on their side of the court. I somehow managed to persuade Karl Flinders from Computer Weekly to join me. We detached ourselves from the claimants and picked our way round the giant pillar to find seats directly behind the po-faced corporate lawyers from Womble Bond Dickinson, who were working for the Post Office. We sat down and opened our laptops. Doing so seemed to generate a ruffle of discomfort. After some *sotto voce* discussions in front of us, a male lawyer approached and asked us to sit somewhere else. I asked why. It turns out he didn't want us seeing confidential information over the shoulders of his colleagues, which might appear on the courtroom screens in our line of sight. I asked if he could force us to move. He told me he couldn't. There was a momentary stand-off as Karl and I contemplated the implications of not moving. On the grounds that any confidential information would have to be flashed up on the Opus screens in at least 36 point type for me to have a chance of reading it, I decided to accede to the lawyer's request. Karl reluctantly followed me. We shifted to the far eastern corner of the court, a full 25 yards from the witness box. I felt faintly humiliated.

---

3 I was surprised to find the seats were neither bolted together nor screwed to the floor, which is a testament to the number of hours I have spent working in public buildings.

Jane Croft and Michael Pooler from the Financial Times were among the other journalists who had come along to mark the opening of the Great Post Office Trial, as had Sam Greenhill from the Daily Mail and Sian Harrison from the Press Association.

At 10.29am the clerk checked the parties were ready and gave the nod to the usher. A hush settled on the court. The usher disappeared into the corridor leading to the judges' chambers. At exactly 10.30am he re-appeared, made one sharp knock on the door and proclaimed: 'All rise!'

We were underway.

Mr Justice Fraser would have commanded respect if he'd pedalled into court on a children's tricycle, playing the kazoo. He is tall, with a slim frame, shaven head, and a practised military bearing. He also seems to appreciate the sartorial advantages of a three-piece suit.

Whilst Fraser's formidable presence and booming voice had the potential to be intimidating, he commanded Court 26 with scrupulous courtesy. Ushers and clerks were thanked for their efforts and nervous-looking witnesses were offered reassuring words before they had to open their mouths.

The barristers, on the other hand, could not get away with anything. Fraser would pounce on and pick apart the slightest lack of clarity in their submissions. Forensic examination of specific points would be sharp and swift, keeping counsel from both parties on their toes whilst ensuring the trial's schedule stayed on track.

The first day was given to opening statements. The parties had submitted several hundreds of pages of written argument to the court, but these had stayed confidential until the trial began. We were finally going to hear, for the first time, the broad thrust of each side's arguments in public.

Patrick Green presented the claimants' case with a tiggerish enthusiasm which gave his arguments a sense of energy and verve. Green told the court the relationship between the Post Office and individual Subpostmasters comprised such an imbalance of power that the Subpostmasters Contract was unfair in law. This was partly because of the way the contract was constructed, partly because so few Postmasters understood its import (or indeed ever saw the contract in the first place) and partly because of the way it was implemented.

Green asserted the power imbalance wasn't just contractual, it was intrinsic to the relationship between the Post Office and Subpostmaster, manifesting itself in access to information, the operation of Horizon, and how each party could and did behave when things went wrong.

During his opening submissions Mr Green referred to a number of interesting documents. One was the Frank Manning email chain written in the light of his site visit to Pam Stubbs' Post Office in Barkham in November 2000.[1]

In this email, you will remember, Mr Manning tells a colleague the problem that has led to a £1,000 discrepancy at Pam's branch '**is Horizon related**,' helpfully in bold type, for emphasis. Nonetheless, Pam was not informed about this diagnosis and was subsequently held liable for (and paid out) the discrepancy.

Manning's email, said Green, directly contradicted the Post Office's central claim (made in its written opening submissions to the trial and, as we know, in its written response to the oral evidence Select Committee hearing in 2015) that no claimant had ever been held liable for branch accounting discrepancies which weren't their fault. The same morning, Patrick Green also raised the infamous 2010 Receipts and Payments Mismatch memo, created a month before Seema Misra's trial. About this, Green told the court:

'There obviously is the ability to write an entry value in a local branch account, because it is recited there as a possible way of doing it, and it sharply shows the degree of control that Post Office and Fujitsu have over not only the Horizon system itself but also how errors that arise – system-related errors that arise – are dealt with.'

The BBC had managed to refer to and quote from the Receipts and Payments Mismatch memo during our 2015 Panorama, but now it was being mentioned in open court, which presumably meant the full document was up for grabs. I wrote an email to Freeths asking for both the memo and the Pam Stubbs email chain.

Over lunch,[2] I managed to persuade Alan Bates to let me take his photo. He really does not like being in front of a camera, but he gave me a shot. We grabbed a sandwich and had a chat. I asked him if he was nervous about being first to take the stand on day two. He told me he wasn't, because he was only required to talk to the judge. I pointed out he

1 See the 'Pam Stubbs' chapter on page 249.

2 Bizarrely referred to in courts across the land as 'the short adjournment' – a Victorian euphemism which suggests even thinking about, let alone consuming, base comestibles is somehow impossibly vulgar.

still had to answer the Post Office's questions. Alan seemed convinced he would do so insofar as they allowed him to give important information to the court. 'I don't even have to look at them,' he said.

Once we were back in the Rolls Building, Alan said, 'There's something I want to show you.' He produced from his pocket several home-made business cards, all of which had the logo of my Post Office Trial website on them, with a link to the Kickstarter page on the back.

'Where on earth did you get these from?' I asked.

'I had them made,' Alan replied.

He told me that whilst the crowdfunding period was live, he'd been handing them out or leaving them lying around at meetings when he came to London.

I was touched. Alan and I have different perspectives on certain issues, to put it mildly. To me, a key protagonist and campaigner in a story which deserves nationwide awareness should be hammering the media for airtime at every opportunity, because I've seen the difference it can make.[3]

Alan, I think, sees journalism as largely ineffective. Certainly not as effective as the courts. I was in awe of what he had achieved as a campaigner, but I always thought his personal lack of interest in the media/public affairs side of things was a serious blind spot.

I looked at the cards in my hand and wondered at the kindness of Alan's gesture. I thanked him.

'No problem!' he chuckled. 'I wanted you to be here reporting all this, because otherwise it meant I'd have to do daily updates to the claimant group myself, and I've got enough on as it is.'

Before the afternoon session started I spotted a small, middle-aged man who had been sitting on his own at the back of court, staring straight ahead. There were, occasionally, tears in his eyes. He didn't seem to be with anyone, so I introduced myself. The man's name was Parmod Kalia. He was a claimant. He didn't know any other claimants. In fact, he didn't know anything about the Postmasters' campaign for justice until 2015. Until then, Parmod had spent more than a decade living in penury after

---

[3] Despite the strength of the JFSA's arguments, by 2018 the story hadn't once been front page news. This was mainly due to the Post Office (abetted by the NFSP) using its enormous clout to suppress the scandal, but when I asked my Post Office insider Colin if it helped that Alan Bates didn't give any interviews, he laughed and said 'Definitely!'

being sent to prison for theft.

Parmod's career began in 1977 as a bank teller at NatWest. He was 18 years old. Parmod worked his way up to the post of assistant manager by the time he left NatWest in 1989. He had handled money all his adult career. Through hard graft and prudent saving, he put enough aside to take over a retail business with a Post Office attached on Chipperfield Road, in Orpington. Parmod successfully ran his Post Office from 1990 to 2001 without a single problem. Then Horizon was installed.

In 2001, Parmod's Post Office was 'audited.' His Horizon system showed a £22,000 hole in his accounts. He was immediately suspended. Parmod says he contacted his local NFSP rep, whose only response was to ask how quickly he could make the discrepancy good to 'keep it out of the courts.'

Desperate, Parmod went to his mother (who knew nothing about the situation) and asked for a loan. He then handed the Post Office a cheque for the full amount.

Once the Post Office had the money, Parmod was sacked and charged with theft. No one suggested for a moment the Horizon system might be at fault, so it was down to Parmod to prove he didn't steal the money at his trial.

Parmod's legal team knew it could end badly. If he was found guilty by a jury, he was almost certainly looking at a prison sentence. They suggested he plead guilty to reduce that risk. Parmod was further advised to make up a story about borrowing the 'missing' money from his branch in order to mitigate his sentence. He did as advised, and was sent to prison anyway.

The years immediately following his conviction were hard. Not knowing what had happened at his Post Office, Parmod blamed himself. His family blamed him too, for the shame he had brought on them and their ruined prospects and reputations within the community. Relationships broke down, increasing Parmod's feelings of worthlessness. He hid what happened from his mother, fearing the truth might kill her. Parmod tried to end his own life on three separate occasions. He thought he was the only one dealing with inexplicable discrepancies at his branch and blamed himself for everything that happened.

Parmod eventually found fulfilment in voluntary and social work, but the 'audit' which ruined his life, his sacking, subsequent prosecution by the Post Office and prison sentence left him fragile. 'It completely broke me, on reflection,' Parmod told me. 'At the time I was dumbstruck. It didn't really hit me as much as it does now.'

Fourteen years after being given a prison sentence, losing everything and trying to bury what happened, Parmod saw the 2015 Panorama.

For Parmod, it was a revelation. He wrote to Paula Vennells, the Post Office chief executive, telling her what happened to him *must* have been as a result of a Horizon error, as per the allegations being made in the Panorama programme. He could see no other reason for it. He sent Ms Vennells all the evidence he had. It is typical of Parmod's decency that he did not demand Vennells re-open or review his case. He just asked for an apology for what the Post Office had done to him.

He received a reply from Angela van den Bogerd. Years later, Parmod sent it to me. Van den Bogerd wrote:

'The Panorama programme you refer to in your letter included a number of inaccurate statements, drawn selectively from limited information, to create a misleading and damaging impression of how and why Post Office undertook prosecutions.'

Van den Bogerd told Parmod the Post Office had 'exhaustively investigated' Horizon and not identified 'any transaction caused by a technical fault with Horizon which resulted in a Postmaster wrongly being held responsible for a loss of money.'

Fifteen months before the Post Office would be admitting in court that remote access was perfectly possible, van den Bogerd told Parmod there was 'no evidence' of transactions recorded by branches 'being altered through "remote access" to the system. Horizon does not have functionality that allows Post Office or Fujitsu to edit or delete the transactions recorded by branches.'

Van den Bogerd finished her letter by telling Parmod,

'If you believe that you have been subject to a miscarriage of justice, you should take independent legal advice. The solicitor who acted for you on the prosecution, or the Citizens Advice Bureau may be able to help you.'

On the day of our first meeting, as Parmod told me his story, I noticed he had difficulty looking me in the eye. It was a condition he told me he'd developed in the years after his release from prison. I asked him why he'd come along to court.

'It's important,' he said. 'There are people here who can put the case forward that there *were* problems in the computer system. And I can understand now that there were many others in the same position as me.'

We swapped numbers.

The afternoon session was given over to the Post Office's 'extremely capable'[4] lead counsel David Cavender QC. Cavender was from One Essex Court, the barristers leading the Post Office's defence. Cavender told Mr Justice Fraser the Post Office has a contractual obligation to Subpostmasters under the terms of the Subpostmasters Contract, and it has always stuck to that obligation. Inventing implied terms of obligation and responsibility to a contract, just because the claimants want it to have some, was, at best, fanciful. Postmasters are agents, the Post Office is the principal, and both go into a business relationship with their eyes open.

'What the claimants are trying to do,' he said, 'is water down the agency/principal relationship – almost to vanishing point.'

Patrick Green had contended that the contract (in all its iterations) was relational, which meant it was 'based upon a relationship of trust… The explicit terms of the contract are just an outline as there are implicit terms and understandings which determine the behaviour of the parties.'

The Post Office said that if the court accepted the JFSA's argument on the Subpostmasters Contract, the Post Office's business model would become untenable. Indeed, in their written submissions, the Post Office contended *Bates v Post Office* represented an 'existential threat' to its way of doing business.

Another argument advanced by Mr Cavender attracted Sir Peter Fraser's close attention. Cavender stated that at no stage would the Post Office ever hold a Postmaster responsible for a discrepancy caused by the Horizon IT system. Section 12:12 of the Subpostmasters Contract, he said, was only interested in a Postmaster's own 'negligence, carelessness or error.' A Horizon error was not a Subpostmaster error, so a Postmaster could never be pursued for a Horizon error under Section 12:12. The kicker to this argument being that if Horizon reported a branch discrepancy, it was perfectly reasonable to infer that the accounting discrepancy existed, because of Horizon's general reliability.

In other words, any Horizon discrepancy became fact by Horizon's reporting of it. And Horizon's existence in the Post Office/Subpostmaster relationship (or its propensity for errors) couldn't make the contract

---

4 According to his chambers' online profile.

unfair because any discrepancy was (in the Post Office's mind) a settled issue before the terms of the contract came into play.

Fraser was sceptical. He concluded an interrogation of Cavender's position with the suggestion the barrister revisit the thrust of his proposition 'because at the moment it is relatively unclear.'

At the end of the day I rushed off to the nearest pub to put together and file my first crowdfunded court report. There was a lot to write about.

ON THE STAND

The next day, on the way into the Rolls Building, I asked James Hartley about the possibility of getting my hands on the daily transcripts. He seemed amenable, but explained the Post Office would need to give their consent as both parties were sharing the cost of producing them.

Alan Bates was sworn in, and his cross-examination at the hands of David Cavender began. This was a big moment in the Post Office story. Alan had waited 15 years for his day in court. We were expecting fireworks. Unfortunately his strategy of answering Cavender's questions whilst staring at the judge made for an awkward start. Although Fraser didn't query the approach, he patently found Alan's tactic odd, and his demeanour demonstrated as much. This threw Alan, who lost focus. Cavender just seemed bemused.

Eventually they settled into a rhythm. Cavender had a lot of questions about the Subpostmasters Contract and Alan's appointment as Postmaster at Craig-y-Don. In his written evidence, Alan maintained he did not see a full Subpostmasters Contract before he took over the branch. Mr Cavender found this incredible. Having painted a picture, which Alan accepted, of an experienced businessman who thrived on detail, how on earth could or would he take on a business without seeing the contract or discussing the nature of his liabilities on the business?

Alan said when he did sign a contract with the Post Office, he thought the three short documents and covering letter constituted the contract, and had no idea that there was another 114-page tome called the Subpostmasters Contract which contained all the detail about his responsibilities if anything went wrong.

'If I had received it,' said Alan 'it would certainly have gone to my solicitors and I certainly wouldn't have signed what I thought was a very straightforward document and returned it almost the same day.'

Cavender seemed to think this was ridiculous. He asked how Alan could possibly have gone into a business deal without seeing the contract which underpinned it? He then suggested Alan was wrong and that actually he had been given the contract. Alan maintained he wasn't given one.

Alan was then asked why, when he signed upwards of 20 documents on the day he took over the Post Office in the presence of a Post Office manager, he didn't read any of them.

'Mr Bates, you are not commercially naïve,' Cavender intoned. 'You are asked here to sign a serious declaration and you've read and understood these extracts.'

'Yes, and I did query them,' replied Alan, 'and I was told, "Oh ... these documents are simply a matter of how we deal with things." '

This, thought Cavender, was hardly the mark of an attention to detail man. And so it went on.

After an excruciating couple of hours, the QC changed tack and started asking about Alan's refusal to follow Post Office procedures once Horizon had been installed at his branch. As we know, when Alan was a Subpostmaster it was possible to deal with a negative discrepancy in three ways:

a) settle it to cash (that is, 'make it good' by cash or cheque);
b) roll it over into the next accounting period as a loss;
c) put it into suspense (with the Post Office's permission) and dispute it.

In 2005 the Post Office removed the latter option and added a 'settle centrally' button which was the same as 'settle to cash' option. This meant accepting the debt without being required to make it good immediately.

Although it remains technically possible on Horizon to this day, the Post Office does not like any Subpostmaster rolling a discrepancy over into another trading period.

As you will remember, with Alan's first bunch of discrepancies, he bundled them up and put the resultant £1,182.81 into suspense. The disputed amount sat in his branch suspense account for two years. The Post Office couldn't work out how the discrepancy arose, so they wrote it off.

Alan got more discrepancies which, rather than putting them into suspense, he just kept declaring them and rolling them over into the next trading period.

When Cavender questioned him on why he didn't put the new discrepancies into his suspense account as before, Alan said there were three reasons:

a) he didn't know it wouldn't come back to him as a debt;
b) he wanted the Post Office to give him the tools to interrogate Horizon properly;
c) he wanted to use these tools to find out himself if he was responsible for the debt.

The QC told Alan he could put his discrepancy into suspense and *still* request the Horizon tools to do his investigations, so why didn't he?

Alan blustered a bit at this. The QC asked the same question again.

The judge then interjected, 'Mr Cavender, you are putting this letter to the witness by concentrating on ceasing the practice of rolling over losses and gains.'

Mr Cavender agreed this was exactly what he was doing.

The judge pointed out this meant he was 'ignoring the first part of the same sentence, and the first sentence on the previous page which requires him to repay the money.'

Cavender admitted that this was, of course, the Post Office's preferred option – Alan just paying up. But Alan still had the option of putting his discrepancy into suspense and the Post Office QC wanted to know why he hadn't.

Towards the end of the cross-examination, Cavender suggested that Alan had become a little fixated on Horizon to the extent he saw it as the source of all his problems – and he had remained fixated ever since. In fact, said Cavender, it was quite conceivable the errors in his branch accounts could have been down to him or his assistants.

'No, it isn't,' replied Alan.

And that was that. The end of Alan Bates' evidence. It wasn't a great performance, but giving evidence isn't necessarily about a performance. Bates was there to give his own perspective. The judge was going to have to decide how useful it was.

After the trial was over I asked Alan how he felt. 'Well,' he reflected, 'I would rather not have gone first.'

I understood what he meant. Second-guessing the conventions of the court, the attitude of the judge and tactics of a highly skilled QC if you've never seen them in action, let alone been in a witness box before, would have a profound affect on anyone's ability to think clearly. Alan was also juggling the wider responsibility of the litigation itself. I thought, under the circumstances, he did well.

Pam Stubbs, however, was different class. It helped that she did not have the weight of the entire litigation on her shoulders, and her circumstances were more recent. The other thing she had in her favour was that she had been subjected to obviously appalling treatment at the hands of the Post Office despite the fact she had not contravened a single Post Office procedure. Cavender could not lay a glove on her.

He started much as he had with Alan Bates, suggesting that Pam's appointment as a Subpostmaster in 1999 was a long time ago.

'It is fair to say,' he ventured 'your memory of the details of those events is probably pretty vague. Is that fair?'

'No, I don't think so,' replied the former games mistress, curtly.

Cavender pushed the point, unwisely using the same metaphor he had put to Alan Bates.

'We are talking about everyday events, not something like a car crash.'

Mrs Stubbs paused and fixed Mr Cavender with a hard stare. 'If you're referring to the events of August 1999,' she said, 'it very much *was* like a car crash. And I remember it vividly.'

Cavender realised his mistake. 'I think you might be referring to your husband's death,' he said.

'Yes,' replied Pam, coolly.

David Cavender said he understood it must have been a very difficult time, but 'I was thinking more about whether you received a particular document or which one you particularly signed. Nineteen years on, you can't be absolutely clear about that, I suspect. Is that fair?'

Pam narrowed her eyes. 'Some documents, yes. Tell me which ones you mean and I will be able to tell you.'

And so we began.

Pam was asked if she understood that her husband was operating under a contract. Pam said she guessed he must be, but she never saw one or saw him consulting it or heard him talking about it. It transpires that the Post Office has no record of Martin Stubbs ever having signed a Subpostmasters Contract. For such an important document, the Subpostmasters Contract was beginning to assume the tantalising proportions of a Snark.[1]

Thoughts turned to Pam's contract.

Cavender said: 'You accept you were regulated by the Subpostmasters Contract?'

Pam replied: 'I assumed I would be taking over the branch on the same terms as my husband ran the branch.'

Pam was questioned about her understanding of the agent/principal relationship a Postmaster had with the Post Office. This came to an abrupt end when Pam pointed out that for the first few months as Subpostmaster she was being taxed at source as an employee. This wasn't

[1] A mythical creature neither seen nor found. Invented by Lewis Carroll in his nonsense poem 'The Hunting of the Snark.'

really helping the Post Office's argument that the Subpostmaster/Post Office relationship was in no way relational. The line of questioning was quickly dropped.

Pam was asked what she signed the day she became Subpostmaster – she maintains she did not see a Subpostmasters Contract for the entire time she was a Subpostmaster. A really long exchange about what sort of documents Pam signed on the day after her husband's death or some weeks later went on for about half an hour before being abandoned.

We eventually alighted on Pam's suspension in 2010. 'Were you surprised?' asked Mr Cavender.

Pam said she was, 'Absolutely staggered … as angry and upset as I've ever been by anything in my life.'

He asked if she ever thought she could be sacked without notice.

'No. Not really,' said Pam.

The QC then asked why she didn't consult her contract to see if she could be suspended in the way she was. Pam told him it was a bit late by then, and she'd been locked out of her temporary Post Office without access to any of the documents.

After Pam Stubbs, across three more days of cross-examination, we heard from Mohammad Sabir, Naushad Abdulla, Liz Stockdale and Louise Dar. The six Postmaster witness stories covered an 18-year period from 1998 to 2016 and a geographic spread from Lenzie in Glasgow to Charlton in South East London. All the cases had striking similarities. The account balances at each witness's Post Office had gone awry, and the Post Office, with minimal or no investigation, demanded money with threats. They then either suspended the Subpostmasters without pay, or sacked them, causing them to lose their investment in their businesses. Naushad Abdulla was angry and combative, giving Cavender as good as he got. Louise Dar was tearful, at one point exclaiming the behaviour of her Post Office contract manager was 'disgusting' and that she should be in court 'answering the questions' instead. Liz Stockdale and Mohammad Sabir seemed as bewildered to be in court as they were by what had happened to them. I had heard dozens of other Subpostmaster stories – including Pam and Alan's – many times before, but here were four strangers who'd suffered varying degrees of loss, having their own situations forensically examined in court, and it all sounded so maddeningly *familiar*.

Once the claimant witnesses had been dealt with, it was time to see what the 14 Post Office witnesses were made of.

Whilst it was certainly compelling to watch the claimants recount their experiences, hearing anything on the record from anyone at the Post Office was even more of an enticing prospect. I had been waiting years for the Post Office's position on Horizon and its treatment of Subpostmasters to be properly picked apart, and we were about to get six days of it.

The first two witnesses, Nick Beal and Paul Williams, both began as counter clerks in 1989 and 1979 respectively. They had 68 years' service between them. Nick Beal had reached the giddy heights of Head of Agents' Development and Remuneration. His responsibilities included managing the Post Office's relationship with the NFSP and Subpostmaster pay. Paul Williams was a Restrictions Advisor who had the responsibility for Alan Bates' Post Office at Craig-y-Don when he was appointed in the late nineties. Unfortunately, he couldn't remember much about it.

Patrick Green spent much of the day dealing with Nick Beal, whose witness statement contained some useful information about the National Federation of Subpostmasters.

Mr Beal had written, 'The NFSP is independent of Post Office' in his witness statement. Beal went on to note that the NFSP had recently become a trade association, wholly funded by the Post Office. According to Mr Beal, a document had been created to 'underline' the NFSP's independence. This was called the 'Grant Funding Agreement.'

Green drew attention to the fact that in its written opening, the Post Office stated, 'The National Federation of Subpostmasters … does not support this action and does not endorse the factual premises of the Claims.'[1]

Mr Beal agreed the NFSP had explicitly supported the Post Office's position on Horizon – and referred to George Thomson's statement to the BIS Select Committee in 2015, in which Thomson had inferred campaigning Subpostmasters were dishonest chancers and that, with regard to Horizon, the Post Office had done 'nothing wrong.'

Mr Green wanted to know more about this, but the judge didn't. 'I'm not particularly interested,' he declared. 'I don't want to sound rude, Mr Green. Everyone comes to this court with a clean slate, whatever the NFSP's view is one way or the other.'

---

1 The NFSP say they had no idea the Post Office were going to use their name in their litigation defence and that, if consulted, they would have requested their name was not used.

Green promised he had a point. 'If your Lordship would bear with me I will make it good.'

Fraser leaned back and let him continue. Over the course of the next half hour Mr Green showed the court an email which had been pulled out of a tranche dumped on the claimants by the Post Office the previous evening. The email was from George Thomson. It was dated 2 August 2013, when the NFSP was in the middle of negotiating a funding agreement with the Post Office. At the time Paula Vennells was looking for the NFSP's support for the Network Transformation scheme, a cost-saving exercise which would cut most Subpostmasters' salaries to the bone.

Thomson was amenable to supporting this project, but wanted 'a signed agreement with the blood of both myself and Paula … on the future of the NFSP' before he put his weight behind the Network Transformation scheme.

Mr Beal reluctantly agreed this meant the NFSP was negotiating its own future as a condition of its support for Network Transformation. Then Mr Green took Mr Beal to the 'signed agreement' which had been secured by the NFSP. The document had only become available after a protracted Freedom of Information Act exchange between Mark Baker (yes, that one) and the Post Office. It was the famous Grant Funding Agreement (GFA) in which the NFSP expressly agreed not to engage in 'any public activity which may prevent Post Office Ltd from implementing any of its initiatives, policies or strategies,' or any 'other activities or behaviour the effect of which may be materially detrimental' to the Post Office. The GFA explicitly stated the terms of the agreement were to remain confidential.

Beal told the court the GFA was always going to be made public. Why then, Patrick Green wondered, did the terms of the contract explicitly state they had to be kept confidential? Mr Beal wasn't sure. Mr Green wondered if the litigation had the potential to be materially detrimental to the Post Office. Mr Beal agreed.

'So the NFSP cannot support this litigation because of the terms of your grant, can it?' asked Mr Green.

'I don't know,' said Beal, helpfully.

The following day's witnesses started work at the Post Office in 1997, 1999 and 1985 respectively – a mere 73 years' service between them. In fact, none of the Post Office's 14 witnesses had less than ten years' service, and most had far more. Their loyalty to their employer appeared absolute. Some were the dimmest of dim bulbs, others were cocksure middle-managers all but winking at each other as they crossed paths between stints in the witness box. The undoubted main attraction was the recently promoted 'People Services Director', Angela van den Bogerd. Ms van den Bogerd was Paula Vennells' wing-woman at the 2015 BIS Select Committee hearing, and many Subpostmasters saw her as Vennells' representative on earth. She was part of the team that told Panorama remote access to the Horizon system without the Postmasters' knowledge was not possible, and she had been operationally responsible for the Post Office's Initial Complaint Review and Mediation Scheme. There was nothing she didn't know about the claimants' grievances, or the Post Office's activities at least since 2013 – although probably longer, as she had worked at the Post Office for 33 years.

I was looking forward to a robust defence of both the Horizon system and the assertions in her witness statement. Instead, everyone in court had to suffer two days of teeth-pulling testimony, delivered in a *tiny* voice, with van den Bogerd's head sinking lower and lower towards her lap as each hour passed. I lost count of the number of times the judge asked her to speak up.

Ms van den Bogerd's central thesis was that Subpostmasters were to blame for whatever difficulties they found themselves in. Each time Patrick Green embarked on a line of questioning, Ms van den Bogerd would give an explanation, which would be examined line by line until it began to fall apart.

When her assertions were contradicted by factual evidence, she might give a minuscule and reluctant acknowledgment of this, whilst refusing to accept it might relate to a wider point about, say, the overall treatment of Subpostmasters or problems with the Post Office's methods of doing business.

There were two other witnesses of note. Elaine Ridge, a Post Office Network Contract Advisor who cheerfully told the judge she wouldn't show the actual Subpostmasters Contract to a prospective appointee because they'd 'run a mile.' When Green pointed her towards some documentary evidence which threw doubt on whether a Subpostmaster should have been suspended, Ridge declared the information to be of no use and told the court she would have suspended the Subpostmaster anyway.

By far the worst performer was Helen Dickinson. Ms Dickinson had been a Post Office fraud investigator for 15 years, rising through the ranks to become a Security Team Leader. She could not have been more different from the Security Team's intimidating ex-coppers regularly described to me by former Subpostmasters. Dickinson is slight, sandy-haired, and, if anything, was more quietly spoken than Angela van den Bogerd.

Ms Dickinson got off to a poor start by telling Patrick Green she had not heard of the Enron scandal. The judge later wrote it was inconceivable that a person of her position had never heard of one of the largest corporate frauds of the past two decades. He found that she was just trying to be unhelpful.

I thought it was entirely plausible Ms Dickinson had not heard of one of the biggest corporate frauds this century, given she went on to demonstrate an almost complete lack of knowledge about a key part of her day-to-day job.

Ms Dickinson had little or no idea how Horizon operated. She wasn't aware there was no way for a Subpostmaster to dispute a discrepancy without accepting it as a debt. She admitted her knowledge of Horizon was 'very basic', mystifyingly telling the court that familiarising herself with the system 'wouldn't work … because then that could cause a conflict with me investigating a matter.' This bizarre approach gave further credence to Second Sight and Professor Charles McLachlan's evidence that Post Office investigators would not consider Horizon to be the source of a discrepancy.

But it was Patrick Green's final question which sent a chill down my spine. He wanted to know about Ms Dickinson's experience of tracking down and seizing Postmasters' assets under the Proceeds of Crime Act. POCA confiscation orders can only be made if a Subpostmaster has been convicted. Green wondered if suspended Subpostmaster cases were sometimes referred to Ms Dickinson's team 'so that POCA could be used to trace the assets?'

'In some cases,' replied Ms Dickinson, 'yes.'

There were two ways of reading the above exchange. The more obvious (and I admit in retrospect, likely) meaning is that when the Post Office wanted to trace Subpostmaster assets through POCA, the cases were referred to Ms Dickinson. At the time I understood Ms Dickinson to be admitting that the Post Office might try to prosecute suspended

Postmasters so the Post Office could use POCA to go after their assets.[2] Either way, I was alarmed enough to put aside my squeamishness about getting involved in the story.

That evening I wrote to the Criminal Cases Review Commission suggesting it was clearly bonkers (I paraphrase) to be making any decisions about the Subpostmaster cases they were reviewing without taking into account the abundance of evidence now pouring out of *Bates v Post Office*.

Vaguely remembering James Arbuthnot had a hand in making sure the CCRC took any Subpostmaster applicants seriously, I forwarded the now-ennobled politician my email. I am still sufficiently deferential to never dream of suggesting a course of action to a peer of the realm – but I very much hoped he would do something. Ninety-five minutes later, I was cc'd in an email to the CCRC from The Right Honourable Lord Arbuthnot of Edrom which suggested that if the CCRC didn't take into account what was happening in *Bates v Post Office*, it might very well open its decision-making process to judicial review.

Exactly a week later, the CCRC wrote to all its Subpostmaster applicants, telling them that, before progressing their cases, the commissioners were going to discuss waiting for the outcome of the Common Issues trial before making any decisions. Good.

Towards the end of the trial I saw a lot more of Jo Hamilton, who, along with the irrepressible Teju Adedayo, probably attended more court days than any other claimant, save for Alan Bates. Jo would have been there every day were it not for the expense of getting to London and her commitments in South Warnborough.

To make ends meet, Jo had spent a large chunk of the previous decade cleaning the houses of the people she knew in her village. By shifting her cleaning days to the weekends, buying what she called an 'old biddies' railcard (Jo turned 60 in 2018) and getting the first off-peak train into London from Basingstoke, Jo realised she could get up to London for £20 return, rather than the £50 peak fare. To make it to court in time, she had to leg it out of Waterloo, catch the 243 bus from a stop outside the

2 Something which, when I heard it in court, sounded completely abhorrent. The Post Office has subsequently supplied me with the relevant version of the CPS Code of Conduct to demonstrate it was a perfectly legitimate consideration under the rules at the time.

station and then run from the Fetter Lane bus stop to the Rolls Building. Jo found that, by doing this, she could get into court at 10.27am, three minutes before proceedings began.

Jo, Wendy, Karen and Teju admitted developing a soft spot for the managing judge.

'There was a bit of a Justice Fraser fan club among us,' said Jo. 'I used to sit right by the [annoying giant concrete] pillar because I found him fascinating. To watch him in action… Every now and then the pen would lift off the desk and you knew he was thinking. And then he'd lean back in his chair, and you thought, "Uh oh – someone's going to get the end of that…" He just took control.'

The Common Issues trial finished on 6 December 2018. Once the closing arguments had been made, Mr Justice Fraser put the parties on notice to expect a judgment some time in January. The second trial – an examination of the Horizon system – was already in the diary for 11 March 2019. Independent IT specialists for both sides had already been appointed, and their preliminary reports had been served. The parties were now focused on the next battlefront, which would expend several million pounds finding out if Horizon was, as the Post Office would have it, 'robust.'

ROLL ROLLS

Whilst we waited for a judgment to the Common Issues trial, Paula Vennells was awarded a CBE in the New Year's Honours List for her services to the Post Office.

The Post Office trumpeted the announcement on its website (now removed), gushing that Vennells had been given the award 'for her work on diversity and inclusion at Post Office, her commitment to the social purpose at the heart of the business and her dedication in putting the customer first.'

Within six weeks Vennells had slipped further into the establishment's warm embrace, announcing she would be leaving the Post Office to take up a board position at the Cabinet Office and chairmanship of Imperial College Healthcare NHS Trust. Whilst at the Post Office, the government had given her one job – to make the organisation profitable. It appeared she had done so, largely by reducing the pay of serving Subpostmasters to such a degree that three quarters are now working for less than the National Living Wage.

On 31 January 2019 I went along to a *Bates v Post Office* case management conference at the Rolls Building. Fraser told the parties they would not get any ruling on the Common Issues before the end of February *at the earliest*. They were also told to be ready for a third trial in the litigation to begin on 4 November. This would deal with issues concerning alleged breach of whatever the Common Issues judgment determined the contract between Subpostmasters and the Post Office to be. After the conference I asked a lawyer if it was unusual to be waiting more than two months for a judgment in a trial of this nature. I was told they can sometimes take more than a year. My anticipation cooled. But at least we were still on track for 11 March.

The Horizon trial would be the most searching independent and public examination of the Horizon IT system in its 20-year history. The Common Issues trial raised a series of questions related to a Postmaster's contractual relationship with the Post Office. The Horizon trial would be about remote access, robustness, data integrity and control measures. The first and most important agreed question for the judge to decide asked:

'To what extent was it possible or likely for bugs, errors or defects … to have the potential … to cause apparent or alleged discrepancies or shortfalls relating to Subpostmasters' branch accounts.'

As well as contributions from Subpostmasters and Post Office witnesses, the Horizon trial would also feature witnesses from Fujitsu and the work of two expert IT witnesses, who had, by early February already spent 11 months seeking information and preparing their analyses.

The Post Office had appointed Dr Robert Worden, a theoretical particle physicist (with specific proficiency in statistics) as their expert. Jason Coyne, whose background was in the implementation (and troubleshooting) of large-scale EPoS and accounting IT systems, was appointed by the claimants. I asked Mr Coyne how he approached something as vast as Horizon from the outside, when all he had to begin with was a blank sheet of paper.

'The first thing that we did,' he replied, 'is we took the Horizon issues – essentially a list of questions that were agreed between the parties – and tried to distil what would be required in order to answer those questions.'

This progressed to a request for information from the Post Office, which had no intention of making things easy. For the purposes of the litigation, the Post Office had appointed a team of internal experts who would decide exactly what information would be released to both Coyne and Dr Worden. Getting his hands on the relevant material proved trying.

'It was the most torturous case I've ever worked on,' Coyne told me, bluntly. 'Disclosure has never been as problematic as it was with the Post Office in anything I've done before.'

One of the earliest, and perhaps most obvious, requests was to see Horizon's Known Error Log. This was the same log requested in 2010 by Professor Charles McLachlan to aid his research into Seema Misra's case. The Post Office's first response was to cast doubt as to whether such a database existed.

Any sane IT operator, especially one running a network the size of Horizon, would keep an error log. Coyne and his team would not be deterred. They asked again for the Known Error Log to be disclosed.

This time, the Post Office acknowledged the error log existed, but claimed it would be irrelevant to the trial. Quite how a system's error log could be irrelevant to a multimillion pound investigation into alleged errors within that system is not just laughable; it is, as Mr Justice Fraser observed, 'obstructive.'

The Post Office's final ploy was to pretend it could not hand over the Known Error Log, because it was held and owned by Fujitsu. This attempt failed when Fraser pointed out, during yet another 'interlocutory skirmish,' the Post Office had the right to access the log under the terms of its contract with Fujitsu.

Coyne got his error log. Or at least, a commitment it would be provided. As with the previous trial, the Post Office dragged its heels on handing over documents in a manner which the claimants complained to the judge was 'far from cooperative or forthcoming.'

On one occasion the Post Office refused Coyne's request to see a list of Horizon's error codes.

'They said, "No, we're not giving you the error code list. You tell us what error code you want to see and we'll tell you what that error code means." And I said, "This is a ridiculous situation. I don't know what I'm looking for. How do I know how to request it?"'

Oddly, Dr Worden seemed to lose his enthusiasm for requesting documents from Fujitsu and the Post Office, at one point refusing to add his signature to a formal request the two men had put together.

Eventually, after seeking and receiving an order from the judge which bypassed the need for Dr Worden's approval, the Post Office grudgingly turned the taps on. The claimants were eventually handed hundreds of thousands of documents and spreadsheets. Coyne estimates his team spent more than five thousand hours grouping them into potential patterns and themes.

'We needed to work out the landscape of the system, because what goes on in a sub-Post Office is just a terminal into lots of other ancillary systems – connections to banks, connections to retail systems, stock re-ordering ... there was lots going on, so we needed to understand how the landscape was mapped out and how all these systems joined together.'

Once the system architecture was understood, they could start examining it.

'Whenever you've got an interface between systems, that is often where you will find bugs, errors and defects, because the way these systems grow up, they're created to do one particular process and then they're modified to be brought into a bigger system, and that's what you had with Horizon.'

Analysing the error logs and the raw data, Coyne began to build a picture of Horizon's structural and historical weaknesses. He and his team worked day and night to supply Freeths and the barristers from Henderson Chambers the jigsaw pieces they needed to build their arguments in court.

'It was every waking hour. Most nights I would sleep with a dictaphone by the bed, because I'd process something whilst I was lying awake and then want to record it so I could go to sleep knowing the idea would be there in the morning.'

Coyne and his team did their job. Patrick Green's written opening pointedly described the Post Office's attitude as 'unhelpful and disruptive,' but by the time March came round, the claimants' legal team felt they had enough ammunition to test the strength of the Post Office's arguments about the robustness of the Horizon system in court.

The trial itself would be held in the same court as the Common Issues trial and follow a similar format. Opening statements would be made by leading counsel – Patrick Green again for the claimants, Anthony de Garr Robinson for the Post Office. Witness cross-examination would follow, then Coyne and Worden would get a grilling. As before, the claimant witnesses were mainly former Subpostmasters, but their ranks would be bolstered by evidence from Richard Roll, the Fujitsu whistleblower.

On Monday 11 March we gathered once more at the Rolls Building. Kay Linnell and Alan Bates took their usual spots in court alongside Freeths. Jo Hamilton and Karen Wilson were among the observers. I took what had become my favoured seat by the wall on the left of the court's heavy double doors. I had switched there from my early perch in the far corner of the court during Angela van den Bogerd's evidence in the first trial. Whilst it meant I could only see the witnesses side on, I could at least hear what they were saying. Sam Greenhill from the Daily Mail, Jane Croft from the FT and Karl Flinders from Computer Weekly joined me to make an unofficial press bench, marking the first day of proceedings.

The trial kicked off with the judge telling everyone that he intended to hand down his Common Issues findings at the end of the week. He then asked both sides' barristers to set out their stalls.

Patrick Green began by reading a confidential Post Office briefing note to the court. It was dated 2017. The memo concluded the company's IT systems were 'not fit for purpose, expensive and difficult to change.' The document urged Post Office directors to 'quickly rationalise and resolve misaligned contracts enacted to support legacy IT, obsolescence, a lack of Post Office technical competence [and] particular focus on Fujitsu and Accenture.'

Anthony de Garr Robinson was not interested in this. He used

Horizon's big numbers to assert that whilst 29 bugs in Horizon had been found by both independent experts in advance of the trial, none of them had affected any of the *claimants'* branch accounts. In fact, he suggested, the claimants were being irrational, and their 'suspicion of Horizon is driven by the natural human scepticism to technology.'

The following two days saw a procession of former Subpostmasters give evidence on oath about errors which, as far as they were concerned, could only be due to Horizon. De Garr Robinson did what he could to persuade them otherwise. On Wednesday afternoon, Richard Roll was sworn in. He confirmed to the court he had worked on third-level Horizon support at Fujitsu's Software Service Centre (SSC) between 2001 and 2004.

The day-and-a-half-long cross-examination was gruelling. Mr Roll is not a man who likes the limelight, admitting to me that before he took to the witness box he was 'nervous as hell.' Mr de Garr Robinson, aided by a report written by one of Mr Roll's former colleagues,[1] was brutal. Roll had always been honest about his poor memory for the specifics of his work at Fujitsu, but he was adamant that part of his job involved wandering into Subpostmasters' branch terminals and tinkering with their account data, whether the Subpostmasters knew about it or not.

The Post Office's tactic was to belittle Mr Roll's expertise, his length of service (2001 to 2004 became '44 months,' which somehow sounded shorter) and his seniority. He would be presented with detailed statements supplied by Fujitsu (for example, 'Mr Roll was not working at a level where he would be required to review code') which directly contradicted his recollection. Roll would then be invited to change his stance, leaving him to give answers like, 'My recollection was that I did work through computer coding of the programmes, but now I'm not so sure.'

The point was pushed home relentlessly by the Post Office QC. Using the Fujitsu-compiled report, he concluded, 'Mr Roll, you didn't regularly identify issues with computer coding that would be flagged for the fourth line support, did you? That's just not consistent with the figures we have been looking at?'

Roll was left floundering. 'The way I remembered it was that we were,

[1] The report was later found by Mr Justice Fraser to be 'inaccurate to a significant degree,' but no one, with the possible exception of its author, knew that at the time of Mr Roll's cross-examination.

as a department, finding issues every week,' he replied, 'but I'm not sure if that is the case now. '

Having done what he could to establish Richard Roll as a low-level grunt, de Garr Robinson used his second day of cross-examination to go in hard on the former engineer's witness statement. Roll had claimed that some errors in Horizon weren't identified properly, which could lead to them being attributed to user error. Unable to give specific examples, other than a hardware fault he discovered in a faulty batch of terminal screens, Roll began to characterise his own claim as a 'belief' or 'feeling.' De Garr Robinson pushed his advantage home, asking:

'In your 44 months at the SSC did you ever encounter a situation where a cyclic redundancy check missed an error of this sort?'

'I can't remember that,' Roll replied.

De Garr Robinson continued. 'I suggest to you, you didn't, Mr Roll. Could I also ask you whether you were ever aware of this – in your experience did you ever actually see this problem happening with a Subpostmaster?'

'I don't think I did, no.'

'You don't think you did?'

'No.'

'So what you're saying – and I don't mean to be rude when I say this – it's an armchair theoretical exercise that you are discussing, it's not something that actually reflected your experience when working at the SSC, is it?'

'No, it was something I was thinking of hypothetically.'

'I'm grateful.'

De Garr Robinson then went back to a claim in Roll's witness statement.

'First of all, you say: "The test team felt they were under enormous pressure to complete the testing within certain timescales which negatively affected the test regime." That's quite a bold claim. The testing wasn't your team, was it?'

'No, they were on the same floor as us, some of them.'

'So you're talking about your recollection of – would it be fair to say office gossip?'

'Yes.'

'From 15 or 19 years ago?'

'Yes.'

'How many conversations of this sort did you have during your time at Fujitsu?'

'I don't recall.'

'Was it a view that was expressed by the entire test team on a regular basis, or was it something that was said to you by one or two people a couple of times?'

'My recollection is that the majority of the team felt pressured.'

'The majority of the team felt pressure. What did they say about this pressure? What did it make them do?'

'I can't remember.'

At one point I thought Roll was beginning to agree with everything the Post Office QC said in the hope his ordeal would come to an end sooner. There was a moment just before lunch on the second day when he went into an unexpected digression about the evidence of one of the Subpostmasters who had been cross-examined before him. Roll groped towards his point before realising he didn't really know what he was trying to say. He gave up, pausing before blurting, somewhat helplessly, 'I'm not making myself very clear. I'm sorry about this.'

By lunchtime on the second day, Roll looked battered. He didn't have to spend two days of his life being progressively taken apart in public, and I wondered if he had any idea what he had signed up for when he agreed to be a witness. From where I was sitting, it had not been a good morning for the claimants.

The afternoon session was a different story. Witnesses are not allowed to speak to anyone during breaks in evidence, but Roll had clearly given himself a good talking to. He returned to the witness box in a far more assertive mood. In response to de Garr Robinson's questions about remote access, he found his mojo.

Mr Roll explained in detail how he was able to go into a Subpostmaster's branch terminal – using the Subpostmaster's login – and change the transaction data without that Subpostmaster's knowledge.

He would log it on the Fujitsu internal system every time it happened. It would be supervised and signed off by another pair of eyes. If the Subpostmaster could be informed they would be, but Mr Roll was clear – he and his colleagues had the power to roam around inside a Subpostmaster's branch terminal without the Subpostmaster having any idea they were there or what they were doing.

De Garr Robinson was taken aback.

'I suggest to you, Mr Roll,' he said, 'that no one at SSC would ever manually change a line of transaction data and then reinsert that transaction data into the message store of any branch. There might be occasions when new transactions were inserted, but it was more than the job of an SSC member was worth to actually start mucking about with lines of existing transaction data.'

Roll bristled. 'Can I say that we were not "mucking about" with lines of transaction data? We were trying to rebuild counters.'

De Garr Robinson told Roll that Riposte (the software Horizon was built on) didn't allow any transaction line in the message store to be individually deleted or changed or edited in any way.

'You couldn't do it through Riposte, no,' said Roll. 'You had to hack the system to do it.'

The QC asked Roll how. Roll explained how he would fool the message store by stripping out 'all of the pre-amble and the post-amble' data on a transaction 'so you're just then left with the basic data as if it had been on the [transaction] stack.' Then you manually change the transaction, and 're-inject that data, which is the process we would have used to rebuild a counter.'

De Garr Robinson was lost and admitted as much, but Mr Justice Fraser wanted to know more.

'I follow what the witness is saying,' he said carefully. 'Keep exploring it.'

De Garr Robinson persevered. 'You could insert new transactions, couldn't you, but what you couldn't do is you couldn't edit or indeed individually delete lines that were in the message store itself?'

Roll was pretty sure he could. 'You would have to delete … all of the messages down to a certain point to the one you wanted to amend and then inject a load more text, or insert more transactions to make the message store and Riposte think that it had been put in by Riposte and by the Postmaster.'

In a reversal of the morning's exchanges, Fraser could see de Garr Robinson was now struggling.

'I think you can probably explore this with the experts,' he suggested.

'I think I probably should,' said the barrister, with some relief.

At around 3.30pm Roll left the witness box and walked past our unofficial press bench. We made eye contact. He raised his eyebrows and blew out his cheeks.

Roll left court and went outside to get some fresh air. The release of emotion caused him to burst into tears. Two claimant Subpostmasters who were making their way out of the building spotted him standing on his own and walked over. On seeing the state he was in, they too burst into tears.

'They gave me a hug,' said Richard, 'and that's when I first realised what I'd been saying must have been quite important. It was good. A very warm moment.'

Richard had come through. No matter that it was a long time ago – a credible witness from inside Fujitsu had stood up in court and directly contradicted the Fujitsu and Post Office party line, under oath, at the High Court.

'He was absolutely amazing,' said Sue Knight, who witnessed it. 'We owe him a lot.'

JUDGMENT NO 3

Very few people beyond both parties' lawyers had seen a draft copy of the Common Issues trial judgment by the time it was handed down. To have given any indication of its contents would have been contempt of court, something the judge made very clear when he gave Kay and Alan permission to view it two days in advance. That said, no one from Freeths, Henderson Chambers, Kay or Alan seemed anything less than breezy as we gathered in court at 11.30am on Friday 15 March 2019. The Post Office was represented by a lone barrister.

There was quite a bit of media interest, which was unusual. Broadcast news crews had set their cameras up outside the Rolls Building and the print hacks were mob-handed inside. Mr Justice Fraser entered court at noon, indicated how paper copies of the judgment should be distributed, said that it was now a public document and left. As soon as he was gone I dived up the centre aisle of the court to grab a copy of the judgment from his clerk, clocking the very broad grin on the face of Patrick Green as he turned to his colleagues. The Freeths team shook each other's hands and then faced the bewildered Subpostmasters at the back of court.

It was a strange moment. A room which had borne witness to hours of tedious formal proceedings was briefly charged. The claimants stood, unsure of who to go to and how to react.

Jo Hamilton looked hopelessly confused as she approached Imogen Randall, a Freeths solicitor.

'What does it mean?' asked Jo. 'What's going on?'

'You've won, Jo. You've won,' said Imogen gently, with an enormous smile on her face.

Jo began to cry. Imogen began to cry. They hugged. The reporters swarmed around Patrick Green, who, still grinning, said the 180,000-word, 1,122-paragraph judgment was a 'complete vindication' of the Subpostmasters' case, and a 'very important legal decision.' The judge had found that the Subpostmasters Contract *was* relational, imputing a duty of care on the Post Office. He also found that many of the terms of the contract were so 'oppressive' as to be unlawful, and he did not hold back on the Post Office's attitude and behaviour both towards its Subpostmasters before and during the litigation.

'Submissions by the Post Office are bold, pay no attention to the actual evidence, and seem to have their origin in a parallel world' ruled Fraser. In another section of the judgment, he stated, 'The Post Office appears, at least at times, to conduct itself as though it is answerable only to itself.' Fraser lambasted the organisation's 'excessive secrecy' and was generally appalled by the senior Post Office staff who gave evidence.

Nick Beal's contribution was described as 'completely unrealistic.' Fraser said Angela van den Bogerd 'seems to have been uniquely exercised to paint the Post Office in the most favourable light possible, regardless of the facts.' The judge went further with van den Bogerd, finding that, 'she did not give me frank evidence, and sought to obfuscate matters, and mislead me.'

Having reviewed their testimony as he was compiling his judgment, Fraser concluded he would only accept any of van den Bogerd and Beal's evidence in future if it was 'clearly and uncontrovertibly corroborated by contemporaneous documents.'

As Sam Stein QC was to say at the Court of Appeal many months later, that 'is the judicial equivalent of not trusting them to tell him if the sky is blue, without going outside to check.'

The judge's comments about the NFSP were equally damning. Fraser referred back to Patrick Green's cross-examination of Nick Beal, which featured George Thomson's signed-in-blood email, and a discussion about the Grant Funding Agreement. He ruled that the GFA *was* intended to be kept secret, and would have likely remained so were it not for the efforts of the 'redoubtable' Mark Baker.

He concluded, 'The NFSP is not an organisation independent of the Post Office, in the sense that the word "independent" is usually understood in the English language. It is not only dependent upon the Post Office for its funding, but that funding is subject to stringent and detailed conditions that enable the Post Office to restrict the activities of the NFSP. The Post Office effectively controls the NFSP… There is also evidence before the court that the NFSP has, in the past, put its own interests and the funding of its future above the interests of its members… In those circumstances, the fact that the NFSP does not support the Claimants in this litigation is entirely to be expected.'

Jo was soon in receipt of a paper copy of the judgment, which she hugged close. She was giving an interview to a reporter in the courtroom when Kathleen Donnelly touched her arm. Jo remembers:

'She said to me, "I just want you to know that's one of the best judgments I've ever seen in my career. I don't think you realise just what you've got in your arms. It is brilliant."'

Outside court Alan Bates gave his first ever press conference.

'We couldn't be happier for the whole group,' he said. 'We've all been working for this for years. But now we're actually there. I'm so pleased.'

I asked him to pick out the parts of the judgment that resonated with him.

'The culture of secrecy that Post Office has, and how they stonewall everybody… There's an awful lot of truth in this document.'

James Hartley was keen to stress that the litigation was by no means over, but the wind was now clearly blowing in the claimants' favour. He said there was now 'an obligation and duty on the Post Office to act with good faith and transparency and cooperation with these claimants.' Crucially, this could now be applied retrospectively, so if future trials found the Post Office hadn't acted with good faith 'then they will be in breach of contract, and they will be responsible for damages.'

The Post Office issued a statement by their Chairman, Tim Parker, which said:

'The Judge's comments are a forceful reminder to us that we must always continue to do better. We have taken his criticisms on board and will take action throughout our organisation.'

But neither he, nor the organisation he represented were going to roll over.

'Post Office will continue to defend the overall litigation,' stated Parker, citing 'areas around the interpretation of our contracts where the Judge's conclusions differ from what we expected from a legal standpoint.'

This, Parker said, meant the Post Office were 'seriously considering' an appeal[1] 'on certain legal interpretations.'

There have been many consequential days in this extraordinary scandal, but 15 March 2019 is the most important to me. It was the moment so many claims made by so many campaigners for so long stopped being disputed. Thanks to the High Court, they had become fact and were reportable as such. The Post Office had spent years ignoring, dismissing and then covering up its treatment of Subpostmasters. Now, for the first time, one of the highest authorities in the land had ruled that the

---

1 Civil judgments made at the High Court, and criminal judgments made at Crown Courts, can be reviewed and potentially overturned at the Court of Appeal, the second-highest tier of courts in England and Wales. The highest court is the Supreme Court.

campaigners were right. It was a heavy blow to the Post Office, and the scope to appeal was limited.

It turns out the Post Office had another trick up its sleeve.

RECUSAL

The claimants' victory in the Common Issues trial had turned the psychogeography of the Subpostmaster scandal into a raging battlefield. The Post Office had lost ground on both its legal and public affairs fronts, and the Postmasters' tanks were now roaring towards Fortress Horizon.

At its new HQ in London's Finsbury Dials, the Post Office was in crisis mode. Senior executives had spent years trying to paint Alan Bates and the JFSA as a tiny bunch of cranks intent on raising imaginary grievances. Now those troublemakers had won a High Court victory which turned the Post Office's entire business model on its head. Revelations about the Horizon IT system had been pouring out of the High Court on a daily basis and were due to continue for another three weeks. The existential threat the Post Office had warned about was potentially coming to pass.

Three days after being found to have tried to mislead the court, Angela van den Bogerd took her seat in the witness box again to be cross-examined for the Horizon trial. This time she seemed to have a rather keener appreciation of her obligations towards telling the truth under oath. Patrick Green took her through her latest witness statements, which were written before the judge's comments as to her credibility. Time and again she was forced to admit they were factually inaccurate. In doing so, her admissions about Horizon-generated errors were extremely damaging to the Post Office's position.

At 5.15pm on Monday 18 March, the same day Angela van den Bogerd had made concession after concession under cross-examination at the High Court, a Post Office board meeting, chaired by director Ken McCall and led by acting Chief Executive Alisdair Cameron, was held. Advice from a 'senior judicial figure' was discussed. A course of action was plotted. A decision[2] which would reverberate throughout the legal world was made.

On Tuesday 19 March Kathleen Donnelly took over from Patrick Green to cross-examine Dawn Phillips, a Post Office witness whose job

---

[2] Which – due to perceived conflicts of interest – both the government representative on the Post Office board, Tom Cooper, and the Post Office chairman, Tim Parker, were not party to. Parker is Chairman of the HM Courts and Tribunal Service, Cooper was representing an executive part of government, which (it was decided) meant he should not be involved in a decision which related to the judiciary.

it was to chase Subpostmaster 'debt.'

The Common Issues trial had established there was no option for a Subpostmaster to dispute a discrepancy on Horizon. This was a massive bone of contention at the start of the litigation as the Post Office maintained that pressing 'settle centrally' on Horizon was the initiation of a dispute process. It was, in fact, and as the judge concluded, a contractual commitment to accept the Horizon-presented discrepancy as a debt.

Ms Phillips was a forceful presence in the witness box. She revealed any Postmaster pressing 'settle centrally' on a Wednesday at the end of a trading period would be sent a debt recovery letter the following Monday, 'so unless they actually made the error on the last day of their trading period then it's likely that they made the error in the previous few weeks.'

Ms Phillips' language unselfconsciously betrayed a damaging reflexive assumption which conflated a branch discrepancy with a Subpostmaster 'error.' She was the living embodiment of a blinkered corporate mindset.

Ms Donnelly asked about the criteria for finding out if there was a dispute attached to a sum settled centrally. Ms Phillips replied that her team would cross-reference the discrepancy with any helpline calls made by the same branch.

'We look for any call in the previous month that could relate to the loss that they have settled. We don't specifically search for settled centrally calls.'

So how, wondered Ms Donnelly, does the Post Office find out if a discrepancy settled centrally is in dispute?

'We try and do everything above £5,000,' replied Ms Phillips.

There was a little moment in court as everybody mentally checked they'd correctly heard what Ms Philips had said. The judge frowned. Even Ms Donnelly seemed surprised.

'So you wouldn't bother checking the helpline log for £2,000?' she asked.

'It's not a case of not bothering, it's a case of how many have settled centrally and how many are large,' came the reply.

Ms Phillips had just described a standard process of initiating debt recovery against Subpostmasters (whether their discrepancies are in dispute or not) if the sum was lower than £5,000. Over the course of the next few minutes, we discovered that the threshold for sending out debt recovery letters apparently shifted according to how busy the department was, but generally it was around the £5,000 mark.

Claiming puzzlement, but possibly out of incredulity, the judge asked

Ms Donnelly to take Ms Phillips through the process again. As she did, we let it sink in. Yup, that's how the system worked.

On the final day of the Horizon trial's second week, the Freeths team were sitting in court watching their screens whilst Patrick Green painstakingly cross-examined Torstein Godeseth, Fujitsu's Chief Horizon Architect. Mr Godeseth helpfully told the court the reason there was no dispute button on Horizon was 'by design … because that keeps our books tidy.' It didn't seem to cause him concern that this meant a Subpostmaster had to legally accept responsibility for a debt before being able to dispute it.

Godeseth also appeared to have gleaned a lot of his information from conversations with his former colleague Gareth Jenkins, who had not been put forward as a witness for the trial, despite perhaps being the most relevant person to the whole proceedings.

Nonetheless, Godeseth was an interesting witness – the judge was later to call his evidence 'considerably more detailed, and of more direct assistance in resolving the Horizon Issues, than any other witness of fact.'

Whilst Patrick Green was gamely plugging away with Godeseth, the Post Office boardroom plan was put into action. An email dropped into the Freeths' team's inboxes.

'It had been sent by the lawyers on the other side,' James Hartley told me, 'who were all sitting there, looking straight ahead. Attached to the email was an application to remove the managing judge.'

A recusal application. This is an invitation for a judge to remove themselves from a trial, which becomes a demand if they don't. It can *only* be made on the grounds of a conflict of interest or because there is a 'real possibility' that a 'fair-minded and informed observer' would conclude that a judge should not try a case because they *cannot* be impartial. This is known as 'apparent bias.' Mr Justice Fraser had, according to the Post Office, demonstrated 'apparent bias' in his Common Issues trial judgment.

The email was forwarded to the barristers' team. Kathleen Donnelly was gobsmacked. 'It was absolutely unbelievable,' she said. 'They had tried so many things as we had gone along… But recusal really was jaw-dropping.'

'It was a watershed moment for us,' remembered Hartley, 'because it told us that the other side were desperate.'

As soon as the morning session finished and the judge had left court, there was a palpable buzz amongst the claimants' lawyers. Instead of filing straight out, like the stony-faced Post Office team, they stayed chatting for a few more minutes than usual. No one else had a clue what was going on, but you could tell something was up. As I tapped away on my laptop, keeping half an eye on the liveliness to my left, Patrick Green bowled past. 'Make sure you're here for the afternoon session,' he said breezily. 'It's going to be *very* interesting.'

I was back in Court 26 nice and early after lunch.

At 2.02pm the judge entered, walked to his chair, and took his place. 'I have received an application…' he began, then stopped. His eyes narrowed. 'Mr de Garr Robinson, do you know anything about it?'

Anthony de Garr Robinson stood up. 'My Lord,' he said, uncomfortably. 'I know that there has been an application. That is almost all I know.'

'Has it been served on the claimants?' Fraser asked.

'My understanding is it has, my Lord, yes.'

Fraser swivelled towards Patrick Green. 'Do you know about it?'

'My Lord, we have just seen it, yes,' replied Green.

'I just saw it five minutes ago,' said Fraser, with a certain steel in his voice. 'It is an application for me to recuse myself as being the managing judge in these proceedings … and also for this trial to stop.'

Despite being outmanoeuvred, the Post Office could not be outgunned. It could always escalate and delay and explore every single legal avenue open to it, because it had access to limitless resources.

Patrick Green was invited to make some remarks on behalf of the claimants, and he left the court in no doubt as to what he believed was going on. He told the judge the recusal application was 'likely, if not calculated, to derail these proceedings.'

And derail them it did. The Horizon trial was halted. Any prospect of a third trial in 2019 was wiped from the calendar. If the Post Office successfully removed Mr Justice Fraser, a new managing judge would have to be found and the Horizon trial would be re-run. Any appeal of the Common Issues trial would consequently carry more weight. Indeed, it was hard to see how the ruling could stand if the judge making it was found to be biased. Within six days, the claimants had gone from landing a seriously damaging blow on the Post Office to facing the prospect of spending hundreds of thousands of pounds, possibly millions, just to defend their place in the game.

From the beginning of the litigation the Post Office had fought every point raised, which had the cumulative effect of running up eye-watering legal costs. James Hartley told me the Post Office 'knew the more they argued points really hard and found ways of generating additional costs, the more pressure they would put the claimants under.' The recusal, for Hartley, was just more of the same, but he admitted 'it did take it to another level.'

On top of the recusal, as expected, the Post Office appealed the Common Issues judgment.

One of the quirks of the judicial set-up at the High Court is that the judge who would hear the initial application to appeal both the Common Issues judgment and the recusal application was … Mr Justice Fraser. If the Post Office failed either or both it could then apply to Mr Justice Fraser to take things forward to the Court of Appeal. If Mr Justice Fraser refused those applications, the Post Office could then apply directly to the Court of Appeal to hear their cases. Them is the rules.

First up was the recusal hearing. This would not be trusted to de Garr Robinson or Cavender. The Post Office wanted to burn some real money. Lord Grabiner QC is One Essex Court's Head of Chambers and one of the most expensive barristers in London. His stately arrival for the recusal hearing turned an already highly-charged litigation into something almost Dickensian. Wheeling Grabiner out to go toe-to-toe with Fraser was a legal hot ticket, and there were plenty of spectators keen to witness the duel.

On the morning of 3 April 2019, before the hearing began, around two dozen members of the Communication Workers Union assembled outside the Rolls Building bearing red and white placards. One said 'The *We'd-Rather-Ditch-The-Judge-Than-Listen* Office' and another was 'The *We-Can't-Handle-The-Truth* Office.' You get the point.

Inside, Court 26 was the fullest I had ever seen it. At least a dozen claimants were in attendance, including Seema Misra, Jo Hamilton, Sue Knight, Lee Castleton and Pam Stubbs.

Ron Warmington from Second Sight was also there, and on the hack front, we were graced by the presence of Joshua Rozenberg, a legend in legal journalism. He came over to say hello, which was nice.

The court was so full, a couple of observers arrived during proceedings and made a dive for the only chairs available, which were on the bench desks next to the claimants' legal team. They plonked themselves down without being invited and became the only members of the public to have their own personal court documentation screen. The solicitors were either too polite or worried about disrupting proceedings to tell the visitors to push off, so there they stayed.[1]

Lord Grabiner is one of the legal world's Big Deals, and he knows it. He has a presence and manner which seemed to suggest everything which had happened over the course of the litigation to date could be disregarded, now he was on the scene.

Grabiner went to work, picking out phrases in the Common Issues trial judgment for their 'invective', 'irrelevance' and potential bearing on future trials.

'The expression "extraordinarily serious behaviour" is a strong expression,' Grabiner told the judge. 'It is an eye-catching expression. And in the context of this debate, there was no warrant for it and, in my submission, it is extremely prejudicial and certainly wasn't necessary for the purposes of the Common Issues.'

He gave another example: 'Your Lordship makes a very general statement about Post Office's house-style of giving evidence. That shows that from now on you are likely to disbelieve Post Office's evidence because it comes from Post Office. In my submission that is how it would be viewed by an objective observer.'

In fact, Lord Grabiner was so assured that towards the end of his allotted time he stopped making arguments and just read out sections of the judgment, adding:

'Well, I mean, your Lordship can imagine what I would be saying about that, but my submission is that the passage speaks for itself.' It was quite something to witness.

The *coup de grâce* was the trap Lord Grabiner laid for the judge at the beginning of the day. Grabiner would read out sections of the Common Issues judgment, selectively omitting Fraser's qualifying statements, one of which might be,

'I make it quite clear that I do not speculate.'

When Fraser attempted to point this out, Grabiner calmly said he was coming to it later.

Eventually he did. These qualifiers were a 'mantra' said Lord Grabiner, which were fooling no one.

'It … would not convince the observer that your Lordship had not

[1] After lunch the same couple came back and sat in exactly the same spot without anyone batting an eyelid.

pre-judged the issues which still fall to be tried by your Lordship… The real question is whether in the eyes of the reasonable observer that is a real possibility that your Lordship has pre-judged matters which are still due to be tried by you … Lord Justice Bingham says, "In most cases we think the answer, one way or the other, will be obvious, but if in any case there is real ground for doubt, that doubt should be resolved in favour of recusal." Your Lordship's use of what I have called, I hope not disrespectfully, the *mantra*, demonstrates your understanding that you should not have made findings, for example, about Horizon or breaches of contract or breaches of duty. Our case is that your Lordship nevertheless went ahead and made those findings.'

After lunch, Patrick Green was required to tell the judge why he shouldn't recuse himself.

Green went in all guns blazing, hooting, 'This is an application without merit and without foundation … it wholly ignores the proper role of context … it appears to proceed on a misapprehension as to the correct approach to analysing apparent bias [and] it proceeds specifically on a misapprehension as to the proper judicial assessment of the proceedings.'

He went on to address the hypothetical 'fair-minded and informed observer,' saying:

'The informed observer is someone who is presumed to actually have been at the trial and know what happened, not commenting on it from afar and not island-hopping between different findings and observations to make assertions about those without having regard to the judgment as a whole … the informed observer test is (a) an objective one and (b) an informed one. So the informed observer knows about the trial as it was presented to your Lordship.'

The main two points he made were that the Post Office were not once saying that any of the judge's findings were wrong, just that they were irrelevant. His second point was that in the context of the trial, the proceedings preceding the trial and litigation as a whole … the judge's findings really were very relevant.

Mr Green ended on a roll, giving the Post Office both barrels. 'They have adopted internally inconsistent positions in relation to the relevance of evidence and essentially tried to ride two horses going off in completely different directions, and your Lordship has had to try and manage the consequence of that, and clarify it, where possible … and then be accused of apparent bias for having done so.'

Whilst everyone was enjoying the theatre, I reckoned the whole charade must have cost at least £10 per second of active proceedings. It was an obscene waste of money.

Unsurprisingly, Mr Justice Fraser did not recuse himself, nor did he give the Post Office permission to appeal the recusal hearing decision. Nor did he subsequently give them permission to appeal the Common Issues trial. Both went to the Court of Appeal. The priority was the appeal of the recusal application decision. Whilst there was still a possibility Fraser could be kicked off the litigation, the Horizon trial could not be concluded. The Post Office were still hoping that if Fraser were removed, the Horizon trial might be re-run. Whether this was because it just wanted to spend more of the claimants' money, or because they saw the trial was already turning into a car crash, or both, is not known.

In May 2019, Lord Justice Coulson handed down the Court of Appeal's decision on the Post Office's recusal appeal. He refused it, describing the application as 'misconceived', 'fatally flawed', 'untenable' and 'absurd.'

Coulson set out his findings in some detail over 19 pages, but emphasises he is only doing so 'because of the volume and nature of the criticisms which have been made and the importance of the group litigation to both parties.' He made it clear he was not giving such a detailed ruling 'because of the merits of the application itself,' which he said was 'without substance.'

The Post Office, he ruled, 'has not come close to demonstrating' it had a case, surmising:

'It is a great pity that the recusal application and this application for permission to appeal have had the effect of delaying the conclusion of the critical Horizon sub-trial. Indeed, the mere making of these applications could have led to the collapse of that sub-trial altogether. Although I can reach no concluded view on the matter, I can at least understand why the [claimants] originally submitted on 21 March that that was its purpose.'

In conclusion, Mr Justice Fraser was not going anywhere. But the Common Issues trial judgment could still be overturned…

NICKI ARCH

Whilst we were waiting for the rescheduled second half of the Horizon trial to get going again (which it did in June 2019) the Post Office official twitter account posted a message:

'Today we've signed the Time To Change Employer Pledge in honour of Mental Health Awareness Week,' it said. The reason behind it was apparently, 'to support employees suffering from mental ill health.'

The tweet was accompanied by a photograph of the Post Office's communications director Mark Davies holding a placard which said, 'We pledge to change the way we think and act about mental health at work.'

He later sent a tweet from his personal account stating:

'No one should have to suffer in silence because of their mental health. So very proud to sign the Time to Change pledge on behalf of the Post Office.'

Given the Post Office were held directly responsible by a large number of Postmasters for destroying their lives, the social media reaction was fierce.

A former Postmaster called David Shepherd tweeted, 'Are you taking the piss POL? Five years on from managing to sell my PO I still suffer with my mental health, which was entirely caused by the way you treat your agents.'

Another Postmaster, Mark Wildblood, posted, 'Proud of a meaningless signature? – what are you going to do about the thousands of postmasters who have been screwed over and have immense mental health and financial issues? Let alone abandoned suicidal and imprisoned pregnant people.'

One of the claimants, Della Robinson, tweeted, 'Absolutely disgusting should be ashamed how dare they use people's feelings to make them look good all the stress and illness they have caused us just shows what callous sick minded things they are.'

It made me realise that my reporting to date had almost exclusively focused on the financial and social effects of what had happened to the Subpostmasters I'd interviewed. I'd never really asked how it affected them internally. Now Post Office employees were engaging in public virtue-signalling about their organisation's supposed commitment to mental health, whilst simultaneously trying to prevent justice for hundreds of people who had suffered the most appalling treatment at their hands.

I thought I'd see if anyone would talk to me about the mental health effects of being accused of a criminal offence. After carefully talking it over with them, three claimants – Tracy Felstead, Nicki Arch and Wendy Buffrey – allowed me to tell their stories, which I posted on my website. They then very kindly allowed me to speak to them again for this book. I am grateful to them. You've read about Tracy and Wendy already. Nicki's situation is slightly different – she 'won.'

Nicki is from Wotton-under-Edge in Gloucestershire. She left school with five O-levels and three CSEs, did her A-levels and then a business degree at Bristol University. She moved to Stroud in 1992 and got a job at Brimscombe Post Office working behind the counter. She stayed at Brimscombe for five years. In 1997 the Brimscombe Subpostmaster sold up to live on a canal boat. Nicki decided she would start doing Post Office relief work – temping as a manager inside a branch for Subpostmasters who needed a break. 'All the Subpostmasters in the area were complaining that they couldn't go on holiday as they couldn't get the relief.'

Nicki was busy. She was asked to do some longer term work at the Chalford Hill branch in Stroud because the Subpostmaster was getting older and didn't feel she could cope on her own. They got on extremely well and in 1998 the Subpostmaster offered Nicki a full time job with holiday pay, so she took it.

The Subpostmaster was diagnosed with cancer. She asked if Nicki would like to take over the retail side of the business – a stationery shop. They came to an arrangement. Nicki invested her savings in stock, worked very hard, and things took off. 'All the villagers were over the moon.'

In 1999 the Subpostmaster died, and the Post Office made her husband Subpostmaster. He had never worked in a Post Office in his life, so he asked if Nicki would keep it going. He took the Subpostmaster salary and paid Nicki a small wage out of it. The shop profits were hers.

Nicki was doing well. Business was good, and she was going steady with her boyfriend Steve, a local tree surgeon.

There were some small two-bed houses being built very close to the Post Office on a shared ownership basis. Nicki and Steve got themselves a mortgage and moved in together.

'We were engaged to be married, we'd just bought our new home. We did everything by the book. And I had a little business, and … it wasn't much, there's no way we could have lived just on my money. But it was steady. So in theory, it was a perfect world, and then suddenly, everything changed. Literally everything.'

In 2000 Horizon was installed at Chalford Hill Post Office. Nicki got one day of on-site training. She was then required to train her part time member of staff, Marlene.

Horizon seemed to work okay, but Nicki found her pension payments kept duplicating, even though her cash was balancing.

'I knew my branch was not balancing correctly on the weekly reports,' she told me, 'and I rang the helpline five weeks on the trot asking for help but I got nothing.'

In November 2000, three people who Nicki thought were Post Office auditors arrived unannounced at her branch.

'When they turned up,' said Nicki, 'I actually thought they were sent to help me. How stupid was I?'

The Post Office men said they had found a £24,000 deficit. Nicki was mortified. Two of the 'auditors' then declared themselves to be Post Office investigators.

Nicki was told her branch was being closed and her counter was being locked. She was driven by the investigators to Stroud Crown Post Office to be interviewed. Nicki was told she was not allowed to make any phone calls or have anyone with her for the interview.

Once they got to Stroud, the interviewers led Nicki into a room, locked the door and started their recorder. The investigators told Nicki she was responsible for the missing £24,000. If she would just admit she stole it, she would be treated more leniently.

'One of the investigators took great pleasure out of saying he was ex-CID – he had met many criminals like me so knew a liar when he saw one. He also asked if the Post Office had paid for my last holiday because he saw a postcard on the wall that I'd sent to Marlene and the customers when I had a week off!'

Nicki was understandably distraught. 'I vehemently denied any involvement in theft or wrongdoing but was ignored. The interviewers were terrifying, threatening me with prison.'

The interview eventually finished at 4pm. Nicki was driven back to Chalford Hill, got in her car and drove straight home, 'sobbing.' She rang her fiancé and family as soon as she got back to tell them what had happened. The Post Office informed Nicki's absent Subpostmaster about the day's events.

Later that evening Nicki received a phone call from the Subpostmaster to say that the Post Office had told him he must suspend her until further notice. She later discovered he was told that if he didn't follow the Post Office advice to suspend Nicki then they would go after him.

'He was an elderly man,' said Nicki, 'who had not long lost his wife of 50 years, so he just followed orders to protect himself.'

Nicki was barred from the Subpostmaster's premises.

'I asked about my shop and how I was meant to earn a living but he said that the Post Office told him he had to do this and he had no choice. Within 24 hours everything had become ashes.'

Nicki found a solicitor. She agreed to be questioned again by Post Office investigators, this time with legal representation. The interviews continued.

'They stripped my life apart. I presented every single bit of financial history from the minute I left university to them. They came to my house to see what was in it. They didn't even have a search warrant. My parents were like, "These are the Post Office, so you work with them and let them do what they want to do." '

Nicki was unable to explain the cause of the discrepancy, because, as far as she was concerned, she hadn't done anything wrong. It didn't stop the investigators suggesting that if she'd just confess to theft, things would go much easier for her.

'They kept saying, "You know, it's in your own interest to just stop this messing around, and stop wasting all our times. We are the Crown. You do realise who we are?" And I'm like, hang on, you're not even police officers.'

Nicki was not impressed by what they were trying to accuse her of, either.

'They had no idea what the hell they were talking about. I was like, "No, that isn't what I did," and they said, "Well, that's what the Horizon printout says," and I would say, "No, it doesn't say that, does it?" and they would say, "Oh, you're just going round in circles now, you're just wasting our time." '

Predictably, Nicki was told she was the only person having problems with Horizon. 'They said, "We've never, ever had a problem with this system." And I'm like, "Well, I'm the first, then, aren't I?" '

The relentless questioning continued.

'I thought they were going to drop it. I thought they're never going to take this to court, surely. And I was saying to my sister they're just going to keep on and on and pressure me, hoping that I'm going to crumble. And I'm not. And that, "We want to question you again, we want to question you again" kept coming. And we'd set up at Stroud police station, in a little room where they'd come, and it was ridiculous. I'm like, are they ever going to charge me with anything, or is this ever going to end?'

After ten months, Nicki was charged with theft, fraud and false accounting. She was sacked from her job as a Post Office manager and told by the Subpostmaster at Chalford Hill to clear her stock out of the retail shop. The case was referred to the Crown Court.

Being a small community, Nicki's prosecution was big news.

The Subpostmaster and Nicki's part time assistant, Marlene, stopped all communication. The Post Office had told them they were needed as prosecution witnesses, so they couldn't speak to her.

The local paper ran a story on Nicki being suspected of theft. She was blanked by her former customers. No one would employ her.

'I just stayed in. I did attempt, several times, to go to the supermarket, and I just felt everybody was whispering, "Oh, that's the woman who steals from pensioners," and I thought I can't … I can't *do this*.'

With only a single income, Nicki and Steve fell behind on their mortgage payments. Their relationship deteriorated.

'Steve wouldn't tell me truly how he felt, because he didn't want to make me feel worse. We weren't married then, so he could walk away. And I kept saying to him, "Why don't you just walk away? Why don't you just go. If you go now, you won't have to be involved in any of it." '

Nicki's biggest concern was what would happen to Steve if she were sent to prison.

'I thought he would never cope. He's completely dyslexic, he can't even cook, and I thought … he wouldn't even know how to pay a bill. And I'm like, "Steve, just walk away. For God's sake, just walk away from this." But luckily, he didn't.'

Steve began to feel very stressed by the situation, struggling with his concentration and making mistakes at work.

'He came home one day and said, "I don't feel right. I'm going to go to the doctors." And I said, "Well, do you want me to write down how you feel, and then you can take it with you? Because you're not very good at expressing yourself." '

Steve agreed. As soon as the doctor saw the note she asked Nicki to make an appointment with her.

'She said, "What on earth is going on?" I said, "Nothing." And she said, "Nicki, I've read that letter. There is something seriously wrong with anybody who writes letters like that." … and I just broke. I just crumbled. She was the first one who delved deep enough to say you can break if you want to. Because I didn't show it to anybody. I thought I can't let Steve know how I feel. You know, because I just thought, God, this is life over.'

The stress started to push Steve and Nicki towards a very dark place.

'It got to the point when Steve said, "Oh, we'll just take a load of pills, and we'll go together. Let's not give them the satisfaction of taking our life away. At least we would have control, you know?" And because we both started on antidepressants at the same time we had access to the pills.'

Thankfully they didn't attempt suicide, but their lives collapsed.

'We were going to have a church wedding, but I said I can't … I can't smile anymore. I don't want to have to pretend in front of people.'

On 28 August 2001 Nicki and Steve went to the local registry office with two witnesses and got married. There were no guests.

'We had no professional photos, no wedding dress and no honeymoon or party. Within half an hour we were back home. We were heartbroken.'

Both Steve and Nicki were now on high levels of medication to keep calm. Nicki says throughout this process, her solicitor seemed out of his depth.

'He sort of was terrified of it. He was like, "Oh my God, I don't know what the hell we're going to do. The Post Office are just going on and on and on, saying the same old thing," he said, "and I can't advise you to say any different to what you're saying, but I don't know how this is going to end. But you need to be prepared for the worst." '

Steve came along to one of the last legal conferences before the trial. Nicki's solicitor told them the Post Office had offered her a deal. The fraud and theft charges would be dropped if she pleaded guilty to false accounting. Her solicitor told her she might want to consider it.

Nicki refused. 'We were walking home, and Steve said, "Are you sure you don't want to just say you've done it, just so that we can actually start a life after?" I said, "No, I'll take whatever they give me. I'd rather do that and be able to live with myself than to do any sort of bargain that I know is a complete load of crap." And he said, "Fine. I'll stand by you, then." '

Nicki's solicitor got a barrister involved for the trial. He offered Nicki a piece of advice. '"Just be yourself,' he said. "Don't try and solve their problems for them," and I said, "What do you mean?" He said, "You keep looking to find solutions to this." He said, "Stop it. That's not your job. That's not what you're here for."'

Nicki was more concerned for Steve.

'My husband is dyslexic and was not domesticated in the slightest so my family promised to help him get through if I went to prison. He promised to wait for me and we shared each night on our own just sobbing and hoping for a miracle.'

The trial was scheduled for April 2002 over three days. The Post Office's case was that Nicki was running a scam, producing duplicate records of pension payouts on Horizon, handing one out to each genuine recipient and trousering the rest.

'You stand in the dock, you've got two prison blokes with you… I was in my early 30s, you know? I'd never, ever been in a courtroom in my life. I'd never been arrested, I'd never done anything. I was from a very strict family, and … I'd done quite well for myself, considering we were from a family of six. All of a sudden, I'm in Bristol Crown Court with two prison officers behind me. My mum was like, "Oh, my God, this is the Queen's business. They're going to send you to prison." They were absolutely devastated. My dad was going through kidney failure, he was in hospital the day the trial started. It was just horrendous.'

Nicki's former boss and Marlene gave evidence as prosecution witnesses.

'They went to court because the Post Office told them to, and they were questioned on oath, and my ex-boss was like, "Well, I've just helped her get her mortgage. I just happened to give her a reference, you see. So no, she hasn't got any money." And he made their barrister look a twat, to be honest. And Marlene went up, and she said, "Well, no, Nicki hasn't got any money." So although they were Post Office witnesses, they might as well have been mine.'

I asked if the Post Office ever explained to the court how she was supposed to be doing this fraud, the actual mechanics of it.

'No,' she says. 'They didn't have a clue. Nor did I.'

Nicki remembers the Post Office barrister getting quite het up.

'He chucked a bundle of dockets at me and said, 'You explain this lot' and I said, "I don't know what you want me to say about it." And he was shouting, and getting louder and louder, saying, "You explain how it all works," and I said, "I don't … I have nothing else to say about them. They are what they are," you know? And he was getting really angry.'

The Post Office then tried to get the prosecution witnesses to explain the fraud. 'They tried. But we were all stood, including myself, in bewilderment to say, hang on a minute, on paper, in theory, your cash is right, your pension dockets are right, it's just your weekly report that's wrong. So how do you know you're owed any money at all? And the Post Office were like, well, Horizon's weekly report tells us we do. And the judge then stepped in and said well, no, your cash is right, your dockets are right, your customers are happy … but the weekly Horizon report is saying different. That's where we're at.'

The whole thing sounds pitiful.

'One of the prison officers was drawing funny little pictures, and passing them to me to try and cheer me up. I do remember that. I've kept one because I felt, oh, bless … I just looked at him, and I was just … I don't know what I'm doing here. And he must have felt sorry for me or something, you know, and he was trying to cheer me up. And he was there all the way through for three days, and I thought, oh God, he'll keep me upright, if I collapse.'

I asked Nicki if she felt the judge smelt a rat, or whether he was straight down the line in his summing up.

'Before the jurors went out to make a decision, I do remember him saying something like, "Make sure you consider whether we've actually got a completely innocent person stood here." It was words to that effect, and I thought, he believes me. My barrister was the same, in all fairness. I have 100% faith that he genuinely knew I was innocent.'

The jury were of a similar mind. They took two hours to find Nicki not guilty.

'I walked out of court and collapsed to the floor sobbing with relief. We got home and I didn't have a clue what to do.'

Penniless, in 2004, Steve and Nicki sold their home before it was repossessed. They entered into an IVA to stave off bankruptcy and moved in with Nicki's parents.

In 2005 Nicki had a complete breakdown. She was admitted to hospital with a number of mental and physical symptoms. Steve could not cope at work – he was making mistakes and becoming a potential liability to himself and others. He started delivery driving, which he does to this day. Nicki was eventually able to get a job with social services. They have slowly rebuilt their lives.

Nicki did not hold back on what she thought of Britain's 'most trusted brand.'

'I hate everything about it. Even now, I will not go into a Post Office, I will not use anything to do with the Post Office. I will drive to somewhere to deliver a letter before I'll post it. I can't bear it. I'm still that bitter, now. It's shocking, really. I just think, oh, get over yourself, but I can't. I'm never going to have a wedding day. I'm never going to have a father walk me up the aisle now because he's dead. It's gone, you know?'

She was particularly scathing about the Post Office's attempt to play the good guys on mental health.

'I couldn't find the words. How bloody dare they? I just do not know how they've got away with it, and I just wonder what on earth is going on in government that nobody has put a stop to it. Because they're vile. I fear for anybody who even considers working for them, let alone all the Subpostmasters now. It's not even humane. I just don't get why they're getting away with it. I just don't understand it. And I think they'll still get away with it. The people who did this to us. They didn't give a shit. Nobody's going to be accountable. The vile people that pushed me into the back of their car … they traipsed me in public through the Crown Post Office in Stroud…'

At the time, Nicki didn't have much hope for the group litigation.

'I don't think we'll get any money, to be honest. By the time everybody's made their profits from it … Freeths are amazing, don't get me wrong, they are brilliant. But at the end of the day, it's a business transaction to them. You know, we are a business transaction, that's all we are. We can get emotionally attached as much as we like. I don't do that anymore… We might get £50 if we're lucky. I don't know. It won't be nothing significant. It won't be life-changing for any of us.'

Despite her views, Nicki told me she was following the trial closely, and was delighted with the Common Issues trial judgment. 'I'm slowly falling in love with Judge Fraser,' she said. 'When I read his verdict, I thought, yeah, you've got it. You've got it. You know exactly where we're coming from.'

Since walking free from court in 2002 Nicki has not heard a word from the Post Office. After her trial, she was on Prozac for a decade. Her longest period without drugs was three years. After joining the litigation as a claimant the anxiety came back. In 2019 Nicki took early retirement from her job in social services and started on the antidepressants again.

She says her marriage to Steve has kept her going.

'Twenty years on, we're solid. Absolutely solid. It's probably one of the strongest marriages you would ever get. And we've got two kids now. Steve is just amazing, though. I don't know how he done it. I think he's more … mind over matter. It was a hideous time, don't get me wrong. At times, we were both on our knees, screaming. And I still can't answer now what on earth made him stay. Because nobody in their right mind would. I can't think of anybody who would want to have lived through what he did. There's nothing, no amount of money, nothing I could ever give that man that he deserves for standing by me and taking this on as his life. Because I'm just … I'm just one screwed up human being, you know? I'm not the same person as I was when he met me. I may look similar, but I'm not the same. I'm bitter, I'm nasty, I can … you know, my moods are shocking. And I'm still like that to this day. Because I'm used to being at rock bottom. I'm confident there. I'm on two Prozac every single day, just to function, just to keep well and contented. It is horrible. It is *horrible*.'

TIME TO CHANGE

After speaking to Nicki, Tracy and Wendy, I emailed Time to Change, the charity whose campaign the Post Office had signed up to. Time to Change's 'global' director, Sue Baker OBE, had sent Mark Davies a tweet shortly after the Post Office signed the charity's pledge. It read:

'Yessss it's happened! Well done Mark.'

Not wishing to puncture the self-congratulatory vibe too much, my email to the charity pointed them in the direction of the outraged responses to the Post Office's tweets. I asked Time to Change for a comment. My email was ignored, so I gave them a call.

I explained I was publishing several pieces from people who were claiming the Post Office had ruined their mental health. Just to be sure they knew the detail of what the Post Office had done to people I sent them Wendy and Tracy's accounts and the link to another story I'd published about Bal Gill, an Oxford Subpostmaster who had also had his life destroyed. I told Time to Change these were people with well-documented mental health problems directly attributed to the way they were treated by the Post Office.

Time to Change replied to say they would not comment.

One of the most frustrating elements of the Post Office Horizon scandal is the institutional inertia around it. Down the years there are dozens of people, organisations and bodies who knew something very serious was happening, because they were told it was. Instead of doing the right thing, they chose to stay silent. HM Government, the NFSP, the justice system and the Post Office itself are cases in point.

I gave Time to Change another bite of the cherry. I contrasted their congratulations for the Post Office with their failure to even acknowledge the complaints made on social media from people suffering mental health problems as a result of the Post Office's actions. I suggested it could seem as if they would prefer to burnish a partner organisation's credentials rather than help actual victims of mental trauma – the exact opposite of the purpose of their charity.

Silence.

EXPERT EVIDENCE

The Horizon trial resumed on 4 June 2019 to hear from both parties' independent IT experts. Between them, Dr Worden and Jason Coyne had found 29 bugs which had manifested themselves in Horizon during its 20 year existence. Their cross-examination took seven full days. Over the course of those seven days we learned the experts' answer to whether Horizon was responsible for causing discrepancies in claimants' branch accounts was either 'possibly' or 'possibly not,' which was a touch frustrating.

Dr Worden in particular appeared to think of Horizon as a fathomless ocean. At one point he told the court:

'It is very hard to explain this, but there are levels of depth and complexity in the way Horizon actually works which the experts have not been able to plumb.'

Really? How could years of knowledge, months of expertise and millions of pounds be spent examining a computer system in order to reach such an exasperating conclusion?

After the trial, Jason Coyne told me. The issue, once more, was lack of disclosure. Horizon issue 1) only asked whether it was *possible* or *likely* that a bug, error or defect had the *potential* to cause shortfalls. The Post Office used this to tell Coyne his requests for individual branch account data and audit logs were off limits.

'Every time we asked for them the Post Office would say, "This is an attempt to identify a particular Postmaster, and a particular Postmaster's accounts. The Horizon trial is not about specific Subpostmasters, therefore this request is rejected." '

Unable to examine individual accounts, Coyne and his team had only been able to look at what was happening to Subpostmasters from the Fujitsu end of the telescope, which *sometimes* gave up useful information, but only in glimpses.

Coyne persevered. He applied what information he did have to build the clearest possible picture of the potential effect of the various bugs the experts had uncovered. In his report he put together their possible seriousness and how they had been dealt with, both by Fujitsu and the Post Office, but he had a tough time of it in the witness box. De Garr Robinson, over four days, won so many concessions out of him I wondered if the 29 bugs Coyne and Worden had identified were bugs of any significance to individual branch accounts at all.

Despite this battering, the judge accepted Mr Coyne's methodology, stating, 'I consider Mr Coyne to have been a helpful and constructive witness, and I find the suggestions made to him that he was biased to the claimants and not independent are criticisms that are not justified.'

Dr Worden approached things very differently. He seemed keen *not* to consider the question of individual branch accounts, or any real world effects of any bugs in the system. He used statistical analysis to satisfy himself that even if the errors he and Coyne found had the *potential* to cause discrepancies, the chances of them doing so was vanishingly small. Patrick Green QC chewed into this, eventually winning the concession from Dr Worden that if you looked at the size of Horizon and the number of transactions over a huge period of time, the statistical likelihood of anyone being materially affected by a Horizon error almost exactly matched the number of claimants.

The judge later described Worden's approach and his methodology as 'conceptually flawed,' 'invalid' and 'of no evidential value.'

The mangling of the interpretation of the issues at stake and the lack of disclosure had undoubtedly hampered the claimants' ability to land many clean blows on the Post Office, but the herculean efforts of the Subpostmasters' legal and IT teams brought the occasional rabbit out of the hat, including:

- An error log noting that one of the patches a Fujitsu engineer had applied to fix a bug hadn't worked, which meant the bug would still be causing problems in branches. Fujitsu had already told the Post Office the bug had been fixed, so to head off any awkwardness they were proposing to dive in before a certain deadline, without the Post Office's permission or any individual Subpostmaster's knowledge, and fiddle around with the relevant branch accounts to sort it all out before anyone noticed.
- The Post Office legal team banning their own independent expert from talking to Fujitsu's engineers. Dr Worden managed to get in one call with Gareth Jenkins, but after that instance, in 2018, he was told that in order to be 'whiter than white' all future communication had to go through Post Office lawyers. Dr Worden never spoke to anyone at Fujitsu again.
- The Post Office warning Dr Worden not to look at Horizon's

back-end working processes. During cross-examination he said he was told it was 'out of scope' which he 'found some difficulty with ... because in a sense things like robustness of Horizon actually depends on all sorts of things.'

- An auditor report from 2001 noting a definite bug in Alan Bates' Horizon branch terminal. The auditor stated: 'A correct assessment of cash holdings could not be made because the Horizon system intermittently adds the previous days cash holdings to the daily declaration.'

One can't help thinking if the latter issue had been sorted out to everyone's satisfaction at the time, the Post Office might have saved themselves several hundred million pounds.

Whilst Patrick Green was cross-examining Dr Worden, the thorny subject of remote access came up. It was finally and incontrovertibly laid to rest when Dr Worden told Green, with specific reference to remote access *without a Subpostmaster's knowledge*:

'We agreed in the joint statement that, more or less, Fujitsu or Post Office could do anything.'

So there we were. After a couple of weeks' break to allow leading counsel to prepare and then submit their closing summaries, the Horizon trial ended, and Mr Justice Fraser went off to write his judgment.

COURT OF APPEAL RULING

Whilst waiting for Mr Justice Fraser's definitive findings on Horizon's efficacy, the Court of Appeal gave its view of the Post Office's attempt to seek permission to appeal the Common Issues judgment. The Post Office had identified 26 areas where it felt Fraser had got the law wrong and submitted detailed legal argument as to how and why.

Lord Justice Coulson, who had called the Post Office's recusal application 'absurd', was not in a mood to be accommodating. He ruled:

'The Post Office has … made sweeping statements about the [Common Issues] trial and the judgment which were demonstrably wrong.'

He added:

'The Post Office describes itself as 'the nation's most trusted brand.' Yet this application is founded on the premise that the nation's most trusted brand was not obliged to treat their Subpostmasters with good faith, and instead entitled to treat them in capricious or arbitrary ways which would not be unfamiliar to a mid-Victorian factory owner.'

The judge dismissed every one of the Post Office's grounds for appeal. First they had failed to remove Fraser, now the Common Issues trial judgment was bullet-proof.

The Post Office's annual report made for an interesting read. In 2017/2018 it had spent £3m fighting the claimants. The only comment it made about the litigation at the time was to suggest Alan Bates' case 'lacks merit.'

During the financial year ending March 2019, the Post Office revealed it had spent £20m on the litigation. This was marked in the Post Office's accounts as 'exceptional' expenditure, which, along with increased amortisation and depreciation, brought the Post Office's overall operating profit down from £47m to £6m.

Such a serious dent on the bottom line appears to have brought about a slight change of tone. The report states that the ongoing litigation, 'reflects the fact that there have been disagreements in the past on the management of contractual relationships. We are determined in future to have the very best working relationship fit for today's business environment, and that we must always strive to do even better.'

As a direct reflection of the impact of the litigation on the Post

Office, every member of the Post Office executive board took a 20% cut to their Short Term Incentive Payments (STIP). This sudden attack of corporate and social responsibility meant the outgoing Chief Executive Paula Vennells saw her STIP drop £52,600 from £196,400 to £143,800.

Thankfully, and by complete coincidence, the Post Office remuneration board decided to increase Vennells' Long Term Incentive Payment (LTIP) from £194,400 to £245,000 *and* gave her a basic salary top up from £253,800 to £255,000. This meant the total net financial cost to Paula Vennells, as recognition of her failures as chief executive, over a period of seven years, was £800.

HIGH STAKES POKER

Although the Post Office had done everything it could to beat up the claimants in the courts, it was not so stupid as to recognise that any prospect of its recusal application or appeal succeeding was small. It had therefore, in early 2019, begun to pursue the idea of a mediated solution.

At first, Alan Bates was resistant. In August 2019 he told his fellow claimants:

'There could well be an optimum time when attending mediation might be in the Group's best interests. But it certainly isn't before the Horizon judgment is released... To start with, the Post Office still refuses to accept it has done anything wrong, otherwise it wouldn't have applied to the Court of Appeal to overturn the findings by the Court of the Common Issues judgment.'

In his view, 'To go to mediation immediately would mean we could find ourselves in the same position we were in at the end of the Initial Complaint Review and Mediation Scheme where, as a number of you will recall, the Post Office turned up at mediation meetings, stated it had done nothing wrong and stated it was "all your fault."'

Mr Bates also said:

'There would be substantial costs involved with attending mediation, so the Post Office would need to demonstrate that it is serious about going into it in good faith and that it is not just a ploy to waste time and deplete our funding. They would need to show they have the funding available to deliver financial redress to the Group and is prepared to redress the wrongs it has done to so many. And this case is not just a matter of money, many claimants still want an apology for the grief that the Post Office has visited upon them and their families.'

Within a couple of months, Bates' tune had changed. The reason, as Kay Linnell told me, was simple. 'We were going to run out of money. We were never going to get to the end of five trials.'

James Hartley agrees. 'It was a difficult decision to embark on the mediation process at all, naturally. But that decision process happened over a period of months whereby we were doing all sorts of financial outcome scenarios, looking in great detail with the leading counsel, the steering committee and ways in which the case might continue and not settle on whichever way round we looked at it. The very clear conclusion was that we needed to find an exit for the Postmasters before they ended up with nothing.'

Although Alan Bates had told me in February 2016 the funds he had at his disposal were unlimited, they weren't. Despite the trouncing the Post Office were getting in the courts, there would come a point at which the litigation funder's success fee and the lawyers' costs would be larger than the maximum amount the claimants could be awarded in damages. Under reforms introduced to the English courts by Lord Justice Jackson in 2013, success fees were not recoverable from a losing party. It was time for some hard-headed financial calculations.

Interestingly, James Hartley felt the result of the Horizon trial was irrelevant to these calculations. On an assessment of what they had seen between March and the eventual conclusion of the trial in July, he told me the claimants had 'factored in' a win. But there was still a great deal of uncertainty around the case. Hartley explained that, despite the action being taken on behalf of a single group of people, there was a risk a proportion of the claimants' cases would fall at fences raised by the Post Office. One simple issue still to be resolved was the statute of limitations. The claimants had yet to prove that all the individual cases more than six years old (which was most of them) were not time-barred.[1] The Post Office had indicated it would contest them all.

'If it had been a personal choice I would have carried on,' Alan told me, 'without the slightest hesitation. But I had to deal with the reality of it. I felt the livelihoods of the individuals would be threatened even further, financially, if something went wrong with the court case.'

Mediation was scheduled for two days, starting 28 November 2019. The Post Office decided to use the same firm of solicitors, Herbert Smith Freehills, who had conducted their losing appeal against the Common Issues judgment. Patrick Green, combining his skills as a QC and trained mediator, led proceedings for the claimants. Although the Subpostmasters' cash pot was running dry, the Post Office didn't know the funding situation, and Green wanted to keep them guessing.

'We did a very good job of making sure we could just about do the next trial, so I could look them in the eye and say, "Fine. Let's roll on to

1 In civil law, something called the statute of limitations means that an action must normally be brought within six years of an event happening. Exceptions, like the emergence of new evidence, can apply.

Heads of Damage"[2] – and mean it!'

I asked what brought the Post Office to the mediation table.

'We were *killing* them,' replied Green, instantly. 'They'd basically lost. Everyone knew they'd lost. The Common Issues ... two visits to the Court of Appeal ... the recusal, which was nuclear. We were beating them hands down every time we went to court. And their strategy of outspending us wasn't working. And I think another thing that unnerved them as well was if they had made a decent guess at to what the funders had put into the litigation, they would have known that it should have run out long ago. So they would be asking themselves how we hadn't already run out money. The whole substrate to this "outspend them" policy hadn't worked. We were still going at it hammer and tongs.'

So mediation it was. The process followed a standard format. Each side sent the mediator (a qualified person agreed by both parties) a statement which set out why it was a good idea to settle the case through mediation and on what basis. The claimants then put a value on their claim; that is, an acceptable settlement sum.

'Normally what happens then,' Green told me, 'is the defendant produces a gigantic spreadsheet where they've analysed all the groups of claims and come to the conclusion they're worth nothing. And you'll say why they're wrong. And on it goes. It's grinding.'

On this occasion, the Post Office's new chief executive, Nick Read, was scheduled to attend, as were five claimant Subpostmasters, including Pam Stubbs, Louise Dar and Jo Hamilton.

Not quite knowing what to expect, on the first day of the mediation the Subpostmasters travelled to Herbert Smith Freehills' headquarters in the City of London. Jo Hamilton walked into a vast boardroom ("I've never seen such a big table!") with the Post Office CEO, his lawyers and flunkies on one side and the claimants' lawyers on the other.

The Subpostmasters had been asked to write their stories down so they could tell them to Nick Read. Jo had prepared something, but told me that when it came to her turn, 'I just decided to look him in the eye and tell him everything they had done to me.'

---

[2] Despite sounding like a metal band, Heads of Damage is a list apportioning values to each aspect of the damages being claimed. In this case, 'Heads' to be argued over included reputational damage, loss of future earnings, deceit by the Post Office, breach of contract, failure to investigate and so on.

It was a powerful moment. Afterwards Read asked if the five Postmasters would come to a separate room so he could talk to them without any lawyers present. Once inside, Jo explained what it was like to be powerless in the face of a brutal bureaucracy.

'I said to him, "We couldn't get anyone to listen to us. No one took us seriously. And we couldn't fight you." '

I asked Jo what she made of Read. 'He appeared to listen,' she said. 'I'd like to *think* he was genuine.'

Although it wasn't due to be made public until 16 December, Mr Justice Fraser allowed the parties to see his draft Horizon judgment before it was handed down.

The two-day mediation stretched to ten. 'It was incredibly intense,' remembers James Hartley. 'Most mediations last about a day. To go to ten is almost unheard of.'

Whilst the lawyers were shuttling back and forth between the parties to see if they could get anywhere, most journalists following the story had 16 December in their diaries.

At 8.30am on 11 December 2019, I was looking at the prospects list in the 5 News morning meeting on the fifth floor of the ITN building in Gray's Inn Road. It was the day before the general election, which would see Boris Johnson's Conservatives confirmed in power for another five years. At 8.48am I got a text from Caroline Wagstaff at Luther Pendragon, Freeths' PR firm. It read, 'I am sending you an email at 9am so you might want to be near a computer.'

The email was the joint announcement of a settlement to the *Bates v Post Office* litigation.

RESULT!

Staring at the ruins of its repeated legal defeats, the huge amounts of money it was shovelling into lawyers' pockets and the growing reputational damage it was sustaining, the Post Office had blinked first. Just.

Expressing 'gratitude' to the claimants, the Post Office thanked 'those who attended the mediation in person to share their experiences with us, for holding us to account in circumstances where, in the past, we have fallen short and we apologise to those affected.'

Alan Bates showered Nick Read in praise for his 'leadership, engagement and determination in helping to reach a settlement of this long running dispute.' Bates stated, 'It would seem that, from the positive discussions with the Post Office's new CEO, Nick Read, there is a genuine desire to move on from these legacy issues and learn lessons from the past.'

Most of the claimants knew the mediation was happening, but the first they knew of the settlement was when it was made public. I forwarded the press release to all my contacts and watched the replies ping back into my inbox.

'This is the best news I have ever heard,' said one claimant. 'Still in disbelief that they would actually acknowledge, let alone apologise for, their behaviour.'

'This has just given me the biggest lift!!!' emailed another.

'Oh my god, I really cannot digest this news,' said another correspondent. 'Not sure how I'm feeling, sick, overwhelmed or relieved. Thank you so much for the update. I just wish we had found out a better way.'

Karl Flinders posted a Computer Weekly article hailing Alan Bates, who had written to the magazine in 2004, saying, 'I fully expect it to take a number of years to bring Post Office Ltd to account for what they have done to us, but we are determined to do it.'

I could not get anyone from the Postmasters' side to tell me how much the settlement was for. Both Freeths and the JFSA said they couldn't give me any information, as they were bound to confidentiality. So were the Post Office, but that didn't stop them calling up Karl within minutes of his piece going live to tell him the final sum was £57.75m.

Five minutes after Karl posted his scoop on Twitter I took a call from someone who knows a lot about this story. 'I hope to Christ that figure is wrong,' he said.

I phoned the Post Office press office to find out exactly what the £57.75m settlement sum was meant to cover. They told me as far as they were concerned it was everything. It was the final sum the Post Office had agreed to give the claimants to make them drop their action.

I asked the press officer several versions of the same question in order to make sure, and he was unequivocal. The £57.75m was not just to cover litigation costs and the funder's success fee. It was the final total sum that the claimants were going to get out of the litigation.

I did some back-of-a-fag-packet calculations, assuming parity across both parties in costs. I was aware litigation funders usually took a multiple of three times their investment, but assumed for the purposes of my example, they had come over all benevolent and only looked to double their money. It meant that in the very best case (and therefore frankly, unlikely) scenario, the 555 claimants would walk away with an average of around £50,000 each.

Shortly after the £57.75m figure had been released by the Post Office I received an email from a former Subpostmaster, who had obviously crunched the numbers himself. He concluded:

'This is nothing but a great win for the Post Office. My losses alone came to £200,000. This compensation will not cover the fraudulent claims that the Post Office took from me. I am 75 and still work to live and pay my mortgage. There will be no celebrating this decision.'

I wondered if there might be other sums the claimants could unlock or access as part of the agreement, but Freeths and the JFSA were adamant they could not comment.

The news value of the settlement and the apology, was not, at the time, overshadowed by the private concerns about the final sum. As a headline figure, £57.75m was a big number. The Post Office had folded and apologised. The Subpostmasters had won!

The settlement press release was accompanied by confirmation that the Horizon trial judgment would be handed down as scheduled. Several dozen Subpostmasters confirmed they would be attending, partly to mark the occasion with their fellow claimants, but also to try to get some more information about what the settlement meant.

Although the litigation had been concluded, the prospect of seeing Subpostmasters gather in number outside court on 16 December and the hitherto unpublished conclusions in the judgment served to pique the interest of the broadcast media. Attention had been diverted on 11 December by the general election, but now there was a potential free hit coming.

On the day of the settlement I wondered if the conclusions in Mr Justice Fraser's judgment and the hearing itself would feel a bit after-the-Lord-Mayor's-show. Instead, they served to tee up a final flourish.

HORIZON TRIAL JUDGMENT

I arrived early at the Rolls Building, wondering who might be around. I had heard rumours some of the campaigners were intending to bring a banner. They had. It was a long strip of red canvas with white lettering which read: 'SOS – Support Our Subpostmasters.' The banner was designed and paid for by Eleanor Shaikh, a one-woman dynamo who had been radicalised by the treatment of her local Subpostmaster, Chirag Sidhpura.

Chirag had a Post Office in the Surrey village of Farncombe. It was raided by Post Office auditors in 2017 who found a £57,000 discrepancy. Chirag was immediately suspended. The next day he got a call from a Post Office security team manager wanting to know how the money had disappeared. It seems from their conversation, the investigations team had finally given up telling Subpostmasters they were the only ones having problems with Horizon.

Chirag expressed his mystification as to how £57,000 could be missing from his Post Office, as, until the 'audit' he was not aware he was running a deficit. He suggested to the security team manager there might be a fault with Horizon. The Post Office investigator responded, 'Everyone says that.'

Chirag was given two options – hand over £57,000 or face prosecution and a possible two years in jail. Terrified, Chirag begged favours from his family. He scraped the cash together and handed it over to the Post Office, who sacked him. Chirag then found he was the latest in a long line of Subpostmasters who had been done over by the Post Office. Unfortunately, he was too late to join the group litigation. He had nonetheless taken a keen interest in the court case, as had the formidable Ms Shaikh, who had bonded with lots of Subpostmasters and was determined to help.

There was a big turnout. On 16 December 2019, Seema Misra, Jo Hamilton, Pam Stubbs, Scott Darlington, Teju Adedayo, Tracey Merritt, Wendy Martin, Tracy Felstead, Wendy Buffrey, Sue Knight, Alison Hall, Deirdre Connolly and Nicki Arch were among the many claimants who assembled outside the Rolls Building. Alan Bates was detained by an unfortunately timed hospital procedure, but his partner Suzanne was there to witness everything.

At 1.45pm, we filed into Court 26 for the final time. Ron Warmington and Ian Henderson came along to witness something which, to them, must have felt like vindication, and history. The place was heaving with claimants, lawyers, journalists and supporters, who were creating quite a buzz. On the instruction of an usher, we fell silent and rose as Mr Justice Fraser entered. Once seated, Fraser told us the judgment was now public. He indicated how the paper copies would be distributed and scribbled an order which brought the litigation to an end. Then he surprised everyone.

'By signing the consent order that I have just signed,' he told the court, 'today is the final substantive hearing day of the Post Office litigation. This means that I am therefore effectively no longer the managing judge.'

We presumed a few minor points of housekeeping would follow. But no.

'Based on the knowledge that I have gained,' Fraser intoned, 'both from conducting the trial and writing the Horizon Issues judgment, I have very grave concerns regarding the veracity of evidence given by Fujitsu employees to other courts in previous proceedings about the known existence of bugs, errors and defects in the Horizon system... After very careful consideration, I have therefore decided, in the interests of justice, to send the papers in the case to the Director of Public Prosecutions, Mr Max Hill QC, so he may consider whether the matter to which I have referred should be the subject of any prosecution.'

The Director of Public Prosecutions runs the Crown Prosecution Service. As Fraser read out the case law which allowed him to make his referral, heads were swivelling and eyebrows were being raised all over the courtroom. The judge then announced that the letter he was sending the DPP would be confidential, and what happened next was entirely up to Max Hill. He wished everyone a Happy Christmas, and left us to it.

The usual bedlam ensued as reporters dived on copies of the judgment whilst simultaneously trying to get comment from all the players in the room. As we filed outside for the press conference, I asked Patrick Green to précis the 1,030-paragraph judgment. He told me the claimants had 'won on all counts.'

Outside court, the Subpostmasters gathered behind Eleanor's red banner and raised their fists in victory for the cameras. There were more photographs and interviews, then the claimants trooped back inside the Rolls Building for a briefing from Freeths. I got in a cab to the BBC's Broadcasting House clutching my copy of the judgment. I'd been invited onto Radio 4's PM programme to discuss the Subpostmasters' victory and was now going to have to speed-read an inch-thick document on the way to pick out some key conclusions. I needn't have worried. They were leaping off the page.

In the back of my cab, I discovered that Mr Justice Fraser had ruled that the first iteration of the Horizon computer system, which became known during the trial as Legacy Horizon, was 'not remotely robust.' After 2010 it became 'slightly more robust than Legacy Horizon, but still had a significant number of bugs, errors and defects.' The upgrade in 2017 made it 'far more robust', but that was too little, too late. The damage had been done.

The Post Office had been prosecuting its own Subpostmasters on the basis of unreliable IT evidence for more than a decade. It had been demanding cash from hundreds more on the same basis. The Horizon trial was set up to ask if bugs, errors and defects could affect Subpostmasters' branch accounts. Fraser went a step further. 'All the evidence in the Horizon Issues trial,' he wrote, 'shows not only was there the potential for this to occur, but it actually has happened, and on numerous occasions.'

Once more the behaviour of the Post Office came in for scathing criticism. Fraser ruled their approach to the litigation 'amounted, in reality, to bare assertions and denials that ignore what has actually occurred… It amounts to the twenty-first century equivalent of maintaining that the earth is flat.'

While MPs, journalists and campaigners were raising questions about Horizon, the Post Office had created a corporate parallel universe.

'A theme contained within some of the internal documents,' wrote Fraser, 'is an extreme sensitivity (seeming to verge, on occasion, to institutional paranoia) concerning any information that may throw doubt on the reputation of Horizon, or expose it to further scrutiny.'

Given Fraser's pronouncements that day in court, it was not surprising that Fujitsu was also heavily criticised. The judgment stated the company had not 'properly and fully investigated … myriad [Horizon] problems, nor did Fujitsu categorise such incidents correctly. They also seem to have moved away, in their investigations, from concluding that there were any issues with the software wherever it was possible for them to do so, regardless of evidence to the contrary, an approach that has been carried into the Fujitsu evidence for the Horizon Issues trial.'

In court, Fujitsu witnesses 'sought to portray the Horizon system – Legacy Horizon and Horizon Online – in a light as favourable as possible to Fujitsu, regardless of its own internal evidence to the contrary, and regardless of the facts.'

I sent a congratulatory email to Alan Bates, letting him know what had happened in Court 26 and asking for a comment. He told me the judgment 'vindicates everything we have been saying for years.' Then he set out the JFSA's direction of travel.

'The real problem we have been left with is the unrecovered expenses which we have had to incur to pursue the litigation and which include considerable litigation financing fees, all of which have devoured most of the £58m damages, leaving little left to be shared between the group.

'It would seem, from some recent excellent research work Eleanor Shaikh undertook, that successive governments have failed in their statutory duty to oversee and manage Post Office and this is something that we are planning to ask our MPs to raise next year. If it turns out to be correct, we will be wanting to recover everything we have had to spend doing the job government should have done.'

He signed off, 'It isn't over yet, just the end of another chapter.'

On my way home from Broadcasting House, an email pinged into my phone. It was from a claimant who had attended the Freeths briefing at the Rolls building after the judgment was handed down.

The message said:

'Battery nearly flat on coach home. In private meeting Freeths said there is going to be £8–£11m for claimants, all the rest go to investors and Freeths. Waste of effort on our part! Very sad.'

I started phoning round. I was told that not only was this figure true but also, if the lawyers and litigation funders had actually taken what they were entitled to, the settlement figure would have been swallowed up completely.

THE FALLOUT

First out of the blocks following the judgment was Lord Arbuthnot. It is a convention that government and parliamentarians refrain from making overt comments about court cases as they happen. The moment they finish, the gloves can come off.

Lord Arbuthnot called the judgment 'an excellent Christmas present, but won at great cost.' He called for an inquiry, saying it needed to be led by a judge, 'since the Post Office has repeatedly given inaccurate information, including to me.'

The next intervention came from Second Sight's Ron Warmington. In his first public comment since the Interim Report was published in 2013, Warmington asked a question which had not been considered by either judgment. If the Postmasters weren't taking money out of the Post Office, and had then been forced to put their own money into the system, where had it all gone?

Back in March 2019, one of the lead claimants in the Horizon trial, Adrees Latif, told the court:

'There is a software glitch that stole our money, you know, that disappeared into magic air where it is not possible.'

Ron Warmington was not so sure. Real money does not disappear 'into magic air' – it has to be accounted for, and he was pretty sure he knew where it had gone.

'The Post Office has improperly enriched itself through the decades,' he thundered, 'with funds that have passed through its own suspense accounts. Had its own staff more diligently investigated in order to establish who were the rightful owners of those funds, they would have been returned to them, whether they were Post Office's customers or its Subpostmasters. When is the Post Office going to return the funds that, in effect, belonged to its Subpostmasters?'

Warmington was in no doubt where the blame lay. 'If the Post Office Board had believed – and acted on, what Second Sight reported … instead of being led by the nose by its own middle management and in-house and external legal advisors, huge amounts of money, and human suffering, would have been avoided.'

For years, the Post Office had leant on Subpostmasters to plug the gaps in its accounts. To the victims it must have seemed like a racket.

Random, inexplicable accounting holes were appearing out of nowhere, resulting in Subpostmasters being screwed for cash, with menaces. The Post Office's contractual muscle, combined with threats of prosecution, allowed it to maintain an attitude which ran from the board to the lowest footsoldier – *give us the money or you will suffer the consequences.*

Rather than front up, Fujitsu did the corporate equivalent of pulling down its baseball cap and leaving by the back entrance. Journalists who asked were given five lines of text asserting the company took Fraser's judgment 'very seriously' and was 'conducting a thorough process to review the court's statements in detail.'

What about the woman in charge of it all? Tom Witherow from the Daily Mail decided to pay Paula Vennells a visit at her house in Bedfordshire. Vennells told Witherow she would not apologise to Subpostmasters and that his question was 'unacceptable.' Jayne Caveen, whose brother, Martin Griffiths, suffered so horribly at the Post Office's hands, told the Mail:

'This woman has driven people to suicide. That was an opportunity to say that mistakes have been made, and we're sorry. I'm really angry and bitter about it. It's shameful she's been in denial all these years. It's heartless.'

Two days later, Vennells sent Witherow a statement, which read:

'It was and remains a source of great regret to me that these colleagues and their families were affected over so many years. I am truly sorry we were unable to find both a solution and a resolution outside of litigation and for the distress this caused.'

Perhaps the most risible reaction to the Horizon judgment came from the NFSP. Calum Greenhow, George Thomson's successor, declared he was 'extremely disappointed by the Post Office's behaviour.' This was because, according to Greenhow, Fraser's judgment implied 'the Post Office has misled the NFSP for years about the reliability of the Horizon system.'

For two decades, the NFSP's leadership had ignored the begging and pleading of desperate Subpostmasters, and decided it would take the Post Office's assurances that all these people were criminals with their hands in the till. Having bought and propagated a lie the Post Office had sold them, it appeared the NFSP was now trying to suggest it was an innocent party. It didn't wash.

DEFENDING THE SETTLEMENT

Once they had deducted their fees, paid the barristers and given Therium their cut, Freeths were left to divvy up what most sources estimate was the remaining £11–£12m from the settlement agreement among 555 claimants. Aware of the outrage in certain quarters, the solicitors tried to explain the situation, reminding claimants:

'At the numerous group meetings that we and JFSA held with many of you, the overwhelming message was that this Group Action was the only chance of getting anything – "anything is better than nothing" was the message to us.'

Freeths had delivered on that aim, but it meant any money coming the claimants' way 'will be significantly less than your losses due to the unrecoverable funding and legal costs paid which were necessary to allow the Group Litigation to be brought.'

In fact, warned Freeths, no one should think about agreeing to 'any expenditure or take on any liabilities in reliance on receiving money' as it was 'unlikely that the amount you will receive will significantly alter your financial circumstances.'

It was a horrible position for everyone to be in. Neither the lawyers nor Therium had taken the full amount they were entitled to. Most of the claimants had not got anything close to what they lost.

The sudden, hard reality of the conclusion to the litigation contrasted markedly with the Postmasters' sense – informed by stunning victories at the High Court and the Court of Appeal – that the Post Office was losing badly and on the run. Many wanted to know how a process which revealed just how unjustly they had been treated could not also compensate them fairly.

In hindsight, the litigation was a superb mechanism for extracting binding judgments which would push the Subpostmasters' case forward. James Hartley is adamant the claimant group regularly had the risks spelled out to them both by Freeths and the JFSA before they signed up to anything. But many Postmasters believed the litigation was their chance for resolution and redress. Some claimants felt they had become collateral, and they didn't like it.

Lee Castleton was in a particularly invidious position. Because he was sued by the Post Office at the High Court, his case was not separated out with the criminally prosecuted claimants. The latter group had a chance at a malicious prosecution claim if they could get their convictions overturned. The settlement meant he no longer has that opportunity. The steering committee signed away Lee's right to further action against the Post Office. In return, he got £20,000.

'I'm not saying that what Alan did is wrong,' he told me. 'I just feel as though we were thrown on a fire a little bit. At the end of the day, I've lost a lot of opportunities going forward that I should be allowed to explore. And I haven't had an awful lot back for that.'

Both Kay Linnell and Patrick Green have separately pointed out to me that Lee had his £300,000 debt to the Post Office cleared, but as Lee says (sarcastically):

'Brilliant. Thank you. That was nothing to do with me. That was put on me because the Post Office told a load of lies in court. Having a debt removed that should never have been mine in the first place doesn't feel like something I should be grateful for.'

Lee did nothing wrong. But his options are gone, apparently for good. He remains philosophical.

'What Alan and Kay did was a brilliant job with a terrible hand. I can't praise them enough for what they did, but completely separate to that, I've been screwed.'

Aware of the disquiet after the headline settlement was communicated to the wider claimant group, Freeths reminded them, 'You all agreed at the outset in the documents you signed, handing over your decision-making to the Committee who acted on legal advice at all times.'

The claimants were also told that due to concerns over potential breaches of confidentiality and legal action which might be brought against them by the Post Office if that were to happen, they would not be sent the entire settlement agreement signed in their name.

A year and a half after the conclusion to the litigation, I met with Patrick Green at Colbert, a grand Parisian-style café which fronts onto Sloane Square in central London. During our conversation Patrick conceded that some of the things said to the claimants about the potential value of the case at the outset may have been 'unguarded.' This led to raised expectations.

'If you've got a number of say, £100m in your mind, and the final settlement figure is £58m, you're going to naturally feel disappointed. But without Alan, the number would be zero.'

I asked why he didn't try to negotiate for £200m.

'The Post Office didn't have £200m. The Treasury's got to give it to them. And getting money out of the Treasury to settle cases is very, very hard. The problem was – if you say you want £200m, they'll say, "Okay, let's spend another £30m litigating, and then we'll see if you're still here." '

On top of this, if you decide to abandon proceedings, as the claimant, you are liable for all costs.

The lack of expectation management by Freeths and the JFSA as the litigation progressed undoubtedly created a problem, but they were in a bind. If they told the claimants they needed to go to mediation because of their rapidly depleting funding pot, it would have been a disaster. The Post Office would have found this out and used the information to its advantage – throwing more money after the tens of millions it had already spent to run the claimants out of road.

But when the settlement landed, it was a shock. The claimants had signed away their legal right to sue the Post Office in exchange for a few grand and a vague apology which contained no mention of liability. Some felt used, and abandoned. Others were more supportive.

'I hear the cries of those upset at the settlement,' said one, 'but had Alan not put his head above the parapet, had Freeths legal team not given their all, had Judge Fraser given in to all the B****S spouted by Paula Vennells and her Mafia friends the payout would be ZERO. We won and have the law on our side, so we can fight another day without having to prove anything. The Post Office have been seen for what they are: bullies with no regard for its employees or working partners.'

Although Alan and his fellow claimants were forced by diminishing returns into a settlement which would only give them a fraction of what they'd lost, the litigation itself had produced two judgments which would have a defining effect on the history of the scandal. They were the work of a 'conspicuously able' judge, but they would not exist without the thousands of hours Alan, Kay, Freeths and the barristers from Henderson Chambers put into preparing and then making their case. Almost without exception, everything positive in the Subpostmasters' universe which has happened since 16 December 2019 can be traced *directly* back to the Common Issues and Horizon trials judgments.

CONTINUING CORPORATE DENIAL

Having got what he needed from the courts, Alan Bates turned his attention to Westminster. In January 2020, he sent the Horizon judgment to Kelly Tolhurst, the Business, Energy and Industrial Strategy[1] minister who had responsibility for the Post Office. He enclosed an invoice for the fees which would otherwise have gone to the claimants in compensation. Railing against the 'tyrannical conduct of Post Office Limited over the years, unchecked by government,' he suggested it was time the executive acknowledge its 'statutory duty to proactively manage' the Post Office.

He concluded:

'By far the most shocking consequence of the failure of successive governments to address the responsibilities they have for Post Office Limited, is the disastrous effect it has had on the lives of the claimant Subpostmaster group, and who knows how many others. Purely because of the way, either intentionally or by ignorance, successive ministers have failed to carry out their duty to actively oversee and manage Post Office Limited.'

The minister replied noting the High Court settlement 'included all legal and other costs' which meant she must 'respectfully refuse' Alan's request for £46m.

Another former Subpostmaster wrote to BEIS asking if anyone at the Post Office was going to be held accountable for the scandal. The reply, from Lauren Wood at the BEIS Ministerial Correspondence Unit, was dismissive.

'Given the major programme of work the Post Office is implementing,' she sniffed, 'the government will not be taking further action at this time. The Horizon IT system was put in place in 1999, with the first issues being raised by postmasters in the early 2000s. Over an almost 20-year period decisions were made by many people, including in relation to the prosecution of Postmasters. There is therefore no single person accountable for what has taken place.'

Refusing to take action over a scandal because too many people were involved and it happened over a long period of time is morally

---

1 The government department formerly known as BIS, hereafter shortened to BEIS. Everyone pronounces it 'bayze.'

reprehensible and Ms Wood (and the government) should know it.

At the end of January the Criminal Cases Review Commission got in touch with the 34 Subpostmasters whose cases it had been sitting on since 2015. It told them it was arranging for a committee of CCRC commissioners to meet in March 'to reach a decision on whether the Post Office cases should be sent for appeal.'

The CCRC also revealed a further 22 Subpostmaster applications had been accepted since the Horizon trial judgment had been handed down.

The Crown Prosecution Service told journalists the DPP had received a letter from Sir Peter Fraser and that it would be asking London's Metropolitan Police Service to investigate Fraser's concerns. The Met confirmed it was looking into the activities of two individuals as a result of the CPS referral.

The government's first public response to the litigation came from the BEIS minister in the Lords. Lord Duncan told peers, 'The old ways of doing things cannot go on' and that, 'the leadership of the Post Office got it very badly wrong' which had led to people experiencing 'unfortunate situations.'

If the word 'unfortunate' used in that context wasn't troubling enough, what followed was. The minister told peers that to keep a close eye on the Post Office, the government would be holding quarterly meetings with the National Federation of Subpostmasters 'as a way of ensuring that there is a better relationship with those who are at the sharp end of the Post Office.' He clearly hadn't read the Common Issues judgment.

In response to a call for an independent public inquiry and Post Office executives held to account, Lord Duncan suggested instead the government would effect 'manifest change' through 'a new national framework.' No one seemed to know what this meant. Lord Duncan further asserted that the Post Office had already somehow undergone 'a change in culture,' thanks to its new chief executive.

It was clear from what Lord Duncan said that ministers had no interest in taking any kind of proactive grip of the situation. The first mention of the litigation in the House of Commons came from Tracy Felstead's MP Lucy Allan who asked, 'May we have a debate in government time to consider what is fast becoming a national scandal?'

The leader of the House, Jacob Rees-Mogg, made a vague commitment to allowing further discussion on the issue, but when another MP asked for a debate which could actually lead to some kind of action, he replied, 'I cannot promise.'

Lucy Allan's contribution sent up a flare at Finsbury Dials. Immediately after she made her comments in the Commons, the Post Office contacted her and suggested a meeting to 'discuss the issues you raised regarding your constituent and the wider outputs of the Group Litigation Order.'

Interested in finding out more, the MP accepted the offer. Two Post Office representatives were dispatched to Portcullis House. One was Patrick Bourke, the Government Affairs and Policy Director who was at the meeting in 2015 when Panorama was not given the correct information about remote access to the Horizon system.

Having been called out for its excessive secrecy, institutional paranoia and punitive enforcement of a contract which was so oppressive as to be in-part unlawful, you might think it was time for a little corporate introspection. Instead, according to Ms Allan, Bourke and his colleague were 'supremely confident to the point of arrogance, that the CCRC would refer "few, if any" cases to the Court of Appeal, and if they did the appeals would fail.'

Ms Allan said the two Post Office men 'were dismissive of the suggestion that innocent people had been wrongly convicted. In their view, I was taking the side of my constituent who was a convicted criminal, without fully understanding the issues.'

Ms Allan, who had spoken at length with Tracy and read both judgments in detail, felt Bourke and his colleague were being 'patronising.'

'They assumed I would just take their word for it and leave it there. I remember feeling that they were high-handed and not interested in the case of my constituent. Their apparent nonchalance shocked me. There was no humility in the light of the judgment.'

The two men also allegedly told the MP that Post Office lawyers would be gunning for each CCRC case to be treated separately, revealing they intended to insist that those who pleaded guilty should be excluded from the process altogether.

Although Ms Allan says she was taken aback by this, it fitted a pattern. Since 2013, the Post Office had been trying to create a parallel universe in which none of the Subpostmasters' cases were connected. Until Second Sight were on the scene the Post Office had no file linking the issues that prosecuted Subpostmasters were raising, then they initially resisted the formation of a group litigation, arguing the campaigning Subpostmasters had little in common. Once the GLO was underway, Angela van den

Bogerd told the High Court she couldn't see any connection between the 500-plus cases.

Ms Allan finished her recollection of the encounter with a weird detail. During the meeting, one of the two Post Office men had put a pencil on the table which bore the logo of Herbert Smith Freehills, the lawyers who had conducted the mediation which led to the High Court settlement.

'I asked them if Herbert Smith had been advising them,' said Ms Allan, 'purely because I had a friend who was a partner there. One of them grabbed the pencil, put it in his pocket and said "No!"'

Before publishing this book, I sought comment from the Post Office regarding this meeting. Both Mr Bourke and the Post Office insist Ms Allan misremembered what was said. Patrick Bourke claims the meeting was constructive and cordial. He specifically denies either he or his colleague asserted any criminal appeals referred back to the courts would fail.

On the issue of trying to have those who pleaded guilty removed from the appeals process, the Post Office says that several months after the meeting with Ms Allan, the Post Office indicated it would not be contesting some of the appeals referred back to the courts by the CCRC, and that this included guilty pleas.

Not long after Ms Allan's meeting with Patrick Bourke, a different Post Office executive was overheard (and recorded) in a pub, blithely contradicting the key finding of the Horizon judgment. 'It's never been proven there's a link between a computer glitch and anyone actually losing money,' he boasted, incorrectly.

The exec went on to suggest that Postmasters with criminal convictions had them for a reason. 'We've got 11,500 Post Offices with £30,000 in cash which *we've* given them. It's public money. Some Subpostmasters might decide to – not necessarily with any particular intent – *borrow* that money for a little while. Some of them downright stole it.'

Asked if he was worried about working at an organisation which had taken such a hit to its reputation in two High Court judgments, the exec was dismissive. 'The vast majority of people have never heard anything about it,' he said, correctly.

BORIS GETS INVOLVED

In February 2020 there was a cabinet reshuffle. Kelly Tolhurst was removed from BEIS and sent to the Department of Transport. She was replaced by Paul Scully, who became the tenth minister with responsibility for the Post Office in as many years.

In the Lords, Lord Duncan was replaced by Lord Callanan, who, on 24 February, brought some new information about the political response to the Post Office scandal into the public domain.

Lord Callanan claimed advice the government had been receiving from the Post Office over the last ten years or so was 'flawed.' He repeated his predecessor's view that 'the government cannot accept any further request for payment.' He went on to say the Post Office was going to set up a scheme 'with the aim of addressing historical shortfalls for Postmasters who were not part of the group litigation settlement.'

Callanan was silent on the need for any sort of investigation into the Post Office, and when challenged directly on whether anyone was going to be held to account, he told his fellow peers, 'the government do not propose to take any further action against current or former directors.'

If that was the settled position of the government, it was given a kick 24 hours later by Boris Johnson. During Prime Minister's Questions the Labour MP Kate Osborne mentioned her constituent, Chris Head, a Subpostmaster claimant and energetic campaigner. 'Will the Prime Minister,' she asked, 'today assure Chris and others that he will commit to launching an independent inquiry?'

Johnson was unequivocal. 'I am happy to commit to getting to the bottom of the matter in the way that she recommends.'

In one sentence the Prime Minister had potentially changed the game. Yes, it was a commitment from a man whose words did not always match his intentions or actions, but the most powerful person in the country had just told parliament that he was happy to commit to an independent inquiry, whether he really meant to or not.

Backbench MPs used the Prime Minister's words to push the government further. A select committee inquiry was announced into the scandal. In the Lords, Lord Callanan claimed the government had been 'misled' by the Post Office, and assured peers there needed to be 'a full examination, with due rigour, of what happened and what the next steps will be.'

Even so, the idea of holding anyone responsible for the scandal was still not on the agenda. 'There is no question but that the Post Office management at the time behaved disgracefully,' said Lord Callanan, 'but none of them is now in post.'

This was not true. Alisdair Cameron, acting chief executive for most of 2019 had gone back to being the organisation's chief financial officer. Lower down, senior managers were clocking up their third and fourth decades of service.

Lucy Allan secured a Westminster Hall debate on 5 March, during which the shadow postal services minister Gill Furniss said she welcomed 'the commitment from the Prime Minister for a full public inquiry ... I have already written to ask him to confirm that that is the case, and to give me timescales.'

One MP, Emma Lewell-Buck, told the story of Kevin and Julie Carter. They had Horizon discrepancies at their Post Office, and reported them, receiving little or no help.

'With shortfalls increasing,' Lewell-Buck continued, 'Julie was invited to an informal disciplinary meeting. The Post Office demanded she pay back the unaccounted monies and accused her of fraud.'

After re-mortgaging their home, Kevin and Julie were forced to pay the Post Office a total of £75,000.

'Julie suffers from multiple sclerosis, and the situation exacerbated her condition. She and Kevin had worked hard. They had a lovely home and employed 14 staff. Their lives have now completely changed for the worse.' Lewell-Buck told the House, 'An exhausted Kevin recently told me, "We've lost our family home. We've lost everything."'

Lewell-Buck then raised the case of another constituent, Dionne Andre.

'After noticing discrepancies, and being a decent, honest person, she too started using her own money to try to put things right. Accused of fraud after the Post Office lost a recording of a disciplinary meeting with her,[1] she was told, "Pay up, or we're sending you to prison." Dionne paid £70,000, but she was never told by the Post Office whether it had dropped the fraud case against her, so she continued to live in constant fear of being arrested. She was then told by the Post Office that she had

---

[1] Something which seems to happen a lot.

to resign. She was forced to sell her business at a £50,000 loss and the Post Office prevented her from selling her second business, for which she had paid a quarter of a million pounds. She lost absolutely everything.'

Lewell-Buck finished her remarks by focusing firmly on the government in a manner which echoed Alan Bates' letter to Kelly Tolhurst at the beginning of the year.

'It is not good enough for successive ministers to wash their hands and repeat the mantra that the Post Office operates as a commercial independent business and they have no day-to-day control over it. Given that it is a state-owned private company, the government have a statutory duty to be involved in the Post Office – a duty that they have abdicated … The Post Office's sheer obstinance and obfuscation has been left unchallenged by the government. It has been left to former Subpostmasters in the depths of despair to organise and fight for justice, but justice is still being denied. Their financial recompense is pitiful, and the lack of accountability and action against those responsible is completely woeful. The government need to take culpability and stop abdicating their responsibility for those who are being denied justice.'

The new minister's response was lame.

'We will certainly look at how we can keep the Post Office on its toes in future,' said Scully, 'and at how to look back to learn the lessons.'

Two weeks later, Paul Scully's tune had changed. Slightly. In yet another backbench debate, Scully told MPs that an inquiry was on the cards, but there would be no announcement yet. 'We are looking at the best way to do it,' he said. 'There will be a further announcement as soon as possible in the very near future. I know that honourable members want progress, but I want to ensure that we get it right, rather than rushing into the terms of reference and other details.'

Between the two debates, the BEIS Select Committee held its first oral evidence hearing. The NFSP's Calum Greenhow was asked about abandoning Subpostmasters and his lack of independence from the Post Office. On the latter point he said the NFSP was independent until 2014 because before then it was a trade union.

Greenhow told MPs, 'What is important at this moment in time, as a trade association, is that what we want to do is make sure that there is no financial barrier in the representation that a Subpostmaster receives from the NFSP. In other words, it is free at point of use.'

Greenhow told MPs 70% of auto-enrolled Subpostmasters 'really valued' the NFSP.

Alan Bates, Tracy Felstead, Wendy Buffrey, Ron Warmington, Ian Henderson and Andy Furey also gave evidence. All were united in their call for a judge-led independent inquiry (something Calum Greenhow notably avoided supporting). A second oral evidence session was scheduled for 24 March at which Paula Vennells' presence was requested. This would be the former CEO's first public appearance since she sat in the same building in 2015 and told the committee's predecessors there had been no evidence of miscarriages of justice. Shortly before her session was due, Vennells stepped down from the Cabinet Office. The government said this was due to a 'wider refresh' of the Cabinet Office board. Vennells did not give a reason for her resignation, stating she had resigned 'along with others.'

Shortly afterwards a senior government source called to tell me that the former CEO had 'been rewarded for failure', her continuing presence in public life was 'outrageous' and she 'had to go.'

In the House, Kevan Jones told MPs Vennells had been 'removed' from her post at the Cabinet Office, but he wasn't satisfied. He wanted to know why Vennells still had her NHS job: 'She knew what was going on, the strategy in the court case and all about the bugs. Why is it that someone who's overseen this absolute scandal is allowed to still hold public positions?' he asked.

The parliamentary activity was becoming relentless. Backbenchers, burning with righteous indignation, were doing everything possible to hold the government's feet to the fire. Their efforts had brought a slim victory – a promise from the government that there would be some sort of investigation into what had happened, but that was it. I found the government's reluctance to do anything troubling. To me, the information which had been pushed into the public domain in *Bates v Post Office* put the Horizon story on the same footing as Windrush or the Infected Blood scandals. *It was all there in plain sight.* Why wasn't the government doing everything it could to find out what went wrong?

As the sound and fury at Westminster grew, the coronavirus pandemic was taking hold across the country. Kate Osborne, the MP who had secured the PM's commitment to a full public inquiry, became the second member of parliament to be struck down by the virus.[1] I had spent most of February and March working on a second Panorama which was due to be aired on Monday 23 March at 8.30pm.

One of our interviewees was Janet Skinner, who suffered a sickening ordeal. Janet began working for the Post Office in her home town of Hull in 1994 as a counter clerk. She loved it, and over ten years worked her way up to becoming a Postmaster on a council estate in Bransholme. In June 2006, after a series of problems with Horizon (all of which Janet reported) four Post Office 'auditors' walked into her branch and found a £59,000 discrepancy. She was suspended on the spot. The next day she was driven to a police station by two Post Office investigators for a 'chat.' The 'chat' was an interview under caution. Janet was not invited to bring a solicitor. She was scared, but as she felt she had nothing to hide, she agreed to take part. The investigators questioned Janet for more than an hour. They weren't interested in what might have gone wrong at the branch. 'They just wanted to know if I had stolen it, what I'd been spending it on and how I was going to give them the money back.'

Janet was charged with theft and false accounting in August 2006, despite there being no evidence of any dishonesty on her part. After a meeting with Post Office prosecutors, Janet's solicitor came to her with a deal. If she pleaded guilty to false accounting, the Post Office would drop the theft charge against her. He advised Janet that if she wanted to stay out of prison, she should accept the offer. In February 2007, a terrified Janet pleaded guilty to false accounting. She was given a nine-month prison sentence.

Janet and I had spoken about the possibility of an interview for a number of years, and in 2020 she kindly agreed to speak to me on camera. My Panorama colleagues were very interested in her story, not least because Janet's former solicitor was now an MP. Karl Turner felt he was misled by Post Office prosecutors over the evidence they had against Janet, and was happy to tell us as much.

Matt Bardo, Tim Robinson and I drove to Hull and interviewed Janet at home. She described the process of being taken from Hull Crown Court to HMP New Hall and being told to remove her clothes. Janet had to undergo an internal examination before being sent to her cell, forced to crouch naked over a mirror whilst a guard watched. She broke down

---

1 Pub quiz fact: Nadine Dorries was the first.

on camera as she told us what it was like to call her teenage children from prison. Whilst she was at New Hall, Janet was considered a suicide risk.

The Post Office had taken Janet's career, reputation and liberty. She was also landed with a compensation order for £11,500. The Post Office secured this by putting a charge on her home. After being released from prison, Janet got a job with a heating company and was trying to rebuild her life – not easy when you have a criminal record with no assets to your name. She sold her house and assumed the Post Office had got the profit on the sale as she didn't see anything from it. In April 2008, a friend called to tell her she was on the front page of the Hull Daily Mail, with a warrant out for her arrest.

Unbeknownst to Janet, when her house was sold, the profit went to her mortgage company, swallowed up in penalty payments for ending the mortgage early. The Post Office sent demands for £11,500 to Janet's old house – the one she had sold and no longer lived at. Janet did not see the demands. She was sent a court summons. Again Janet did not see the summons because it was sent to her old address. At a hearing Janet did not attend, a judge issued a warrant for her arrest. Janet was in severe danger of being sent to prison again.

After the call from her friend, Janet drove to Sheffield Crown Court (the nearest to where she was) and handed herself in. She was put in handcuffs and led to a cell. At a hastily arranged hearing a judge had to be persuaded that Janet shouldn't receive a five-year prison sentence. Shortly afterwards, Janet suffered a complete physical breakdown. Her immune system had turned on itself. Janet became paralysed from the neck down and spent four months in hospital. Doctors told her she might never walk again. Thankfully, Janet is made from very, very tough stuff. She almost willed herself to a partial recovery and refuses to be cowed by her experience. Even though I knew Janet and had some idea of what she had been through, it was quite an experience listening to her describe it in the quiet of her front room.

As we put the finishing touches to the programme, word came through it might not get screened. Confirmation was received shortly after we delivered the final cut to BBC1. The Prime Minister would be using Panorama's prime time evening slot to announce an immediate total lockdown, in an attempt to arrest the escalating coronavirus pandemic.

CCRC REFERRAL

The next few weeks were difficult. For many it was touched by tragedy. The horror of the pandemic as it laid waste to thousands of lives will stay lodged in the national consciousness for decades. Practical considerations about safety and day-to-day living put everything else into sharp relief.

Despite the personal strain on individuals and their families, those who weren't immediately affected found a way to keep ticking over. The day after the Prime Minister announced the lockdown, settlement money started appearing in some claimants' accounts. Freeths confirmed they were making emergency interim payments to as many people as possible whilst they paused to work out how on earth they, like every other organisation in the country, were going to be able to function.

It was, in the grand scheme of things, a tiny moment, but it was powerful. After more than 15 years of single-minded attrition, in the face of overwhelming odds, Alan Bates had managed to walk a wheelbarrow into the Post Office's vaults, load it up with millions of pounds, and hand it back to his followers. It was nowhere near enough. He knew that. But it was something. Getting the rest might feasibly require a similar effort.

Two days later, on 26 March, the CCRC's commissioners referred 39 Subpostmaster cases to the Court of Appeal. Jo Hamilton, Seema Misra, Noel Thomas, Wendy Buffrey, Tracy Felstead, Scott Darlington, Rubbina Shaheen, Susan Rudkin and Kamran Ashraf were among them, as were the late Peter Holmes and Julian Wilson. We were also told twenty-two more applicants were being considered.

Janet Skinner was also on the CCRC's list. On the day her conviction was referred to the Court of Appeal I called her to see how she was.

'I feel absolutely f***ing amazing,' she replied. 'I can't believe it. I opened that email and I read the first couple of lines and I just started shaking. I am so happy. If any of the commissioners were standing in front of me right now, I would kiss them. I really would ... I feel like I've won the lottery. I feel like screaming.'

Tracy Felstead was equally excited. 'I'm over the moon,' she said. 'I've waited my whole adult life for this.'

The CCRC made it clear it was only able to refer the cases because of Mr Justice Fraser's findings in the Horizon trial judgment. All 39 Subpostmasters had been prosecuted on the basis of Horizon evidence.

The judge had found Horizon to be unreliable. There was therefore a 'real possibility' the convictions might be considered unsafe, the test which needed to be met to allow the referral. I was surprised to see neither Parmod Kalia or Teju Adedayo had made it onto the list of CCRC referrals.

I gave them both a call. It seems the sticking point was the stories they had fabricated after pleading guilty to mitigate their sentences. Or as the Post Office would have it, not just admitted guilt, but confessed. Parmod and Teju were understandably distressed. They both swore to me that they were innocent and they had made the stories up under extreme duress, as they were both terrified of going to prison. Not that it helped Parmod.

The Post Office's response to the referrals was intriguing. It basically said it was going to wait until it had received the CCRC's 'statement of reasons' before commenting further, but there was a sentence which leaped out.

'We have,' it said, 'been doing all we can to ensure that, in the light of the findings in the Horizon judgment, further disclosure is provided as appropriate in other cases where Post Office acted as prosecutor, not just those reviewed by the CCRC.'

What other cases? There were 61 convicted Postmasters among the civil litigants. Assuming they formed the majority, or perhaps all, of the 61 cases being reviewed by the CCRC, how many others were out there?

I went back to the Post Office and asked how many 'other' prosecutions they were looking at. I then started digging through documents which were already publicly available. These were Freedom of Information requests[2] made before the group litigation started. They only gave a partial picture, but when put together they showed there had been 251 Post Office prosecutions between 2004 and 2017.

In a decade of looking into the story, I had (perhaps foolishly) assumed most of the Post Office prosecutions were sound. How could they not be? I had been told as a child our justice system rests on the principle it is better ten guilty people go free than one innocent person is

2 Made through and published by the truly exceptional website resource www.whatdotheyknow.com.

convicted.[1] The principle goes to the heart of what a just society is. It was already unconscionable the CCRC thought there was enough evidence to suggest *at least* 39 people may have been prosecuted unfairly, and that there were *at least* 61 Subpostmasters who were fighting to clear their names. The idea there could be, say, 10? 20? 50? more potentially unsafe prosecutions was head-spinning.

On 3 April 2020, after some chasing, the Post Office emailed to tell me they were actually looking at 'around 500 additional cases … which resulted in convictions.' I stared at the message. Five hundred. *Five hundred* people prosecuted by the Post Office, who had ended up with criminal convictions.

I started running through the possible scenarios. If five hundred more convictions were being reviewed and … say … ten per cent were found to be unsafe, that was another 50 'new' cases, meaning it was possible more than a hundred people could have been wrongly convicted.

Also, if the Post Office had prosecuted 251 people between 2004 and 2017 – assuming not all of those people had been given criminal convictions – then at least 250 people were prosecuted during a four-year period between the rollout of Horizon in 1999 and 2003. That was more than one a week.

Convinced I was sitting on possibly the biggest scoop of the scandal so far, I got in touch with Tom Witherow at the Daily Mail. Tom and I had been sharing information for a while and we had developed a good working relationship. Tom, like me, was staggered by the idea that the Post Office had managed to secure the convictions of hundreds of Subpostmasters using Horizon evidence. He took the information to his editor, who agreed that on a normal news day, the story was a front page splash. Unfortunately, it was not a normal news day. It was not a normal news year. People were dying in their thousands from a killer virus. The nation had other, very serious problems on its mind. On Saturday 11 April 2020, the news that the Post Office was reviewing the criminal convictions of five hundred Subpostmasters got into the Daily Mail on page 27.

Whilst researching the number of prosecutions made by the Post

---

[1] A principle known as Blackstone's ratio: 'It is better that ten guilty persons escape than that one innocent suffer.' The idea as stated was crafted in the 1760s by William Blackstone, an English legal commentator and judge. By the nineteenth century the ratio had become a legal maxim in England and the US. The concept has antecedents going back to the Old Testament.

Office, I found another Freedom of Information request, which had been answered in 2012. It was made by someone called Alan Bates. Bates wanted to know how long the Post Office kept records of its prosecutions. He was told they only went back to 2005. I vaguely remembered this surfacing during the research into our 2015 Panorama. At the time it made me give up on ever finding out if there was a big jump in prosecutions when Horizon was introduced. As my senior colleague Matt Bardo noted – even if there was a leap in prosecutions, the Post Office could always say that better data meant more thieves were being caught.

The new statement from the Post Office made it clear that either the information about the number of post-2004 prosecutions was not true, or more likely, the Post Office did have information about pre-2004 prosecutions. I went back to the Post Office, asking if they would give me the true number of prosecutions and convictions going back to 1990.

NEW LEGAL SUITORS

As well as giving us an interview for Panorama, the Labour MP Karl Turner encouraged a lawyer friend of his, Neil Hudgell, to take a closer look at the scandal. James Hartley and the Freeths team did not specialise in criminal law, which left a number of convicted claimants looking around for representation. James knew Neil, and soon Freeths were helping those who wanted to hand over the reins to Hudgells. Neil and I made contact in April 2020. He explained what seemed to be a very straightforward plan. Represent as many convicted appellants as he could find, steer them through the criminal appeal process *pro bono*, and then go after the Post Office for malicious prosecution, either with legal aid funding or on a no-win, no-fee basis.

Neil was not alone in offering his services, but he was by far the most proactive, and soon Hudgells were representing most of the convicted claimants.

As the pandemic took hold, I began to correspond with another lawyer, this time a barrister called Paul Marshall. Mr Marshall had worked with the MP Kevin Hollinrake on helping victims of the HBOS banking fraud[2] and he saw plenty of parallels with the way the Post Office had behaved, both historically and over the course of the litigation. Marshall published an opinion piece on LinkedIn which stated the Post Office had gone about its business 'without proper – or seemingly any – regard to the facts and without regard to the harm and damage, in financial and human terms, that institutional disregard for facts may have.'

Soon, Marshall began to take a serious interest in the Horizon scandal, and had the time to do it. In 2017 he was diagnosed with stage 4 metastatic cancer, which required chemotherapy, the extraction of half his liver and the removal of large parts of his bowel. He was now spending a lot of time sitting around at home trying not to catch coronavirus. Marshall decided to use whatever time he had to help Subpostmasters where he could.

Fortuitously, the solicitor Nick Gould, a partner at Aria Grace Law, read some of Marshall's writing on LinkedIn and made contact. The two

[2] In which six bankers working for HBOS in Reading stole millions of pounds from struggling businesses.

men decided to work together *pro bono* to help Subpostmasters with their appeals.

The team was completed by the arrival of Flora Page, a criminal barrister who had seen some of Nick's posts drawing attention to Marshall's writing on social media. Flora wrote to Aria Grace saying she would be happy to help – again *pro bono*. It was agreed Flora Page would become Paul Marshall's junior.

At the beginning of May 2020, to widespread cynicism, the Post Office launched its 'Historical Shortfall Scheme.' Like 2013's doomed Mediation Scheme, the Historical Shortfall Scheme was open to serving and former Subpostmasters who felt they had been forced to give in to demands for cash from the Post Office, without a proper investigation into whether its shonky IT might be responsible.

Unlike the 2013 scheme, the Historical Shortfall Scheme was not open to Subpostmasters with criminal convictions, and although the Post Office didn't mention this in the press release announcing the scheme, claimants in *Bates v Post Office* were also specifically excluded.

The Post Office said it was liaising with the NFSP, CWU and the JFSA in order to publicise the scheme, but applicants had to be quick. The cut-off date for joining was half way through August, a 17-week window. This did not seem fair. The scheme was not going to get any news coverage due to the pandemic, and even if it did reach the right people, they didn't have long to take legal advice and get their claim in order. Furthermore, paperwork might take a while to track down, and with people's minds focused on keeping themselves and their relatives alive, there was concern the deadline was far too soon. The Post Office said the 17-week application window was approved during the settlement negotiations, but this did not seem to take into account how much the world had changed since December 2019.

Aside from the short window to get the claims in, there were concerns over the scheme's lawyers – Herbert Smith Freehills. HSF helped the Post Office appeal the Common Issues judgment with arguments, according to Lord Justice Coulson, 'founded on the premise that the nation's most trusted brand was not obliged to treat their SPMs with good faith, and instead entitled to treat them in capricious or arbitrary ways.' Hardly a good start. They had also advised Lloyds Bank on the establishment of a compensation scheme for victims of the HBOS banking fraud.[1] The scheme was later found to be 'unfair' to some of those who applied.

Paul Marshall described appointing HSF to run the Post Office scheme as 'putting the fox in charge of the chicken coop.'

The Historical Shortfall Scheme did have a number of unusual terms, including the rather Kafka-esque condition that applicants with claims of more than £10,000 had to sign away their right to legal action against the Post Office *before* being told the sum the Post Office was prepared to pay them.

Neil Hudgell listed his concerns in a blog post, noting the Post Office was financing the scheme as well as being responsible for its overall governance and administration. He also noted its 'independent advisory committee' would be selected by the Post Office.

Mr Hudgell wrote, 'Reference is made to "information sharing" with the Justice for Subpostmasters Alliance, something which appears not quite to be the case following a conversation with campaign group founder Alan Bates, who possessed no more detail than you or I.'

Hudgell concluded, 'One can therefore reasonably assume a high level of cynicism from all support groups, commentators and ultimately potential applicants.'

Herbert Smith Freehills seemed mystified anyone could think the Post Office was an organisation with anything but the best interests of Postmasters at heart. They fired off a letter, telling Hudgell:

'Our client is determined to ensure the success of the Scheme and promotion of the principles agreed as part of the GLO settlement. The Postmaster community should not unnecessarily be discouraged from applying when the Scheme has been specifically designed to be simple and accessible and to offer a final resolution of these matters without the time and cost of formal civil litigation.'

[1] Lloyds bought HBOS, and in doing so assumed responsibility for compensating victims of the Reading fraud.

THE APPORTIONING

The same week the Post Office launched the Historical Shortfall Scheme, final payments from the *Bates v Post Office* settlement began to land in claimants' accounts.

Some were delighted. 'Still trying to process. Thank you!' said one who got nearly £40,000.

Others weren't so happy. One former Subpostmaster, who received £23,000, told me, 'the actual amount I have received does not even cover the debt I am still paying off … like everyone else I feel it is a bitter pill to swallow, better than nothing, but less than 2.5 percent of my losses…'

Nicki Arch, who was falsely prosecuted for theft by the Post Office, tweeted:

'My total recompense for two decades of hell is £5,059.70. How soul destroying is that? Truly devastated.'

With their payments, Freeths sent claimants a seven-page document called 'Post Office Group Litigation: Methodology Underpinning Preparation of the Claim Proceeds Account.'

It listed 16 different categories of loss, namely:

> Shortfalls, Loss of appointment, Loss of earnings during suspension, Contractual notice losses, Handicap on the open labour market, Stigma/reputational damage, Personal injury, Bankruptcy expenses, Harassment, Legal fees for civil proceedings, Legal fees incurred, Professional fees, Staff redundancy costs (for Subpostmasters who were terminated or forced to resign), Loss of value in the business premises, Loss of residential home (for example, where repossessed), Loss of value in any other personal/tangible property.

The methodology document reminded claimants the value applied to each category was based on information provided to Freeths via their initial statement, a detailed questionnaire and any additional information provided to Freeths during the litigation.

One claimant who hadn't even been suspended by the Post Office received tens of thousands of pounds in compensation. Janet Skinner, who went to prison, received £8,500.

Another who suffered horrendously at the Post Office's hands told me, 'I am not happy. And as a group we need to know the breakdown of the payments to all claimants.'

Some members of the JFSA told me they thought the money from the settlement should have been shared equally, matching the all-for-one-and-one-for-all mentality which typified the claimants' approach at the outset.

Freeths have told me the advice given to the claimants was correct and appropriate at all times, but the outpouring of dissatisfaction from some quarters appeared to have caught the Justice for Subpostmasters Alliance on the back foot.

Alan Bates moved to address claimants' concerns by sending out a circular.

'We know many of you are disappointed with what you have received,' he said, 'but hopefully by now you are clearer on why the available sums are at the level which they are.'

Bates warned any legal claim against Freeths or the JFSA would be 'a complete waste of time and money and would go nowhere.'

In a sign of how seriously Freeths were taking the threat, Bates revealed the firm had actually held back some of the final settlement to cover the cost of 'any legal challenge which is being considered against the apportionment.'

The JFSA founder told claimants if they didn't like the situation they were in, they shouldn't have got involved in the first place.

'Don't forget,' he said, 'you saw the terms of the group action before you signed up to it, and if you attempt to challenge it, all you are doing is spending more money with lawyers instead of giving it to claimants. But it is your decision.'

I asked Kay Linnell if she had any sympathy for claimants angry at how little they got. 'No, I don't really,' she said. 'We have given them back their reputation – we have proved the Post Office behaved disgracefully, and we have proved the Horizon system did not work.'

The defensiveness and public lack of sympathy from Kay and Alan was perhaps understandable, but for some, it struck the wrong chord. Many claimants were fragile. Their mental health had been severely damaged by their experience of the Post Office, and the litigation had re-opened deep wounds.

I received one email which said, 'I have lost my business, my house and most importantly, my integrity. I have no money. Those I classed as friends now ignore me. All my family thought I was gambling. My marriage is broken. I've tried again but I'm an alcoholic. I've tried suicide three times. I wish I had succeeded. The Post Office has wrecked my life.'

I called the claimant who sent it. He told me the cash he received from the settlement had knocked his self-esteem and mental health right back, just when he thought he was beginning to turn the corner. He sounded broken.

A SCANDAL YOU CAN SEE FROM SPACE

I usually work in television, which I enjoy. You get to go to interesting places, meet interesting people and film them doing interesting things. Radio does not need pictures. Whilst there is a lot to be said for travelling somewhere to record a conversation with someone on location, with radio you don't *have* to. You can just give them a call.

Due to the UK-wide restrictions on travel introduced on 23 March 2020, the TV industry came to a grinding, and very sudden, halt. We had just managed to get the Panorama in the can, and whilst it would stay in the can for a number of weeks, we had, at least, been able to finish it. Through sheer convoluted fluke, my next assignment was in radio, specifically a ten-part series for Radio 4 about the Post Office. Creating it would be fraught with logistical difficulty, but we were confident we could do it. I strapped together a mini-studio in my bedroom with some portable recording kit and a duvet, for rudimentary soundproofing. The series producer, Bob Nicholson, directed operations from his flat in London. The lack of traffic and human activity outside my house kept external noise to a minimum. Like thousands of people all round the country, we had figured out a way of making it work.

The first part of the series was due to go out on Monday 25 May. The Friday before that date was hectic. I was sitting under my duvet bashing away at a shared Google doc whilst arguing the toss with Bob over Zoom until we agreed which and how many words might fit into the edit gaps created by the post-soundscaping[1] final edit. Once the words had been agreed I would then try to record them using varying manners of emphasis and speeds of delivery, before realising we'd created a repetition or potentially misleading nuance which needed to be argued over, changed, re-agreed and re-recorded before starting the process all over again.

During a break in proceedings, my phone rang. I didn't recognise the number. Normally I would let it go to voicemail, but when you are at the sharp end of a transmission deadline you become more inclined to answer a number you don't recognise. Every call you get *might* be someone you've never met with information crucially important to the successful

---

[1] Soundscaping is a posh word for incidental music and sound effects.

delivery of your programme. It could be a lawyer, a courier, a publicity person or the Head of Network. If it's irrelevant, you can politely but firmly suggest you have the conversation another time. If it *is* relevant you will be thanking your lucky stars you picked up.

My call that afternoon was from a nice man at the Post Office. He told me my Freedom of Information request pertaining to Post Office prosecutions had been published. I was not sure what to say. No one from any organisation, including the Post Office, had ever called me up to tell me they had answered an FOI request I had made. Taking this surprising piece of customer care at face value, I thanked the nice man for troubling to call. He suggested I might want to have a look at the Post Office response to my FOI, and then told me he expected it would be up on the Post Office website later that evening. Preoccupied with the job in hand, I thanked the man again and got back to arguing with Bob. At 7.36pm an email arrived from the Post Office press office.

It said, 'Following detailed record searches into the oldest cases from more than two decades ago, [we have] currently identified around 900 cases prosecuted since the introduction of Horizon which may have relied on Horizon data.'

Nine hundred. *Nine hundred*?! The email contained a link to the Post Office website, which gave more information, plus a link to my FOI request on the What Do They Know website. I opened it up, and found myself staring at the true scale of the scandal.

Prefaced with a caveat that the numbers had been generated by a process which had still not been finished and that the data was likely to be incomplete, the Post Office had provided a table showing the number of convictions by year since 1990. Totting up the figures, there were 766 convictions since 1999 with a further 104 which were not dated. Interestingly the number of convictions in the six years leading up to Horizon's introduction totalled 46. In the six years after there were 330, a seven-fold increase.

Organisations love putting out bad news on a Friday afternoon. Everyone is either itching to go home or get to the pub. Deadlines for the Saturday papers are earlier than during the week and broadcast news media has already allocated most of its relatively meagre weekend resources. Unexpected announcements from corporate organisations can occasionally go unnoticed. And if a late-dropping story gets any weekend coverage at all, it is usually a passing mention – just enough to stop any news editor bothering with it on Monday morning.

I called BBC Radio 4's Today show and spoke to a producer I know. They felt the 900 figure was unlikely to get much coverage that particular weekend as the programme had a big Dominic Cummings exclusive. The producer proposed holding the story for Monday. Providing Monday's programme editor liked it, providing no other news outlet got to the story first and providing nothing more newsworthy happened to squeeze it out of the running order, the 900 prosecutions figure could be beamed into millions of people's cars and kitchens on the same day The Great Post Office Trial started. If all went well, the Today team might also be kind enough to plug the series' first episode.

Amazingly, everything came together. No one touched the story over the weekend, so it went out on Today on Monday 25 June. The presenting team kindly signposted the start of our series. The Great Post Office Trial's two-week Radio 4 run was topped off by BBC1's decision to run the delayed Panorama – Scandal At The Post Office – the Monday immediately after the series finished.

By June 2020, Alan and Kay were on manoeuvres again. The JFSA announced a crowdfunding campaign to raise money for a complaint to the Parliamentary Ombudsman. Bates wanted the government to compensate the group litigation claimants for the £46m they had to pay in fees from the £57.75m settlement. His argument was simple – the claimants had drawn attention to serious problems at the Post Office, something the government had either failed to notice or do anything about, which was a failure of its statutory duty.

The JFSA had initially approached a specialist QC about suing the government for the £46m, but was advised it had a low chance of success.

'His advice,' said Bates, 'was that it might be possible, but it would be very expensive and we would be looking at years again, so realistically that wasn't looking to be a practicable option. However … [the QC] suggested that there might be a better, quicker and cheaper route to follow.'

The office of the Parliamentary Ombudsman was established by an Act of Parliament in 1967. The Ombudsman can investigate complaints from members of the public who believe that they have suffered 'injustice' because of 'maladministration' by government departments or certain public bodies.

Maladministration, according to a Commons briefing paper, can be defined as a public body not having acted properly or fairly, or having given a poor service and not put things right. As the Office of the Ombudsman was being established, the Leader of the House of Commons told MPs maladministration included 'bias, neglect, inattention, delay, incompetence, inaptitude, perversity, turpitude, arbitrariness and so on.'

The Ombudsman has the right to 'summon persons and papers, (that is, to require the attendance of witnesses and to have access to information), and absolute privilege to protect his or her reports. These powers are analogous to the powers of a judge of the High Court.'

So far so good, but there's always a catch. This one is pretty serious. If the Ombudsman finds in a complainant's favour, it has no executive powers to alter the 'decision' which led to the complaint or award compensation, precisely what Bates and his fellow claimants were after.

The Ombudsman's powers only extend as far as *suggesting* a 'remedy', which might include financial compensation. In 2009, a former Ombudsman, Ann Abraham, published her 'principles for remedy,' which state, 'Our underlying principle is to ensure that the public body restores the complainant to the position they would have been in if the maladministration or poor service had not occurred. If that is not possible, the public body should compensate them appropriately.'

The word 'should' in the above sentence is doing a lot of heavy lifting. There is no requirement on the government to do what the Ombudsman thinks it 'should.' If a government chooses, for whatever reason, not to accept a decision, there is one more stage of escalation: the Ombudsman (if *it* chooses to) can lay a 'special report' before parliament. The government can also ignore this, but can expect to take a lot of parliamentary heat if it tries to do so.

Bates wanted £98,000 in donations to pay for an experienced legal team to prepare the complaint and represent the claimants. He told his followers:

'During the civil action the Post Office threw everything it could at us, including four legal teams, the Court of Appeal and trying to sack the judge. Be absolutely certain that the government will try every trick in the book to have our submission dismissed. We will only have one chance of following this route.'

Within six weeks, he'd raised the money.

VENNELLS RIDES AGAIN

Whilst Alan Bates was bunkering down with his new legal friends, focused on winning compensation for the claimants he'd led into the group litigation, two simple questions began to loom large over the Post Office Horizon IT scandal: a) how could this have happened? b) who was responsible?

For years the government had tried to persuade MPs, journalists and campaigners that the decisions taken by the Post Office were entirely driven by the Post Office board. Successive ministers would be wheeled out to state that the Post Office was an 'arm's length' organisation and the government did not get involved in operational decisions.

This construction conveniently ignored the truth of the matter. As a company owned, subsidised and underwritten by the state, the Post Office could not do *anything* risky or controversial without government approval.

The board of the Post Office was made aware that credible concerns were being raised about the Horizon IT system in 2010 (at the very latest), thanks to the Ismay report. Even though the report gave false comfort, it should have started ringing very loud alarm bells. Three years later, the board *knew* it had a serious problem on its hands when Simon Clarke called an immediate halt to the Post Office's criminal prosecutions strategy.

It is unthinkable that senior officials at BEIS and HM Treasury didn't know by 2014 the Post Office may have been responsible for committing grave harm against dozens, possibly hundreds of individuals. Every subsequent material decision made about the scandal would have to be approved by the government, because they were now underwriting the risk – from the sacking of Second Sight in 2015 to blowing more than £100m at the High Court.

As the scandal began to unravel, it is perhaps no surprise that by the time we got to 2020, the government was keen to do absolutely nothing to assist finding out who was responsible, possibly because its civil servants were working cheek-by-jowl with the Post Office board and its ministers should have known exactly what was going on.

Shortly after the Panorama went out I was contacted by a senior government source who confirmed that ministers were going to announce a 'review' of the scandal but:

'We are limited in what we can do – the terms of the review were kicked between BEIS and No 10 before they finally reached an agreement on what the terms should be and how it should be structured, but the officials [civil servants] weren't happy with anything. They didn't want a review, they didn't want an inquiry or anything. They wanted it all to go away.'

Lord Callanan, the business minister, could not understand why Paula Vennells' had escaped censure. He wrote to his counterpart at the Department of Health, Lord Bethell, telling him, 'The decisions and conduct of POL while Paula was CEO were heavily criticised in the Horizon Litigation .... This includes attempts to confuse and obscure true facts ... haphazard practices ... behaving with impunity towards Postmasters; fostering a culture of secrecy and excessive confidentiality and failing to be transparent when necessary.'

Callanan wondered whether Paula Vennells was 'a fit and proper person to be the Imperial College NHS Trust chair in light of those criticisms.'

Vennells clung on. Whilst the national lockdown had put paid to her scheduled evidence session before the BEIS Select Committee, the MP who chaired the committee, Darren Jones, was determined to try to hold the former Post Office CEO and other key execs to account. Jones contacted Paula Vennells, her successor Nick Read and Rob Putland, Fujitsu's Senior Vice-President. Each letter contained a list of carefully formulated questions. The replies Jones received and published on behalf of the Select Committee are telling.

Paula Vennells' account of her seven-year tenure can be summarised thus:

1) Nothing was her fault.
2) A lot of it was definitely Fujitsu's fault.
3) The government was completely aware of and involved with every consequential decision the Post Office made.

Vennells starts her reply to Jones by saying she will do her 'best' to 'assist' the Committee's investigations, but when it comes to discussing miscarriages of justice 'I do not and do not intend to waive any privilege of Post Office or myself.' She adds, 'I wish to state for the record that I do not accept any personal criminal misconduct.'

Vennells is soon telling Mr Jones about the existence of an 'ad-hoc' board sub-committee set up specifically to deal with Second Sight and the issues arising from Second Sight's initial investigation. The existence of this board had never been publicly acknowledged before. Paula Vennells told Jones she sat on the sub-committee, alongside Alice Perkins and the ShEx[1] director Susannah Storey (now the top civil servant at the Department for Media, Culture and Sport). Alwen Lyons attended the sub-committee, as did the Post Office interim General Counsel, Chris Aujard, who had been parachuted in after Susan Crichton's exit.

When Second Sight began their investigation in 2012, they were given unfettered access to every Post Office document they had wanted to look at, including Post Office prosecution files. It was Vennells' board sub-committee which made a decision, more than a year later, to stop Second Sight from being given access to the internal prosecution files. In her letter to Jones, Vennells said this was:

'Firstly because the documents were legally privileged and, as I understood it, it had never been agreed that Second Sight would be given access to privileged material. Secondly, it was the view of Post Office that the conduct of prosecutions was outside the scope of the Scheme. Thirdly, Second Sight, as forensic accountants, had no expertise to consider legal matters.'

Firstly – so what? Just because a document is legally privileged, it doesn't mean it has a witchy spell on it. If the Post Office wanted Second Sight to see those documents, all it had to do was waive legal privilege by handing them over.

Secondly – so what? You either want your independent investigators to see and report the truth or you don't. You don't start arguing about scope.

Thirdly – Second Sight were experienced investigators. They were perfectly capable of making pronouncements on internal prosecution files which were within their area of expertise and either recommending or commissioning further specialist legal interpretation as required.

---

1 Since 2012 there has been a government representative sitting on the Post Office board. The government director was from a body called SharEx or ShEx, which stood for Shareholder Executive. ShEx was an advisory body within HMG which had responsibility for overseeing the performance of all government-owned businesses. In 2015 ShEx was rolled into the Treasury-controlled UK Government Investments (UKGI), but the function of the director on the Post Office board remained the same – keeping HMG fully informed of what was happening in Post Office land, so the government could intervene where necessary.

Vennells' sub-committee's decision directly contradicted the assurance given by the Post Office to Subpostmasters in 2012, when the Post Office told the JFSA and all serving Subpostmasters that Second Sight, 'will be entitled to request information related to a concern from Post Office Limited, and if Post Office Limited holds that information, Post Office Limited will provide it to Second Sight.'

The effect of the board sub-committee's decision was that documents which could have been examined and which might have revealed potential miscarriages of justice were withheld from Second Sight. Not only that, whilst the Post Office was withholding information from Second Sight, Paula Vennells went to parliament to tell the BIS Select Committee, 'If there had been any miscarriages of justice, it would have been really important to me and the Post Office that we surfaced those.'

On the subject of remote access, Vennells was more sure-footed.

'I raised this question repeatedly, both internally and with Fujitsu, and was always given the same answer: that it was not possible for branch records to be altered remotely without the sub-postmaster's knowledge. Indeed, I remember being told by Fujitsu's then CEO when I raised it with him that the system was "like Fort Knox." He had been a trusted outsource partner and had the reputation of a highly competent technology sector CEO. His word was important to me.'[2]

Finally, when it came to government involvement, Vennells wanted it known that BEIS and UKGI were *all over* the Post Office.

'The UKGI directors were fully engaged in the discussions and Post Office (including myself and each subsequent Chair) had conversations with their senior line director and the Chief Executive of UKGI too from time to time. The present UKGI incumbent director [Tom Cooper] joined the Board in 2018 ... He was fully engaged on the Board, sub-committee and with ministers and lawyers at BEIS.'

Vennells' evidence appeared around the same time it slipped out that she had quietly stepped down from her position on the Church's ethical investments advisory group. Tom Hedges, a church member who had been prosecuted by the Post Office, wrote to the Bishop of St Albans,

---

2 Who exactly the Fujitsu CEO Vennells was referring to has become a mini-saga in its own right. Two national newspapers have named someone who vehemently denies it, setting off a legal complaint. As the issue was in dispute, I contacted Ms Vennells, through her representatives, to ask if she would be so kind as to name the person behind the alleged 'Fort Knox' comment. She declined to respond.

who looked after the Bromham Benefice where the Reverend Vennells preached. Mr Hedges asked if the Bishop would take any disciplinary action against Vennells. The Bishop wrote back saying he had taken legal advice, and couldn't attribute the wrongdoing of the Post Office to Ms Vennells.

Vennells' successor, Nick Read, had far less skin in the game, but his letter to Darren Jones appears designed to steer MPs away from uncomfortable truths into a harmonious golden future where relationships are reset, lines are drawn under things, and everyone is focused on finding the best way forward. He does start by saying 'Bluntly, there can be no new beginning without an appropriate reckoning with the past,' but then singularly fails to do any reckoning with the past at all.

On the issue of remote access, Read says: 'As I was not involved at the time, I do not wish to speculate how Post Office's knowledge of remote access issues evolved.'

Mr Read is also not that interested in addressing the issue of who at the Post Office was telling porky pies to the government. Lord Callanan told peers the government had been 'misled.' Mr Jones wanted to know how the Post Office had misled the government and who had given the misleading advice.

Mr Read replies: 'I am not able to comment on matters before my time.'

There is one interesting and unequivocal statement – in response to a question on the Post Office's prosecution function, Mr Read tells the committee the Post Office has no intention of prosecuting anyone ever again.

In his letter to the Post Office chief executive, Darren Jones had asked, 'Do you now accept that there was a major problem with Horizon and, if so, when did Post Office Ltd identify this problem and what was the nature of that problem?'

Read answers by claiming the Horizon judgment 'did not determine whether bugs, errors or defects did in fact cause shortfalls in the individual claimants' accounts but it found that they had the potential to create apparent discrepancies in Postmasters' branch accounts.'

This is true. However, the Horizon judgment was *never* going to determine *anything* about individual claimants' accounts, because that was not what the Horizon *trial* was about. The Horizon trial was set up to determine whether Horizon had the potential to cause discrepancies in branch accounts. The answer was not only yes there was the *potential*, but that, according to Mr Justice Fraser, 'it actually has happened, and on numerous occasions,' a clause Mr Read made no reference to.

Mr Read's comments came six months after another Post Office exec was recorded in a pub saying: 'It's never been proven there's a link between a computer glitch and anyone actually losing money.'

Taken together, both statements could suggest a culture of denial still pervades the Post Office. I'd hoped to explore this further, but Mr Read has so far refused my requests for an interview. The Post Office stands by his evidence to parliament.

AHEM, FUJITSU?

Forgive me for dwelling on Fujitsu's response to the Select Committee inquiry. It is the most comprehensive public statement the company has given in its 20+ year operation of the Horizon system, and it deserves some scrutiny.

Unsurprisingly, in his reply to Darren Jones' letter, Fujitsu's Rob Putland is quite certain everything is the Post Office's fault.

Jones asked for a comment on Mr Justice Fraser's finding that during the Horizon trial Fujitsu employees gave 'a very one-sided picture which was to omit any reference to important contemporaneous documents that criticise or demonstrate any deficiencies with Horizon.'

Mr Putland replies, 'Whilst Fujitsu employees gave evidence, it was the Post Office who determined all aspects of its case including the choice of witnesses, the nature of their evidence and the associated documents. Nonetheless, we take Mr Justice Fraser's criticisms extremely seriously and we have now stopped the provision of any new witness evidence to the Post Office.'

This seemed to be suggesting that somehow those evil swines at the Post Office managed to manipulate sweet, innocent Fujitsu staff into the sort of folk who might wish to defend the Horizon system to the detriment of truth and justice. Fujitsu's solution, you will note, is not a constructive commitment to work with the Post Office to do things properly in future, or to ask their own staff to think about telling the truth in court, but a refusal to let the poor bambinis get involved in any more of the Post Office's legal proceedings.

Mr Jones asked Mr Putland why it took 'a highly expensive court case' to establish that Fujitsu employees could roam around in branch accounts, adjusting them without Subpostmasters' knowledge.

Mr Putland replies, 'This is a matter for the Post Office; they determined the litigation strategy and their conduct towards the Subpostmasters.'

Litigation strategy has nothing to do with remote access. Fujitsu had ten years of watching the Post Office make incorrect public assertions. It wouldn't have taken much to correct them or threaten to contradict them if they were made in public again.

Later in his letter, Mr Putland starts to get very slippery. Jones had asked, 'How reliable is Horizon now and what steps are Fujitsu taking to ensure full disclosure of errors and bugs?' and, 'How many bugs, errors and discrepancies have been logged for each year since they began to be recorded?'

Putland replies, 'no complex IT system will ever be completely free of errors and bugs', telling Jones:

'The system has recorded thousands of incidents since the inception of Horizon, as would be expected of a system of this complexity and size. However, in respect of material incidents, Mr Justice Fraser highlights 29 bugs, errors and defects, some of which had the potential to impact a Subpostmaster local branch account.'

This simply does not answer the question. Jones did not ask how many material incidents the recent court case found. During *Bates v Post Office*, a vast amount of Horizon error logs were not disclosed to the court or to either of the independent IT experts who were assigned to examine the Horizon system. Those IT experts worked with their teams through the logs they had been given to ascertain what they could. With the limited information, resources and time-span they had available, the IT experts were able to find 29 bugs which had the potential to impact branch accounts.

Putland knows, or could find out, the real number of bugs/errors/defects which caused material incidents over Horizon's 20-year history and he could have presented that number to the inquiry. He didn't.

Jones had asked, 'Can you provide a breakdown by error type and its implications for the integrity of a local Horizon terminal and for the system as a whole?'

Putland replies, 'In the Appendices to his judgment in *Bates v Post Office Ltd*, Mr Justice Fraser provides significant detail on the history of Horizon and a summary of bugs, errors and defects since the inception of Horizon in 1999 including those that had the potential to impact a Subpostmaster's local branch account.'

Again, the MP's question had nothing to do with the court case. The court case was a snapshot of the system used to establish general facts. Earlier in his letter, Putland got on his high horse about the Post Office's presentation of evidence to the High Court, but now he was deploying exactly the same approach to the Select Committee inquiry.

Moving on to wider questions, Jones asked, 'What lessons have you learnt from Horizon and how can you reassure my Committee that the type of issues detailed in *Bates v Post Office* will not happen again?'

Putland starts by saying the provision of witness evidence to support prosecutions under the direction of the Post Office 'should not have been allowed to happen' and confirms, 'Fujitsu will not provide any witness evidence in the future to support Post Office-led prosecutions of Subpostmasters.' Then his answer gets worrying. He states Fujitsu 'will provide information if requested by the Police or an appropriate judicial authority but only after such request has been fully considered, and with the approval of a UK board director.'

It's obviously a good thing that Fujitsu are not going to let themselves be led by the nose into prosecution cases against Subpostmasters without properly thinking about it at board level, but this also smacks of a company which is going to become very unwilling to hand over information about many things to anyone. Given the judge found Fujitsu staff were continually overlooking Horizon errors, either to suggest they weren't their responsibility, or were caused by individuals external to the company, or to paint a misleading picture in court, it does not bode well for anyone trying to get the truth out of the organisation in the future.

Jones finished his letter by asking about accountability at Fujitsu. Had anyone been disciplined over the Horizon disaster?

Putland says, 'In many cases key employees and decision-makers are no longer working at Fujitsu. If it emerges that any current employee intentionally misled the court or otherwise failed to meet the standards expected from Fujitsu, then they will be dismissed.'

Here, for the record, is what Mr Justice Fraser said about three members of Fujitsu staff.

> **Andy Dunks**, IT Security Analyst, Fujitsu:
> 'Mr Dunks expressly sought to mislead me by stating that there was no "Fujitsu party line" when it came to the contents of drafting witness statements about audit records for legal proceedings. There plainly is... I found Mr Dunks very unsatisfactory as a witness. He was both plainly aware of the Fujitsu "party line," or corporate position, regarding the words asserting accuracy of audit data, and he was very anxious to keep to it, whilst initially denying that there was one. He sought to mislead me.'

> **Stephen Parker**, Head of Post Office Application Support, Fujitsu:
> 'Mr Parker chose specifically to give the impression in his first witness statement that Fujitsu did not have the power (the word

Mr Parker expressly chose) to inject transactions into the counter at branches, even though he knew that it did. This paints him in a very poor light as a credible witness… I do not consider that Mr Parker was interested in accuracy in any of his evidential exercises, and I do not consider that he was objective in the way he presented his evidence, although he sought to give the impression that he was… Although Mr Parker agreed, as it was put to him more than once, that accuracy is important, I do not consider his evidence in his witness statements to have been remotely accurate, even though he stoutly maintained that it was… I found him a very unsatisfactory witness, who presented in his witness statements a misleading and one-sided sanitised version of actual problems and events that Fujitsu had experienced.'

William Membury, Central Quality Partner, Fujitsu:
'Mr Membury's statement … omitted some highly material matters… I consider that Mr Membury's evidence is of limited, if any, assistance in resolving the Horizon Issues. It does however continue the very one-sided picture presented by all the Fujitsu witness statements, which was to omit any reference to important contemporaneous documents that criticise or demonstrate any deficiencies with Horizon.'

From Putland's answers to the chair of the BEIS Select Committee, Fujitsu certainly didn't seem to be doing much corporate soul-searching over its own culpability. When, for the purposes of this book, I asked Fujitsu about its role in the scandal and specifically about Mr Putland's evidence to parliament, it refused to comment.

THE SETTLEMENT AGREEMENT

In August 2020, while some of us were being encouraged by the government to Eat Out to Help Out,[1] the Post Office published the litigation settlement agreement. Although Freeths had explained its contents to their clients, they hadn't shared the actual agreement in its entirety with anyone from the claimant group, citing concerns about breach of confidentiality. Now, thanks to a persistent FOI campaign by a scandalised activist called Peter Bell, anyone could have a look. It was, as you might expect, revealing.

After the settlement agreement was announced in 2019, both Freeths and the JFSA referred to decisions about the litigation being made by the 'Claimant Steering Committee.' It was this powerful group which had essentially signed off everything on behalf of the wider group. Whilst I was working on the Great Post Office Trial for Radio 4, I asked Alan Bates who exactly sat on the steering committee. He gave me a four-paragraph reply, which stated:

> 'As with other large Group Actions, a Steering Committee is contractually appointed at the outset of the case by the Claimants, to make all decisions on behalf of the Group (and in the interests of the Group as a whole) based on the legal advice of Leading Counsel and the solicitors. That is what happened in this case.
>
> 'One of the main reasons for that structure in Group Actions is to ensure that confidential strategic decisions can be made without important strategic information about the strengths and weaknesses of the case getting into the opponent's hands, as that would likely be very damaging to the Claimant Group's case.
>
> 'The Claimants have been advised of the detailed and complex

---

[1] Throughout August 2020 the government ran a scheme in England to encourage people who might be wary of catching coronavirus to go out to eat in restaurants and cafés. It allowed every qualifying food outlet to offer a 2-for-1 deal on food and soft drinks sold to diners up to the value of £10 per customer. It turned out people were right to be wary of coronavirus as the pandemic returned with a vengeance just a few weeks later.

legal and economic risks, issues and matters underpinning the legal advice that was given to the Steering Committee by Leading Counsel and Freeths, and Freeths will continue to speak directly to each of the Claimants who would like further clarity on any issue.

'Beyond that, you will appreciate that as with any legal case of this type, there are legal confidentiality constraints that we should all observe.'

Which was useful context, but it didn't answer my question.

Clause 1.1 of the 'Confidential Settlement Deed,' published by the Post Office, was more succinct. It stated that the members of the 'Claimant Steering Committee' were 'Alan Bates and Kay Linnell.'

I asked the barrister Paul Marshall if he thought it was fair that one claimant, working with another non-claimant, had responsibility for decisions which affected the entire claimant group. He described it as 'plainly unsatisfactory.' I asked him why.

'Alan Bates had no experience of the trauma that a large number of claimants had,' replied Marshall, 'because he had been largely successful in resisting the Post Office's claims against him. Kay Linnell was a professional accountant and had no direct personal experience of the Post Office's conduct. That meant that effectively the only claimant who had experience of the Post Office's conduct was Alan Bates himself, and he was not representative of the experience of many. The obvious consequence, in a nutshell, was that the steering committee was wholly unrepresentative of the experience of most of the claimants. Arguably, in any sensible meaning of the word, it was not a committee at all. It certainly was not a representative committee.'

Over coffee at Colbert in Sloane Square, Patrick Green QC told me it wouldn't have made blind bit of difference who was on the steering committee.

'They *could* have put more people on it, if they were selfish, because they could have hidden behind them. It would *only* have been in Alan and Kay's interests to do that. Not the claimants.'

I put it to Patrick that surely a claimant who had been to prison or who had a criminal conviction would have at least offered an alternative perspective?

'We pleaded a case against the Post Office,' said Green, 'of malicious prosecution, which could never, *ever* succeed until the convictions of the claimants had been quashed. So their claims were stayed by the court. So the claimants with convictions had no claim during the litigation. From a governance perspective, putting people whose claims were not ongoing on a steering committee in charge of those whose claims *were* ongoing would be a conflict of interest.'

This at least made sense of the other surprising thing about the settlement agreement, which was that the Post Office had not given convicted claimants a penny, stating 'the Defendant has not made, or agreed to make, any payment to or for the benefit of any Convicted Claimant.'

Earlier in the year Kay Linnell had explained to me the reason the payments to convicted claimants were so small was because if they got their convictions overturned, they would be able to go after the Post Office for malicious prosecution and potentially get some serious compensation. The settlement agreement revealed just how closely Alan and Kay's hands were tied. The convicted claimants had essentially been given what little money they had received *by their fellow claimants.*

Scott Darlington, a Subpostmaster who was convicted of false accounting, was mystified. He told me:

'The terms of the settlement didn't quite add up to me – particularly people with criminal convictions being written out of it. After all the traipsing up and down for years going to all the meetings to find out I'd been written out of the settlement apart from if the others wanted to give us some money stuck in my craw.'

I asked Scott if he had been told by the JFSA at any stage that his claim, and that of other convicted Subpostmasters, was neither part of the litigation, nor its settlement.

'No. I only found out when I read the settlement agreement.'

The agreement is a fascinating document, and on reading it you can make a case for Alan Bates having achieved more to improve the lot of serving Subpostmasters than any other individual in the history of the Post Office.

When it was announced in May 2020, the Post Office said its Historical Shortfall Scheme 'followed' the settlement of the *Bates v Post Office* group litigation. The litigation agreement reveals it was actually a negotiated *condition* of the settlement. Schedule 6 of the agreement states:

'Post Office shall establish a group led by the Post Office General

> Counsel and/or a senior manager to deal with any issues in respect of shortfalls which arose between 2000 and the Effective Date of this Agreement (the "Historic Shortfall Group"); The purpose of the Historic Shortfall Group shall be to set up a scheme (the "Historic Shortfall Group Scheme") to bring finality to SPMs in respect of all outstanding issues in respect of shortfalls incurred between 1 January 2000 and the Effective Date of this Agreement.'

At great cost to themselves, the claimants had opened the door for those who had not been part of the litigation to recover losses suffered at the hands of the Post Office.

The settlement agreement also forced the Post Office to commit to more Subpostmaster training, more trainers, new business support managers, a new handover process, a new branch support model including new area managers, new branch support tools, increased Subpostmaster remuneration, better quality control on transaction corrections, a new team to deal with disputed transaction corrections, dedicated case handlers to investigate discrepancies, better access to Horizon data from Fujitsu, a completely different approach to 'losses' (which suggests they won't automatically be treated as Subpostmaster debts), better audits and better phone support. Quite a list.

BACK TO COURT

In June 2020, there was yet another Lords debate. This time Lord Cormack told the House that the Post Office had behaved with 'malevolent incompetence.' The business minister, Lord Callanan, agreed. It was clearly time for the government to act. Despite the civil service's reluctance to do anything, sustained cross-party pressure from backbenchers and peers (aided by resolute demands from the Labour front bench), had forced the issue.

A formal 'review' of the Post Office Horizon Scandal was announced by Paul Scully on 10 June 2020. It would be chaired by a retired High Court judge, Sir Wyn Williams. Crucially, it was not to be given statutory powers. A statutory inquiry has the power to subpoena documents and compel witnesses to attend cross-examination. Without statutory status, Sir Wyn's 'review' was toothless.

The review was further emasculated by its scope. It was put in place to 'consider whether Post Office Ltd has learned necessary lessons from the Horizon dispute.' It was not allowed to consider who was responsible for the disaster. Furthermore, the review's terms stated that the Post Office's 'prosecution function, matters of criminal law, the Horizon group damages settlement, the conduct of current or future litigation relating to Horizon and/or the engagement or findings of any other supervisory or complaints mechanisms, including in the public sector' were off-limits.

Lord Arbuthnot called it 'a cynical cop out.' Alan Bates was furious. 'It is utterly pointless our taking part,' he told JFSA members. 'There is nothing in it for us, and all we would be doing is giving our stamp of approval to their pointless internal whitewash.'

Bates vowed to press on with his complaint to the Parliamentary Ombudsman. While we waited for that, all eyes turned towards to the biggest question of all – had the Post Office been responsible for sending innocent people to prison?

After its initial tranche of 39 Subpostmaster referrals in March, the CCRC had referred a further eight cases in June. It had also asked the Attorney General and the Ministry of Justice Select Committee to review the state of private prosecutions in England and Wales. It transpired that no one had even been counting private prosecutions, let alone reviewing them. The potential for another scandal was obvious.

In its formal statement of reasons for referring the Postmaster cases, the CCRC advanced two arguments. Both came under the general heading 'Abuse of Process.'

The first category (interchangeably referred to as a 'ground' or 'limb'[1]) concerned the Post Office's alleged failure to:

a) properly investigate the circumstances behind a discrepancy before bringing a prosecution, and/or;

b) its alleged failure to disclose relevant material to the people it was prosecuting.

This, said the CCRC, meant it was not possible for the trial process to be fair.

The second category considered the Post Office's prosecutions to be an 'affront to the public conscience.' This was a profoundly serious charge. Whereas category one abuse could be put down to error or incompetence, category two was essentially an allegation that the Post Office deliberately pursued a prosecution strategy that it knew was unconscionable. The consequences of a finding on second category abuse were far-reaching. First of all, it could invite an investigation into whether there had been prosecutorial misconduct at the Post Office; secondly it potentially put decision-makers at the Post Office and Fujitsu in the frame for perverting the course of justice.

In both instances, the CCRC argued Horizon data was essential to the convictions of the Subpostmasters. It therefore believed that in the light of the High Court's findings about Horizon, there was a 'real possibility' all 47 convictions could be quashed.

The referred Postmasters now became appellants. Six of the 47 convictions were at magistrates' courts, which meant they had to be dealt with at a Crown Court. The remaining 39 cases would be addressed by a 'constitution' of three Court of Appeal judges at the Royal Courts of Justice – coincidentally sitting in the same court used by Master Fontaine to give the group litigation order the green light in January 2017.

In my naïvety I thought once a Subpostmaster had got a referral from the CCRC, the rest would be a formality. The 'real possibility' test sounds easy enough, but the CCRC refers less than 5% of the cases it accepts.

---

[1] And therefore referred to interchangeably in legal documents, in court and by me throughout this book. All three words – category, ground, limb – in this context mean exactly the same thing.

Surely the Post Office would not spend public money contesting the appeal of some poor soul who'd gone through everything required of them to persuade a super-cautious CCRC they had a case. What would be the point?

Whilst the Post Office considered its position, the appellant Subpostmasters confirmed their legal representation. Most, including Jo Hamilton, Karen Wilson and Wendy Buffrey, signed up with Hudgells. Tracy Felstead, Janet Skinner and Seema Misra went with Paul Marshall, Flora Page and the team at Aria Grace. Kamran Ashraf signed up with Sandip Patel QC, who had stuck his neck out on our 2014 One Show investigation to say that in his view there was 'sufficient cause for concern … that innocent people might have been wrongly convicted.'

This was his opportunity to prove it.

The Post Office's confidential review of its 900-odd prosecutions had grown over the course of 2020 into one of the biggest internal investigations in British corporate history. It involved 60 barristers sifting through more than 4.5 million documents. The firm of solicitors picking up the fees was Peters and Peters.

The purpose of the review was two-fold. Firstly, the government and the Post Office board needed to know there weren't any more nasties in the closet. The group litigation (including the settlement) had cost the Post Office more than £100m. With 1,200 applicants by early autumn, the Historical Shortfall Scheme was likely to cost at least the same again. There was now the prospect of multiple convictions being quashed, each of which would come with a claim for malicious prosecution to be successfully defended, settled or lost. Judging by its previous years' accounts, the Post Office's operating profit was going to be wiped out by its litigation liabilities. One more unexpected detonation under the balance sheet and the Post Office would cease to be a going concern.

The second reason for the review was to ensure that, after 20 years, the Post Office would finally start properly fulfilling its disclosure obligations, beginning with the appellants referred to the Court of Appeal.

As Peters and Peters and their team of barristers worked their way through the Post Office's internal prosecution files, they began to form their own conclusions about the 47 individual cases referred by the CCRC. According to their objective analysis, the Post Office's auditors, contract managers, investigators and prosecutors had indeed, over an extended period of time, got a lot of deadly serious things, very badly wrong.

INTERNATIONAL WRONGFUL CONVICTION DAY

On 2 October 2020 – international wrongful conviction day – the Post Office announced it was not going to contest 44 of the 47 cases referred by the Criminal Cases Review Commission. There were several administrative hoops to clamber through, and the courts had to rubber-stamp everything, but for more than three dozen Subpostmasters, they finally had the news they had been waiting years to hear – their convictions would be quashed and their names would be cleared.

With the government's tacit backing, the Post Office board had spent millions of pounds of taxpayers' money trying to deny it had been responsible for some of the most appalling behaviour in UK corporate history. Now it was admitting responsibility for prosecuting 44 innocent people. Almost exactly ten years after she was found guilty of theft at Guildford Crown Court, the Post Office had conceded Seema Misra did not get a fair trial, and that her conviction was an abuse of process. I called her up, but she was too emotional to speak. She sent me a message saying:

'Thank you very much to everyone for your support. I don't have many words apart from a tear of joy.'

Scott Darlington was having a strange moment. He said he was 'genuinely surprised' the Post Office weren't going to oppose his appeal, saying, 'The first few years of walking around as convicted criminal and the devastation to my life that this dealt me are difficult to put into words. I knew I was innocent, my family and friends also believed I was innocent. But the public and former customers and colleagues and the people of the town where I live must have thought I was guilty, I was, after all, convicted in a Crown Court of false accounting. The next step is suing them for malicious prosecution, which I know is a whole different ball game. But today, I'm happy. Very happy.'

Wendy Buffrey, Jo Hamilton, Noel Thomas, Susan Rudkin, Julian Wilson, Rubbina Shaheen, Tracy Felstead, Peter Holmes and Janet Skinner were also among the 44. Janet was a bit giddy. She described herself as 'floored' but 'in a good way. I didn't expect it to be positive at all. Now my emotions are all over the place.'

The disturbing thing for many Subpostmasters, who had gone forward in their campaign together, was the three appellants the Post Office had decided to contest. Whilst Wendy Buffrey said her own celebratory moment was 'wonderful,' it was 'tinged with a little sadness that we were not all given the same news.'

Alan Bates refused to comment. He too was focused on the three contested referrals and wanted to find out more about them before making any public pronouncement. The Post Office declined to explain why it had contested three of the referrals or, indeed, why it *wasn't* contesting the vast majority. The Post Office Chairman, Tim Parker, simply said he was 'sincerely sorry on behalf of the Post Office for historical failings which seriously affected some Postmasters.'

The Post Office also didn't mention that it was busy putting a little fly in the ointment.

OUT ON A LIMB

Here was the fly: of the 44 appellants whose cases were not being resisted by the Post Office, only four – Jo Hamilton, Noel Thomas, Allison Henderson and Alison Hall – were not being contested on *both* grounds of the CCRC's referral. The Post Office accepted the remaining 40 did not have a fair trial, but it refused to accept they should never have been prosecuted, as the CCRC had argued. To many appellants this was a detail – either route led to exactly the same result: a quashed conviction. But Seema Misra, Tracy Felstead and Janet Skinner were not happy about it. They believed their prosecutions were as much an affront to the public conscience as those of Jo, Noel, Allison and Alison. They too wanted complete exoneration.

The majority of the remaining appellants did not see the point in arguing the toss at the Court of Appeal over what they saw as a legal technicality, irrelevant to the outcome. They had been waiting far too long to have their convictions quashed as it was. Why delay things? Their lawyers took a similar view. As far as they were concerned, limb 2 was simply not something that needed to be addressed. It would be far easier, and quicker, to get the convictions quashed on limb 1 and then raise all the affront to the public conscience stuff in a malicious prosecution claim against the Post Office at the High Court.

Seema, Janet and Tracy disagreed. After long discussions in which the various possible outcomes were separately explained to them by Aria Grace Law, Flora Page and Paul Marshall, the three women independently confirmed to their legal team that they intended to see out limb 2. It was a matter of public interest and principle. Yes, it would take a lot of work to prepare the arguments against the Post Office. And they would need the court to accept that arguing limb 2 was a sensible demand on its time, but the prize was a ruling that Janet, Seema and Tracy's prosecutions should never have been brought.

If they succeeded, it could make every appellant's claim for malicious prosecution weightier *and* it would prepare the ground for hundreds more appeals. It would also remove the Post Office's last remaining shred of credibility or authority. But, as well as potentially slowing the appeals process down, there was a risk attached. If the court sided with the *Post Office* on limb 2 it could potentially skewer *every* convicted appellant's malicious prosecution claim. Proving the malice in malicious prosecution with a ruling explicitly against limb 2 might be tricky.

The lawyers for 37 of the 40 appellants who were home on limb 1 decided they were not going to assist on making the case to argue limb 2. It would be down to Marshall and Page.

Things took a nasty turn when some of those 37 appellants took it on themselves to call or text Seema, Janet and Tracy to try to persuade them to drop their attachment to limb 2. One text said, 'I was hoping to get my conviction quashed by Christmas. Thanks.' Another told them their barristers should 'stand down' as they obviously didn't know what they were doing.

Janet did not take kindly to this.

'Seema had gone to India to bury her dad. And she was getting the same sort of messages I was getting whilst she was going through her dad's funeral. And Tracy took it really bad. Really bad. She was in absolute floods of tears. I was absolutely fuming. I thought, "How dare they?!" '

Unused to coming under fire from their own side, Seema, Janet and Tracy could have wobbled, but they stuck to their guns. The Court of Appeal arranged its first hearing into all 41 Subpostmaster cases under its jurisdiction on 18 November 2020. It was decided for the sake of convenience that the six other appellants who had been convicted at magistrates' courts would be dealt with at Southwark Crown Court – just over the river from the Royal Courts of Justice. A hearing to discuss how that would unfold was pencilled in for 11 December 2020.

CONTEMPT

As the Court of Appeal hearing approached, the appellants' legal teams continued to receive documents from the Post Office through Peters and Peters' disclosure exercise. On 22 October, Paul Marshall spotted something which piqued his interest. It was a document which stated that the Post Office board had been notified about evidence given during a court case by a Fujitsu engineer called Gareth Jenkins.

Marshall asked Aria Grace to write to the Post Office for more information. He wanted to know 'why the board of the Post Office was being advised about the evidence of one witness.' He was particularly interested in Jenkins because he had been the independent expert witness for the Post Office at Seema's trial in 2010.

On 12 November, six days before the first hearing into his clients' appeals, the Post Office sent Aria Grace another tranche of information. It contained the Clarke Advice. Within a few minutes of picking it up Marshall realised its importance.

'In my almost 30 years' experience at the bar I have never come across information that has been so electrifying,' he said. 'It almost caused my teeth to fall out when I read it.'

The document revealed the Post Office knew in 2013 that Fujitsu's Gareth Jenkins had given incomplete and therefore potentially misleading evidence in at least six Post Office prosecution cases. 'That fact,' said Marshall, 'put the Post Office in breach of its obligations to the court as a prosecuting authority.'

Marshall immediately set about reversioning his submissions to the Court of Appeal. He also sent the Clarke Advice to the Metropolitan Police officer who had been investigating Mr Justice Fraser's grave concerns.

On 13 November the Metropolitan Police told Computer Weekly its investigation had now become a criminal investigation.

With Britain experiencing its second serious wave of coronavirus infections, the restrictions in Court 4 of the Royal Courts of Justice were severe. Social distancing requirements meant every person allowed into court needed two clear metres of space around them, radically reducing the court's capacity.

I managed to get a place, but it wasn't a good one. When I turned up, polite but firm ushers were operating a strict list of pre-arranged invitees who were given personalised, protected spaces in the courtroom. The sheer number of legal folk involved in representing their various Subpostmaster clients squeezed almost everyone else out. With three judges, a clerk and ushers, nine leading counsel, their juniors and various solicitors assisting, places were at a premium.

A satellite court linked by a temperamental comms set-up would be in operation for the 18 November hearing. Subpostmasters were asked to attend remotely. Having registered my interest a number of times I was assigned a seat in the main court at the back of the public gallery. Victorian court galleries seem to be designed with the express aim of making the public feel as uncomfortable and unwelcome as possible. They are often placed some distance above the action, with restricted views and naff acoustics as standard. Court 4 at the Royal Courts of Justice is a classic of the genre. But at least I was in.

There were three judges presiding over the Subpostmaster appeals: Lord Justice Holroyde, Mrs Justice Farbey and Mr Justice Picken. Tim Moloney QC represented the Hudgells appellants. Paul Marshall had to attend remotely because of his health situation. Flora Page was in Court 5. The Post Office team was led by Brian Altman QC, who I couldn't see. Altman was the first to speak and thankfully he had a good courtroom voice. I started live-tweeting.

Before getting to the main business of the day, the Post Office QC told the court he wanted to draw their attention to an email. It had been sent to the Post Office press office the previous evening by a Daily Telegraph journalist called Lewis Page. In his email, Mr Page told the press office that Seema, Janet and Tracy's legal team had let him see a document received 'under disclosure rules' by the Post Office.

It was the Clarke Advice.

'It will become public very soon,' wrote Page. 'Naturally, the Post Office should have the right of reply. Apologies for the timing, but I've only just seen the document and pitched the story myself. I'll keep you informed of publication, etc, as I know more.'

It is a wise rule of journalism not to tell anyone where you got your sensitive information without your source's express permission. I still don't understand why Lewis Page told the Post Office who had given him sight of the Clarke Advice,[1] but now Mr Altman was in possession of that information, we were about to see the damage he could do with it.

Mr Altman told the court that what the Clarke Advice 'deals with, in essence, is the topic of the evidence Gareth Jenkins had given in sample cases, witness statements he had made, his duties as an expert witness, and the fact that he had been tainted because Mr Clarke and the Post Office had been told by Mr Jenkins in the conference of 28 June 2013 – so a little before this Advice was written – that it was Mr Jenkins who had divulged to Second Sight, the accountancy firm, for the purposes of an interim report they wrote on 8 July 2013 that Horizon had some bugs.'

Mr Altman drew the judges' attention to a disclosure management document which dictated how information arising from the Peters and Peters investigation would be shared with the appellants and their legal teams.

Altman noted that it warned, 'The unauthorised use or onward transmission of any disclosed material for any purpose, other than the preparation for and conduct of appeal proceedings, is a breach of the common law … and constitutes a contempt of court punishable by a fine, or imprisonment, or both.'

At the word 'imprisonment,' I started to feel nauseous. This was serious *merde*.

The Post Office QC continued, 'We submit that the provision by the legal representative (or representatives, we know not which) of Aria Grace, as openly stated by Lewis Page in his email of yesterday, to a member of the press … amounts, arguably, to a contempt of this court.'

'Lewis Page,' said Mr Altman, pausing just long enough to summon an imaginary flourish, 'is the brother of junior counsel, Flora Page.'

Mr Altman helpfully provided the court with examples of case law which underlined the gravity of the situation, and continued to explain the civil, criminal and common law contempts which may or may not come into play. He was putting everything before the court, he said, simply out of his 'professional duty to do so.'

Maybe. But his kite was flying beautifully. The judges could not resist.

Lord Justice Holroyde immediately called Altman's submissions a

---

1 I asked Lewis about this a few months later. He told me, 'There was never any realistic prospect of keeping the identity of my source confidential, and I didn't think that was an issue.'

'potentially serious' matter. He invited Paul Marshall and Flora Page to respond.

Flora Page admitted she had passed the Clarke Advice to her brother but said she did so because the social distancing rules and advanced registration system meant he would not be able to attend court. She told the court that giving her brother the document in advance 'was a pragmatic decision based on the fact that if there were to be no reporting restrictions, and if the document was fully mentioned in court today, then it would be a document which, potentially, could be reported upon.'

This seemed to me to be a reasonable thing to do. But I am not a Court of Appeal judge.

'Miss Page,' said Lord Justice Holroyde, 'I am afraid we take a serious view of this... We must warn you that among the matters to be considered, are whether Her Majesty's Attorney General should be invited to consider a possible contempt of court and/or whether there should be a report to a professional body.'

I felt sick to the pit of my stomach. I had just watched the Post Office and the courts combine to potentially turn a public-spirited young barrister's career to dust, in a matter of minutes. For the briefest of seconds, I had a fraction of a sense of how it must feel to be a helpless and frightened Subpostmaster dragged into an environment which had the power to destroy them in an instant.

After lunch, Lord Justice Holroyde told Flora Page she would be required to attend a special hearing the next morning. She was also told to contact her brother and secure the return of the Clarke Advice, plus his 'assurance that he will not use it or any copy of it, or the contents of it, because, to put it bluntly, you should not have given it to him, and he has no right to it.'

Holroyde warned that, 'If he is not willing to give that assurance ... we will expect to see him at 10.15am tomorrow; and if he chooses not to come then, then he must expect that we will take some steps to secure his attendance.'

By now laying it on with a trowel, Holroyde finally told Altman to get the Director of Public Prosecutions involved too, 'because of the concern about the possible effect' on the ongoing criminal investigation by the Met Police.

Things were not looking good for Flora.

I reported what was said in court, including Brian Altman's description of the contents of the Clarke Advice. I then sought comment from various sources, including Ed Miliband, the shadow Secretary of State for Business. Ed had given me a call[1] the same week our Panorama had gone out in 2020. He told me he was determined to hold the government's feet to the fire over this scandal and was just setting up a line of communication with me. It was time to test that line. Ed kindly put me in touch with Charlie Falconer, a Labour party grandee and former Lord Chancellor. We had a chat about what I witnessed in court. Falconer told me he had no doubt the Clarke Advice was 'a smoking gun.'

The following day, Flora Page and her brother attended court. Paul Marshall was not present nor dialled in. For the first half hour Brian Altman, Richard Bentwood (Ms Page's own hurriedly-appointed barrister) and the three judges discussed whether what had transpired was a civil, criminal or common law contempt, or a simple error of professional judgment, or not even that. They also knocked about ideas regarding who should be dealing with this potential contempt case, and when. Everything was progressing in a slightly surreal manner when the court received an email from Detective Sergeant Hayley Bloom of the Metropolitan Police.

DS Bloom notified the court she had been sent the Clarke Advice by Paul Marshall the day before the hearing on 18 November, with a covering email stating:

'This is what we filed with the court yesterday for the hearing tomorrow.'

DS Bloom also told the court Mr Marshall had re-sent her the Clarke Advice that very morning with the note:

'This document was referred to in court yesterday.'

Lord Justice Holroyde expressed the court's 'very considerable disquiet' at this turn of events. He ordered Mr Marshall to attend a hearing on 3 December alongside Flora Page. He also warned of the potential 'unhappy consequences' for Seema, Tracy and Janet 'not excluding, at this stage, the possibility that their cases may have to be separately dealt with in some way.'

Holroyde then asked Mr Altman to formulate a charge of contempt for the hearing on 3 December and to do the work 'with one eye to the

---

1 I was sitting on my sofa at home watching daytime telly, eating cereal and possibly fighting off a hangover the first time we spoke, so I found it all a bit disorienting. He had messaged me to say he'd call, but I didn't actually think he would.

possibility that there may be charges to be considered against two rather than one.'

The whole thing was turning into a car crash. Both Flora and Paul felt it was essential the arguments for limb 2 of the CCRC's Abuse of Process should be heard by the court. Now they were fighting for their careers.

Given her invidious position, Flora felt unable to continue representing her clients. She stood down from the case.

Demoralised, and furious at the Court of Appeal's treatment of his junior, Marshall called Lord Arbuthnot, who he had spoken to a number of times as a result of their mutual interest in the Post Office scandal. As a former barrister, Lord Arbuthnot had an understanding of the pressure both Page and Marshall were under and the position they found themselves in. Marshall told Arbuthnot he was going to resign from the bar in disgust at Flora's treatment.

Arbuthnot instructed Marshall that he 'absolutely must not' do anything of the sort. He was needed.

Marshall understood where the peer was coming from, but he wasn't having a great time of it. The idea of preparing for the limb 2 hearing against the vastly over-resourced Post Office, without the assistance of the other appellants' barristers, was not necessarily something he felt he could do alone. The volume of work required just to pull the arguments together was daunting enough. The prospect of dealing with Holroyde and a dangerous, highly-skilled opponent like Altman in open court felt disadvantageous, especially after what had just transpired.

On top of all this, Marshall's fundamental problem was that he did not trust the courts. He would later say in a speech, 'Were the English criminal justice system to be an airline, no one would fly it, such is the repeated incidence of disastrous failure.' The idea of trying to achieve a desirable outcome in what he perceived as a hostile environment seemed futile. He couldn't see how he was going to get a fair hearing.

Having delivered his instruction to Paul Marshall, James Arbuthnot went back to the House of Lords and started swinging. The Clarke Advice – as far as he was concerned – was proof the Post Office had lied to parliament during its evidence to the BIS Select Committee in 2015, specifically when it stated in its written evidence that it was, 'under an absolute duty to disclose any evidence that might undermine a prosecution case or support the case of a defendant… To date no such evidence has been provided.'

As far as Arbuthnot was concerned, the Clarke Advice was clear evidence of miscarriages of justice, notified to the Post Office in 2013. He believed the Post Office's 2015 statement, denying any miscarriages of justice, potentially put it in contempt of parliament. Arbuthnot alerted the Speaker of the House of Commons and the Lord Speaker. He also wrote to Lord Callanan, stating unequivocally that the Post Office had lied. Lord Callanan declined to disagree.

THE OMBUDSMAN COMPLAINT

Whilst the extraordinary contempt shenanigans were playing out at the Court of Appeal, Alan Bates was putting the finishing touches to his crowdfunded Parliamentary Ombudsman complaint. In January 2020 he had sent an invoice for £46m to the BEIS minister Kelly Tolhurst. This was rejected. Then, in October 2020, he sent a formal complaint to BEIS. This too was rejected. It was time to fire his next salvo.

The complaint to the Ombudsman, submitted on 1 December 2020, accused the Post Office of 'running amok' over a 20-year period, abetted by the government.

The JFSA contended that had the government been doing its job properly, the Post Office 'would not have been able to destroy the lives of the Complainants and the Complainants would not have been required to fight a high profile, lengthy and expensive legal campaign in order to uncover POL's actions and bring to light the truth behind the Horizon scandal.'

Bates' complaint comprehensively exposed the lie that the Post Office was in some way acting unilaterally after the introduction of Horizon, and instead detailed the manner in which the government was fully aware of Horizon's unreliability, the prosecution spree, the cover-up and the disastrous litigation strategy.

'We can say with confidence,' wrote Bates, 'that HMG could quite easily have taken steps to stop POL's heinous conduct at any time during the Relevant Period. Or to put it another way, if HMG as 100% owner could not put a stop to POL's heinous conduct, there is no one that could.'

Bates didn't just demand his £46m litigation costs back. He calculated the true amount of money lost to the 555 claimants over the 'Relevant Period' and adjusted his claim to a cool £300m.

By complaining to the Ombudsman, Alan Bates had pulled a large statutory lever. Would anything happen?

SIDESHOW BRIAN

The 3 December hearing at the Court of Appeal was a farce. Paul Marshall could only attend remotely. Flora sat alone at the front of court. Both had instructed two QCs who by now had the benefit of two weeks' preparation.

The Post Office was again represented by Brian Altman. Having fathered the issue of contempt on 18 November, Mr Altman now seemed very keen to leave the court with his baby.

Addressing Lord Justice Holroyde, who again was sitting with Mrs Justice Farbey and Mr Justice Picken, Altman declared, 'I should like to make clear that the Post Office has not made an application for anyone's committal for contempt. That has not been our application and I am permitted to say that we are not instructed, and indeed have never been instructed, to make any such application.'

Altman seemed to be suggesting that he and the Post Office were victims of unfortunate circumstance. Or as he put it, 'We have sought to assist the court as we were invited to do.'

Mr Altman suggested it might be better if the court considered taking custody of his contempt allegation and getting a new team of barristers involved, to provide 'a clean break, as it were.'

Page and Marshall's representatives were not going to let him get away with this. Edward Henry QC, the barrister representing Flora Page, listed the number of different ways the court appeared to have been led in the wrong direction over the matter by the Post Office. As a result, he said Ms Page had been questioned unfairly, 'and it would be a very, very regrettable thing if this court were to proceed on the basis that there was no procedural unfairness because … we respectfully submit the unfairness is pellucidly clear.'

Patrick Lawrence QC, who had been appointed as Paul Marshall's barrister, wanted to know what contempt his client was being accused of and by whom. No one seemed to be sure. Lawrence said the Post Office had raised the complaint and how it moved forward should 'now properly to be regarded as a matter for the Post Office.' If the Post Office didn't want to pursue it, it shouldn't need to be pursued.

Altman resisted. 'The Post Office may, in one sense, be an aggrieved or injured party in the one sense but there's far greater interest, and that's the administration of justice.'

He invited the court to take up its responsibilities. The judges seemed keen, but met considerable resistance from Henry and Lawrence as to what those responsibilities could actually be. The battle raged for hours. Just before he sat down at the end of the day, Edward Henry asked for permission to appeal.

Holroyde seemed more than a little exasperated. 'Sorry? Permission to appeal against what to whom?'

Mr Henry wanted to seek permission to appeal from the Court of Appeal to the Supreme Court should it make an adverse finding against his client.

Mr Altman helpfully suggested that legally, there was no need. Mr Henry was 'getting ahead of himself.'

Eventually the judges left court, conferred for 27 minutes and returned with their decision. Holroyde, Farbey and Picken were going to set the contempt issue aside, ordering it be settled by a different panel of judges *after* the Subpostmaster appeals had been heard in March 2021. The faint rustling of long grass could be heard. I left court feeling rather glad I was not a lawyer.

Despite any immediate threat dissipating, Page and Marshall were still facing career extinction. Now they just had longer to dwell on it. Marshall also had two weeks, without a junior, to prepare for the hearing into limb 2 on 17 December. He would have to make the case alone.

Whilst all the journalists who had an interest in the Post Office scandal were watching what was going on at the Court of Appeal, Paula Vennells announced she would be stepping down from her post as Chair of the Imperial College Healthcare NHS Trust, two years early. No reason was given for her departure, but Lord Arbuthnot thought he knew. He commented:

'Can it be a coincidence that shortly after it became clear that the Post Office lied to parliament, Paula Vennells announced she was stepping down from the Health job?'

Alan Bates wasn't surprised, telling me he was 'utterly amazed they appointed her in the first place. Don't they read newspapers or undertake due diligence when they appoint someone?'

Tom Witherow at the Daily Mail managed to confirm off-the-record that 'the decision was made due to the ongoing IT scandal.'

It was the third job Vennells had lost in the space of 12 months, but her status as a pillar of the community remained. The Reverend Vennells continued to preach on moral matters throughout the Church of England's Bromham Benefice in Bedfordshire and, more lucratively, she remained a non-executive director on the boards of Morrisons supermarket and the home and garden retailer, Dunelm.

Former Subpostmaster, Tom Hedges, who, as well as being a committed Christian was also a former company director, wrote to the boards of the two retailers and asked why they continued to employ the Reverend Vennells. Hedges supplied the companies with just a small amount of the evidence that had come to light over the course of the litigation.

Mr Hedges received a bumptious reply from the Chairman of Morrisons, Andrew Higginson. Higginson told Hedges:

'In terms of Paula's suitability to be a Director of Morrisons, I have learnt through my career to take people as I find them, and, indeed, this is a fundamental part of my job.'

Higginson continued, 'It is both my own and my colleagues' assessment that Paula is an excellent Non-Executive Director, who brings great experience and a strong moral compass to the table.'

When serious and well-founded concerns are communicated in good faith to rich and influential people, they should be investigated, not glibly dismissed.

FIRST CONVICTIONS QUASHED

Kamran Ashraf was one of the six people the CCRC had referred to Southwark Crown Court after being convicted at a magistrates' court. Since his referral in March he had endured eight months of silence, waiting to find out what would happen. On Monday 7 December 2020 he received a two-line email from Southwark Crown Court. His case would be 'listed for mention' on Friday 11 December.

'If you wish to attend, you can,' wrote the court officer, 'but your attendance is not required.'

Kamran was confused. What did 'listed for mention' mean? Having received the email at the same time as their clients, the Subpostmasters' legal teams were similarly caught on the back foot. They soon clattered into action. I was forwarded some correspondence which made it plain that whilst no one was entirely sure what was meant to be happening that Friday, there was a 'possibility that the convictions will be dealt with.'

Dealt with.

Wait. What? Overturned?!

I tried to get some kind of direct confirmation from anyone, including the court itself, that this could be true. By Wednesday, it looked as if it might be. The process of overturning a conviction at a Crown Court is different from the Court of Appeal. Formally, the trial is re-heard, and the court can then allow the appeal or dismiss it. There appeared to be some legal obstacles relating to the guilty pleas, but it was becoming apparent that the Post Office was proposing to deal with the re-trials (triggered by the CCRC referrals) by offering no evidence. The fight over limb 1 or limb 2 sat outside this process. The appellants' legal teams were in agreement – why bother kicking things into 2021? Representations were made to the court. By Thursday, everything seemed to have fallen into place. Barring some kind of disaster, Friday was going to be a landmark occasion.

Exactly a year to the day after the email which announced the settlement of the *Bates v Post Office* litigation, a gaggle of us gathered at Southwark Crown Court. Kamran Ashraf, Vipin Patel, Jasvinder Barang and Chris Trousdale all attended. Susan Rudkin was too ill to make the journey down in person, so she dialled in via video link. Julie Cleife was not represented, nor did she attend. I was working for ITV News that day so arranged for a cameraman to be stationed outside court to pick up arrival shots. Susan and Michael Rudkin agreed to allow a Midlands-based ITV crew into their home in Ibstock to film their reaction to the verdict.

The first person I bumped into in the courthouse was Vipin Patel's son Varchas. I'd got to know Varchas quite well, but I'd never met his dad. We were introduced. I hadn't realised Vipin still ran the same convenience store which he and his wife Jayshreeben had bought in 2002, and which had once housed a Post Office counter. Vipin told me the Horizon terminal was long gone, but he hadn't touched the counter itself since his conviction in 2011. The Patels' shop was in the genteel village of Horspath in Oxfordshire.

At 10am the appellants, their families and the legal teams filed into court. I was the only journalist present. Once the judge was sitting, Simon Baker,[1] the Post Office barrister, introduced himself and the appellants' barristers to the judge. It took him what seemed like less than sixty seconds to sketch out the details of the Subpostmasters' original convictions and the circumstances which had led to the retrial. After dealing with a legal point which (on the nod from the judge) vacated the Postmasters' guilty pleas, Mr Baker proceeded, 'straight to what I know the appellants have been looking to for some time, which is that in respect of each of those six appellants the respondent offers no evidence.'

There was a bit of pointless legal jousting, a discussion about costs, the by-now-compulsory comms link blow up, which eventually concluded with Her Honour Judge Deborah Taylor simply saying, 'We allow the appeals and enter not guilty verdicts in relation to all appeals.'

She added, with jarring insensitivity, 'I am sure that all of the appellants are grateful for the approach that the Post Office has taken finally to this matter and that it can be put to rest for them.'

When you read back and look at what the Post Office had stolen from the six appellants in terms of their finances, family life, dignity, health and reputation, I am not sure 'grateful' was the most appropriate word.

The judge left. We were all standing in silence. Jasvinder began to cry. She hugged Kamran. The families, conditioned by nine months of social distancing, murmured congratulations to each other from behind their masks. The moment of victory was basically marked with a collective sigh

[1] For the avoidance of doubt, not the former Post Office project manager featured earlier in this book – a namesake.

of careworn fatigue.

Outside court Jasvinder told me and my cameraman that living with the effects of her conviction had been 'very stressful.' She thanked her family and friends 'and our group! We've been keeping together with all the other Subpostmasters and Subpostmistresses ... when we've had our down days we've been there for each other. I can get on with the rest of my life now. It's the worst thing to be found guilty for something that you haven't done. I am a law-abiding citizen. Today is just absolutely wonderful.'

Kamran and Siema had never spoken on the record before. They had had to live with what happened longer than most. On the court steps, Kamran was composed. 'It's been 17 years,' he said. 'Way too long. Way, way too long, but the main thing is, we've got there in the end. I'm just shell-shocked. I don't know how to react. So many mixed emotions, but at the same time when you think back and think about the things that have happened over the last 17 years, not just to me and my family but what we've been through as a group. It's just been horrendous.'

Normally I'd be delighted to be the only journalist getting a scoop on the big story, but I found it depressing that no one else was around.

Having hoovered up the remaining interviews, including a quote from Neil Hudgell, who made it crystal clear that this was the 'tip of the iceberg,' I asked the Patels what their plans were. They told me they were heading straight back to Oxfordshire. I asked if I could film them in their shop. They agreed. Due to social distancing regulations I was unable to travel with them or my cameraman, so I jumped in a cab to Paddington and got on a train to Oxford. We met again a couple of hours later outside Horspath Stores.

It was fascinating to see how the mood of the Patels had changed from bewilderment tinged with anger, to a growing sense of joy and release as they were welcomed back into their community. Horspath Stores had been locked up for the day so the whole family could attend court. They arrived back just as school was finishing. The store was quickly reopened and Jayshreeben went into the shop. She reappeared with free chocolate bars for all the children gathered outside and a big smile on her face. Mrs Patel was almost giddy with happiness, chatting to the children's parents and posing for photos with the kids as they waved their free chocolate in the air. Vipin shook hands with the many villagers who came by to tell him how pleased they were. I took my cameraman inside. Varchas showed me the old Post Office counter with a blind reading 'Closed!'

which had been pulled down across the window for the last nine years.

Vipin is an old man now and his health has suffered. He can only walk with sticks or crutches. We filmed him behind his old counter talking about the experience of being prosecuted for a crime he didn't commit. Then we took a quick break to think about the next shot. In the middle of a technical discussion with my cameraman, I glanced at Vipin to see if he was okay. He was still behind the counter looking around in something of a daze. He seemed so vulnerable.

LIMB 2 IS GO

Two days before the Court of Appeal hearing which would decide whether Seema Misra, Tracy Felstead and Janet Skinner would be allowed to argue their convictions were an 'affront to the public conscience,' Paul Marshall resigned.

He sent a nine page letter to Lord Justice Holroyde, Mrs Justice Farbey and Mr Justice Picken detailing the circumstances which led to the disclosure of the Clarke Advice and subsequent contempt allegation made (and then disavowed) by the Post Office.

He then listed the unsatisfactory way the proceedings were apparently taken over and handled by the court. These included making him subject to an order of the court, 'in proceedings to which I am not a party, in the course of a hearing at which I was not present, of which I was given no notice that any issue in connection with my conduct was to be raised, less made, the first notice of which was given to me four days after the order was made, where the document founding criticism of my conduct by the court was provided to me 11 days after the hearing, and then only upon my specific request.'

He concluded, 'Having carefully and anxiously reviewed the proceedings on 18 November, 19 November and 3 December 2020, and the terms of the order made on 3 December 2020, I consider that I am inhibited from continuing fearlessly to represent my clients before this court.'

It is part of the Bar Standards Board code of conduct that a barrister must 'fearlessly and by all proper and lawful means' promote their clients' best interests and 'do so without regard to their own interests.'

Marshall felt compromised.

'I am consequently disabled,' he wrote, 'from discharging my professional duty to my clients. Accordingly, it is in my clients' best interests to be represented in these appeals before this court by other counsel. I have also been advised that, given my recent remission from metastatic cancer, my continuing participation in these proceedings has become medically significant.'

Marshall didn't leave his charges in the lurch. Four days before firing off his missive to the Court of Appeal, he crafted a skeleton argument making the case for limb 2, and left it in the hands of one of his colleagues at Cornerstone chambers, Lisa Busch QC. I asked her how she came to pick the case up.

'My senior clerk called me at six o'clock on a Friday evening and he said, "Paul Marshall's got this Post Office case. He can't do it so you're doing it." And so I said "Okay." And that was that!'

I asked Lisa how close she was to Paul and how much she knew about the story before agreeing to take the responsibility on.

'Oh gosh, I've known Paul for probably around 15 years. We've always got on very well and I'm immensely fond of him, but I had no idea about his involvement in the Post Office case. In fact, I have to say my knowledge *of* the Post Office case was pretty much nil.'

It was a big decision, quickly made.

'In theory I could have said no, not least because this was a case at the criminal division at the Court of Appeal and I do not have *any* experience of criminal law, but as a general rule, if a colleague asks you to take over a case, we help each other out.'

Ms Busch's secret weapon was her specialism, which covers public and constitutional law. 'The crucial point about this case was that it wasn't really a criminal law case. It was a constitutional law case, because all this stuff about category 1 and category 2 abuse of process is very much about constitutional law principles. And that's why I agreed to take it on.'

Not that she didn't have second thoughts.

'I was worried, because I think you can end up getting distracted by silly things,' Lisa told me. 'My main concern was that I knew nothing about criminal procedure – I knew nothing about where I was supposed to be standing in court for heaven's sake – but that wasn't enough to stop me from doing it.'

Ms Busch assembled two juniors from her chambers, Olivia Davies and Dr Sam Fowles (the latter's PhD helpfully being in constitutional law), and got to work.

'Paul had written volumes and volumes of excellently drafted stuff, but he's a commercial lawyer, and I just thought – there's masses and masses and masses of material that I need to get on top of, I have just got to do it in the way I've got to do it.'

Lisa and her team read through all the documentation related to the case and started picking through.

'I read through all of Paul's submissions and I just took what I thought were the gems and pretty much discarded the rest. I thought that if I am going to win this at the first stage – that is the right to argue limb 2 – then I've got to present it in as simple and clear a way as I possibly can.'

It wasn't an ideal situation, but bringing a fresh pair of eyes – or three fresh pairs of eyes – to the material helped.

'The defining feature of public law is that it's conceptual,' said Lisa, 'so we were used to working in situations where there's no real dispute about facts and evidence. The other criminal lawyers were much more forensic and focused on the minutiae. But my approach was – we've already got masses of evidence in the form of the findings of Mr Justice Fraser. The only question was – do these findings which substantiate a category 1 abuse also lend themselves to a finding on category 2 abuse? Everything else can just go.'

Lisa told me she 'didn't sleep for a few days' whilst poring over the *Bates v Post Office* judgments and the CCRC Statement of Reasons before drafting the best skeleton argument she could.

'I tried to not get emotionally involved, but when I was reading through the judgments … it was jaw-dropping stuff, but I couldn't allow myself to dwell on that, for obvious reasons.'

Lisa Busch shaped her arguments around a central point. Category 1 abuse was about the relationship between the prosecutor and the defendant. Category 2 abuse 'implicated the court.'

It takes a certain bravery to get on top of complex legal arguments from a standing start three working days before a court hearing. Especially a hearing in which your ability to recall, defend and build on your arguments in a credible manner will be tested to destruction in front of three senior judges.

Ms Busch had the added pressure of being in court amongst seven other potentially hostile criminal QCs, a clutch of hacks and her three Subpostmaster clients, for whom this was a deadly serious business.

The court hearing was set up to answer two questions – whether Subpostmasters had the *right* to argue limb 2, and if they did not have the right, whether the court should allow them to do so.

The first point was rather easily dealt with. The barrister appointed by the court concluded there was no settled right in law for the Subpostmasters to go after limb 2. After reading his submissions, the court was in agreement – the judges would therefore have to be persuaded to give the Subpostmasters permission.

Invited to go first, Busch was disarmingly open about the limited preparation time she'd had in coming to the case. She nonetheless was certain a ground 2 consideration was achievable within the four-day timescale scheduled for the full hearing in March 2021. It was also, she told the court, the right thing to do, because of 'the really terrible, terrible time the appellants have had.'

Busch admitted that the latter point was 'not a legal submission as such,' but 'one could take the view that the least could be done' for the appellants 'is to afford them an opportunity to vindicate their reputations.'

The lack of support for her position was striking. The representatives of the other Subpostmasters felt that going for ground 2 and fighting the Post Office on a fact-specific basis for each appellant would drag things out. If the outcome was going to be the same what was the point?

Indeed, as Tim Moloney (who represented the vast majority of appellants) noted, some of his clients had already had their convictions quashed at Southwark Crown Court, via the simple expedient of not raising limb 2 at all.

Holroyde seemed a little put out by events in Southwark. 'I don't recollect anyone mentioning to us at any stage in the proceedings in this court that the Crown Court appeals were going to be heard last week,' he said, adding, 'The first I knew about it was when I saw it on Twitter!'

Glad to be of service.

The first hint things might go Tracy, Janet and Seema's way was when Mr Justice Picken asked Moloney if his position would change if limb 2 were 'considered at the general level, which may mean that the fact-specific never needs to be got to.'

Moloney said this *would* be something his clients might be open to, telling the court, 'We do not accept the Post Office's position in relation to ground 2... If the court allows argument on ground 2 we will hopefully take a full role in the arguments in relation to ground 2.'

Brian Altman was there to pour cold water on the idea that a limb 2 finding could be made in the time the court had set aside for the full hearing. It was all going to be far too much unnecessary trouble.

'When one comes to consider then who knew what and when,' he said, 'that's not a simple question to answer (in fact there's more than one question, but overall there's a rolled-up question), because one would have to look at the particular cases affected. Presumably we would have to think about inviting the Post Office to investigate and interview lawyers affected, some of whom might still work for the Post Office, some of whom won't ... one would have to look perhaps up and down corporate governance and so on and so forth about what was happening in the Post Office during that period ... and it's not just the Post Office, because it would inevitably involve Fujitsu.'

In Altman's hands, it sounded like limb 2 would potentially be another investigation on the scale of the *Bates v Post Office* civil litigation but with an unknowable, unfathomable goal. Altman asked the court, 'What would the ambit of ground 2 be? What's its ultimate purpose? Does it have a different outcome? No, if successful. Does it disable the court from making appropriate comments in the course of a judgment on limb 1? No, if based on the evidence before it.'

The Post Office was quite clear that if the Subpostmasters wanted vindication on limb 2, they could get it through a claim in the civil courts for malicious prosecution.

The other Subpostmasters' QCs sided with the Post Office, all effectively saying that a proper 'ventilation' of the arguments needed to persuade the judges to make a ground 2 ruling would require vast amounts of work, which could not possibly be completed in the three months to March 2021.

The court was not convinced. Mr Justice Picken even suggested it was 'slightly odd to have appellants who aren't interested in ground 2,' and after lunch allowed Lisa Busch to answer the Post Office and her fellow appellants' points.

Busch argued that most of the facts required had been found, both via disclosure and the two civil litigation judgments.

'We are categorically not seeking an open-ended fishing expedition,' she said. 'What's in issue in this case is not so much a matter of the evidence; it's a question of legal implications to draw from the evidence.'

She then addressed the Post Office's arguments on expedience, and reversed them.

'Part of the Post Office's case, and indeed that of the other appellants, is that proceedings should not be delayed given there's already been so much delay and the convictions should be quashed forthwith. However, Mr Altman is now suggesting that in fact there *should* be a delay until the resolution of the malicious prosecution cases. So, whereas, at least on our case, all these issues could be resolved in March, the Post Office is now suggesting that we should wait until further down the line, and civil proceedings for malicious prosecution.'

Lord Justice Holroyde twigged. 'So, your point is – if they deserve to be vindicated why should they have to wait until the end of a civil process, which may take a long time starting from now.'

Busch nodded vigorously. 'Exactly ... it *must* be the case that the category 2 issue is relevant itself to the malicious prosecution proceedings. It's hard to imagine a finding on ground 2 would *not* have a bearing on those proceedings, and indeed might make them capable of being dealt with more efficiently and effectively.'

This was, Busch said, about 'maintaining the integrity of the justice system' which was hardly likely to be achieved if 'the Post Office can dictate the manner in which the proceedings are run by conceding an appeal on one ground and leaving outstanding what we say is a hugely important issue of principle that directly affects my clients' rights.'

In short order, Lisa Busch had told the court that ground 2 could easily be argued in the time available, punting it towards the civil courts was both inappropriate and *created* delay, and then she got her main point home – this wasn't just about the Subpostmasters or the Post Office. It was about justice, and the court should not abrogate its responsibility to make a finding on potential abuse of the justice system itself.

It was a bravura performance, and carried all before it. At the end of the day, the judges ruled that no extra court time or lengthy investigation was needed, and limb 2 could – and would – be argued alongside limb 1. The hearing was scheduled to begin on 22 March 2021.

MORE REFERRALS

In January 2021, the CCRC referred four more Subpostmasters back to the courts, two of whom were Parmod Kalia and Teju Adedayo. Parmod and Teju had been crushed when the CCRC declined to refer their applications in 2020 alongside the first tranche of litigation claimants, many of whom had become supportive and welcoming friends during the civil court case. Their applications had been held up because they had pleaded guilty then confessed to their alleged crimes. Both insisted these confessions were made on advice, under duress, with a view to mitigating the sentences their guilty pleas would inevitably bring. Hudgells had managed to successfully demonstrate to the CCRC that the confessions were fictions, and the CCRC was now satisfied their cases could go forward.

I called Parmod and Teju. They were obviously delighted, but they'd been put through the mill by the referral process. Now they were so close to getting their convictions quashed, they didn't want to jeopardise or jinx them by offering a single word on the record. They both seemed all over the place. I could understand why.

The third appellant of the four was Roger Allen. He had been prosecuted by the Department for Work and Pensions using Horizon data. The DWP refused to tell me the name of Mr Allen's solicitors, or when his first court hearing might be. They also told me they didn't have any information on who or how many people it prosecuted using Horizon evidence over the last 20 years due to data protection rules. The failure to keep proper records is shocking, but it appears that the destruction of data is actively encouraged by statute, guideline and government agencies across the board. Therefore, 'DWP Policy is that data is retained only if there is a business need.'

I asked for more information, and got chapter and verse:

> 'All fraud documents ... should be destroyed after 14 calendar months... Completed official notebooks must be retained for not less than three years from the date of the last entry or six months after the expiry of a successful appeal against conviction, whichever is the longer. Official notebooks containing information about investigations which have resulted in a custodial sentence being imposed should be kept until the sentence has been completed...

> In England and Wales, in order to comply with the Criminal Procedure and Investigations Act … documents should not be destroyed prior to release from prison when the claimant receives a custodial sentence… Unless DWP receives notification that the convicted person has been released early, documents should be retained until the sentence imposed by the court is spent… Audio or video tapes and compact or DVDs should be destroyed or securely disposed of at the same time as documents … the Data Protection Act (DPA) requires that personal data is not kept longer than is necessary. This generally means that details of cases would not be kept beyond five years.'

Data protection laws have unquestionably made it harder for journalists to get important information out of public and private institutions. If they are also contributing to the wholesale destruction of historically important information, then there is a bigger problem which needs addressing, and fast.

The fourth appellant was Pamela Lock, who pleaded guilty to false accounting in 2001 at Swansea Crown Court after £26,000 allegedly went missing at her branch. From what we now knew about it, Horizon during that period frequently became a random number generator. Ms Lock was given 80 hours' community service, which is an indication of just how guilty the judge thought she might be. But I bet the conviction blighted her life. Having made enquiries into the three other referrals, I weighed the advantages of finding out more about Ms Lock's. There was nothing online, save a reference in a contribution to a parliamentary debate by her MP Tonia Antoniazzi.

I decided not to follow it up, realising I no longer had the time or resources to make contact with every Subpostmaster caught up in this scandal. There are too many. The detail of what Pamela Lock went through, and how badly she was treated, would be for someone else to put on the record. I had to accept that, for the purposes of what I was trying to do, she had become a statistic, which in itself is faintly depressing.

This story is littered with hundreds of individual human tragedies rendered almost unremarkable by the scale of what went wrong. One miscarriage of justice should make us angry. Five hundred miscarriages of justice should make us five hundred times more angry, but it doesn't. As human beings we're not capable of processing information in that way.

The inevitable consequence is that people responsible for the widespread destruction of multiple livelihoods are never punished proportionately (if they get punished at all). In this, as in other cases, they should be. The Post Office, the government, Fujitsu, the NFSP and the justice system ruined hundreds of people over two decades. The individuals responsible should not be allowed to get away with it, but I suspect they will.

Pamela Lock was convicted at a Crown Court, so she could join the cohort of appellants at March's Court of Appeal hearing. Parmod and Teju were convicted at magistrates' courts, so they would need a separate hearing at Southwark Crown Court. Roger Allen was convicted at a Crown Court but as the respondent for the big hearing in March was the Post Office, he too would need to be dealt with separately.

SHAME, BREAKDOWNS AND RECURRING MENTAL ANGUISH

Before the Court of Appeal session rolled round, in January 2021, Sir Wyn Williams held the first focus group of his Post Office Horizon IT review.

Oral testimony can be surprising. Anyone who has taken part in a job interview or panel discussion will know the answers you give to questions can develop on the hoof into new ideas over the course of a sentence or two.

In a loosely structured three-hour discussion, the contributors at the first inquiry session were given free rein to visit and revisit various themes. One of the contributors was the Postmaster and CWU activist, Mark Baker.

During the session Mark spoke of the guilt he felt about not being able to help everybody the Post Office was trammelling, telling Sir Wyn:

'I do have this sense of being on a rescue boat and I've grabbed someone's hand, who was drowning in the water and I've tried to get them on the boat to save them and they've slipped away. That is a recurring thought that goes through my mind.'

The other male contributor was Pete Murray, who I got to know quite well over 2020 by writing up and publishing his story. Pete took over Hope Farm Road Post Office after Martin Griffiths took his own life. He was not told about what happened to his predecessor. The Horizon problems which blighted the last four years of Mr Griffiths' life continued for Pete. When Post Office auditors found a large discrepancy at the Hope Farm Road branch, Pete was suspended, just as Mr Griffiths had been.

Pete suffered a stroke, as well as losing goodness knows how many tens of thousands of pounds in lost income and forced repayments, under the threat of legal action. In the oral session Pete described his experience of being nearly ruined by the Post Office:

'It's left me completely devastated. It's caused absolute havoc in my family. I feel alienated from my children. I've had several nervous breakdowns ... the last three Christmases have been destroyed by breakdowns... Falling into tears at the drop of a hat over nothing... I feel ashamed, even though I still know that I've done nothing wrong... I've now had it confirmed that I'm suffering from PTSD, which has been a great weight off my shoulders, 'cause I've shared that information with my kids. I feel like they understand a bit more.'

The third contributor was Shann Rodgers, still serving as Subpostmaster at Goldsithney Post Office in Cornwall. Shann's story perfectly illustrated the fear felt by serving Postmasters about the hated Horizon system. After 17 years working for Post Office HQ in London, Shann was bored. Newly divorced, she moved 300 miles west with her nine-year-old daughter, to start over as a Subpostmaster.

Shann's 'bubbly' personality made her a natural pillar of the community and she was welcomed into the village. Life was good until Horizon started playing up. Despite regular 'blue screen of death' crashes, she was told she was the only one having problems with the system, and she was held responsible for inexplicable Horizon discrepancies. Although she was never suspended, repayment threats meant she had to cash in a savings account she had set up to help her daughter at university.

During the oral evidence session Shann told Sir Wyn Williams that she feels unable to give up her job because the village depends on her, but she 'dreads' going into her Post Office. Without her, the branch would close – no one would take it on as a business, as it is no longer a going concern. As for her employers:

'I hate the Post Office. I hate them… This was our dream and they turned my dream into a nightmare.'

At the end of the session Sir Wyn was either taken, or affected to be taken, by the testimony. He also said he was 'not very happy' to hear Shann's account of repeatedly being told she was the only person having problems with Horizon, adding that if it was or had been replicated around the country, 'then it's not too strong for me to say that that would be reprehensible.'

Sir Wyn asked Mark Baker to supply him with a record of all the cases he had heard 'you're the only one' mentioned.

After watching the focus group session, I realised it had been nearly two months since the Parliamentary Ombudsman had been sent the JFSA's 50-page complaint. I called up the Ombudsman's press office to see how much progress had been made. The press officer had never heard of the Horizon scandal, nor the JFSA, nor its complaint. She told me the Ombudsman investigates in private, but she couldn't put a timescale on how long it might take. She said she'd call me back with more information. She didn't.[1]

1 In June 2021, seven months after it was submitted, the Ombudsman told me it was still deciding whether or not to investigate the JFSA's complaint.

PRESUMPTIONS ABOUT MACHINES AND AI

With Christmas out of the way, and January's Covid lockdown keeping many people at home, the appellants' barristers got to work on how they would present their clients' cases to the Court of Appeal. Between them, Flora Page, Paul Marshall and Lisa Busch had got limb 2 on the table without any prospect of delaying a result. Now it was up for grabs, Lisa began to collaborate with Tim Moloney.

'Tim and I had a very good working relationship,' Lisa told me. 'He was a tremendously nice chap and was immensely helpful. There were days when he was doing murder trials in the Crown Court and I would ring him and he would talk to me over lunch.'

The two QCs and their respective juniors helped each other out on various procedural and legal points, bringing Sam Stein QC into their discussions to cut down on unnecessary duplication and create a unity of purpose.

During this preparatory period, there was more activity in parliament. The chair of the BEIS Select Committee, Darren Jones, took a stab at dismantling the legal presumption underpinning the Subpostmasters' convictions.

Although his inquiry into Horizon was on indefinite hiatus (thanks to the launch of the government review) Mr Jones had retained a strong interest in the Horizon scandal and was trying to get some movement elsewhere. In a COVID-compliant parliamentary debate, Mr Jones laid into the 22-year-old legal presumption of reliability in computers, telling the Culture minister Matt Warman:

'If the Post Office had been required to prove its computer system was operating reliably, it would not have been able to do so, because we now know it wasn't.'

Jones wanted the Law Commission's legal presumption (that 'in the absence of evidence to the contrary, the courts will presume that mechanical instruments were in order at the material time') modified to reflect reality. He told the minister, 'If people found it difficult to prove a computer was operating reliably in the early 1990s, we can only imagine how difficult it might be to do that today, with the likes of machine-learning algorithms coming to conclusions for reasons even the computer programmer doesn't understand.'

The minister promised to go away and look at it, but didn't sound too hopeful. He did, however, tell Jones, 'The judiciary criminal procedure rule committee could consider making changes … [and] I look forward to taking the matter up with the Ministry of Justice and the Lord Chief Justice.'

DOCUMENT SHREDDING

On 22 March I made my way up to London for the first day of the appeal process hearing, again in Court 4 of the Royal Courts of Justice. Although Britain's latest wave of coronavirus was subsiding, the lockdown was still in full effect and strict social distancing rules remained in place. Through some fairly intense lobbying, I had managed to secure myself a place in the well of the court rather than up in the gods, or worse, listening in via the court's industrial tech-core white noise generator, which doubled as a comms link.

I arrived early and bumped into Seema, Janet and Tracy. It was also lovely to see Nicki Arch, who'd come up from the West Country to support her friends. We took some photos and made our way into court.

Once the judges were sitting and we were settled, I began to live-tweet.

Tim Moloney began by telling the court of the 'shame and humiliation' his clients had experienced, and the 'enormous psychological toll' of being prosecuted and convicted. 'Many immediately went to prison, some saw their marriages break up, others suffered bankruptcy, and some are dead... One of these appellants ... is suffering from terminal brain cancer.'

He then went on to lay out what the Post Office knew and when – the concerns over Horizon before its rollout, the extensive bugs which were uncovered internally, unresolved and ultimately blamed on Subpostmasters and the refusal to investigate, even when the board became aware of the Subpostmasters' campaign.

'The lives of Subpostmasters were irreparably ruined', Moloney told the court. 'Some took their own lives, but still the respondent did not commission an external, independent investigation into the reliability of Horizon. Instead, as part of its internal review of challenges to Horizon, in August 2010, the respondent discussed in the Ismay report its ultimate refusal to order an independent review of the system's integrity.'

Moloney raised the Ismay report as being a key document, because one of the reasons for the recommendation that there be no investigation into Horizon was because, as the report stated, 'All criminal prosecutions would have to be stayed. It would also beg a question of the Court of Appeal over past prosecutions and imprisonments.'

Mr Moloney said, 'A great many heads of department in POL had sight of that report, including the head of criminal law, Rob Wilson, and the principal civil lawyer. We say the failure of the respondent in all the circumstances to commission such an independent report is shameful and culpable.'

Moloney was soon reciting to the court a litany of conscious decisions made by the Post Office in order to deny Subpostmasters a fair trial – the confidential Receipts and Payments Mismatch memo which should have been disclosed, the press article that was put on a Schedule of Sensitive Material and an expert witness report about the reliability of Horizon which was withheld from Jackie McDonald's defence team. Jackie was the Subpostmaster who was so terrified when she saw Seema go to prison that she pleaded guilty to all the charges against her and was sent to prison anyway.

Mr Moloney turned to the behaviour of the prosecution team, noting how plea bargain deals were routine, and that even when theft charges had been dropped, a guilty plea to false accounting might only be accepted by the Post Office 'if the defendant confirmed in writing that "there is no criticism made towards the functioning and reliability of the Horizon system." '

We already knew Jo Hamilton had been prosecuted for theft, despite an internal report stating clearly 'there is no evidence of theft' at her branch. What we didn't know was that the Peters and Peters disclosure exercise revealed Post Office prosecutors had communicated what Moloney said was, 'an express intention to add charges of theft to an indictment alleging false accounting if those charged with false accounting did not plead guilty.'

Moloney quoted a document assessing Subpostmaster prosecutions which stated, 'If any seeks a trial, then I will add charges of theft.'

Shortly before the publication of this book, the Post Office supplied me with a copy of this document. They were not able to tell me who authored it, but they believe it was almost certainly written by a Post Office lawyer with prosecuting responsibility.

When I showed it to a barrister friend of mine, he told me the idea of a prosecutor threatening to add a more serious charge as a means of encouragement to plead to the lesser was 'scandalous' and 'plainly abusive conduct.'

My legal friend said, 'There is an obvious requirement for the author of that document to be identified and referred to the Solicitors

Regulation Authority.'

When Mr Moloney had finished, Sam Stein QC, representing Scott Darlington, Rubbina Shaheen and Peter Holmes (among others), got to his feet. Mr Stein called the Post Office 'the nation's most untrustworthy brand' and its client organisation, the NFSP, contractually 'fettered' – that is, obliged to support the Post Office, not its members. He told the judges, 'I doubt if any one of us has ever seen an entire system which embodies the victim, the brand and the prosecutor warped against its users, and those it prosecuted, to such a degree.'

Whilst quoting liberally from the two Fraser judgments, Stein made the point that Mr Justice Fraser, in the civil litigation, was not in possession of the information which had been made available to the criminal court through the Peters and Peters review.

'If he had the material we have,' said Stein, 'his comments – already demonstrating an elegant and descriptive damning of the Post Office – would have spirited him into a further call for those responsible for concealing the true extent of the faults of the Post Office to go into a handy police station as quickly as possible.'

Sam Stein then went into specifics. In the course of doing so he publicly revealed the existence of the second Clarke Advice. You will remember this is the document written by the barrister Simon Clarke in 2013, telling the Post Office its instructions to shred material relating to problems with Horizon was almost certainly perverting the course of justice.

Stein told the court, 'The Post Office's reaction to the attempt to set up a system that might possibly deal with disclosure is one of dishonesty. It is one of destruction of documents.'

Whilst I have been able to slot the existence of the Clarke Advices into their chronological context for the purposes of this book, the existence of the first Clarke Advice (regarding disclosure) had only been known outside the Post Office since November 2020. Now, in March 2021, we were being told there was a 'shredding' Clarke Advice too. Sitting in court, I again had one of those moments where I couldn't believe what I was hearing. *The Post Office had ordered the shredding of documents?!*

As we were just about to break for lunch on the first day, Sam Tobin from the Press Association leapt to his feet and asked Lord Justice Holroyde if he would allow the applicants' counsel to supply journalists with their skeleton arguments. Normally this would be a formality, but the paranoia surrounding proceedings since Flora Page and Paul Marshall's alleged contempt meant that documents which were usually handed over to journalists as a matter of course were no longer reaching us.

Lord Justice Holroyde acceded. 'There has been comprehensive reference to those documents,' he said. 'I just cannot imagine any objection to disclosure of them? I see lots of head movement indicating that is so.'

Seeing an opportunity, I stood up and asked if this now included the Clarke Advices. Before Holroyde could respond, Brian Altman butted in.

'My Lord, the Clarke Advice which has been referred to so far is the one of 2 August 2013; the one Mr Wallis is interested in is the one of 15 July 2013. I don't know if Mr Stein is coming to that this afternoon or not?'

Stein replied, 'I am and, if it assists the court, my own view is that they will be covered in such detail as they should be, then disclosed.'

Holroyde agreed. Finally, eight years after they should have been, the Clarke Advices were about to be made public.

After lunch, Lisa Busch QC rounded up the appellants' main arguments. She focused on the fact that the prosecution of so many people, using such obviously flawed methodology, by an organisation which was not concerned with fairness, was not just an affront to the people it prosecuted, but an affront to the court – to justice itself. This tack had been particularly effective in the hearing before Christmas, and she pursued it now.

'In category 2 cases,' said Ms Busch, 'the court is directly implicated and has a special constitutional responsibility to ensure the integrity of the criminal justice system is maintained.'

Persuading the court it was self-evident the Post Office had behaved in a way which was an affront to justice was just part of the battle. Ms Busch's role was to convince the judges it was their absolute duty to proactively go after any hint of it. She used a logic train.

'If the Post Office had acted with clean hands, the appellants would not have been prosecuted and the short step from that is the conclusion they should not, and should never have been prosecuted.'

Ms Busch summarised, 'In this case, the Post Office not only misled the appellants in the course of prosecuting them, they have also systematically misled the criminal courts, and have sought to mislead the civil courts in the group litigation.'

Once more, Mr Altman was on hand to pour cold water on these grandiose ideas. General findings about the courts' 'conscience' were a bit silly, he seemed to be saying, when 'abuse of process is a fact and time-sensitive exercise.'

Mr Altman said the Post Office accepted that lack of disclosure with regard to problems about Horizon had a material effect on the fairness of 39 of the 42 appellants in court (which, we should not forget, is a stunning admission in itself) but the Post Office did not, and would not, accept that in 35 of those 39 cases, on a fact-specific basis, what happened 'was so bad … that it made it an affront to the public conscience.'

Mr Justice Picken wanted to know if Mr Altman's argument was that, unless there was something specific to each appellant, then 'the material we have had described to us today, including the Clarke Advices, for instance, is just irrelevant?'

Not just each appellant's case, said Mr Altman, but also the time of the alleged Post Office abuse. The first Clarke Advice was written in 2013, and it was about Gareth Jenkins. It can only be of relevance to the Post Office cases, Altman contended, where Mr Jenkins gave evidence.

Over the course of the week's hearing, Mr Altman told the Court of Appeal it would have to decide whether it was just or fair to 'take a broad brush overview of everything that happened over 13 years and say that all those points cumulatively apply to every single case every time? Or does one have to look at each case to see … the impact of any individual facets of the argument?'

Mr Altman invited the judges to accept the latter point, that it *should* look at individual time and fact-specific issues as they applied to each case. As that was not possible within the confines of a four-day hearing, the court should not make a generic ruling on limb 2.

Tim Moloney countered this, saying, 'Of these cases where ground 1 has been conceded, there is nothing in any of them which would excuse the conduct of the respondent such as to preclude the finding of ground 2 abuse, because it is systemic. It is not simply a non-disclosure in one case, it is not simply a non-investigation in one case, it is systemic non-disclosure. It is systemic failure to investigate what should be obvious to any rational, responsible business.'

Mr Justice Picken took this up, asking if Mr Moloney was saying this 'amounts to … a degradation of the system, the criminal justice system?'

Mr Moloney was indeed. Between them, Moloney, Busch and Stein represented 38 appellants. One of the remaining four was Dawn O'Connell, whose story I had never come across before. I bumped into her brother Mark and son Matt, outside court. We got chatting and swapped numbers. Dawn was one of the three deceased appellants. She had died just a few months before she got the chance to clear her name. Her story is harrowing.

Dawn O'Connell's barrister was Ben Gordon, who spoke by video link. After two days of dry legal argument, Mr Gordon took the time to spell out exactly what the Post Office had done to his client. It was a straightforward submission, made at the end of a long day, but it stunned the court. I fancy it may have brought home to the judges the real world, human impact of the Post Office's actions. I have, with minor editing for clarity, reprinted Mr Gordon's submission to the court in full. He said:

> 'My Lord, Ms Dawn O'Connell is not here today, having passed away in September of last year. I myself never had the chance to meet Ms O'Connell. Her appeal against her conviction is advanced or continued in her son Matthew's name. Matthew O'Connell and Dawn's brother, Mark, as I understand it, are present in court today, next door, in the overflow court.
>
> 'In the years following her conviction in 2008, and the serving of her suspended sentence, Ms O'Connell's health, both physical and mental, declined dramatically. According to her family and loved ones, her personality also changed, irrevocably. She became increasingly isolated, ultimately reclusive, as described by her family, and struggled desperately to deal with the stigma of her conviction.
>
> 'She suffered with severe bouts of depression. She did receive treatment, medication and counselling, but she sunk inexorably into alcoholism. In her latter and final years, my Lord, I understand that Ms O'Connell made repeated attempts upon her own life. In September of last year, her body succumbed to the damage caused by her sustained abuse of alcohol and she died tragically at the age of 57.
>
> 'On behalf of her son, her brother, and all her surviving family

members and friends, I feel compelled to tender to the court their sincere regret and deep anguish that Dawn is not here today to hear her case being argued.

'Ms O'Connell's conviction dates back to August of 2008 and Harrow Crown Court, where, upon her own pleas of guilty, she was convicted of five counts of false accounting. One further count alleging theft of approximately £45,470 was ordered to lie on the file on the usual terms and was not proceeded with. A pre-sentence report was ordered and, a month later, in September, Ms O'Connell was sentenced to 12 months' imprisonment suspended for two years, with a requirement for the completion of 150 hours of unpaid work.

'Between 2000 and 2008, Ms Dawn O'Connell worked as a branch manager, a Post Office branch manager in Northolt. As with many others which are before the court today, Ms O'Connell's case was one in which the Horizon data was central, central to the prosecution and her conviction. The prosecution arose from an unexplained shortfall, or deficit on the system at her branch. When audited, Ms O'Connell reported the shortfalls and indicated that she was unable to explain the anomaly. Initially, as she explained, she had hoped that the error would correct itself, but over the ensuing months it grew and accumulated.

'Ultimately, having admitted falsifying the accounts in an attempt to conceal the deficit in the hope of preserving her job, she pleaded guilty to the offences of false accounting. Throughout the audit, throughout the investigation and throughout the prosecution, Ms O'Connell repeatedly and strenuously denied theft. As I have said, this count was left to lie on the file.

'As conceded by the respondent in relation to her appeal, there was no evidence of theft or any actual loss at her branch, as opposed to a Horizon generated shortfall. There was no other evidence to corroborate the Horizon data. On the contrary, evidence was collected from other employees which attested to Ms O'Connell's honesty and probity.

'As further conceded by the respondent in her case, no attempt was made by the Post Office, as private prosecutor, to obtain or interrogate the [underlying Horizon] data. There was no investigation into the integrity of the Horizon figures, and it is recognised that the appellant herself was severely limited in her ability to challenge the Horizon evidence and therefore that it was incumbent upon the Post Office to ensure that the reliability of the evidence was properly investigated and, my Lord, this was not done.

'The Post Office failed in its duty as a private prosecutor both to investigate properly the reliability of the system by obtaining and examining the data, and to disclose to the appellant or the court the full and accurate position in relation to the reliability of the system. No disclosure was forthcoming in Ms O'Connell's case, in relation to any concern or enquiry raised into the functionality of the system.

'Ms O'Connell's case file demonstrates that the focus of the investigation in her case was on proving how the accounts were falsified, which of course she had admitted, rather than examining the root cause of the shortfall. In fact, as it seems, no effort was made to identify or discover the actual cause of the shortfall or deficit. During the internal audit process, and her interviews under caution, Ms O'Connell raised the issues she had encountered with the system and its recurring anomalies. No investigation or disclosure followed.

'Ms O'Connell was a lady of hitherto good character, about whom people were, it seems, lining up to attest to her honesty and integrity. In the papers I have seen, I have counted somewhere in the region of 30 character statements, which I think were obtained on her behalf. It is conceded by the respondent that for these reasons it was not possible for Ms O'Connell's trial to be a fair one, thereby amounting to first category of abuse of process.

> 'However, as set out only a short while ago by Mr Moloney on behalf of his clients, and as set out in our skeleton argument, dated 21 January, we would respectfully submit that for the same set of reasons, or in respect of the same failures in the investigative and disclosure exercises, the prosecution against Ms O'Connell was rendered unconscionable, and that bringing it was an affront to the national conscience.
>
> 'Accordingly, my Lord, on her son Matthew's behalf, we respectfully invite the court to quash her conviction on both grounds, or both limbs of abuse of process.'

There was a tangible silence after Ben Gordon's contribution. Then Lord Justice Holroyde brought the day's proceedings to a close.

TRUE PROSECUTION NUMBER

The final day of the Court of Appeal hearing concerned the three Subpostmasters whose appeals the Post Office was resisting. Here Brian Altman went into detail about each of the cases to explain their alleged misdemeanours and spell out to the court why Horizon data was not essential to their prosecutions. The only reason the CCRC had felt able to make *any* referrals was by connecting the dots between Horizon's unreliability and that data's importance to a Post Office prosecution. If the Post Office could successfully break that connection, the convictions would almost certainly stand.

Stanley Fell was Sam Stein QC's client. Mr Fell is a pensioner and was, until his suspension and prosecution in 2007, a third-generation Post Office employee. He had run Newton Bergoland Post Office in Leicestershire from 1976 without a problem until Horizon arrived. Mr Fell was not comfortable with the Horizon system and required repeated extra training after it was installed. He also suffered unexplained discrepancies, which he had to make good.

Unfortunately, it seems that by the mid-2000s Mr Fell had also tied himself into a grocery contract which required him to shift £2,000 worth of stock each week. He ended up subsidising his retail business with money from the Post Office till, which is not allowed. His branch trading statement was not adjusted to record this, which was potentially illegal. After he raised issues about a lack of ready cash at his counter, the Post Office sent in an area manager. Mr Fell admitted 'borrowing' money from the Post Office till to buy stock for his shop. The court heard he told the manager 'he thought he would have been found out a while back.'

Without stopping to question what sort of master criminal would take money from his Post Office counter and then essentially report it to the Post Office, Stanley Fell was suspended and prosecuted for false accounting. Mr Fell pleaded guilty and wrote a note of contrition via his solicitors which said, 'I admit that I acted dishonestly in falsifying the monthly trading statement… I wish to confirm to the court that at no time did I intend to permanently deprive the Post Office of the monies in question. It was always my intention to pay back that which I had borrowed, as I now have. I didn't intend to steal the money.'

As I listened in court, I got the sense of a person who needed help rather than destroying and ruining, but maybe I'm soft. Mr Fell's statement to the court finished, 'The burden of my actions became so unbearable that I planned to end my life… I wish to offer the Post Office and my family an unreserved apology for my financial negligence but wish to reaffirm without prejudice that at no time have I sought to steal or defraud the Post Office of any stock or cash whilst in my custody. It has always been my intention to repay the money to the Post Office.'

Mr Altman told the court that the circumstances of this case had nothing to do with Horizon data. This was not about an unexplained shortfall in Mr Fell's accounts, but an explained one.

Similar scenarios played out with the other two appellants, Wendy Cousins and Neelam Hussain. The CCRC had contended Horizon data was 'essential' to their prosecutions. If it wasn't, little else mattered. The convictions would stand.

After the revelations of the first two days, the end of the week was less newsworthy, but it did throw up an interesting statistic – what was thought to be the final, confirmed number of Horizon-related prosecutions. The court was told the Post Office had prosecuted 736 people between 2000 and 2014 using Horizon evidence – down from the 900+ estimate which was made in May 2020, but still averaging out at just over one a week.

Intriguingly, the number of shortfall offences in the four years leading up to the introduction of Horizon had also changed.

When the Post Office responded to my FOI request in May 2020, they produced a chart which showed between 1996 and 1999 there were 86 prosecutions of Subpostmasters and other staff. Between 2000 and 2003 there were 242. This figure was used at the Court of Appeal by the appellants to draw attention to a big leap in prosecutions when Horizon was in use. Now the figures were different. The Post Office said the first Horizon prosecution was in 2000, but that in the four years leading up to that date, it had in fact prosecuted 163 people for possible shortfall-related offences.

This uplift in the number of pre-Horizon prosecutions made for a less dramatic difference between the pen-and-paper days and Horizon's arrival. There are all sorts of inferences you could draw from that – not least that there was a lot of account fiddling before Horizon came along and Horizon just helped expose it.[2] On closer inspection it looked like there was some smoke and mirrors at work. To arrive at its pre-Horizon total prosecutions, the Post Office said it had excluded all robbery and burglary prosecutions from the prosecution totals, but the numbers it ended up with were taken from a spreadsheet which, 'included a category of offences described as "other." It has not been possible to ascertain what offences this referred to and so they have been included as they may relate to shortfall cases.'

The hearing drew to an end. Judgment on the 42 cases in hand was reserved until 23 April 2021.

For the purposes of this book, I asked the Post Office for clarification about the 'other' category mentioned above. Following my request, Peters and Peters separated likely shortfall cases (for example, theft, false accounting, cash loss, audit shortage) and those which were likely not (for example, giro suppression, P&A fraud, overclaims, laundering, stock loss, allegations affecting the character), and concluded in the four years leading up to Horizon's introduction there were 68 'likely' shortfall-related convictions, and in the four years after Horizon's introduction there were 226.

Finally, more than ten years after the question was first asked, I can tell you Horizon's arrival brought about an immediate 232% increase in Post Office prosecutions of Subpostmasters for shortfall-related offences. The fact no one at the Post Office considered this strange suggests they did think (as my colleague Matt Bardo had posited in 2015) Horizon was merely identifying criminality which already existed within the system.

---

2 Or that the Post Office was already zealously over-prosecuting before Horizon arrived.

READ SIDES WITH BATES

Whilst we were waiting for the Court of Appeal's ruling, the Post Office chief executive Nick Read came out with the strangest of statements.

In a speech to senior staff about the scandal, Read announced that the number of applicants to the Historical Shortfall Scheme and the amount of money they were claiming was unexpected, and more than the Post Office could afford.

'The Post Office,' he said, 'simply does not have the financial resources to provide meaningful compensation.'

It would later transpire the Post Office guessed the total number of claims to the scheme would top out at £35m, and budgeted accordingly. By the time the scheme closed it had accepted 2,400 applications, 2,200 of which were claiming a total of £311m, with the remaining 200 still being assessed.

David Cavender's warnings about Alan Bates' civil claim being an 'existential threat' to the business were correct. As of April 2021, the Post Office ceased to be a going concern. Read's solution was to go to the Treasury.

'I am urging government to work with us,' he told staff, 'to find a way of ensuring that the funding needed for such compensation, along with the means to get it to those to whom it may become owed, is arranged as quickly and efficiently as possible.'

Then came the strange bit. 'We must ensure that all Postmasters affected by this scandal are compensated and compensated quickly.'

All Subpostmasters? Not just the ones on the Historical Shortfall Scheme, but the claimant group who settled with the Post Office at the High Court? Apparently so.

'Although the parties entered into a full and final settlement of the Group Litigation in good faith,' he continued, 'it has only become apparent through various news reports since quite how much of the total appears to have been apportioned to the claimants' lawyers and funders.'

Given the Post Office's litigation strategy appeared to be based on emptying the claimants' pockets as slowly and expensively as possible, it's hard to believe Mr Read hadn't guessed the likely destination of much of the settlement cash. Whatever, it meant the two men who had signed the

Bates v Post Office settlement agreement were now both saying it wasn't fit for purpose. Nick Read had lined up behind the Postmasters against the government.

Read told his staff the Post Office needed to, 'confront and face up to its recent past... We have to accept that it is the Post Office that caused what for some has been very deep pain... We failed.'

In his speech Mr Read also announced that the much-loathed Horizon IT system was on its way out, claiming:

'Ways of working with Postmasters will be underpinned by a new IT system which will be more user-friendly, easier to adapt for new products and services, and cloud-based, to ensure easy maintenance and ready interoperability with other systems.'

This was exactly the same bright new dawn offered by the Post Office back in the late nineties. At the time, Horizon was described as the biggest non-military IT system in Europe.

In his 2021 speech, Mr Read said Horizon's replacement will be 'among the biggest, if not the biggest, IT rollout in the country.'

Disconcerting echoes. I hope it works.

A week after Read's bizarre speech, Alan Bates wrote an opaque editorial for Computer Weekly, telling readers that the settlement agreement to *Bates v Post Office* was not actually a complete and final settlement. This was because, 'In trying to agree a settlement figure, the only issues that could be used to calculate a financial figure were based on those legal points we had won as part of the judgments in the two trials that had been held.'

There were, Bates said, a further eight points still to be contested as part of the litigation. He stopped short of saying whether or not he'll be going after the Post Office or the government to open them up, but concluded:

'When you see the Post Office, the Department for Business, Energy and Industrial Strategy (BEIS) and Her Majesty's Government bandying around the phrase "full and final settlement," in actuality they are only referring to the issues that formed part of the first two trials, although they would have you think everything had been addressed. Some people might think they were deliberately trying to mislead everyone.'

JUDGMENT DAY

I arrived at 8.06am and saw Wendy Buffrey first. She was standing on her own outside the Royal Courts of Justice, waiting patiently whilst Jo Hamilton was positioned in front of a camera, ready to be interviewed remotely by the BBC Breakfast presenters in Salford. It was a bright spring morning, which you could tell was going to develop into a gloriously sunny day. Thanks to the tall buildings which block out the sun to the east and south of the RCJ, we were in shadow.

Jo hadn't brought her coat and was suffering. After her interview I suggested to the BBC crew that if they wanted Jo for another live hit, they might like to sit her in the front of their satellite van so she could warm up. They immediately obliged and Jo jumped into the driver's seat, shivering. I went to get her a coffee.

Due to social distancing concerns, Subpostmasters had been discouraged from bringing too many friends and family to court. A gathering of more than 30 outside the gates of the Royal Courts of Justice could cause problems.

The only people allowed inside court were claimants, their legal teams and a few journalists. Many Subpostmasters brought friends or family who would have to wait out on the street, where an atmosphere was building. Karen Wilson had come down the night before from Worcestershire with her brother David where they met up with Karen's step-daughter Emma and Julian's older brother Trevor. Marion Holmes, Peter's widow, had got the train from Newcastle to Leeds from where her son drove her the rest of the way down. Marion is a gentle, white-haired woman in her seventies. We'd been exchanging emails for months, and it was a delight to finally meet her. Noel Thomas had a 5am start, getting the train from Bangor with his two children, Sian and Edwin. Scott Darlington drove down from Macclesfield and arrived with his brother Steve, giving me the opportunity to congratulate Steve in person for his authorship of Howe and Co's submission to the BIS Select Committee inquiry in 2015.[3] Seema brought Davinder up by train from Woking. Janet arrived the evening

---

[3] So good, I have quoted different sections of it in the 'Going In Hard' and 'Paula Vennells Speaks' chapters of this book.

before from Hull. She bowled up to the gates of the court in shades, looking very cool, with her equally glam niece and daughter. Alison Hall brought her husband Richard. Rubbina and Mohamed Shaheen introduced me to Mahebub Chatur, the man who took pity on them when he found them sleeping in a van.

Other members of the *Bates v Post Office* claimant group came in solidarity – I spotted Chris Head, Nicki Arch and Lee Castleton. Kamran Ashraf and Chris Trousdale, who previously had their convictions quashed at Southwark Crown Court, were also there to lend their support. It was great to see Chris and Kamran (with Siema at his side, as ever), smiling and looking relaxed.

I tried to gauge the mood among the appellants, but it was tricky. Given the travel involved, many of them were already running on fumes, and a common refrain was how badly everyone had slept. But there were smiles of recognition and greeting at the growing number of familiar faces.

TV crews from Sky and ITV tracked into view. Eleanor Shaikh unfurled her Support Our Subpostmasters banner and stood proudly outside court, giving the TV crews something to film and the snappers something to snap. Chris Head had a campaigning t-shirt, which the professional photographers made a lot of. Chris Trousdale was offering Justice for Subpostmasters Alliance face masks to all and sundry. He had also brought his own bright blue JFSA banner. I commented on his move into JFSA merchandise.

'It's pretty easy when you work in a print shop!' he laughed.

I left them to it and went inside. Wandering through the Great Hall, I found Seema, Janet and Tracy chatting with Lisa Busch and Olivia Davies. Seema gave me a big smile, but you could see the nerves fluttering around her expression. Janet, Tracy and Seema didn't have as much riding on the outcome as Stanley Fell, Wendy Cousins and Neelam Hussain, but they had stuck their necks out on limb 2, and were looking for vindication.

Noel Thomas, Vijay Parekh and Tom Hedges secured a place in the well of Court 4. Seema, Jo, Tracy, Alison Hall, Harjinder Butoy and Neelam Hussain were in the gallery. Janet Skinner, Scott Darlington, Marion Holmes and Matt O'Connell had places in Court 5. Wendy Buffrey was in Court 7 with Mohammed Rasul, Karen Wilson and Della Robinson. Many more waited outside. I climbed the steps to the jury box in Court 4 and started tweeting in anticipation of the judges' arrival.

At 10.30am, Holroyde, Picken and Farbey filed in. Lord Justice Holroyde began reading a summary of the judgment.

On ground 1, he said, the Post Office 'knew there were serious issues about the reliability of Horizon... Yet it does not appear that POL adequately considered or made relevant disclosure of problems with or concerns about Horizon in any of the cases at any point during that period. On the contrary, it consistently asserted that Horizon was robust and reliable.'

Holroyde said those at the Post Office concerned with prosecutions of Subpostmasters 'clearly wished to be able to maintain the assertion that Horizon data was accurate, and effectively steamrolled over any Subpostmaster who sought to challenge its accuracy.'

On ground 2, Holroyde announced, 'We conclude that the Post Office's failures of investigation and disclosure were so egregious as to make the prosecution of any of the "Horizon cases" an affront to the conscience of the court.'

In other words, all the Postmasters who succeeded on ground 1 had succeeded on ground 2. The court ruled, 'By representing Horizon as reliable, and refusing to countenance any suggestion to the contrary, the Post Office effectively sought to reverse the burden of proof: it treated what was no more than a shortfall shown by an unreliable accounting system as an incontrovertible loss, and proceeded as if it were for the accused to prove that no such loss had occurred.'

There was a sting in the tail. For the three Subpostmasters whose appeals hung in the balance, the judges concluded the reliability of Horizon data was *not* essential to the prosecution case. Their convictions were considered safe and would not be overturned.

I said a prayer for Stanley Fell, Wendy Cousins and Neelam Hussain. There was enough of a 'realistic possibility' for the CCRC to believe their convictions could be quashed, but there was not enough evidence to convince the Court of Appeal. I knew that in the media frenzy to come, they would be ignored and possibly forgotten. I had never met them, and have no idea what happened at their Post Offices, but this seemed like a painful way for them to find out their fate.

Holroyde finished by listing the appellants whose convictions had been quashed. Their prosecutions were an affront to the public conscience and an affront to the conscience of the court. They should never have been prosecuted. They are completely vindicated. They are:

Josephine Hamilton, Hughie 'Noel' Thomas, Allison Henderson, Alison Hall, Gail Ward, Julian Wilson (deceased), Jacqueline McDonald, Tracy Felstead, Janet Skinner, Scott Darlington, Seema Misra, Della Robinson, Khayyam Ishaq, Tom Hedges, Peter Holmes (deceased), Rubbina Shaheen, Damien Owen, Mohammed Rasul, Wendy Buffrey, Kashmir Gill, Barry Capon, Vijay Parekh, Lynette Hutchings, Dawn O'Connell (deceased), Carl Page, Lisa Brennan, William David Graham, Siobhan Sayer, Tim Burgess, Pauline Thomson, Nicholas Clark, Margery Williams, Tahir Mahmood, Ian Warren, David Yates, Harjinder Butoy, Gillian Howard, David Blakey and Pamela Lock.

As her name was read out, Tracy Felstead gave a small yelp of emotion from behind her mask, and the tears began to flow. Because of social distancing, Tracy was alone in court as when she was convicted in 2002. There was no one to give her a hug.

The full Court of Appeal judgment is far shorter than the two monsters Mr Justice Fraser produced at the High Court, but it still stretches to 51,136 words over 447 paragraphs. To summarise, Holroyde, Farbey and Picken ruled the Post Office had been doing Bad Things.

First they decided the two Clarke Advices suggested 'there was a culture, amongst at least some in positions of responsibility' at the Post Office of 'seeking to avoid legal obligations when fulfilment of those obligations would be inconvenient.'

The second Clarke Advice, don't forget, warned a 'failure to record and retain material' if taken partly or wholly in order to avoid future disclosure obligations 'may well amount to a conspiracy to pervert the course of justice.' The judges found the idea that a government-owned company should *in 2013* have to be warned about the legality of shredding documents in these circumstances and perverting the course of justice was 'extraordinary.'

Holroyde, Farbey and Picken also state: 'The Post Office knew that there were problems with Horizon. The Post Office knew that SPMs around the country had complained of inexplicable discrepancies in the accounts. The Post Office knew that different bugs, defects and errors had been detected well beyond anything which might be regarded as a period of initial teething problems. In short, the Post Office knew that there were serious issues about the reliability of Horizon.'

They conclude:

'The consistent failure of the Post Office to be open and honest about the issues affecting Horizon can in our view only be explained by a strong reluctance to say or do anything which might lead to other Subpostmasters knowing about those issues.'

As a crumb of comfort to the Post Office, the judges decided they were 'not persuaded' by the argument that the corruption stretched to any 'improper financial motivation' for pursuing prosecutions with 'a view to obtaining confiscation or compensation orders.'

Having handed down their conclusions, the judges departed. Still standing, everyone else began to file out. I looked across to Seema, who gave a little thumbs up as she left the public gallery above me. It was all over.

'Be kind!' murmured Brian Altman as I stepped down from the jury box. I raised my eyebrows and headed back outside into the mêlée.

Press scrums are largely predictable, but they can develop a strange dynamic. This particular one was hopelessly disorganised because of the COVID-inspired one-way system at the court gates, which meant the usual location for after-court media statements was blocked. The assembled TV crews were reluctant to suggest the Subpostmasters group together anyway – pictures of loads of Subpostmasters huddled in front of a bunch of microphone stands could see journalists accused of encouraging people to break social-distancing rules. Without any consensus on what to do, the whole thing became a free-for-all.

Harjinder Butoy didn't realise he was one of the first Subpostmasters to come out of court. He may have got something of a shock to see the faces yelling at him as he came down the steps with his family. His response was to burst into tears and hug his wife and father. As Harjinder made his way for the exit gate he was rushed by TV crews, photographers and journalists who stopped him from getting any further.

Wendy Buffrey didn't even get a chance to leave the building. She was called by her BBC local radio station as she left Court 7. As she waited to go on air, Wendy moved away from the people filing out of court to find somewhere quiet. I've listened to a recording of the interview. In it, Wendy's words take on an almost ethereal quality as they bounce off the RCJ's stone walls.

'I'm very tearful,' she told the presenter, between sobs. 'I can't believe it's all over… Nearly 14 years… It's horrendous we were all put in this position in the first place. It's just … how do you replace that time? It's just … *gone.*'

Wendy called the ruling a huge weight off her shoulders, and in the interview you can hear the relief, joy, sadness and anger tumbling out of her in waves. Crying freely, Wendy said she wanted to thank Alan Bates, Kay Linnell, her family, Freeths, Hudgells and her employer Andrew Taylor. Then she pulled herself up and said a little more clearly: 'Now all we need is for the people who are responsible for this to be held accountable.'

Outside, as more Subpostmasters were exiting the building, they found themselves backing up behind Harjinder, who was still trapped by the TV crews and reporters. On spotting more Subpostmasters coming up behind him, journalists began interviewing the newcomers through the iron railings. It was chaotic, but there was no danger. Not having any immediate broadcast commitments, I stood back and admired the mess. Ron Warmington and James Arbuthnot wandered into view, both grinning. Flora Page arrived and posed for souvenir victory photos with Janet, Seema and Tracy.

'We decided we had to fight it,' Janet triumphantly told reporters. 'We needed to prove it was an affront to the public conscience and we did. We smashed it!'

Eventually the snappers took control and corralled the appellants into place between the red and blue banners. Tom Hedges loudly popped the cork in a bottle of fizz and poured a plastic glass for Marion Holmes. As he did so, he addressed the assembled media:

'When I told my mother, who's 93, I was coming to court she said, "Get yourself down to Aldi and get some prosecco." She said, "Just remember your name is Hedges not Rothschild, so get prosecco, not Bollinger!" '

Noel Thomas paid tribute to the absent Alan Bates, who he called a 'rottweiler.'

Karen Wilson had once more brought Julian's ashes to court. She stood alongside her daughter and Julian's brother, holding a portrait of her husband. She was understandably very emotional, telling me she was 'speechless … crying with one eye, and happy with the other.' Karen wanted everyone to know the judgment proved 'that Julian was right.

That's the main thing. From the High Court, to here… He was right. And so were all the others.'

The multiple reporters did their jobs, and the scenes of jubilation and emotion found their way into millions of homes that day. The Post Office said it 'sincerely' apologised for 'serious failures' in its 'historical conduct of prosecutions of postmasters.' Paula Vennells said she was 'deeply saddened by the Subpostmasters' accounts' heard during the Court of Appeal proceedings, adding, 'I am truly sorry for the suffering caused to them as a result of the convictions which the Court of Appeal has today overturned.'

REDRESS AND ACCOUNTABILITY

By the Monday morning after Friday's ruling, what was left of Paula Vennells' career was toast.

She stepped down from the boards of Dunelm and Morrisons with immediate effect, and announced she would no longer be active within the Church of England, telling her flock, 'My involvement with the Post Office has become a distraction from the good work undertaken in the Diocese of St Albans and in the parishes I serve.'

The Communication Workers Union called for Vennells to be stripped of her CBE and demanded a criminal investigation into those at the Post Office 'who put these loyal Postmasters in this situation. No doubt many senior figures wish to run from this situation, but to do such a thing is unacceptable.'

Lord Arbuthnot agreed, saying, 'It is high time the police began to take a serious look at whether the Post Office management have been perverting the course of justice.'

With the appeals process out of the way, Flora Page and Paul Marshall attended a hearing at the Court of Appeal to see if they were going to be charged with contempt. A panel of judges put the idea out of its misery, leaving both barristers without a stain on their reputations.

Two weeks to the day after the Court of Appeal judgment was handed down, the Post Office said it was writing to 540 of what it was *now* saying was 738 people who had been prosecuted using Horizon evidence between 2000 and 20*15*,[4] with a view to 'helping' them consider making appeals. A further 100 cases were under consideration. It also quietly introduced a 'Review or Dispute' option to Horizon, which now appears on the screen between the 'Make good - cash' and 'Make good - cheque' buttons.

In May 2021 the government finally announced that Sir Wyn Williams' inquiry into the Post Office Horizon scandal would be put on a statutory footing. Witnesses could now be compelled to attend and cross-examined by a barrister. Documents can be subpoenaed.

Paul Scully became the first minister in nearly ten years of asking to give me an on-the-record interview. I was allocated 15 minutes.

---

4 It was previously thought the Post Office ceased to prosecute people using Horizon evidence in 2014.

I started by asking Mr Scully what it was that Paula Vennells had done to deserve her CBE. He said it was because 'the financial outlook of the Post Office considerably improved' during her tenure and 'that, as I understand was the basis of it.' So she had made the Post Office profitable. I asked about the other issues which were live throughout Vennells' tenure, including the miscarriages of justice, the cover-up, and the fact that the Post Office's move to profitability was done on the backs of Subpostmasters, who'd seen their pay shrink almost across the board whilst she was in charge.

Mr Scully said finding answers to those questions, particularly the 'Horizon situation,' as he put it, was 'exactly what Sir Wyn's inquiry is there to do.' Whether Vennells could or should be stripped of her CBE was a matter for the government's forfeiture committee. Scully declined to give an opinion on whether Vennells should lose her CBE but said it was 'good' that she had effectively withdrawn from public life.

On the subject of government accountability for the scandal, Scully told me all the civil servants who sat on the board of the Post Office were 'led to believe that the Horizon software was robust at all times.'

When I argued that the Post Office board had colluded to keep evidence of miscarriages of justice from MPs and campaigners, and that a senior government civil servant was sitting on the board when those decisions were taken, Scully told me, 'government is not above accountability.' I pushed him, and he told me Sir Wyn Williams could call who he wanted to the inquiry and no one – Post Office, NFSP, Fujitsu, civil servant or minister – would be able to hide.

For a good 12 months up to May 2021 the government had been repeating the mantra that the settlement agreement for Alan Bates' group of 555 Subpostmasters was 'full and final.' During our interview, Scully's position appeared to shift a bit. He said, 'I can't just pledge to step in at this moment in time. But I want to make sure that I can have good conversations with Alan Bates and the Postmasters within the 555, just as much as I want to have good conversations with other wronged Postmasters, because they need justice and they need fair compensation.'

Shortly afterwards, Mr Scully's handlers brought the conversation to an end. Since that interview, Alan Bates has had meetings with both Paul Scully and Sir Wyn. The first oral evidence sessions of the reformulated Williams inquiry are due to start in 2022.

I wondered if Paula Vennells might now feel ready to give me an interview, in my seventh year of asking. Speaking through her lawyers, she refused to talk to me directly, so I decided to go and see her.

I met a producer colleague at Bedford railway station on a blustery late spring day. We drove through the countryside in his ancient Land Rover to find Vennells' house. It didn't take long. As you might expect for someone who was paid nearly five million pounds over the course of her tenure as Post Office Chief Executive, the Reverend lives in a grand, rambling old cottage, set in perfectly manicured grounds. It is the sort of house Jo Hamilton had to clean to make ends meet.

We parked up on public land within sight of Vennells' drive to see if there were any signs of life. There was no one coming or going and we couldn't see any lights on. As dusk fell, we abandoned the Land Rover and traipsed towards the main property, past a lake and an enormous old barn. Vennells' house is set back to front – you approach it from the rear and the drive swings round towards the front of the building. From the lack of activity we'd observed I fully expected to find the place deserted. Then, a surprise. As I started to track towards the front door, I could see a room with some lights on. As our approach continued and our line of sight widened, I saw the room was a kitchen, and standing in it was Paula Vennells. We made eye-contact. Delighted to see she was home, I jogged up to the front door and knocked, announcing who I was and why I wanted to speak to her. No response. I knocked again, loudly. I walked back to the kitchen window. The lights had been switched off and the room was empty. Two untouched plates of what looked like pork chops and hot veg were steaming away in the semi-dark. What was Vennells doing now? Hiding?

I went back to the front door and knocked again. No response. I went round the house to another door and knocked there, hoping she could hear my polite but direct entreaties for an interview. I tried knocking on a third door and then gave up. My colleague and I walked back up the drive, rather disconsolately.

In London, on Friday 14 May, Parmod Kalia and Teju Adedayo finally got their convictions overturned at Southwark Crown Court. I was delighted for them both. On 19 July, a further twelve Subpostmasters had their convictions quashed at the Court of Appeal, including John Dickson, the Subpostmaster from Pleasley in Mansfield whose email had spurred me to stay with this story a decade previously. Mr Dickson told his local newspaper after his conviction he 'didn't want to leave the house for a very long time. I knew I was innocent – but I was so worried about what people thought of me.'

On 22 July, the government said it was going to make interim payments of up to £100,000 to Subpostmasters whose convictions had been quashed ahead of any final sum awarded through dispute resolution or the courts.

In August 2021, a full 17 months after opening its investigation, the Metropolitan police confirmed it had interviewed two former Fujitsu employees under caution in connection with the Post Office Horizon scandal. The investigation is ongoing.

There are already 63 people whose reputations have been restored through the courts. That means the *interim* compensation bill alone is guaranteed to be in the millions, but resolution seems a long way off – even for those who have had their convictions overturned. The lack of a definitive ruling on limb 2 in the Crown Court has emboldened the Post Office to refuse interim compensation payments to several Subpostmasters, which suggests it is spoiling for a fight over some of the malicious prosecution claims being prepared for the civil courts.

The Post Office's success in ensuring Stanley Fell, Wendy Cousins and Neelam Hussain's convictions were upheld has also set a precedent – it is currently opposing the appeals of a growing number of former Subpostmasters who have come forward in recent months. Roger Allen, who was prosecuted by the DWP using Horizon evidence, has been joined by three other appellants. The DWP lost its ability to prosecute people in 2012, so the respondent in the DWP cases is now the Crown Prosecution Service. The CPS has indicated it might not be happy to accept the same limb 2 finding which the Court of Appeal has acknowledged applies to the Post Office's actions, which signifies some potentially protracted legal skirmishes to come.

And don't forget the cost... by my conservative estimate, the Post Office and government have already spent, or committed to spend, around half a billion pounds fighting, investigating, mediating or compensating campaigning Subpostmasters. That's before any of those with quashed convictions get the full amount due to them.

While the wheels of state machinery slowly grind along, it can become easy to lose track of some of the fundamentals of this scandal. I hope this book, and the stories within it, can serve as a reminder.

Horizon was a badly-procured and atrociously-implemented IT disaster. It was operated in an environment where flawed and incompetent people were able to destroy people's lives without a shred of accountability.

I have no doubt most people at the Post Office still believe the NFSP's George Thomson was right when he described the campaigners' fight for justice as a 'cottage industry' by dishonest people 'chancing their luck.' Entrenched cultural belief does not simply disappear with a few apologies and a new chief executive.

In September 2021 I took part in a remote seminar for former Subpostmasters. It was chaired by Lord Arbuthnot, and set up to allow participants to talk about routes to accountability and the proper investigation of what or who enabled this scandal to happen. Many of the people present are named in this book, and it was good, if a little surreal, to see their faces lined up on a computer screen as the discussion took place. Those who spoke gave informative and constructive advice to the academics hosting the event. The anger, anguish and trauma which informed some of the contributions was visceral, and deeply affecting.

Proper redress for *all* the victims of this scandal is essential. The Prime Minister said as much to Tracy Felstead, Dionne Andre and Michael Rudkin when he held a private conversation with them on 30 April – seven days after the Post Office's 20 year prosecution campaign was ruled an affront to the conscience of the court. As for any individual being formally censured or punished for their role in causing, perpetuating or trying to cover-up the Great Post Office Scandal, well… I'm not going to hold my breath.

WHO'S WHO

Abdulla, Naushad	Subpostmaster, Charlton Post Office, London. Witness in the Common Issues trial *Bates v Post Office.*
Adedayo, Teju	Subpostmaster, Kent. Conviction for false accounting quashed on 14 May 2021.
Allan, Lucy MP	Tracy Felstead's MP.
Allen, Nigel	Post Office employee. Pam Stubbs' former contract manager.
Allen, Roger	Subpostmaster prosecuted by the Department for Work and Pensions using Horizon evidence.
Altman, Brian QC	Barrister who acted for the Post Office at the Court of Appeal 2020-2021. Wrote General Review of prosecutions for the Post Office in October 2013.
Andre, Dionne	Subpostmaster of two Post Offices in South Shields. Threatened with prosecution for fraud by the Post Office.
Arbuthnot, Lord (James)	Campaigning politician. Former MP for North East Hampshire (Jo Hamilton's constituency). Now Lord Arbuthnot of Edrom.
Arch, Nicki	Post Office manager, Stroud, Gloucs. Prosecuted for theft, fraud and false accounting. Jury found her not guilty.
Ashraf, Kamran	Post Office manager, Hampstead, London. Siema Kamran's husband.
Aujard, Chris	Post Office Interim General Counsel from November 2013 to January 2015.
Bailey, Adrian MP	Chaired the 2015 BIS Select Committee inquiry into the Post Office Mediation Scheme.
Bajaj, Amar	Subpostmaster who was featured in Computer Weekly's groundbreaking investigation in 2009.
Baker, Colin	General Secretary of the National Federation of Subpostmasters (NFSP) 1991-2007.
Baker, Mark	Serving Postmaster. National Executive Officer of the NFSP from 2001 to 2010. Now CWU National Organiser for Subpostmasters.

Baker, Simon	Senior project manager at the Post Office. Left in September 2013.
Baker, Simon QC	Barrister working for the Post Office.
Baker, Sue	Time to Change's global director.
Barang, Jasvinder	Subpostmaster, convicted of fraud. Conviction quashed at Southwark Crown Court on 11 December 2020.
Bardo, Matt	Senior producer, BBC Panorama.
Bates, Alan	Subpostmaster, Craig-y-Don. Founder of the Justice for Subpostmasters Alliance (JFSA). Lead claimant in *Bates v Post Office*. Strategic genius.
Beal, Nick	Post Office Head of Agents' Development and Remuneration.
Bell, Peter	Activist who obtained the *Bates v Post Office* settlement agreement via FOI.
Bentwood, Richard	Barrister who represented Flora Page at the Court of Appeal.
Binley, Brian MP	Member of the BIS Select Committee in 2015 who was involved in the inquiry into the Post Office Mediation Scheme.
Bloom, Hayley	Detective Sergeant from the Metropolitan Police tasked with investigating Fujitsu employees.
Bourke, Patrick	Post Office Government and Policy Affairs Director.
Brennan, Lisa	Post Office counter clerk from Merseyside. Convicted of theft. Conviction quashed at Court of Appeal on 23 April 2021.
Bridgen, Andrew MP	Campaigning politician. Michael Rudkin's MP.
Bristow, David	Subpostmaster, Odiham, Hants. Appeared in 2011 BBC Inside Out South broadcast.
Brooks, Richard	Private Eye journalist. Co-author of the 2020 Private Eye Special Report 'Justice Lost in the Post.'
Brown, Alan	Subpostmaster, Callendar Square, Falkirk. Featured in Computer Weekly's groundbreaking investigation in 2009.

Brown, Tom	Subpostmaster whose prosecution was dropped following Second Sight's interim report.
Buffrey, Doug	Wendy Buffrey's husband.
Buffrey, Wendy	Subpostmaster, Up Hatherley, Glos. Conviction quashed at Court of Appeal on 23 April 2021.
Burgess, Tim	Subpostmaster, convicted of false accounting at Teesside Crown Court. Conviction quashed at Court of Appeal on 23 April 2021.
Burgess-Boyde, Sarah	Subpostmaster, Starbeck Avenue branch, Newcastle. Sacked, charged with theft. The Post Office prosecution against her collapsed when they offered no evidence.
Busch, Lisa QC	Barrister who represented Seema Misra, Tracy Felstead and Janet Skinner after Paul Marshall stood down.
Butoy, Harjinder	Subpostmaster, Sutton-in-Ashfield, Notts. Sent to prison. Conviction quashed at Court of Appeal on 23 April 2021.
Cable, Sir Vince	Secretary of State at BIS from 2010 to 2015.
Callanan, Lord	BEIS minister in the House of Lords from 2020.
Cameron, Alisdair	Post Office Chief Financial Officer, acting CEO for the middle part of 2019.
Capon, Barry	Subpostmaster convicted of false accounting. Conviction quashed at Court of Appeal on 23 April 2021.
Carter, Julie	Subpostmaster, Newcastle-Upon-Tyne. Featured in Neil Tweedie's Daily Mail piece 25 April 2015.
Cash, Andy	Simon Clarke's former colleague at Cartwright King.
Castleton, Lee	Subpostmaster, Bridlington, Yorkshire. Sued by the Post Office at the County and High Courts. Indefatigable campaigner.
Caveen, Jayne	Martin Griffiths' sister.
Cavender, David QC	Barrister. Post Office lead counsel during the Common Issues trial *Bates v Post Office*.
Chatur, Mahebub	Forensic accountant who helped and advised Mohamed and Rubbina Shaheen.

Clark, Nicolas	Subpostmaster. Convicted of false accounting at Grimsby Crown Court. Conviction quashed at Court of Appeal on 23 April 2021.
Clarke, Simon	Former senior criminal barrister at Cartwright King.
Cleife, Julie	Subpostmaster, Over Wallop, Hants. Convicted of fraud. Conviction quashed at Southwark Crown Court on 11 December 2020.
'Clint'	Fujitsu Horizon Development Manager 1998-1999. Clint is not his real name.
'Colin'	Post Office communication and marketing exec. Colin is not his real name.
Collins, Tony	Former Editor, Computer Weekly. Commissioned the first piece of investigative journalism into Post Office's Horizon IT scandal.
Connolly, Deirdre	Subpostmaster, Killeter, Co Tyrone. Sacked and forced to make good a £15,000 discrepancy.
Cooper, Joe	Camera operator for the first Panorama programme in 2015.
Coulson, Lord Justice	Court of Appeal judge who heard the appeals against the recusal and Common Issues judgment.
Cousins, Wendy	Subpostmaster referred to the Court of Appeal by the Criminal Cases Review Commission. Her appeal failed.
Coyne, Jason	Claimants' independent IT expert who investigated Horizon for *Bates v Post Office.*
Craddock, Jenny	Former BBC Inside Out South producer.
Crichton, Susan	Post Office's General Counsel until 2013.
Croft, Jane	Financial Times court reporter.
Dar, Louise	Subpostmaster, Lenzie, Glasgow. A lead witness in the Common Issues trial, *Bates v Post Office.*
Darlington, Scott	Subpostmaster, Alderley Edge, Cheshire. Prosecuted for false accounting. Conviction quashed at Court of Appeal on 23 April 2021.
Davies, Mark	Post Office Director of Communications between 2012 and 2019.

Davies, Olivia	Barrister assisting Lisa Busch QC.
Davison, Margaret	Subpostmaster, West Boldon, South Tyneside.
de Garr Robinson, Anthony QC	Barrister. Post Office lead counsel in Horizon trial, *Bates v Post Office*.
Dickinson, Helen	Post Office fraud investigator. Witness in Common Issues trial, *Bates v Post Office*.
Dickson, John	Subpostmaster, Pleasley, Notts.
Dinsdale, Mark	Post Office security team.
Donnelly, Kathleen	Barrister, Henderson Chambers.
Duncan, Lord	Lord Callanan's predecessor as the BEIS Business Minister.
Dunks, Andy	Fujitsu, IT Security Analyst.
Falconer, Lord (Charlie)	Labour party grandee and former Lord Chancellor.
Farbey, Mrs Justice	One of the judges in *Hamilton v Post Office* at the Court of Appeal.
Fell, Stanley	Subpostmaster, Newton Bergoland, Leics. Referred to the Court of Appeal by the CCRC. His appeal failed.
Felstead, Tracy	Crown Office worker, Camberwell Green, London. Sent to prison. Conviction quashed at Court of Appeal on 23 April 2021.
Flinders, Karl	Computer Weekly staff journalist.
Fontaine, Senior Master	High Court judge presiding over the GLO application in January 2017.
Ford, Julie	Subpostmaster, Yeovil, Somerset. Bankrupted. Featured in Computer Weekly's groundbreaking investigation in 2009.
Fowles, Dr Sam	Barrister assisting Lisa Busch QC.
Fraser, Mr Justice (Peter)	Managing judge at the High Court group litigation *Bates v Post Office*.
French, Jane	Former BBC Inside Out South editor.
Furey, Andy	CWU, Assistant Secretary.

Furniss, Gill MP	Former chair of the All Party Parliamentary Group (APPG) on Post Offices.
Gahir, Rajinder	Post Office auditor who visited Pam Stubbs.
Garrard, Roch	Retired probation officer who spotted the link between the Post Office stories of Noel Thomas and Jo Hamilton.
Gilhooly, Donna	Post Office Chairman and Chief Executive's Correspondence Manager.
Gill, Bal	Subpostmaster, Cowley Road, Oxford. Kashmir's son.
Gill, Kashmir	Subpostmaster, Cowley Road, Oxford. Prosecuted for false accounting. Conviction quashed at Court of Appeal on 23 April 2021.
Glover, Amanda	Shoosmiths partner.
Goddard, Jane	BBC South film-maker.
Godeseth, Torstein	Fujitsu's Chief Architect on Horizon.
Gordon, Ben	Barrister acting for Dawn O'Connell.
Gould, Nick	Aria Grace Law partner. Solicitors acting for Seema Misra, Tracy Felstead and Janet Skinner at the Court of Appeal.
Grabiner, Lord	Barrister. One Essex Court's Head of Chambers, instructed to represent Post Office at the recusal hearing.
Graham, William David	Subpostmaster. Convicted of false accounting at Maidstone Crown Court. Conviction quashed at Court of Appeal on 23 April 2021.
Green, Patrick QC	Barrister, Henderson Chambers. Lead counsel for claimants throughout *Bates v Post Office* group litigation.
Greene, David	Partner at Edwin Coe solicitors.
Greenhill, Sam	Daily Mail Chief Reporter.
Greenhow, Calum	NFSP, Chief Executive. George Thomson's successor.
Griffiths, Gina	Martin Griffiths' widow.
Griffiths, Martin	Subpostmaster, Hope Farm Road, Wallasey. Martin took his own life in September 2013.
Griffiths, Matt	Martin Griffiths' son.

Hadrill, Keith	Barrister. Seema Misra's counsel.
Hall, Alison	Subpostmaster, Hightown, West Yorkshire. Convicted of fraud at Leeds Crown Court. Conviction quashed at Court of Appeal on 23 April 2021.
Hami, Mohamed	Rubbina Shaheen's husband.
Hamilton, David	Jo Hamilton's husband.
Hamilton, Jo	Subpostmaster, South Warnborough, Hampshire. Convicted of theft. Conviction quashed at Court of Appeal on 23 April 2021. JFSA stalwart.
Harrison, Sian	PA Media. Editor, Law Service.
Hartley, James	Freeths partner, litigation and dispute resolution specialist.
Head, Andy	BBC Panorama executive producer, Northern Ireland unit.
Hedges, Tom	Subpostmaster, Hogsthorpe, Lincs. Prosecuted for false accounting. Conviction quashed at Court of Appeal on 23 April 2021.
Henderson, Allison	Subpostmaster, Worstead, Norfolk. Convicted of false accounting. Conviction quashed at Court of Appeal on 23 April 2021.
Henderson, Ian	Second Sight, director.
Henry, Edward QC	Barrister who represented Flora Page at the Court of Appeal.
Hill, Max QC	Director of Public Prosecutions.
Hogg, Issy	Solicitor (previously with Coomber Rich). Acted for Jo Hamilton and Seema Misra.
Hollinrake, Kevin	Co-chair, APPG on Fair Business Banking.
Holmes, Peter	Subpostmaster, Jesmond, Newcastle-upon-Tyne. Conviction posthumously quashed at Court of Appeal on 23 April 2021.
Holmes, Marion	Peter Holmes' widow.
Holroyde, Lord Justice	Senior judge presiding over *Hamilton v Post Office* Court of Appeal hearing.

Hooper, Sir Anthony	Retired Court of Appeal judge who chaired the Mediation Scheme Working Group.
Howard, Gillian	Subpostmaster, New Mill, West Yorkshire. Convicted of fraud at Bradford Crown Court. Conviction quashed at Court of Appeal on 23 April 2021.
Hudgell, Dr Neil	Hudgell Solicitors' Executive Chairman. Represents dozens of Subpostmasters seeking to have their convictions overturned.
Humphrys, John	Former BBC Today programme presenter.
Hussain, Neelam	Manager, West Bromwich Post Office. Convicted of theft. Referred to the Court of Appeal by the CCRC. Her appeal failed.
Hutchings, Lynette	Subpostmaster. Convicted of false accounting at Portsmouth Crown Court. Conviction quashed at Court of Appeal on 23 April 2021.
Irranca-Davies, Huw MP	Member of the APPG on Post Offices.
Ishaq, Khayyam	Subpostmaster, Birkenshaw, West Yorkshire. Convicted of theft at Bradford Crown Court. Conviction quashed at Court of Appeal on 23 April 2021.
Ismay, Rod	Post Office Head of Product and Branch Accounting at the time Horizon Online was rolled out in 2010.
Jenkins, Gareth	Fujitsu Horizon System Architect.
Johnson, Boris	Prime Minister from July 2019 to present.
Jones, Bryn	BBC Journalist who has investigated several Subpostmaster stories. Worked on the Taro Naw investigations into the Horizon IT system.
Jones, Darren MP	BEIS Select Committee chair. Former solicitor.
Jones, David MP	Alan Bates' MP and member of the APPG on Post Offices.
Jones, Dylan	BBC journalist, former presenter of Taro Naw.
Jones, Kevan MP	Member of the APPG on Post Offices.
Kalia, Parmod	Subpostmaster, Orpington, Kent. Theft conviction quashed at Southwark Crown Court in May 2021.

Kamran, Siema	Subpostmaster, Hampstead, London. Kamran Ashraf's wife.
Knight, Nigel	Sue Knight's husband.
Knight, Sue	Subpostmaster, St Keverne, Cornwall. Prosecution dropped following Second Sight's interim report.
Latif, Adrees	Subpostmaster, Caddington, Bedfordshire. Lead witness Horizon trial, *Bates v Post Office*.
Lawrence, Patrick QC	Barrister who represented Paul Marshall at the Court of Appeal.
Letwin, Oliver MP	Tracey Merritt's MP.
Lewell-Buck, Emma MP	Kevin and Julie Carter's and Dionne Andre's MP.
Lilley, Peter MP	Secretary of State for Business in 1996.
Linnell, Kay	Forensic accountant who works with Alan Bates. Claimants' steering committee member during the *Bates v Post Office* litigation.
Lock, Pamela	Subpostmaster, Cwmdu, Swansea. Convicted of false accounting. Conviction quashed at Court of Appeal on 23 April 2021.
Lohrasb, Sio	Former Fujitsu technical lead, responsible for the live rollout of Horizon.
Longman, Jon	Post Office security team investigator.
Lyons, Alwen OBE	Former Post Office Company Secretary.
Mandelson, Peter MP	Former Secretary of State for Business, Innovation and Skills.
Manning, Frank	Post Office manager who visited Pam Stubbs' branch.
Marshall, Paul	Barrister. Worked with Flora Page and Aria Grace Law representing Seema Misra, Tracy Felstead and Janet Skinner.
Martin, Wendy	Subpostmaster, Crichton Lane, York. Claimant in *Bates v Post Office*.
McCormack, Tim	Blogger and former Subpostmaster.

McDonald, Jackie (Jacqueline)	Subpostmaster, Broughton, Lancs. Sentenced to 18 months in prison. Conviction quashed at Court of Appeal on 23 April 2021.
McFadden, Pat MP	Postal Affairs Minister at the Department for Business, Innovation and Skills in 2010.
McLachlan, Professor Charles	Independent IT expert appointed by Seema Misra's defence team.
Meggitt, Graham	BBC Wales cameraman.
Membury, William	Fujitsu Central Quality Partner.
Merritt, Tracey	Subpostmaster, Yetminster, Dorset. Prosecuted for false accounting. Case collapsed. Claimant in *Bates v Post Office*.
Miliband, Ed MP	Shadow Secretary of State for BEIS. Former Labour leader.
Misra, Davinder	Seema Misra's husband.
Misra, Seema	Subpostmaster, West Byfleet, Surrey. Sent to prison in 2010. Conviction quashed at Court of Appeal on 23 April 2021.
Moloney, Tim QC	Barrister representing Hudgell Solicitors' appellants.
Murray, Ian MP	Participated in the Westminster Hall debate in December 2014.
Murray, Pete	Postmaster at Grove Road in Wallasey. Became Martin Griffiths' successor at Hope Farm Road, Great Sutton.
Nicholson, Bob	Great Post Office Trial series producer.
Norris, Adrian	Post Office auditor who visited Seema Misra's branch.
Noverre, Keith	Post Office auditor who visited Seema Misra's branch.
Oates, Graham	Subpostmaster who attended JFSA inaugural meeting in 2009.
O'Connell, Dawn	Subpostmaster, Northolt, London. Convicted of false accounting. Conviction posthumously quashed at Court of Appeal on 23 April 2021.
O'Connell, Mark	Dawn O'Connell's brother.
O'Connell, Matt	Dawn O'Connell's son.

Osborne, Kate MP	Elicited promise of public inquiry from Boris Johnson.
Owen, Albert MP	Participated in the Westminster Hall debate in December 2014.
Owen, Les	Post Office non-executive director in 2012.
Page, Carl	Subpostmaster, Rugeley, Staffs. Convicted of theft at Stafford Crown Court. Conviction quashed at Court of Appeal on 23 April 2021.
Page, Flora	Barrister who worked with Paul Marshall and Aria Grace Law representing Seema Misra, Tracy Felstead and Janet Skinner.
Page, Lewis	Journalist. Flora Page's brother.
Parekh, Vijay	Subpostmaster, Willesden, London. Convicted of theft. Conviction quashed at Court of Appeal on 23 April 2021.
Parker, Stephen	Fujitsu's Head of Post Office Application Support.
Parker, Tim	Post Office Chairman from 2015 to present.
Patel, Sandip QC	Barrister acting for Kamran Ashraf and Vijay Parekh at the Court of Appeal.
Patel, Vipin	Subpostmaster, Horspath, Oxon. Convicted of false accounting and fraud. Conviction quashed at Southwark Crown Court on 11 December 2020.
Perkins, Alice	Post Office Chairman from 2012 to 2015.
Phillips, Dawn	Post Office Team Leader for Agent Accounting. Witness in the Common Issues trial *Bates v Post Office*.
Picken, Mr Justice	One of the judges in *Hamilton v Post Office* at the Court of Appeal.
Pooler, Michael	Financial Times journalist.
Prodger, Matt	BBC's former Social Affairs correspondent.
Putland, Rob	Fujitsu, Senior Vice-President, Head of Global Legal and Commercial.
Randall, Imogen	Freeths, Senior Associate.
Rasul, Mohammed	Subpostmaster. Convicted of theft at Manchester Crown Court. Conviction quashed at Court of Appeal on 23 April 2021.

Read, Nick	Post Office Chief Executive since 2019. Successor to Paula Vennells.
Rees-Mogg, Jacob MP	Leader of the House of Commons since July 2019.
Ridge, Elaine	Post Office Network Contract Advisor.
Robinson, Anna Marie	BBC Journalist who has investigated several Subpostmaster stories. Worked on the Taro Naw investigations into the Horizon IT system.
Robinson, Della	Subpostmaster, Dukinfield, Manchester. Convicted of false accounting. Conviction quashed at Court of Appeal on 23 April 2021.
Robinson, Tim	BBC Panorama journalist and former Inside Out producer.
Rodgers, Shann	Subpostmaster, Goldsithney, Cornwall. Gave evidence to Sir Wyn Williams' inquiry in 2021.
Rolfe, Martin	Fujitsu staff member who gave Michael Rudkin a tour of Fujitsu HQ in Bracknell, Berkshire.
Roll, Richard	Fujitsu Horizon technical support operator from 2001 to 2004. Whistleblower.
Rozenberg, Joshua	Legendary legal journalist.
Rudkin, Michael	Subpostmaster, Ibstock, Leics. Former member of NFSP Executive Committee. Wife, Susan, prosecuted for false accounting.
Rudkin, Susan	Post Office manager, Ibstock, Leics. Convicted of false accounting. Conviction quashed at Southwark Crown Court 11 December 2020.
Sabir, Mohammad	Subpostmaster of two branches in Bingley, West Yorkshire. Terminated by Post Office. Lead witness in Common Issues trial, *Bates v Post Office*.
Sayer, Siobhan	Subpostmaster, Erpingham, Norfolk. Convicted of fraud at Norwich Crown Court. Conviction quashed at Court of Appeal on 23 April 2021.
Scott, John	Post Office Head of Security from 2006 to 2016.
Scully, Paul MP	Postal Affairs Minister from 2020 to present.
Sercombe, Suzanne	Alan Bates' partner.
Sewell, Lesley	Post Office Chief Information Officer in 2012.

Shaheen, Rubbina	Subpostmaster, Greenfields, Shrewsbury. Convicted of false accounting and sent to prison. Conviction quashed at Court of Appeal on 23 April 2021.
Shaikh, Eleanor	Campaigner and activist. Customer of Chirag Sidhpura's at Farncombe Post Office.
Sidhpura, Chirag	Manager, Farncombe Post Office, Surrey. Former Subpostmaster.
Simpson, Alan	Post Office security team member.
Singh, Jarnail	Post Office senior criminal lawyer.
Singh, Nippi	NFSP official.
Skinner, Janet	Post Office manager, Bransholme, Hull. Sent to prison for false accounting. Conviction quashed at Court of Appeal on 23 April 2021.
Smith, Dave	Post Office's Managing Director at the time Horizon Online was rolled out in 2010.
Smith, Jacqui MP	Raised issue of problems with Horizon in parliament in 2010.
Smith, Martin	Simon Clarke's colleague at Cartwright King.
Smith, Sandy	BBC One Show Executive Editor from 2010 to 2019.
Spackman, Conor	BBC Panorama researcher in 2015.
Stanley, Peter	Post Office exec in 2010.
Stein, Sam QC	Barrister representing several Subpostmasters at the Court of Appeal.
Stockdale, Liz	Subpostmaster, Sandsacre, East Yorkshire. Terminated by the Post Office. A lead witness in Common Issues trial *Bates v Post Office.*
Storey, Susannah	Government appointed Post Office director who also sat on the ad-hoc Post Office board sub-committee set up to deal with the Horizon issues in 2013.
Stubbs, Martin	Pam Stubbs' husband.
Stubbs, Pam	Subpostmaster, Barkham, near Wokingham, Berkshire. A lead witness in the Common Issues trial, *Bates v Post Office.*
Sturgess, Geoffrey	Franchise lawyer.

Sweeney, John	Journalist, reporter and author. Presented first Panorama film on the Post Office Horizon Scandal called Trouble at the Post Office.
Sweetman, Stuart	Post Office Managing Director in 1996.
Swinson, Jo MP	Minister for Postal Affairs at the Business, Innovation and Skills Department 2012-2015.
Tatford, Warwick	Barrister for the Post Office in Seema Misra's trial.
Taylor, Her Honour Judge (Deborah)	Judge who quashed Subpostmasters' convictions at Southwark Crown Court.
Tecwyn, Sion	BBC Wales Taro Naw reporter and presenter.
Thomas, Eira	Noel Thomas' wife.
Thomas, (Hughie) Noel	Subpostmaster, Gaerwen, Anglesey. Sent to prison for false accounting. Conviction quashed at Court of Appeal on 23 April 2021.
Thomson, George	NFSP General Secretary 2007-2016. NFSP Chief Executive 2016-2018.
Thomson, Pauline	Subpostmaster, Matfield, near Tunbridge Wells, Kent. Convicted of false accounting. Conviction quashed at Court of Appeal on 23 April 2021.
Thomson, Rebecca	Journalist who broke the story of the Post Office Horizon scandal in Computer Weekly in May 2009.
Tobin, Sam	Journalist, PA Media.
Tolhurst, Kelly MP	BEIS minister 2018-2020.
Trousdale, Chris	Subpostmaster, Whitby, North Yorkshire. Convicted of false accounting. Conviction quashed at Southwark Crown Court on 11 December 2020.
Turner, Karl MP	Janet Skinner's former solicitor.
Tweedie, Neil	Daily Mail journalist.
Valters, Jon	BBC Inside Out South producer.
van den Bogerd, Angela	Post Office exec.
Vennells, Paula	Post Office Chief Executive 2012 to 2019.
Verity, Andy	BBC's economics correspondent.

Wagstaff, Caroline	Luther Pendragon, Freeths' PR firm.
Wakely, Mike	Alan Bates' area manager.
Walker, Janet	James Arbuthnot's Chief of Staff.
Ward, Gail	Subpostmaster, Wells, Somerset. Convicted of false accounting. Conviction quashed at Court of Appeal on 23 April 2021.
Warmington, Ron	Second Sight Managing Director.
Warren, Ian	Subpostmaster, Hedingham, Essex. Convicted of theft. Conviction quashed at Court of Appeal on 23 April 2021.
Williams, Paul	Post Office Restrictions Advisor.
Williams, Rachel	Subpostmaster.
Williams, Sir Wyn	Retired judge appointed to oversee the statutory inquiry into the Post Office scandal.
Wilson, Julian	Subpostmaster, Astwood Bank, Redditch, Worcs. Convicted of false accounting. Conviction posthumously quashed at Court of Appeal on 23 April 2021.
Wilson, Karen	Julian Wilson's widow.
Wilson, Rob	Post Office prosecutor, rising to Head of Criminal Law team by 2010.
Witherow, Tom	Daily Mail Business Correspondent.
Withers, Jim	Subpostmaster, Cromer, Norfolk. Appeared in Neil Tweedie's Daily Mail article in 2015.
Wood, Mike MP	Participated in the Westminster Hall debate in December 2014.
Worden, Dr Robert	Post Office independent IT expert who investigated Horizon for *Bates v Post Office*.
Wyllie, Kim	Subpostmaster whose prosecution was stopped immediately following the publication of Second Sight's first report.
Yates, David	Subpostmaster convicted of theft at Guildford Crown Court. Conviction quashed at Court of Appeal on 23 April 2021.
Zahawi, Nadhim MP	BIS Select Committee – 2015.

TIMELINE

1994

August
Government tenders £1bn PFI contract to create swipe-card system for the Benefits Agency and the Post Office.

1996

May
Fujitsu/ICL win the contract.

1997

September
Scheduled trial rollout abandoned.

November
Benefits Agency and the Post Office serve Fujitsu with a formal notice of breach of contract.

1998

January
Benefits Agency abandons Horizon project.

April
Post Office assumes full line management of Horizon project.

May
Alan Bates takes over Craig-y-Don Post Office.

June
Government commissions an independent review of the Horizon project.

December
Fujitsu demand a renegotiation of the Horizon contract.

1999

October
Horizon rollout begins.

2000

Prosecution of Subpostmasters using Horizon evidence begins.

The Post Office secures the criminal conviction of six people using Horizon evidence.

2001

January
Richard Roll joins Fujitsu.

The Post Office secures the criminal conviction of 41 people using Horizon evidence.

2002

The Post Office secures the criminal conviction of 64 people using Horizon evidence.

2003

August
Alan Bates is given three months' notice.

The Post Office secures the criminal conviction of 56 people using Horizon evidence.

2004

Alan Bates sets up the Post Office Victims website.

The Post Office secures the criminal conviction of 59 people using Horizon evidence.

2005

The Post Office removes the branch suspense option from Horizon.

The Post Office secures the criminal conviction of 68 people using Horizon evidence.

2006

The Post Office secures the criminal conviction of 69 people using Horizon evidence.

2007

January
The Post Office takes Lee Castleton to the High Court. He is bankrupted.

The Post Office secures the criminal conviction of 50 people using Horizon evidence.

2008

August
Michael Rudkin, Subpostmaster at Ibstock, visits Fujitsu HQ.

The Post Office secures the criminal conviction of 48 people using Horizon evidence.

2009

May
Computer Weekly publishes Rebecca Thomson's investigation into Horizon.

September
S4C broadcasts the first Taro Naw documentary.

October
James Arbuthnot MP is contacted by suspended Odiham Subpostmaster, David Bristow.

November
First meeting of the Justice for Subpostmasters Alliance (JFSA).

The Post Office secures the criminal conviction of 70 people using Horizon evidence.

2010

January
Jacqui Smith MP raises Horizon problems and treatment of Subpostmasters in parliament.

The rollout of Horizon Online begins.

April
The Horizon Online pilot scheme is put on red alert by Fujitsu and temporarily halted.

August
The Ismay report is sent to the Post Office board and senior leadership. Ismay asserts Horizon is robust.

October
Seema Misra is sentenced to 15 months in prison.

The Post Office secures the criminal conviction of 55 people using Horizon evidence.

2011

February
BBC Surrey and Inside Out South investigation is broadcast. Seen by Richard Roll.

April
Ernst and Young review of Horizon (and other Post Office processes/IT).

July
James Arbuthnot tells the Post Office Chairman Alice Perkins there's a problem with Horizon.

August
The first pre-action letter is sent by Shoosmiths solicitors to the Post Office.

September
The Post Office Horizon IT Scandal first appears in Private Eye.

The Post Office secures the criminal conviction of 44 people using Horizon evidence.

2012

January
Post Office non-executive director Les Owen references the Private Eye article at a Post Office board meeting. He is assured Horizon is robust.

February
Meeting between MPs, Subpostmasters and Shoosmiths.

March
The fourth major Horizon problem in nine months leads to a total paralysis of the network for several hours.

Post Office report (after the Ismay report) states there are no problems with Horizon.

April
Paula Vennells is appointed Post Office chief executive.

May
James Arbuthnot and Oliver Letwin are invited to meet Paula Vennells and Alice Perkins. A decision is made to get a firm of independent forensic accountants to investigate Horizon.

July
Second Sight's appointment is announced. Approved by the JFSA and MPs.

September
Ian Henderson from Second Sight visits Fujitsu. Gareth Jenkins tells him there is remote access to Horizon.

The Post Office secures the criminal conviction of 50 people using Horizon evidence.

2013

May
Ron Warmington expresses concerns to James Arbuthnot about the lack of cooperation from the Post Office.

June
Drafts of Second Sight's Interim Report are circulated to the Post Office and the JFSA.

Post Office holds the first of six full board meetings in five weeks.

July
Cartwright King Sift Review begins in secret.

Second Sight deliver their Interim Report.

Jo Swinson announces the Post Office will set up a working party to complete the review of cases started by Second Sight.

July
The Clarke Advice on disclosure is delivered to the Post Office. It recommends a review of all Post Office prosecutions.

Post Office Head of Security orders the shredding of documents relating to Horizon problems.

A second Clarke Advice warning against shredding documents is sent to the Post Office.

August
Initial Complaint Review and Mediation Scheme is launched.

August
Shoosmiths parts company with the JFSA.

A Grant Funding Agreement is set up between the NFSP and the Post Office.

October
Detica NetReveal reports problems with the Post Office's fraud repellency, business processes and IT.

Post Office commissions barrister Brian Altman QC to review prosecution and disclosure obligations.

November
Chris Aujard replaces Susan Crichton as General Counsel of the Post Office.

The Post Office secures the criminal conviction of 56 people using Horizon evidence.

2014

January
Post Office decides to stop routinely prosecuting Subpostmasters.

July
Second Sight produce Briefing Report Part One.

August
Second Sight produce Briefing Report Part Two (first version).

Post Office refuses to accept Second Sight's Briefing Report Part Two and produces a rebuttal document.

November
James Arbuthnot calls a summit with the Post Office to discuss the Mediation Scheme.

December
BBC's John Humphrys interviews Post Office Communications Director Mark Davies on the Today programme.

James Arbuthnot calls an Adjournment Debate on the Post Office in the House of Commons.

2015

January
Business, Innovation and Skills Select Committee launches an inquiry into Horizon and the Post Office Mediation Scheme.

February
NFSP General Secretary tells BIS committee inquiry Horizon is 'exceptionally' robust.

Paula Vennells tells BIS committee inquiry there is no evidence of any miscarriages of justice.

March
Post Office terminates the Mediation Scheme Working Group.

Criminal Cases Review Commission starts accepting Subpostmaster cases.

James Arbuthnot raises the collapse of the Mediation Scheme at Prime Minister's Questions.

Post Office final report into the Mediation Scheme is published on its website.

BIS Select Committee inquiry concludes.

April
Second Sight produce Briefing Report Part Two (second version).

Post Office again disavows Second Sight's report and produces another rebuttal document.

August
BBC broadcasts Panorama: Trouble At The Post Office. Richard Roll is interviewed.

Post Office calls Panorama partial, selective and misleading.

The NFSP says it has not taken any calls from Subpostmasters querying Horizon and states the system is fundamentally sound.

The Post Office secures the criminal conviction of 2 people using Horizon evidence.

Total since 2000 =738

2016

January
JFSA assembles a legal team and funding to sue the Post Office.

April
Bates v Post Office is filed at the High Court.

2017

January
Post Office admits remote access is possible at a High Court hearing.

March
High Court grants Group Litigation Order for *Bates v Post Office*.

July
More than 500 claimants sign up to *Bates v Post Office* group litigation.

2018

August
CCRC writes to claimants saying it has nearly finished its investigations into their cases.

November
First trial in *Bates v Post Office* – The Common Issues – begins.

CCRC decides to wait at least for the judgment of the Common Issues trial before making any decisions.

December
Paula Vennells is awarded a CBE in the New Year's Honours List for her services to the Post Office.

2019

March
Horizon trial begins.

Common Issues judgment is handed down, ruling in the claimants' favour.

Post Office makes an application to recuse Mr Justice Fraser. The Horizon trial is halted.

April
Paula Vennells leaves the Post Office to take up a board position at the Cabinet Office and the chairmanship of Imperial College Healthcare NHS Trust.

Post Office's recusal application is dismissed by the High Court.

Horizon trial resumes.

May
Court of Appeal refuses the recusal appeal.

June
Post Office asks the Court of Appeal for permission to appeal the Common Issues judgment.

Expert evidence is heard from Jason Coyne and Dr Worden after a two month interval.

July
Horizon trial ends.

November
Lord Justice Coulson rejects the Post Office's Common Issues judgment appeal.

JFSA and the Post Office begin mediation.

December
Post Office and Subpostmasters agree a £57.75m settlement. Most of the settlement goes to lawyers and funders.

Horizon trial judgment is handed down. Mr Justice Fraser passes a file to the Director of Public Prosecutions.

2020

January

Alan Bates sends the Horizon judgment to BEIS minister Kelly Tolhurst, with an invoice for fees incurred by the Subpostmasters. The request is refused.

DPP passes Mr Justice Fraser's file to the Metropolitan Police. They begin an investigation.

February

Paul Scully replaces Kelly Tolhurst as BEIS Minister.

During Prime Minister's Questions Boris Johnson appears to commit to an independent inquiry into the scandal.

Paul Scully rejects a request for the Subpostmasters' legal costs to be paid.

March

Private Eye Special Report 'Justice Lost in the Post' is published.

Paula Vennells steps down from the Cabinet Office.

CCRC refers 39 Subpostmaster cases to the Court of Appeal.

May

Post Office launches the Historical Shortfall Scheme.

Payments from the remaining settlement agreement cash are made to Subpostmasters.

Post Office reveals the scale of its prosecution activity for the first time saying it believes around 500 Subpostmasters may have been convicted using Horizon evidence.

The Great Post Office Trial series is first broadcast on BBC Radio 4.

Angela van den Bogerd leaves the Post Office.

Post Office announces it has identified around 900 prosecutions which may have relied on Horizon data.

June

BBC broadcasts Panorama: Scandal At The Post Office.

JFSA announces a crowdfunding campaign to raise money for a complaint to the Parliamentary Ombudsman.

Darren Jones sends questions on behalf of the Select Committee to Paula Vennells, Post Office CEO Nick Read and Fujitsu.

Paula Vennells resigns from her position on the church's ethical investments advisory group.

A non-statutory 'review' of the Post Office Horizon scandal is announced by Paul Scully.

CCRC refers a further eight cases to the Court of Appeal.

August

Post Office publishes the litigation settlement agreement.

October
Post Office announces it will not contest 44 of the 47 cases referred to the Court of Appeal.

Alan Bates sends a formal complaint to BEIS which is rejected.

November
Barristers Paul Marshall and Flora Page, who represented Seema Misra, Tracy Felstead and Janet Skinner at the Court of Appeal, are given the Clarke Advice.

Metropolitan Police says its investigation is now a criminal investigation.

Paul Marshall sends the Clarke Advice to the Metropolitan Police.

Flora Page gives a journalist (her brother, Lewis Page) the Clarke Advice. Lewis contacts the Post Office.

Post Office complains to the Court of Appeal the Clarke Advice has been given to a journalist.

Flora Page ceases to represent Tracy Felstead, Janet Skinner and Seema Misra.

December
Alan Bates complains to the Parliamentary Ombudsman, demanding more than £300m from the government.

Paula Vennells steps down from her post as Chair of the Imperial Healthcare NHS Trust.

The first six Postmaster convictions are quashed at Southwark Crown Court.

Paul Marshall ceases to represent Janet Skinner, Tracy Felstead and Seema Misra, handing over to Lisa Busch QC.

Court of Appeal allows the limb 2 argument to go ahead.

2021

January
CCRC refers four more Subpostmasters back to the courts.

Sir Wyn Williams holds the first focus group of his non-statutory inquiry.

March
Four-day Court of Appeal hearing begins. The existence of the 'shredding' Clarke Advice is revealed.

April
Post Office CEO Nick Read claims he was unaware how much of the *Bates v Post Office* settlement would be spent on fees and asks the government to make up the difference.

Boris Johnson has a remote meeting with three Subpostmasters. He assures them they will get proper redress.

The Court of Appeal quashes 39 convictions on limbs 1 and 2 of the CCRC referral.

Paula Vennells steps down from the boards of Morrisons and Dunelm and is no longer active within the Church of England.

May

Post Office announces 540 of its Horizon prosecutions may be unsafe and is reviewing 100 more.

Government announces Sir Wyn Williams' inquiry will be put on a statutory footing.

Two more Subpostmaster convictions are quashed at Southwark Crown Court.

July

Twelve more convictions are quashed at the Court of Appeal.

Government announces that Subpostmasters whose convictions have been quashed will be eligible for an interim payment of up to £100,000.

August

Metropolitan Police says it has interviewed a man and a woman in connection with the Post Office Horizon scandal.

GLOSSARY

Actus non facit reum nisi mens sit rea	Latin for 'An act does not make a person guilty unless the mind is also guilty.' See also *mens rea*.
Actus reus	Latin for 'Criminal act.'
After the event insurance (ATE)	Insurance purchased after an event has taken place, but before any legal costs are incurred. The insurance will normally cover the legal costs a claimant is liable to pay if they lose their case at trial.
API	A set of definitions and protocols for building and integrating application software. APIs allow two applications to talk to each other.
Arm's length body	An organisation which operates with a degree of independence from the government.
Artificial Intelligence (AI)	Broadly, the use of computers to assist decision-making using data.
Auditors	People employed to inspect accounts. To act as an auditor, a person should be certified by the regulatory authority of accounting and auditing or possess certain specified qualifications. This was not a requirement of the 'auditors' the Post Office employed to inspect Subpostmaster branch accounts.
Automated Teller Machine (ATM)	Cashpoint.
Balancing to zero	Requirement that a Subpostmaster verifies their cash and stock figure matches that produced by Horizon. Every branch has to balance to zero before they can start the next trading period.
Bates and Others v Post Office Ltd	A group litigation brought against the Post Office at the High Court by former Subpostmaster Alan Bates and more than 500 other individuals. Bates' claim was filed on 11 April 2016 and the claim was settled on 11 December 2019.
BBC	The British Broadcasting Corporation. Licence-fee funded content provider across TV, radio and internet.
Blackstone's ratio	A 280-year-old principle which underpins modern notions of justice: 'It is better that ten guilty persons escape than that one innocent suffer.' The concept has antecedents going back to the Old Testament.

Branch suspense account	An account into which Subpostmasters could place discrepancies temporarily while disputed transactions were investigated by the Post Office. This option was discontinued in 2005.
Branch Trading Statement (BTS)	A statement produced at the end of each trading period. The Post Office treated this as a 'settled' account. In law, knowingly producing a false settled account (with dishonest intent) is the crime of false accounting.
Callendar Square bug	A Horizon bug which caused the Riposte message store to lock, stopping it from replicating certain instructions and messages. This was 'a bug with potential lasting impact, and indeed it did cause actual impact' between 2000 and 2010. Also known as the Riposte Lock/Unlock bug.
Case Questionnaire Response (CQR)	Document filled out by applicants to the Mediation Scheme giving information about their case.
Case Review Report (CRR)	Review by Second Sight after receiving an applicant's CQR and the Post Office's POIR – Post Office Investigation Report.
Category A bug	The worst sort – could render your IT system inoperable.
Category B bug	A serious bug.
Category C bug	A bug you can live with, but will need a patch.
Centre for Effective Dispute Resolution (CEDR)	An independent non-profit organisation and registered charity specialising in mediation and alternative dispute resolution.
Common Issues	A list of questions to be decided by the judge after being agreed by both parties in *Bates v Post Office*. The Common Issues trial at the High Court ventilated both parties' perspectives on the Common Issues. The Common Issues judgment, written by Mr Justice Fraser, settled the matter.
Common Issues trial	The Common Issues trial was part of the *Bates v Post Office* group litigation. It took place during November and December 2018, with judgment handed down on 15 March 2019.

Communication Workers Union (CWU)	The main trade union in the UK for people working for telephone, cable, digital subscriber line and postal delivery companies. The CWU represents directly-employed Crown Office staff and has, over the last ten years, started representing Subpostmasters. It is not recognised by the Post Office in its latter capacity.
Computer Weekly	A digital magazine and website for IT professionals in the UK. Computer Weekly has been covering the Post Office scandal since 2009.
Contempt of court	Wrongful conduct which consists of interference with the administration of justice.
County Court	The County Court deals with civil (non-criminal) matters, e.g. businesses trying to recover money they are owed from individuals, or other businesses.
Court of Appeal	Second highest court in England and Wales after the Supreme Court. It hears appeals to High Court and Crown Court judgments.
Credence system	Recorded data going in and out of Subpostmaster accounts.
Criminal Cases Review Commission (CCRC)	A public body, set up in 1997, with a statutory mandate to put right miscarriages of justice.
Crown Court	A single entity with 77 court centres across England and Wales (Scotland and NI have separate legal systems). The Crown Court deals with serious criminal cases, including theft from a Post Office.
Crown Post Offices (or Crown Offices)	Branches that are owned and managed by the Post Office directly.
Crown Prosecution Service (CPS)	Prosecutes criminal cases which have been investigated by the police and other investigative organisations in England and Wales.
Data dictionary	A centralised repository of information about data such as meaning, relationships to other data, origin, usage, and format (as defined in the IBM Dictionary of Computing).
Debt notice	A notice sent from the Post Office to the Subpostmaster requiring them to make good a discrepancy. Also called a debt recovery letter.

Department for Business, Energy and Industrial Strategy (BEIS)	Department of the government of the UK. Formerly known as Department for Business, Innovation and Skills (BIS).
Director of Public Prosecutions (DPP)	The head of the Crown Prosecution Service.
Disclosure	The process of handing over information to an interested party in civil and criminal legal proceedings. There is a basic principle that disclosure should be comprehensive and timely. Withholding information which could damage your case is not allowed.
Electronic Point of Sale (EPoS)	Combination of hardware and software which captures cash and electronic payments and can generate detailed reports.
False accounting	Making a false statement to the benefit of yourself or the detriment of another.
Fujitsu	A Japanese multinational information and communications technology equipment and services corporation. One of the world's largest IT services providers. Fujitsu UK is one of the largest providers of IT services to the UK government. Fujitsu UK bought ICL in 1990. Fujitsu/ICL won the £1bn PFI contract to automate the Post Office in 1996. Fujitsu created Horizon and ran it for the Post Office for more than 20 years. Its role in this scandal has yet to be properly unpicked.
Full Authority Digital Engine Control (FADEC)	A computer-managed aircraft ignition and engine control system used in modern commercial and military aircraft to control all aspects of engine performance digitally, in place of technical or analog electronic controls.
Gains	Surplus money in a Horizon branch account.
General Post Office (GPO)	The state postal system and telecommunications carrier of the UK until 1969.
Grant Funding Agreement (GFA)	Agreement between the Post Office and NFSP in which the NFSP expressly agreed not to engage in 'any public activity which may prevent POL from implementing any of its initiatives, policies or strategies,' or any 'other activities or behaviour the effect of which may be materially detrimental' to the Post Office.

Group Litigation — Sometimes called a class action. Class action is more readily understood but there is a technical difference. Generally in the US 'class action' is used to mean a type of representative action, i.e. an action brought on behalf of all members of a defined class, who don't need to do anything to be part of it. However, a Group Litigation Order (GLO) only binds the claimants who specifically sign up to it.

Heads of damage — A list apportioning values to each aspect of the damages being claimed.

High Court — Where complex and high value civil claims are decided, including appeals to County Court judgments.

Horizon — The software used to run Post Office branch terminals and the hardware which housed it. Horizon Online, the updated version of what became known as Legacy Horizon, was introduced in 2010.

Horizon cash account — Not an account in the traditional sense of the word. A Horizon program which crawled through every transaction on each terminal in each branch at the end of the day's trading which then came up with a figure. The figure should correspond exactly with the amount of physical cash on the premises.

Horizon Issues — A list of questions to be decided by the judge after being agreed by both parties in *Bates v Post Office*. The Horizon trial at the High Court ventilated both parties' perspectives on the Horizon Issues. The Horizon trial judgment, written by Mr Justice Fraser, settled the matter.

Horizon Trial — More formally known as the Horizon Issues Trial, the Horizon trial was part of the *Bates v Post Office* group litigation. It took place between March and July 2019, with judgment handed down on 16 December 2019.

Initial Complaint Review and Mediation Scheme (ICRAMS) — The mediation scheme set up by the Post Office at the urging of MPs and the JFSA to allow Subpostmasters to air their complaints.

Inside Out — Now defunct regional current affairs strand which ran on BBC1 on Monday evenings.

Integrated Services Digital Network (ISDN) — A set of communication standards for simultaneous digital transmission of voice, video, data, and other network services over the digitalised circuits of the public switched telephone network.

Interlocutory applications	Applications made by one or other of the parties pending the hearing of the main case.
Internal suspense account	A Post Office account where unreconciled balances were held until such time as the Post Office credited the amounts to their Profit and Loss account. The Second Sight report stated that 'it was probable that some of those entries should have been re-credited to branches to offset losses previously charged.'
International Computers Limited (ICL)	British computer company bought by Fujitsu in 1990. Won the contract to automate the Post Office in 1996. The ICL Pathway project became Horizon. ICL disappeared as a brand at the turn of this century.
Investigation Branch (IB)	The Post Office feared in-house investigators. Became the Investigation Department (ID), then Post Office Investigation Department (POID), the Post Office Security and Investigation Services (POSIS), then Security Group.
Jackson reforms	Reforms to the civil litigation costs system made by Lord Justice Jackson. They came into force in 2013 and created a market for litigation funders.
Justice for Subpostmasters Alliance (JFSA)	The group founded by Alan Bates to get justice for those Subpostmasters who had been treated badly, and in many cases prosecuted, by the Post Office.
Known Error Log (KEL)	A record of the errors and bugs within an IT system.
Legal privilege	A rule of confidentiality governing communication of information between a person or company and their legal advisors. Legally privileged information does not have to be disclosed, even to a court. It is considered to be a fundamental condition on which the administration of justice as a whole rests, but it can also be used by organisations to keep sensitive and damaging information secret.
Limb 1	The first part or ground of an argument made by the CCRC when referring its first Subpostmaster cases back to the courts. The CCRC argued the Post Office's alleged failure to properly investigate the circumstances behind a discrepancy before bringing a prosecution, and/or its alleged failure to disclose relevant material to the people it was prosecuting meant it was not possible for the trial process to be fair.

Limb 2	The second part or ground of an argument made by the CCRC when referring its first Subpostmaster cases back to the courts. The CCRC argued that the Post Office's prosecutions were so fundamentally misguided, they were an affront to the public's conscience and should never have been brought.
Litigation funding	Funding options available to bring or fight a claim, to cover not only their legal costs but their potential exposure to having to pay the other side's costs if they lose. Options include: conditional fee agreements (CFAs), damages-based agreements (DBAs), after the event (ATE) insurance and third party funding.
Magistrates' Courts	A lower court which holds trials for summary criminal offences and preliminary hearings for more serious ones. This could include theft, fraud or false accounting.
Malicious prosecution	The wrongful institution of criminal proceedings against someone without reasonable grounds.
Mens rea	Literally, guilty mind. This is the mental element in a crime (i.e. criminal intention). In most cases a criminal offence requires both a criminal act and a criminal intention.
Message store	A program within the Horizon system, containing some of its fundamental operating instructions.
National Audit Office (NAO)	Independent parliamentary body that scrutinises public spending.
National Federation of Subpostmasters (NFSP)	Organisation founded in 1897 which represents the overwhelming majority of Subpostmasters in the UK.
Overnight Cash Holding (ONCH)	The amount of cash held in a Post Office branch overnight.
Panorama	The BBC's flagship current affairs programme.
Parliamentary privilege	The protection of free speech within parliament. Legal action cannot be brought against an MP for saying something in the Houses of Parliament. It ensures that Members of Parliament are able to speak freely in debates, and protects parliament's internal affairs from interference from the courts. Certain proceedings (i.e. select committee inquiry oral evidence sessions) are partly protected by parliamentary privilege, which gives participants, including non-MPs, the opportunity to speak more freely than they might otherwise.

Patch	A software update which effects change, or a set of changes, to a program or its supporting data.
Pathway	Name of the consortium which won a £1bn contract to auto- mate the Post Office. Majority-owned by Fujitsu/ICL it quickly became wholly owned by Fujitsu/ICL, who rebranded it ICL Pathway. Project Pathway became Horizon..
Police and Criminal Evidence Act 1984 (PACE)	An Act of Parliament which instituted a legislative framework for the powers of police officers in England and Wales to combat crime, and provided codes of practice for the exercise of those powers.
Post Office Investigation Department (POID)	Formerly the Investigation Branch, later becoming Post Office Security and Investigation Services (POSIS), and then finally, Security Group.
Post Office Investigation Report (POIR)	Report produced by the Post Office after an applicant to the Complaint and Mediation Scheme submitted a CQR – Case Questionnaire Response.
Post Office Limited (POL)	A company providing a wide range of products including postage stamps and banking to the public through its nationwide network of Post Office branches. It is wholly-owned by the government. The Post Office's nominal shareholder is the Secretary of State for Business, Energy and Industrial Strategy, but it is run and funded via UK Government Investments (UKGI), a branch of HM Treasury, which looks after all wholly-owned government companies.
Post Office Security and Investigation Services (POSIS)	Formerly the Post Office Investigations Department and now called Security Group.
Postmaster	Nowadays a completely interchangeable term with Subpostmaster. 100 years ago there was a very clear distinction – Postmasters or Head Postmasters were directly employed by the Post Office and responsible for the entire mail operation in a given region. Subpostmasters were self-employed small business owners acting as agents of the Post Office.
Pre-action letter of claim	Letter sent to a person or organisation before commencing legal action. It should include the basis on which a claim is being made, a summary of the facts, what the claimant wants from the defendant, and if money, how the amount is calculated.
Private Eye	A satirical magazine, with a nice line in cartoons and investigative journalism.

Proceeds of Crime Act 2002 (POCA)	An Act which allows the courts to make orders to recover money or property gained from criminal activities.
Prototype	A model which can demonstrate proof of concept.
Public Finance Initiative (PFI)	A way of using private money to fund public sector projects.
Reasons to Urge (RTU) meeting	A disciplinary meeting whereby a suspended Subpostmaster must 'urge' the Post Office to reinstate or not sack them.
Receipts and Payments Mismatch	A Horizon bug triggered by a particular sequence of button presses on a Horizon terminal. The effect was to clear a discrepancy so far as the user in the branch was concerned but not at Horizon's back-end, causing a mismatch.
Recusal	The withdrawal of a judge from a case because of a possible conflict of interest or lack of impartiality.
Relational contract	A developing area of contract law around implied terms of good faith. A business contract can be said to be relational if it is long-term, both parties intend 'that their respective roles be performed with integrity, and with fidelity to their bargain,' there's a commitment to 'collaborating with one another,' a 'high degree of communication, cooperation and predictable performance based on mutual trust and confidence, and expectations of loyalty' and a 'degree of significant investment' or a 'substantial financial commitment' by one party (or both) in the venture.
Rem Out DisPatched (RODP)	Four letter code produced by Horizon when the pouches containing cash are ready to be despatched to CashCo.
Rem Out StandBy (ROST)	Four letter code produced by Horizon when the Subpostmaster tells Horizon how much cash will be in each pouch.
Reversal bug	A bug introduced by the release of Horizon version S30 where the value of transactions reversed by Subpostmasters would double rather than cancel the value of the transaction. It was found that the wrong mathematical sign had been used in the software code of the routine that actioned this process (a + instead of a -).

Riposte message store	Third-party software within the Legacy Horizon system, containing Horizon's fundamental operating instructions. It was not used in Horizon Online.
Roll over	Rolling over from one accounting period to the next. Postmasters were required to balance to zero at the end of each accounting period. Discrepancies had to be settled, agreed to be settled or (pre-2005) requested to be put into suspense.
Royal Mail Group (RMG)	The Royal Mail was a department of the Post Office until Royal Mail Group was created. Royal Mail Group had three divisions – Parcelforce, Royal Mail (which dealt with letters and small packages) and Post Office Counters Ltd (which later became Post Office Ltd). In 2012 Post Office Ltd was carved out of Royal Mail Group and the latter was privatised. The Post Office remains 100% owned by government.
Schedule of Sensitive Material	A document allowing prosecutors to withhold information from a defendant. There has to be an overwhelming public interest reason not to disclose evidence to a defence team – for instance, a matter of national security.
Second Sight	Firm of independent forensic accountants hired to investigate Horizon.
Select Committee	A small group of backbench MPs or members of the House of Lords who investigate a specific issue in detail or perform a specific scrutiny role. Select committees launch inquiries and may call in officials and experts for questioning. They can also demand information from the government. Select committees publish their findings. The government is expected to respond to any recommendations that are made.
Settle Centrally	Acknowledging a branch discrepancy as a debt to the Subpostmaster, but delaying settling it. The debt is placed in a holding account (called a branch or local suspense account) to be paid at a subsequent date by the Subpostmaster.
Settle to Cash or Cheque	Acknowledging a branch discrepancy as a debt to the Subpostmaster, and making it good immediately by placing cash or a cheque into the branch till or safe.
Software Support Centre (SSC)	Specialist technical support operated out of Fujitsu HQ in Bracknell, dealing with hardware and software errors and bugs. Richard Roll worked in Fujitsu SSC from 2001 until 2004.

SPMR/SPM	Post Office shorthand for Subpostmaster.
Statute of Limitations	The law that sets the maximum amount of time that parties involved in a dispute have to initiate legal proceedings.
Stock units	Horizon cash and stock balances relating to the physical till trays operated by individual Subpostmasters and their assistants in each branch. Every Horizon user would be responsible for their own Horizon stock unit which should exactly match the contents of their physical till trays.
Strict liability offence	A criminal offence where the issue of criminal intent does not have to be proved in relation to one or more elements of the criminal act. Theft, false accounting and fraud are not strict liability offences. Speeding is.
Subpostmasters	Small business owners, operating as agents of the Post Office who nonetheless enjoy certain benefits more common to employees. Their contract with the Post Office has been deemed 'relational,' though the Post Office fought hard to reject this characterisation. The CWU is trying to have Postmasters legally recognised as 'workers,' which will give them certain employment rights.
Taro Naw	Now defunct Welsh-language current affairs programme made by BBC journalists in Wales for S4C – the Welsh Channel 4.
Transaction Acknowledgement (TA)	A correction to a Subpostmaster's accounts sent by the Post Office to a branch via Horizon. It has to be accepted.
Transaction Correction (TC)	A correction to a Subpostmaster's accounts sent by the Post Office to a branch via Horizon. It can be disputed.
Unders and overs tin	Place to store small amounts of surplus money which can be used to make up a deficit.
United Kingdom Government Investments (UKGI)	The government body looking after all large government-owned businesses. Staffed by civil servants and high-flying business types. Reports to HM Treasury. A UKGI-nominated director sits on the Post Office board, and has done since 2012, making the government fully complicit in all Post Office board decisions since then.

Westminster Hall	A parliamentary debating room which is much less grand than the hall it is named after and adjoins. Westminster Hall debates give MPs an opportunity to raise local or national issues and receive a response from the relevant government minister.

SOURCES

Most of this book has been put together from my own interviews or documents which have come my way via court processes and/or various helpful individuals. I have published quite a bit already (including court transcripts) on the Post Office Trial website (postofficetrial.com), which is intended to act as an online resource for students of this scandal. There are many other useful online documents, websites, newspapers, magazines and books which I have found invaluable. I have listed the main ones below.

Online resources

Hansard – hansard.parliament.uk – an archive of what is said in parliamentary debates and select committees. Complemented by parliament.uk and old.parliament.uk which archive written evidence to select committees and parliamentary research documents about the Post Office.

Justice for Subpostmasters Alliance – jfsa.org.uk – a reasonably comprehensive repository of documentation and media coverage related to the scandal.

British and Irish Legal Information Institute, better known as Bailii – bailii.org – which collates and publishes court judgments, including all six *Bates v Post Office* judgments, *Post Office v Castleton* and *Hamilton v Post Office*.

Post Office corporate site – corporate.postoffice.co.uk – which archives statements and press releases. Information can suddenly disappear or change, so it's worth exporting and saving pages with interesting information on them.

Wayback Machine – web.archive.org – a bot which crawls the internet, archiving pages as it goes. If you put any active or inactive link into the wayback machine's search box, it will bring up a calendar showing the number of times it has visited and archived the page, allowing you to read pages which have been taken down and see how information on live pages has been altered.

Computer Weekly – computerweekly.com – the original 2009 investigation is still available, as is a comprehensive and regularly updated timeline, documenting each twist and turn of the story.

Private Eye – private-eye.co.uk – not much of Private Eye's first rate journalism is posted online, so I recommend subscribing to the printed magazine. However, Lord Gnome has made the 2020 special report 'Justice Lost In The Post' available to read online.

BBC News, BBC Sounds and BBC iPlayer – bbc.co.uk – you can find lots of regional news items about individual Subpostmasters here, as well as broader takes on the story. The Great Post Office Trial can be heard on BBC Sounds.

Daily Mail – dailymail.co.uk – a national newspaper which in recent years has done some excellent work detailing the scandal. Search 'Subpostmasters' once you are on the site to bring up relevant articles.

Digital Evidence and Electronic Signature Law Review – journals.sas.ac.uk/deeslr – run by the indefatigable Stephen Mason. It contains a number of articles related to the law's failures when it comes to interpreting electronic evidence, plus the transcripts from Seema Misra's trial.

Exeter University Post Office Project – evidencebasedjustice.exeter.ac.uk/current-research-data/post-office-project/ – an ongoing piece of work looking at the various legal, governmental and corporate failures which led to so many people being wrongfully convicted.

Hudgells – hudgellsolicitors.co.uk – Neil Hudgell has done quite a bit of writing on his clients and how they have been affected by the scandal. Hudgells have also commissioned a very moving film which puts the Postmasters' stories front and centre.

Post Office Horizon Inquiry – postofficehorizoninquiry.org.uk

– detailing the work of the statutory inquiry.

The Postal Museum – postalmuseum.org – a huge searchable archive of source documentation.

Books

The National Federation of Subpostmasters: 100 Years of Proud History 1897 - 1997 (Published by the NFSP)

Masters of the Post: The Authorised History of the Royal Mail – Duncan Campbell-Smith (Penguin Books)

ACKNOWLEDGMENTS

This book has been put together with the help of hundreds of people. To name them all would:

a) be a nightmare, because I would definitely forget someone;

b) take another 500 pages; and

c) end some careers, which I don't want to do.

Instead, I would like to pass on my deepest thanks to anyone and everyone who has helped in any way, especially the many hundreds of people who have kindly donated to my tip jar or crowdfunding campaigns or bought into this book when it was just an idea. Hand in hand with that, of course, goes the special thank you to anyone who has given me the tiniest scrap of useful information or documentation over the course of the last 11 years. I am also deeply grateful to Helen and David and everyone from Bath Publishing, especially the marketing, editorial, design and legal teams who put up with the endless emails, phone calls and revisions to the manuscript, right up to the wire. In my defence, it is still a developing story! I am, of course, indebted to every broadcast and print editor who has previously commissioned me to work on this story, as well as all the lawyers, politicians, IT professionals, forensic accountants, auditors, academics, journalists and former and existing Post Office and Fujitsu staff who have given me the benefit of their insight and expertise.

To my colleagues – thanks for your help, advice and enthusiasm. You have been incredibly generous and gracious in your support. To my friends and family – thank you for the unstinting tolerance and love.

Finally, and most importantly, I would like to thank all the former and serving Subpostmasters, managers, assistants and their families who sent me information, invited me into their homes, responded to my emails and told me their personal stories. I am humbled and honoured to have met you and worked with you. Reporting this scandal has been one of the greatest privileges of my career.

Oh, and thank you to Matt and Olly from the Modern Mann podcast. A deal is a deal.

INDEX

A

B

C

D

E

F

J

N

O

P

R

S

T

Y

Z

Printed in the USA
CPSIA information can be obtained
at www.ICGtesting.com
LVHW031604110124
768539LV00001B/7

9 781739 099206